Proconsuls

Delegated Political-Military Leadership from Rome to America Today

This book is a study of proconsulship, a form of delegated political-military leadership historically associated with the governance of large empires. Opening with a conceptual and historical analysis of proconsulship as an aspect of imperial or quasi-imperial rule generally, it surveys its origins and development in the late Roman Republic and its manifestations in the British Empire. The main focus is proconsulship in American history. Beginning with the occupation of Cuba and the Philippines after the Spanish-American War, it discusses the role of General Douglas MacArthur in East Asia during and after World War II, the occupation of Germany (focusing on General Lucius Clay), and proconsular leadership during the Vietnam War and the occupation of Iraq and Afghanistan at the turn of the twenty-first century. An additional chapter provides an overview and assessment of the evolution of American political-military command and control and decision-making after the end of the Cold War.

Carnes Lord is Professor of Military and Naval Strategy in the Center for Naval Warfare Studies, United States Naval War College. As a political scientist, his interests lie in international and strategic studies, national security organization and management, and political philosophy. Lord holds PhD degrees from Cornell University and Yale University and has taught political science at Yale University, the University of Virginia, and the Fletcher School of Law and Diplomacy. He has held several senior positions in the United States government, including director of international communications and information policy on the National Security Council staff (1981–1984), assistant to the vice president for national security affairs (1989–1991), and Distinguished Fellow at the National Defense University (1991–1993). Lord is the author of, among other works, *The Presidency and the Management of National Security* (1988), *The Modern Prince: What Leaders Need to Know Now* (2003), and *Losing Hearts and Minds? Strategic Influence and Public Diplomacy in the Age of Terror* (2006).

Proconsuls

Delegated Political-Military Leadership
from Rome to America Today

CARNES LORD

CAMBRIDGE
UNIVERSITY PRESS

CAMBRIDGE UNIVERSITY PRESS
Cambridge, New York, Melbourne, Madrid, Cape Town
Singapore, São Paulo, Delhi, Mexico City

Cambridge University Press
32 Avenue of the Americas, New York, NY 10013-2473, USA

www.cambridge.org
Information on this title: www.cambridge.org/9780521254694

First published 2012

Printed in the United States of America

A catalog record for this publication is available from the British Library.

Library of Congress Cataloging in Publication data

Lord, Carnes.
Proconsuls : delegated political-military leadership from Rome to America today / Carnes Lord.
  p. cm.
Includes bibliographical references and index.
ISBN 978-1-107-00961-5 (hardback) – ISBN 978-0-521-25469-4 (paperback)
1. Military government – History. 2. Military occupation – History. 3. Great Britain –
Colonies – Administration – History. 4. United States – Territories and possessions – History.
5. Proconsuls, Roman. I. Title.
JV412.L67 2012
355.4′9–dc23   2011041603

ISBN 978-1-107-00961-5 Hardback
ISBN 978-0-521-25469-4 Paperback

For Rebecca, Blair, and Sarah

Contents

Acknowledgments   *page* ix

 1 On Proconsular Leadership   1
 2 Roman Origins   23
 3 Wood in Cuba   47
 4 The Philippines   67
 5 MacArthur in the Far East   91
 6 Clay in Germany   109
 7 Vietnam   133
 8 Clark in the Balkans   167
 9 Bremer in Iraq   186
10 Petraeus in the Middle East   208
11 American Lessons   228

Index   241

Acknowledgments

A number of obligations have been incurred in the course of writing this book. I have benefited from the advice and criticism of several colleagues at the Naval War College, notably Donald Chisholm, Bradford Lee, Michael Pavkovic, and Robert Rubel. I am also grateful to Robert Rubel for some stimulating discussions of potential reform of the Unified Command Plan from a naval perspective, which importantly influenced my thinking in the final chapter, as well as for reviewing the chapter on Wesley Clark. Particular thanks also to Arthur Eckstein of the University of Maryland for his careful reading of the chapter on ancient Rome. Alice Juda of the Naval War College Library provided cheerful and patient research assistance. I have benefited from generous financial support provided by the Smith Richardson Foundation; special thanks are owed to Nadia Schadlow for her support of my efforts, in this and other writing projects. I am also much indebted to my literary agent, Donald Gastwirth, for interesting Cambridge University Press in the manuscript, as well as for his constant encouragement and friendship; thanks are owed, too, to Lewis Bateman, my editor at Cambridge, as well as his assistant, Anne Lovering Rounds. Nancy Greenwood was a careful reader of the manuscript. Finally, I thank my wife, Meredith Lord, for holding the ring on the home front, and Rebecca, Blair, and Sarah, for their sweetness and laughter. This book is dedicated to my daughters.

I

On Proconsular Leadership

They that dig foundations deep,
Fit for realms to rise upon,
Little honour do they reap
Of their generation . . .
Rudyard Kipling[1]

In spite of the often bitter disputes among Americans of different political persuasions over the nation's ongoing struggles in Iraq and Afghanistan, it would probably be widely agreed that the difficulties the United States has encountered in the Middle East since the events of September 11, 2001, are not simply a reflection of policy failure in Washington. Some of them may have been unavoidable, or a function of the "fog of war," or for that matter simple bad luck. Yet political-military decision-making by American officials in the field has also left something to be desired. This was most clearly the case in Iraq in the immediate aftermath of U.S. military operations there in mid-2003.[2] At the same time, in at least one conspicuous case – the "surge" in American ground forces in Iraq in 2007 – a dramatic improvement in American fortunes can be traced primarily to the initiative, strategic vision, and operational virtuosity of the American field commander, General David Petraeus. Recently, in a time of great uncertainty concerning the future of the American involvement in Afghanistan, Petraeus was given a further opportunity to provide what can fairly be described as national leadership in meeting a fundamental and

---

[1] Rudyard Kipling, "The Pro-consuls" (1905), a eulogy of Lord Alfred Milner, British High Commissioner of South Africa, 1897–1905.

[2] For accounts of this period from several contrasting viewpoints, see Thomas E. Ricks, *Fiasco: The American Military Adventure in Iraq* (New York: Penguin, 2006); Ali A. Allawi, *The Occupation of Iraq: Winning the War, Losing the Peace* (New Haven, CT: Yale University Press, 2007); L. Paul Bremer III, *My Year In Iraq* (New York: Simon & Schuster, 2006); and Douglas J. Feith, *War and Decision: Inside the Pentagon at the Dawn of the War on Terrorism* (New York: Harper, 2008).

daunting challenge to the security interests of the United States, its friends and allies, and the international community as a whole.

What role do or should subordinate officials have in providing national-level or strategic leadership? What scope do they actually have for independent action? What is the relationship between such officials and their superiors, and how should that relationship be managed? These are the fundamental issues this study sets out to address. Remarkably little thematic attention has been paid to them in the relevant academic and policy-oriented literature of recent times. There seem to be a number of reasons for this. Perhaps the most significant is the lingering influence within American social science of the distinction between "policy" and "administration." This distinction, traceable to an essay of Woodrow Wilson's of the late nineteenth century, was originally intended to have normative force – that is, it was supposed to lay the groundwork for a new, more professional, and less political approach to public administration than that previously obtaining in the United States. Over time, however, it has leached into the mental picture that academics and practitioners alike tend to hold of the actual workings of policy-making in contemporary democracies. According to this understanding, policy and administration are sharply distinguished, with subordinate officials seen as mere implementers of decisions taken at the higher policy or political levels of the government.[3]

There can be little doubt that in other societies and earlier historical epochs, the situation was rather different. In feudal societies, the higher nobility generally controlled extensive territories and commanded military forces personally loyal to themselves. Such men were political leaders in their own right, not merely administrators, and their political interests and concerns had to be taken into account by their feudal overlords if their cooperation was to be ensured. In extensive empires such as those of Persia, Rome, China, the Ottoman Turks, and the Spanish Hapsburgs, covering vast areas and with primitive communications at best, control could only be sustained by delegating extensive authority to local officials. These officials often became powerful magnates in their own right, and their loyalty could not always easily be commanded. Particularly in times of weakness or turmoil at the imperial center, these men often went into business for themselves, sometimes ruling autonomously in return for a pro forma acknowledgment of imperial suzerainty, sometimes proclaiming actual independence, and at other times attempting to seize power at the center for themselves. Our English-language political vocabulary has been enriched by a number of terms designating essentially this phenomenon: "satrap" (an ancient Persian word), "viceroy" (of Spanish origin), and – of comparable terms the one clearly enjoying the most currency today – "proconsul."

The word "proconsul" derives from a Latin phrase meaning "in place of a consul." In the Roman Republic of classical times, executive power was wielded

[3] Woodrow Wilson, "The Study of Administration" (1887), in Frederick C. Mosher, ed., *Basic Literature of American Public Administration, 1787–1950* (New York: Holmes and Meier, 1981).

by two annually elected officials known as consuls. In the course of Roman expansion in central Italy during the fourth century BC, the Romans discovered that it could be highly inconvenient to recall a consul in the middle of a military campaign after his term of office had expired, particularly as the military requirements of an expansionist foreign policy were becoming more and more demanding. The solution they hit upon was to create a new type of official capable of substituting for a consul in a major military command, that is to say, one endowed with the prestige and authority of high political office and an ability to take important decisions on his own responsibility. Roman proconsuls under the Republic were therefore never mere administrators, although their freedom of action might vary significantly according to circumstances. Some of them, at any rate, were surely statesmen by any description. If there is a single simple way to characterize proconsular rule in general, it would perhaps be this: delegated political-military leadership that rises in the best case to statesmanship.[4]

To describe a subordinate official of a contemporary democracy as a proconsul is generally not intended as a compliment. A proconsul is typically thought of today as a powerful official of high military or political rank in a remote territory who uses his power in an independent, unauthorized, or high-handed fashion. This negative connotation no doubt reflects in some measure the role that powerful dynasts of consular or proconsular rank – notably, Julius Caesar – played historically in the wreck of the Roman Republic in the first century BC. Is there then no legitimate role for proconsular leadership in the world today? The answer to this question is by no means evident.

There are a number of reasons for thinking that proconsular leadership is not really possible today, at any rate in the advanced democracies. In the first place, contemporary democracies are virtually by definition states that abide by the rule of law and a constitutional order that firmly subordinates military to civilian authority. Second, what might be called the bureaucratic character of contemporary democracies constrains the behavior of subordinate officials in ways that effectively check proconsular-type ambitions, which tend to thrive only in traditional aristocratic societies like that of classical Rome. Finally, modern communications have largely overcome the tyranny of distance that made older empires so vulnerable to the ambitions of local governors.

The sociologist Max Weber famously distinguished three varieties of legitimate modes of governance in world history: traditional, rational-legal, and charismatic. In this formulation, "rational-legal," or bureaucratic, governance is the dominant mode in the modern world; "traditional" governance

---

4 Consider Sir Henry Taylor, *The Statesman*, ed. David Lewis Schaefer (Westport, CT: Praeger, 1992 [1842]). This neglected work, the earliest treatise on public administration in modern Britain, makes the case that delegated leadership in some circumstances may well qualify as a form of policy leadership or statesmanship. For the concept of statesmanship or statecraft generally see Carnes Lord, *The Modern Prince: What Leaders Need to Know Now* (New Haven, CT: Yale University Press, 2003).

characterizes older, more personalized aristocratic societies; and "charismatic" governance is personalized rule based on the appeal of a religion, ideology, or individual personality.[5] Yet it is not difficult to see that these "ideal types" are by no means mutually exclusive. While the bureaucratization of government in recent times is a phenomenon that should not be underestimated, it should also not be exaggerated. It is striking to what extent the traditional order persisted even in Europe well into the twentieth century, and still today survives in parts of the world in thinly disguised bureaucratic garb. It would also be a mistake to underestimate the possibilities of charismatic leadership today, not least in the advanced democracies. It is perhaps sufficient to say that human nature remains more of a constant in political life than is allowed by Weber's formulation. Consider, notoriously, the case of General Douglas MacArthur. MacArthur was an American aristocrat who consciously modeled himself on the political and military heroes of Roman antiquity. More than that, and what made MacArthur potentially dangerous, was a charismatic political presence that held wide popular appeal and could well have vaulted him into the White House.[6]

The case of MacArthur is sufficient to show that modern democracies have not completely solved the problem of civil–military relations. There seems little reason for the United States or any other well-established democracy today to worry about the prospect of a military coup (although it might be recalled that some French generals attempted one against Charles de Gaulle as late as 1962), but the unique culture of military organizations and their estrangement from the civilian world, even – or rather particularly – in contemporary democracies remains a constant source of policy disagreements and personal friction and misunderstanding.[7] A perhaps surprising dimension of the problem is the political profile of military proconsuls. On more than one occasion, MacArthur used the prospect of his candidacy for the presidency on the opposition ticket to intimidate his commander in chief and enhance his own proconsular freedom of action. Though admittedly an extreme case, MacArthur's situation was not unique in the American record. In very recent years, this issue has reemerged on the scene in the person of General David Petraeus.

As for the second argument, the basic point is that the bureaucratization of contemporary life that is so obvious in the experience of ordinary citizens is much less operative at senior levels of government. Senior American officials in particular are, to be sure, enmeshed in a complex web of congressionally mandated studies, internal strategy reviews, presidential directives, and public policy documents that might seem to preclude any real freedom of action for

---

[5] Max Weber, *Economy and Society*, ed. Guenther Roth and Claus Wittich, 2 vols. (Berkeley: University of California Press, 1978), II, ch. 14.

[6] See especially Michael Schaller, *Douglas MacArthur: The Far Eastern General* (New York: Oxford University Press, 1989).

[7] See, e.g., Eliot A. Cohen, *Supreme Command: Soldiers, Statesmen, and Leadership in Wartime* (New York: Free Press, 2002).

individuals other than those at the very top. Yet the reality of all this is much less than meets the eye. The American national security bureaucracy remains unusually decentralized and fragmented. Partly because of the sheer scope of the responsibilities facing those at the helm of the world's only surviving superpower, the attention the top policy-makers are able to accord any single problem is limited no matter how pressing or important. Even when a policy decision is made, it is often not really made, but remains open to continuing challenge depending on the external circumstances and the shifting alliances of the bureaucratic players involved. The autonomous role of Congress in the American political system adds a further element of uncertainty, providing as it does a ready avenue for executive officials to obstruct or circumvent normal policy channels. Further, disciplining officials for perceived failure or for less than cooperative or even insubordinate behavior is difficult and tends to be avoided wherever possible, given the political complications it usually entails.[8] Even within the military, where discipline and respect for the chain of command are more integral to the institutional culture, the sacking of generals or admirals is rare. The relief of General Stanley McChrystal as senior American commander in Afghanistan in 2010 is a striking exception to this rule.[9] A final and related point is the role of the contemporary media in distorting the workings of bureaucratic processes in democracies today, and again particularly the United States. General Douglas MacArthur was a careful student of the press and used it to full advantage to increase his political profile at home and strengthen his independence of action. He learned this from an earlier American proconsul, General Leonard Wood.

Thirdly, there is the question of communication between governments and their proconsuls. It is natural to assume that the scope for proconsular leadership was drastically diminished by the invention of virtually instantaneous electronic communications in the course of the nineteenth century. The key development here was the laying of transoceanic telegraph cables beginning around mid-century, which allowed Great Britain in particular to reduce from weeks or even months to hours the time necessary to communicate with the far-flung officers of its empire. The fact of the matter, however, is that Britain's most memorably independent-minded proconsuls actually postdate this development. Personalities, leadership style, and organizational relationships all contribute to the proconsular phenomenon. And more important than the technology of communication itself, it can be argued, are the protocols and practices that structure communication and the problem these are designed to

---

[8] For a revealing account of bureaucratic infighting in Washington at the time of the invasion of Iraq, see Feith (then Under Secretary of Defense for Policy), chs. 8–9, 14. See more generally Carnes Lord, *The Presidency and the Management of National Security* (New York: Free Press, 1988).

[9] McChrystal was cashiered for derisive comments about senior civilian officials purportedly made by the general or his staff to a reporter. The relative frequency of firings of senior military personnel by then-current Secretary of Defense Robert M. Gates very much reflects his own leadership style rather than any shift in this area in the culture of official Washington.

avoid – communication content that is vague, misleading, contradictory, or simply muddled. For an understanding of intragovernmental communications today, it is vital to grasp the net loss in intellectually disciplined staff work caused by growing reliance on casual email exchanges and PowerPoint briefings. Although this is certainly not unique to the United States, it is almost certainly more advanced here than elsewhere. One has only to sample the archives of American political-military decision-making during and after World War II – or, for that matter, British diplomatic dispatches at any time in the nineteenth century – to sense the secular decline in the basic clarity and strategic logic of American intergovernmental communications today. An unintended consequence of this is a weakening of bureaucratic constraints on our proconsular leaders.

None of this is meant to suggest that MacArthur is the typical (and still less the "ideal type") American proconsul. It is rather to argue that there has been more scope for proconsular leadership on the American political stage in the past than is generally recognized. Nor is this necessarily a bad thing. The leadership deficits the United States has had to face recently in the Iraq and Afghan theaters are nothing new. Similar problems plagued the American effort in Vietnam in the 1960s and 1970s, although this fact has tended to be overshadowed by the gross errors that marked the military dimension of that war. At the same time, however, it is also clear that they are not somehow an inevitable by-product of the structure of the American government or of American political culture. If Iraq and Vietnam seem to point to the inability of the American Republic to carry out a classic imperial policy abroad, other episodes in the American experience point in the opposite direction. American military officers in a proconsular role – MacArthur himself most notably – achieved startling success during the occupation of Nazi Germany and Imperial Japan after World War II, as well as in earlier undertakings such as the reconstruction of Cuba (1898–1902) and the long American occupation of the Philippines (1898–1936) following the Spanish-American War. In fact, though, even Iraq and Vietnam are not simply examples of American proconsular failure. Indeed, both are unusually instructive cases because they tell a mixed story, one that enables the observer to understand the underlying causes of both failure and success in proconsular leadership in a single operational theater.

This is a study, then, in what may be called, with all due qualification, imperial governance. Its focus, however, is not on imperial leadership as such or the central machinery of imperial governance, but rather on the manner in which central authority is exercised on the imperial periphery by subordinate officials. More specifically, we are interested in subordinate officials of a certain type – not simply imperial administrators, but consequential leaders who contributed importantly to the formulation and execution of policy on the marches of empire. For the sake of convenience and clarity, we shall refer to such officials as proconsuls in the proper sense of the term. Proconsular leadership calls for the exercise of statecraft of a high order – indeed, sometimes of the highest order, if the founding of what are (in effect if not in name) new states or regimes can be considered the highest task of statecraft. Part of its scope is suggested by the contemporary terms "nation-building" and "stability and reconstruction operations." Perhaps most characteristically, it involves in some combination the instruments of both political and military power. Indeed, its most difficult challenge is the proper coordination of these instruments. It faces secondary but scarcely less daunting challenges, however, with respect to material resources, economics, and finance, as well as ethnicity, religion, and culture – the latter a potentially explosive arena that empires too frequently neglect at their great peril, as the recent American experience in Iraq attests.

It is perhaps advisable to step back here to address the vexed question of how "imperialism" as a contemporary as well as a historical phenomenon should be described and assessed. It can be predicted with a high degree of confidence that this study will not be greeted with enthusiasm by those who resent the role of American power in the world today and see no difference between the behavior of the United States in its dealings with lesser states and that of the conquering territorial empires of times past. Let it be said as clearly as possible at the outset, then, that it is not the purpose of the present work to provide a brief either for imperialism generally or for American imperialism in particular. Nor, for that matter, does it accept the idea that there actually is an "American Empire." The vocabulary of "empire," "proconsul," and similar terms is used throughout this study as a literary and heuristic device and for stylistic convenience, and is in no way intended as an adequate substantive characterization of what is being discussed, let alone as an endorsement of it. Having said this, however, I find myself obliged to note that I do not find everything associated with imperialism – especially the "liberal imperialism" of Britain but even the imperialism of ancient Rome – irremediably evil or without useful positive lessons for contemporary democracies. If that were the case, this book would not have been written.

To clear the conceptual decks before proceeding, it will perhaps be well to offer a brief discussion of the meaning of "empire" and the considerations that can lead one to conclude that the United States is not an empire in any useful sense of that term. In the course of this discussion I will contrast my own perspective with that of Niall Ferguson, a leading proponent of an imperial role for the United States in the world of today. I begin with an account of another empire of classical times, that of Athens, the world's first democracy.[10]

After the Athenians led a coalition of willing Greek city-states in a successful war of resistance against the invading Persian Empire early in the fifth century BC, they remained for decades thereafter the *hegemon* ("leader") of

---

[10] What follows draws on Carnes Lord, "Dreams of Empire," *Claremont Review of Books* (Fall 2004): 11–12. On Athenian imperialism see, for example, Michael Doyle, *Empires* (Ithaca, NY: Cornell University Press, 1986), ch. 3.

a maritime-oriented alliance designed to control the waters of the Aegean and thus contain Persian power. Initially, most of the allied cities, even very small ones, contributed ships to the coalition's naval forces. As time passed, however, and with the acquiescence if not encouragement of the Athenians, cash subsidies came to replace actual military forces as the allied contribution to the common defense. Gradually, too, as the Persian threat came to seem less immediate, the allies grew restive with Athens' sometimes heavy-handed leadership, particularly when the Athenians appropriated league funds for a major public works building program at home (we owe the Parthenon to it, among other things). Eventually, Samos, one of the more powerful of these allies, rose in revolt against Athens; it was subdued only after a lengthy and bitter struggle. From this point on, it was clear to all that the nature of Athens' leadership in Greece had taken a fateful turn: what began as hegemony had ended in "empire" (*archê*, meaning simply "rule").

There are certainly suggestive parallels between this ancient history and the evolution of the Atlantic Alliance under the leadership of the United States following World War II. Particularly interesting is the complicity of the allies themselves in the drift toward empire, reminding one of the long decline in the military capabilities of NATO Europe relative to the United States and its growing psychological dependence on America as the global security provider. It is also worth emphasizing the relatively mild character of the Athenian empire. Many of Athens' dependencies were democracies that were friendly to the metropolis for ideological reasons and looked to it for support against internal political opponents; but even non-democratic cities tended to enjoy a high degree of political autonomy.

At the same time, the fundamental difference between Athens and America is clear. The allies of the United States have both "exit" and "voice" to a much greater degree than did those of the Athenians. The United States never sent the Sixth Fleet against France when it withdrew from the military component of NATO in the 1960s or opposed the invasion of Iraq in 2002, as the Athenians sent their navy against the Samians. Nor, of course, has the United States sought to plant or acquire colonial dependencies (with exceptions relating primarily to the Spanish-American War), as did the Athenians, the Romans, and especially the European maritime powers of modern times. Most tellingly, when the United States did engage in territorial conquest, notably in Europe and in the Pacific in the course of the Second World War, it showed no interest in permanent domination or exploitation of these areas (unlike the Athenians, for example, in their invasion of Sicily, or its own quasi-imperial rival, the Soviet Union); rather, its policy was to rebuild and rehabilitate them as part of a broad alliance of democratic states that came to be known as the Free World. From this point of view, it has to be said that a great deal of the current talk about an emerging American "empire" is simply lacking in elementary historical perspective and represents a gross misuse of language.

Is the United States really an empire in any meaningful sense? Niall Ferguson, one of the most distinguished younger historians writing today, answers this question with an emphatic yes.[11] Ferguson denies that there is any real distinction between hegemony and empire. The fact that the United States, unlike conventional empires, has for most of its history eschewed direct rule of foreign peoples is not sufficient to deny it the name of empire, for as the British (or, for that matter, the Romans) showed, imperial rule can also be indirect – rule exercised through native elites or through the promotion of extreme economic dependency, as in the case of British financial domination of Chile and Argentina in the nineteenth century.[12] From the earliest days of the republic, Ferguson contends, Americans had "intimations" of empire, albeit an "empire of liberty," in Thomas Jefferson's well-known phrase. Washington himself called it a "nascent empire." That the new nation would expand was a foregone conclusion as early as July 1776, when the Continental Congress rejected a proposal to set western boundaries for the states. Although dollars and diplomacy contributed as much to the acquisition of its vast territories as military force, the United States was far from hesitant to take up arms against Indians, the Mexicans, or other inconvenient claimants to those lands. And from an early period it was also clear that America's "manifest destiny" would be pursued beyond its own shores, especially in Central America and the Caribbean and later in the Pacific. The Monroe Doctrine signaled the nation's intention to establish a hegemonic sphere of influence in Latin America. The acquisition of Hawaii in 1898 marked the beginning of an openly imperial phase. More typical, however, and of greater relevance for the present, was the growing involvement of the United States in the political and economic affairs of Mexico and other countries in Central America and the Caribbean early in the twentieth century in an effort to foster good government and protect perceived American interests in the region. As President Theodore Roosevelt put it in his "Corollary" to the Monroe Doctrine (1904): "Chronic wrong-doing, or an impotence which results in a general loosening of the ties of civilized society, may . . . ultimately require intervention by some civilized nation." Although American enthusiasm for nation-building and democratic development in places like Nicaragua, Cuba, and Haiti did not long survive the realities encountered there, the strategy of "dictating democracy" has retained at least latent appeal throughout the American political class as the best way to deal with international troublemakers and failed states.

For Ferguson (an economic historian by trade and a Briton), the United States is in a deep sense the successor to the British Empire as part of a larger enterprise he calls "Anglobalization." The "liberal empire" established by the

[11] Niall Ferguson, *Colossus: The Price of America's Empire* (New York: Penguin, 2004). See also his *Empire: The Rise and Demise of the British World Order and the Lessons for Global Power* (New York: Basic Books, 2002).

[12] Ferguson, *Colossus*, 8–12. The distinction between empire and hegemony is accepted by Doyle but denied by various other commentators either explicitly (Chalmers Johnson, *The Sorrows of Empire: Militarism, Secrecy, and the End of the Republic* [New York: Henry Holt, 2004], 30) or implicitly (Henry A. Kissinger, *Does America Need a Foreign Policy? Towards a Diplomacy for the 21st Century* [New York: Simon & Schuster, 2001], 325 ff.).

British differed qualitatively from previous empires. Though careful not to airbrush Britannia's warts, Ferguson rightly emphasizes Britain's role in promoting global free trade and economic development and disseminating liberal political ideas and institutions. Winston Churchill once characterized British imperialism in this way: "[to reclaim] from barbarism fertile regions and large populations . . . to give peace to warring tribes, to administer justice where all was violence, to strike the chains off the slave, to draw the richness from the soil, to plant the earliest seeds of commerce and learning, to increase in whole peoples their capacities for pleasure and diminish their chances of pain. . . . " In suitably updated language, Ferguson thinks, this could serve equally as an advertisement for contemporary American foreign policy.

Ferguson's case is in many ways persuasive, yet it seriously overstates the continuities between America and imperial Britain. He fails to emphasize sufficiently, for example, the extent to which American continental expansion was driven by individuals rather than the state, as well as the resistance consistently and for at least a time successfully shown by a succession of Congresses toward various annexationist projects (Canada, Texas, the Dominican Republic, Samoa, Hawaii, Cuba, the Philippines). Although many of Britain's imperial acquisitions were no doubt undertaken in part for defensive reasons, this was more clearly the case for the United States. Further, the republican character of the country made it very difficult for Americans to hold alien peoples in permanent or even semi-permanent subjection, as the Philippine experiment so plainly showed. Finally, while the processes of "Anglobalization" are certainly real, it is less clear in what sense these processes are inherently imperial or imperialistic. To speak, as Ferguson does, of Britain's "imperialism of free trade" or America's "imperialism of anti-imperialism" begins at some point to drain this term of all useful meaning. In any event, Ferguson himself goes on to argue that whether or not the United States is objectively an empire, Americans are reluctant, not to say inept imperialists. Americans are imperialists "in denial;" they still cling to an antiquated vision of their country as the slayer of empires. America is hobbled in its imperial mission by three "deficits": an economic deficit, a manpower deficit, and an attention deficit. Ferguson is excellent on the economic dimension of modern so-called imperialism, noting that, contrary to the notion popularized in the 1980s by the historian Paul Kennedy,[13] America is far from suffering from "imperial overstretch": For the United States today (and the same was true for Britain in the nineteenth century), the cost of empire is remarkably low. The United States currently fields the mightiest army in the history of the world for a very modest fraction of its gross national product. The real problem is the nation's unbridled appetite for consumption and its apparent entrapment in an upward spiral of social welfare costs. Americans have, in other words, little interest in sacrificing personal comfort for the honor of ruling the world.

---

[13] Paul Kennedy, *The Rise and Fall of the Great Powers* (New York: Random House, 1987).

In spite of the development of a genuinely democratic politics in Britain in the course of the nineteenth century, one might add, its traditional aristocracy retained important political and social roles in national life at least up to the First World War; one of these roles was in imperial and colonial governance. As in classical Rome, an aristocratic class ambitious for honor in war and political preferment found a natural outlet in an expanding overseas empire. This helped to create and sustain an imperial dynamic that had no real counterpart in the American experience – although echoes of it could certainly be found there. For similar reasons, Ferguson points out, Americans are unwilling to create the additional legions or underwrite and officer the auxiliary forces (some equivalent, that is, of Britain's Indian army) necessary for policing the world effectively. Finally, Americans are fixated on the short run and lose interest in imperial projects before they are fairly launched, as we have arguably done in Iraq as well as Afghanistan. All of this would seem to argue strongly that the United States should not be in the empire business.[14]

While there has been a flood of scholarly and more popular writing on the general subject of empire in recent years, proconsular leadership as a generic political phenomenon seems never to have been systematically studied and

---

[14] William E. Odom (a former U.S. Army general) and Robert Dujarric have recently offered an analysis that has many parallels with Ferguson's, especially in their appreciation of the importance of liberal economic institutions and practices for the success of the new American imperium: *America's Inadvertent Empire* (New Haven, CT: Yale University Press, 2004); valuable too is its focus on aspects of American power that tend to be neglected or at least not considered sufficiently in such discussions – demography, education, science and technology, and the media and mass culture. Odom and Dujarric argue that the extent of American superiority in each of these areas makes it a phenomenon that is historically *sui generis* and alters the normal rules of international behavior. Against the dominant "realist" school of international relations theory, they argue that the liberal character of the American imperium – that is to say, of the advanced democracies more or less associated with the U.S. alliance system – creates a kind of "constitutional" structure that helps make American international behavior self-limiting and thereby obviates traditional "balancing" against the U.S. by potential major power adversaries. They go beyond Ferguson in insisting that the American global order, if an empire at all, is "an empire of a new type." Along similar lines, Frank Nincovich argues: "In a real sense, the center of the story is not imperialism, or American empire, but the system of globalization that has replaced old imperial ways of doing business.... If, metaphorically speaking, this new global order is indeed the new empire, it is an empire without an emperor, an empire in which the United States is at best an embattled general manager." "The New Empire," in Kimberley Kagan, ed., *The Imperial Moment* (Cambridge, MA: Harvard University Press, 2010), 168. Recent full-throated defenses of "American imperialism" include Thomas F. Madden, *Empires of Trust: How Rome Built – and America is Building – a New World* (New York: Dutton, 2008) and Deepak Lal, *In Praise of Empires: Globalization and Order* (New York: Palgrave MacMillan, 2004). Lal, an economist, native of India, and one-time Indian nationalist and socialist (an uncle was a member of Nehru's cabinet), is an interesting convert to the cause of the Raj and American-inspired global capitalism. For a more nuanced assessment see Charles S. Meier, *Among Empires: American Ascendancy and its Predecessors* (Cambridge, MA: Harvard University Press, 2006), who also refuses to decide whether the United States is an empire. A forceful statement of the skeptical case is Victor Davis Hanson, "What Empire?" in Andrew J. Bacevich, ed., *The Imperial Tense: Prospects and Problems of American Empire* (Chicago: Ivan R. Dee, 2003), 146–55.

remains a neglected – indeed, virtually an unrecognized – topic of scholarly investigation and analysis.[15] In the Roman context, there has been a powerful tendency in modern historiography to credit the Roman Senate with greater direction and control of foreign policy from the center than seems to have been the case following the extension of Roman power beyond the Italian mainland in the third century BC, and, accordingly, to slight the policy role of proconsular and other subordinate officials under the Republic. Although recent scholarship has modified this picture in important ways, it remains an influential paradigm.[16] In the British case, while there have been numerous studies of individual imperial officials,[17] with one important exception to be discussed shortly, there has been so far as I know no systematic analysis of British proconsular leadership as such. In the American case, there has indeed been heightened interest in very recent years in the increasingly prominent role assumed by America's peacetime regional military commanders in the shaping of American policy in the post–Cold War world. It is of more than passing interest that the formal title of these military proconsuls was recently changed from "commanders in chief" (CINCs) to "combatant commanders" (COCOMs) as a way to reemphasize their primarily military role.[18] Again, however, there has been no attempt to look at this development or at the recent performance of senior American military and diplomatic figures in ongoing theaters of conflict in the light of the country's considerable experience in comparable situations over the course of its history. Nor have earlier American proconsuls attracted much recent attention by historians or biographers.[19]

[15] See, however, L. H. Gann and Peter Duignan, eds., *African Proconsuls: European Governors in Africa* (New York: Free Press, 1978), esp. 1–16.

[16] The most important recent study is Arthur M. Eckstein, *Senate and General: Individual Decision Making and Roman Foreign Relations, 264–194 B.C.* (Berkeley: University of California Press, 1987).

[17] See notably Mark Bence-Jones, *Clive of India* (New York: St. Martin's, 1974); L. H. Gann and Peter Duignan, eds., *The Rulers of British Africa, 1870–1914* (Stanford, CA: Stanford University Press, 1978); John A. Benyon, *Proconsul and Paramountcy in South Africa: The High Commission, British Supremacy, and the Sub-continent, 1806–1910* (Durban: University of Natal Press, 1980); David Gilmour, *Curzon: Imperial Statesman* (New York: Farrar, Straus and Giroux, 1994); C. W. R. Long, *British Proconsuls in Egypt, 1914–1929* (London: Routledge, 2004); and Roger Owen, *Lord Cromer: Victorian Imperialist, Edwardian Proconsul* (Oxford: Oxford University Press, 2004).

[18] The "commander in chief" title was apparently considered to derogate from the authority of the Commander in Chief proper, that is, the president. On the larger issue see especially Andrew J. Bacevich, *American Empire: The Realities and Consequences of U.S. Diplomacy* (Cambridge, MA: Harvard University Press, 2002), ch. 2 ("Rise of the Proconsuls"), and Derek S. Reveron, ed., *America's Viceroys: The Military and U.S. Foreign Policy* (New York: Palgrave MacMillan, 2004).

[19] The exception is General Douglas MacArthur, well-served in an authoritative biography by D. Clayton James, *The Years of MacArthur*, 3 vols. (Boston: Houghton Mifflin, 1970–85). See also Jean Edward Smith, *Lucius D. Clay: An American Life* (New York: Henry Holt, 1990), and Jack McCallum, *Leonard Wood: Rough Rider, Surgeon, Architect of American Imperialism* (New York: New York University Press, 2006).

If there is a single trend in the literature on empire over the last half-century or so, it is a growing recognition of the importance of the "periphery" in determining the character of empires relative to the imperial "center" or "metropole."[20] Much contemporary theorizing about empire tends to assume that what drives the creation or expansion of empires is not simply the motives animating key policy-makers in the imperial capital, but rather a complex bargain between these policy-makers and forces and circumstances at work on the imperial periphery. The latter include most obviously the native population in all its variety, but also individuals and groups originating in the mother country – traders, settlers, missionaries, adventurers, and, not least, colonial soldiers and administrators. Typically, at the center of this bargain is a collaborative relationship of some sort with the native population or elements of it, especially indigenous elites of various kinds, because it is rare for empires to be imposed and sustained by force alone.[21] Certainly not to be neglected is the role of private individuals and organizations. As noted earlier, the westward expansion of the United States was largely driven by such forces rather than by the designs of its government. The role of trade in the development of the British Empire is fundamental; it is particularly striking that the foundations of British India were laid not by the British state but by a private trading organization, the East India Company. But what, then, of the representatives of the imperial government in the periphery? Are they best understood simply as extensions of the center – or as independent or potentially independent peripheral actors? For the most part, if only implicitly, the first answer is the one given.

Yet the opposite case is not difficult to make. In a brief but suggestive discussion of the "proconsular phenomenon" in imperial Britain, Ronald Hyam observes:

One of the most striking features of imperial administration and expansion was the power of the "man on the spot." Throughout the century governors ignored or exceeded their instructions, especially in India and Africa.... Sir George Grey's desire for independence of action [in South Africa] led him to behave with extraordinary tactlessness and intolerance toward the colonial office; for years he got away with it. Sir John Pope-Hennessy [in West Africa] also disobeyed explicit but unwelcome instructions;

[20] The seminal study is Ronald E. Robinson and John Gallagher, "The Imperialism of Free Trade," *Economic History Review*, 2nd. Ser., 6 (1953–54): 1–15. See also Ronald E. Robinson, *Africa and the Victorians: The Official Mind of Imperialism* (London: MacMillan, 1961), as well as his "Non-European Foundations of European Imperialism: Sketch for a Theory of Collaboration," in Roger Owen and R. Sutcliff, eds., *Studies in a Theory of Imperialism* (London: Longman, 1972, 117–42); D. K. Fieldhouse, *Economics and Empire 1830–1914* (Ithaca, NY: Cornell University Press, 1973); and the overview and assessment of the "peripheral" approach in W. Roger Louis, ed., *Imperialism: the Robinson and Gallagher Controversy* (New York: New Viewpoints, 1976), as well as Wolfgang J. Mommsen, *Theories of Imperialism*, trans. P. S. Falla (Chicago: University of Chicago Press, 1980), 86–112. For a recent scholarly overview of the imperialism issue broadly see Herfried Münkler, *Empires: The Logic of World Domination from Ancient Rome to the United States*, trans. Patrick Camiller (Cambridge: Polity, 2007).
[21] See notably Colin Newbury, *Patrons, Clients, and Empire: Chieftancy and Over-rule in Asia, Africa, and the Pacific* (Oxford: Oxford University Press, 2003).

the colonial office might criticize and rebuke, but generally backed him up. His career also showed the power a governor had to make or break subordinates at will. Lord Ellenborough had always opposed advance in the Indus Valley, but within a few months of arriving in India he confirmed in 1842 the annexation of Sind, having given his trust and support to Sir Charles Napier. Ellenborough was recalled, but Sind remained. The entire cabinet was against the blatantly aggressive annexation. . . . The personal views and ambitions of Ellenborough and Napier enabled them, in an era of slow communications, to carry the day against the whole weight of the British government and the East India Company.

Lest the reader mistakenly conclude that the slow communications of this period were a decisive factor in all this, Hyam continues:

Commodore Goodenough fulfilled his commission to investigate in Fiji requests for annexation by accepting the cession of the islands [1874]. . . . The grandiloquent, willfully enthusiastic Lytton disobeyed orders as viceroy [of India], so dragging Britain into an unwanted war in Afghanistan [1878–79]. The colonial office on more than one occasion between 1903 and 1906 had doubts about Lugard's forceful advances in Nigeria, but it had in the last resort to rely on his analysis of how serious any given rising might be. . . . Generally, the British government reluctantly accepted the initiatives of its proconsuls, and it did so increasingly as the century wore on. Rhodes, Mackenzie, Warren and Baden-Powell, who brought expansion to the northern frontiers of the empire in South Africa in the 1880s and 1890s, all ignored instructions which conflicted with their conceptions, and from 1884 they defied the colonial office with impunity. The last years of the Unionist rule [1895–1905] were the heyday of proconsular authority. Cromer's position in Egypt was unchallenged. [Prime Minister Arthur] Balfour complained that Curzon raised India to the status of an independent and not always friendly autocracy. But as he recognized all too well, it was difficult to override prestigious officers who had detailed local knowledge.[22]

What was behind these extraordinary assertions of individual authority, not seldom in direct contravention of official orders? Personal factors were certainly at work. Men were often drawn to office in the Empire for reasons such as a desire for freedom from conventional restraints, disgust with politics in the mother country, or simply a desire to wield autocratic power. Some of them had charismatic and forceful personalities that were difficult for others to resist. At another level, however, they simply took advantage of opportunities available to them in the circumstances they faced. Generally speaking, they assumed power that was there to be assumed. In the best case, they assumed power not for self-interested or idiosyncratic reasons, but because it was necessary to carry out their imperial missions. As such, one can argue, they played a unique and indispensable role as mediators between the periphery and the imperial center, especially in the case of what might be called peripheral subsystems of major strategic significance.

---

[22] Ronald Hyam, *Britain's Imperial Century, 1814–1915: A Study of Empire and Expansion* (New York: Harper and Row, 1976), 148–50.

Such, in brief, is the argument developed by South African historian John Benyon, in what remains the single most important analytical treatment of the proconsular phenomenon.[23] Although his discussion is based wholly on the British imperial experience, it plainly has wider application and deserves careful attention. Benyon begins by noting the vagueness of the term "proconsul" as generally used, while suggesting that its main, generally accepted connotation would seem to be "semi-independent and extraordinary capacity to shape the periphery" of an empire. A proconsular official is therefore more than simply the metropole's "man on the spot," for semi-independent decisions can be made at many levels of a colonial hierarchy, including governor, lieutenant governor, frontier soldier, district commissioner, or mere magistrate. He tentatively suggests that perhaps the most straightforward way to distinguish a true proconsul is charisma – a "masterful and magnetic personality." Frederick Lugard, for example, is remembered as a proconsul of the first rank not so much for what he actually accomplished in the imperial backwater of northern Nigeria but because by force of his personality and a "penchant for publicity" he developed a doctrine of imperial administration that became gospel for two generations of British colonial officials. Benyon also underscores the importance of "opportunity" for the fullest development of proconsular power and influence. Opportunity includes such matters as limitations on imperial communications, the varying degrees of interest and involvement in imperial affairs by governments at the center, and the dynamism of imperial expansion at a given historical moment (he notes that "the halcyon days of peripheral 'opportunity' were largely over by 1918"). But the most important factor for him is the extent of the "challenge" actually posed by the imperial territory for which an imperial official is responsible. This challenge is in each case rooted in the geographic and strategic realities of the empire at large.

There were, Benyon maintains, six strategic points or "keys" to maintaining the integrity of the British Empire and its global mastery of the seas: the Straits of Dover, the St. Lawrence River, the Straits of Gibraltar, the Suez Canal, the Cape of Good Hope, and the Straits of Malacca. Around these points grew up six regions of transcendent strategic concern for Britain – "paramountcies," as he calls them – which would become the seats of Britain's true proconsuls:

A Governor-General presided over the grouping of British North American colonies along the St. Lawrence. If allied to a Great Power, Ireland threatened the Western approaches to the Straits of Dover; a Lord Lieutenant . . . had therefore to neutralize the age-old hostility of Catholic and Celtic Erin "come what may." Between the Straits of Gibraltar and Isthmus of Suez a Mediterranean proconsulate grew up under the Governor of Malta and Lord High Commissioner of the Ionian Islands. Modestly named British Agent and Consul General, the successor-proconsul in Cairo would preside over the later North African version of this Levantine paramountcy as it extended from Suez

[23] John A. Benyon, "Overlords of Empire? British 'Proconsular Imperialism' in Comparative Perspective," *Journal of Imperial and Commonwealth History* 19 (1991): 164–202. See also his *Proconsul and Paramountcy in South Africa* (1980).

to the very headwaters of the Nile. A High Commissioner would eventually rule as proconsul over virtually the whole of the Southern African sub-continent. Under the proconsulate of its Governors-General (later, "Viceroys") India was of course the greatest of all strategic satellites. Consequently, the paramountcy which would emerge under a Governor and later High Commissioner around the Straits of Malacca and Singapore would evolve in circumstances of dependency – and show resultant peculiarities.[24]

In addition to their strategic position relative to the Empire as a whole, he continues, these imperial subsystems or paramountcies are typically characterized by the following: the presence of serious communal cleavages on ethnic, racial, or religious lines; the existence of several foci of imperial authority calling for greater coordination as a single strategic entity; "open and turbulent" frontiers generating pressures to extend the umbrella of imperial authority; a corresponding need for military forces under centralized proconsular control; the complication of actual or potential great power involvement and hence a need for local/regional diplomacy; and, finally, formal or informal recognition at the center by way of far-reaching special concessions, charters, mandates, and the like.

The "portmanteau" commissions of the proconsuls, which made them "High Commissioners" or "Governors-General," or conveyed local diplomatic competence, together with a variety of letters patent and special statutes, directly or implicitly acknowledged the fact that regional aggregations of colonies, fortresses, extra-territorial jurisdictions of protectorates and protected states, and spheres of influence (as opposed to single dependencies), were growing up under their aegis to be significant power-systems or proto-states in their own right. Far from being passive transmitters of metropolitan or peripheral impulses, these proconsuls were hardly the meekest of "mediators." In ways usually denied to ordinary governors the proconsuls could manipulate their masters at home and marshal their colonial collaborators in order to shift the structural determinants in the imperial relationship and realign them with their individual – often idiosyncratic – programmes.[25]

The principal functions of imperial proconsuls, Benyon argues, had to do, first and above all, with security; second, with constitutional development and the consolidation of imperial political control; and third, with maintaining and strengthening imperial political and diplomatic influence in their region. He emphasizes particularly the role of proconsuls in "originating major constitutional dispensations," noting that they were often able through personal lobbying to "carry the men at home along with them," something generally not within the reach of ordinary colonial governors.[26] Less obvious, although

---

[24] "Overlords of Empire?" 168–69. He concludes this paragraph by adding: "Finally, beyond Asia, the imperial drive had begun to fade, so the High Commissioner for the Western Pacific would find his watery proconsulate inconveniently etiolated." This is a reference to the short-lived dual appointment of the Governor of Fiji, Sir Arthur Gordon, as High Commissioner of the Western Pacific in 1877 (189–91).

[25] Ibid., 170.

[26] Ibid., 177.

"perhaps more significant in the long run," were the administrative innovations that proconsuls were able to carry out, often without any prior instruction from London. The efforts of Hastings and Cornwallis, for example, to reform and professionalize the East India Company's service were vital in cementing the bases of British power in India. Finally, the role of proconsuls in regional diplomacy was often of considerable importance. The governors-general of Canada in the early part of the nineteenth century had an important role in managing Britain's relationship with the United States; the High Commissioner in South Africa managed diplomacy with the independent Boer republics; and perhaps most remarkably, large areas of British foreign policy in Asia were virtually contracted out to the "Foreign Department" of the government of India.

It could be argued that given the global reach and complexity of the British Empire at its height, the proconsular phenomenon as found there is in fact not typical of empires throughout history. A case could be made that in some respects its proconsuls operated under even looser controls than proconsuls in the Roman Republic – and much looser certainly than provincial governors in the Roman Empire. Nevertheless, there are striking parallels between the British and Roman cases. The American case is obviously not entirely comparable, given not only the much smaller scope and duration of American imperial experiments but the weaker commitment to an imperial mission in the country and – a corollary to this – the lower threshold on the part of the political class or the public in general for tolerating proconsular freelancing. Still, the least that can be said is that there are American analogs for all of these aspects of the proconsular phenomenon in its British incarnation, and that the British case therefore provides a highly useful lens for viewing and interpreting the American experience.

What sort of person typically fills the proconsular role? To this point we may seem to have assumed that proconsuls must always be military officers of senior rank. This is not at all the case. American proconsuls have been generals, politicians, businessmen, and diplomats; on occasion they have been former cabinet members or potential presidential candidates. British proconsuls were probably more typically civilian than military, although often from an aristocratic and military background.[27] But it needs to be recognized that the distinction between civilian and military officials was often much less sharp in

---

[27] Rather, this was increasingly so as the nineteenth century progressed and a civilian colonial service was fully established. However, the historical roots of Britain's proconsuls are to be sought in the military governors of imperial garrison towns in the sixteenth and seventeenth centuries. See Stephen Saunders Webb, *The Governors-General: The English Army and the Definition of the Empire, 1569–1681* (Chapel Hill: University of North Carolina Press, 1979), a rich account of the relationship of center and periphery in the formative period of the British Empire. For additional background, of particular relevance for an understanding of the American Revolution, see Jack P. Greene, *Peripheries and Center: Constitutional Development in the Extended Polities of the British Empire and the United States, 1607–1788* (Athens: University of Georgia Press, 1986).

the past than it is today. General Leonard Wood was never accepted as a real soldier by the American Army, for example; General Lucius Clay was appointed American proconsul in Germany because of his demonstrated administrative abilities, not any particular military talent or achievement (in fact, he had never seen combat). Clive and Hastings, the founders of British India, were essentially civilians, although both commanded military forces and won major battles. In classical Rome, in order to rise to positions of political leadership it was necessary to prove oneself as a soldier; Roman armies were therefore officered fundamentally by civilians (although often civilians who had served as military commanders for many years), and it was thus natural that such figures would assume roles in civil government abroad whenever that proved necessary. In many historical situations, moreover, proconsular leadership has not been unitary, but a shared function involving a military and a civilian official (or on occasion competing military or civilian officials, when their respective areas of operation were not clearly defined). In such cases, not surprisingly, divided authority has frequently been a recipe for inaction or disaster.

Any study of leadership needs to be sensitive to both the personal and the policy and institutional dimensions of this subject. The psychological aspects of proconsular leadership will be an important theme of this study. Delegated leadership as distinct from supreme leadership requires a delicate balancing of deference and initiative that can be difficult to achieve and to maintain, especially as the distance of the proconsul from the center and the demands (or opportunities) of autonomous decision-making increase. Psychological traits such as arrogance and ambition can have large effects.[28] At a more intellectual level, it will be necessary to look at the inherited and acquired mental equipment of proconsuls as well as their ways of conceptualizing their environment, tasks, and strategies. This becomes all the more important to the extent that the environment in which the proconsul operates is a culturally alien one. How proconsuls understand and cope with the alien "other" of the imperial periphery will be another theme of this study.[29]

With regard to the policy and institutional side of proconsular leadership, the critical issue is plainly the relation of the proconsul and the organizations he commands to the central structures of imperial decision-making. The core of the proconsular function is political-military leadership; its chief challenge is the coordination of civil and military authority in the periphery and its alignment with political-military leadership in the center. Civil authority at the properly proconsular level has two distinct components: on the one hand, the engineering of what Benyon calls "major constitutional dispensations" and, on the other, what one might describe as "foundational administrative reforms" (as distinct from routine administrative acts within a settled political and

---

[28] Some interesting reflections on this topic may be found in Hyam, 135–50.
[29] Consider again Hyam, ch. 2; and note also Susan B. Mattern, *Rome and the Enemy: Imperial Strategy in the Principate* (Berkeley: University of California Press, 1999).

institutional framework).[30] These include measures across a wide variety of economic activities, public health, infrastructure and transportation, education, and religion and culture. Further, there are the relationships (often largely informal rather than institutional) between proconsuls and local authorities and elites, both native and foreign. Finally, there is the proconsul's role, formally mandated or informally assumed, in conducting diplomatic relations with foreign powers or entities whose interests impinge on his peripheral sphere of action.

This study of course makes no claim to comprehensiveness. It does not deal at all with empires ancient or modern other than Rome and Britain, although an excellent case could be made for surveying the experience of ancient Persia or China or the modern Ottomans or France,[31] or for a more extensive study of the British imperial experience. Expanding the project in this way would have been impractical, however, given in particular the limited usefulness of the existing secondary literature on this subject. Nor does it attempt to provide more than a sketch of the relevant historical background of the periods it covers, or anything approaching a full account of a particular proconsul's life or deeds.

At the same time, I have avoided following the problematic (and frequently abused) practice in political science of focusing only on selected "case studies." For Rome, I have surveyed if only in cursory fashion the development of the proconsular phenomenon generally over the last several centuries of the Republic. For the United States, an effort has been made to include at least some discussion of all of the most important figures who can plausibly be identified as proconsuls in the properly functional sense of the term, from the Spanish-American War to the present.[32] The most prominent among them are General Leonard Wood and William Howard Taft in Cuba and the Philippines in the early twentieth century; General Douglas MacArthur in the Philippines, Japan, and Korea from 1936 to 1951; General Lucius Clay in Germany in the late 1940s; the intelligence operative Edward Lansdale in the Philippines and Vietnam in the 1950s; Ambassador Henry Cabot Lodge and General Maxwell Taylor in Vietnam in the early 1960s; General Creighton Abrams, Ambassador

---

[30] Though not a proconsul, Hamilton's reform program in the first decade of the American Republic is exemplary in this sense: Forrest McDonald, *Alexander Hamilton: A Biography* (New York: W.W. Norton, 1979). For the British Empire, the outstanding figures would be Hastings, Cromer, and Curzon.

[31] For France, mention should be made of Barnett Singer and John Langdon, *Cultured Force: Makers and Defenders of the French Colonial Empire* (Madison: University of Wisconsin Press, 2004), a comparative study of the major French proconsular figures of the nineteenth century. See also Douglas Porch, "Bugeaud, Gallieni, Lyautey: The Development of French Colonial Warfare," in Peter Paret, ed., *Makers of Modern Strategy from Machiavelli to the Nuclear Age* (Princeton, NJ: Princeton University Press, 1986), 376–407.

[32] It should be added that a case could perhaps be made for including certain proconsular-style military figures from the Mexican War, the Civil War, or the American occupation of Germany following World War I.

Ellsworth Bunker, and pacification chief William Colby in Vietnam in the late
1960s and early 1970s; General Wesley Clark in the Balkans in the late 1990s;
Ambassador L. Paul Bremer in Iraq in 2003–04; and General David Petraeus
in Iraq and Afghanistan from 2006.

It is important to underline to what extent such an effort is constrained
by the availability of pertinent historical materials. Some though not all of
these men composed autobiographies; even where such documents are available, however, they are frequently incomplete, when not actively obfuscatory
and self-serving. Primary reliance therefore must be placed on diaries, private
letters, and archival materials of various sorts gathered by biographers, some
of which were originally classified and therefore unavailable to researchers
until decades after the events. (This is notably the case, for example, with
General Lucius Clay, who has therefore received less attention and credit in
standard historical accounts of his tenure in postwar Germany than he plainly
deserves; MacArthur's reputation, on the other hand, has tended to suffer.) As
we approach the present, such materials remain for the most part out of reach,
and we must depend instead mostly on journalistic accounts of varying thor-
oughness and reliability – although it has to be noted that high-level decision-
making in the United States today is remarkably subject to virtually real-time
journalistic exposure compared to earlier eras and other societies. Even when
an extensive historical literature exists, however, key decision-makers – including presidents themselves (notably, for our period, McKinley and Franklin
Roosevelt) – often remain surprisingly opaque. It can only be hoped that this
study will pique the interest of future historians, who will carry further this
investigation of the proconsular story, in the United States and elsewhere.

In the American context, proconsular leadership appears in different guises
and has accordingly never been examined as a single phenomenon. As noted
at the outset, there has been a marked renewal of interest in this subject in
view of recent developments in Iraq and Afghanistan. As I argue, it encompasses activities as diverse as postconflict military occupations such as those
of the Philippines and Cuba following the Spanish-American War and Germany and Japan after World War II, nation-building and counterinsurgency in
Vietnam and Iraq, and the quasi-autonomous political-military roles that have
been increasingly assumed by the uniformed American regional combatant
commanders since the end of the Cold War, especially in the Balkans and the
Middle East. One could also make a case for considering the claim of ambassadors or special envoys confronting certain kinds of political-military crisis
situations, although again the limitations of the historical record are in many
such cases prohibitively severe.[33] The aftermath of the American invasion of
Iraq in 2003 offers a powerful case for the importance of proconsular leadership – both for better and worse. The combination of inept civilian leadership

---

[33] Some examples might be Amb. Ellsworth Bunker in the Dominican Republic in 1965, Amb.
Deane Hinton in Panama following the U.S. invasion of that country in 1989, and Amb. Robert
Oakley in Somalia following the U.S. intervention there in 1992.

in the person of Ambassador L. Paul Bremer and unimaginative military leadership in the persons of General George Casey and General Ricardo Sanchez, as well as the uneasy coexistence between them and the lack of effective direction from Washington, contributed substantially to the severe challenges the United States has had to confront in that country in the years since. At the same time, the military leadership of General David Petraeus and, perhaps as important, Petraeus' fruitful collaboration with Ryan Crocker, the very able U.S. ambassador to Baghdad, has demonstrated that effective proconsular leadership is possible in a very unpromising setting. The Afghan theater has similarly seen a changing cast of military and civilian leaders of varying capacities and achievements, culminating in 2010 in the appointment of General Petraeus as – in effect if not in name – the overall commander of American operations in that country. In the summer of 2011, however, both Petraeus and U.S. ambassador (and former general) Karl Eikenberry were replaced, with Petraeus agreeing to end his military career and accept appointment as director of the Central Intelligence Agency. While it is clearly too soon to provide an overall assessment of Petraeus' achievements, it is difficult to disagree with former Secretary of Defense Robert M. Gates when he characterized the general as the most distinguished soldier of his generation.

Concluding this study is a chapter that attempts to distill the lessons of the American proconsular experience for the present. There has been considerable hand-wringing in this country in recent years over the alleged militarization of U.S. foreign policy caused in significant part by the growing influence of the regional military "combatant commanders." Yet the history of proconsular leadership as reviewed here very largely fails to support the notion that the principal potential danger posed by American proconsuls is by generals insensitive to political contexts and requirements or ambitious for their own preferment. The fact of the matter is that the worst American proconsuls have been civilians – most prominently in our study, ambassadors Henry Cabot Lodge and L. Paul Bremer.[34] MacArthur is an outlier among military figures, but even his record is far from simply negative. The chief underlying problem, to state it simply, seems to be that civilians are less equipped to deal with military challenges than military officers (or at least superior ones) are to adapt to and master the various civil dimensions of postconflict situations. Such a conclusion has wide ramifications. It suggests that the U.S. military has erred fundamentally in attempting to shed the military government function it had embraced and performed so effectively at the end of World War II, while on the civilian side there has been a corresponding failure to come to grips in a serious fashion with the highly demanding postconflict – or, for that matter, "low-intensity conflict" – strategic and organizational environment.

This having been said, it is certainly legitimate to question the current organizational framework of the American military's overseas presence. I argue that

---

[34] Lesser figures include Francis Burton Harrison in the Philippines and Elbridge Durbrow in Vietnam.

the "combatant commands" as delineated under the authority of the venerable Unified Command Plan are obsolete artifacts of the Cold War and need to be fundamentally rethought. The current strategic environment calls for a holistic or global approach to managing U.S. military forces that is in tension with the regional approach imposed by current practice. Further, to the extent that the American "empire" remains in need of a regionally based organizational infrastructure, there is every reason to transition that infrastructure from a predominantly military to a predominantly civilian and interagency one. Finally, however, none of this is meant to suggest that proconsular leadership is a thing of the past. The key challenge we face in this regard is to recognize a potential requirement for proconsular leadership under certain circumstances and work toward incorporating such a requirement within the structures and processes of American national security decision-making.

2

Roman Origins

"Peccavi."
Sir Charles Napier[1]

In 327 BC, Quintus Publilius Philo, one of Rome's two consuls for that year, was commander of an army besieging the city of Neapolis (modern Naples), which had sided with the neighboring Samnites in their long struggle with Rome for dominance in central Italy. By immemorial custom, consuls – the chief executive officers of the Roman Republic – held office for a single year and were not normally eligible for (immediate) reelection. When the elections of magistrates for the coming year were held, however, it was deemed advisable not to replace the senior commander in the middle of these ongoing operations. Instead, the popular assembly passed a motion that "Quintus Publilius Philo should on the expiration of his consulship conduct the campaign in place of a consul [*pro consule*] until the war with the Greeks was concluded," according to the preeminent historian of the Republic. Thus did the Romans create their first "proconsul."[2]

Before exploring further the nature of proconsular decision-making in classical Rome and its historical evolution there, some basic points need to be made. To the extent that the notion of proconsulship or proconsular rule remains of interest today, it is in the context of discussions of (a putative) American "empire" and the role of regional American military commanders within it. In the Roman context, however, proconsulship in the proper and interesting sense of the term is a product of the Roman Republic, not the Roman Empire. The Roman Empire (27 BC–476 AD) indeed inherited institutional forms and terminology from the Republic that preceded it, proconsulship included; but imperial

---

[1] Latin for "I have sinned," cable famously attributed to the British general Sir Charles Napier on his unauthorized seizure of Sindh (now a province of Pakistan) in 1843.

[2] Titus Livius (Livy) 8.23.11–12, 26.7. Neapolis had been settled originally by Greek colonists.

proconsuls were something quite different from their republican counterparts. As we shall see, the reorganization of the Roman government effected by the first emperor, Caesar Augustus, set out to solve the fundamental problem that proconsular authority had come to pose for the Republic. It did so by reducing "proconsul" to an essentially honorific title with largely administrative duties and – the critical point – no command of military forces.

A second reason for focusing our discussion on the Roman Republic rather than the Roman Empire is simply that, to the extent that classical Rome remains pertinent to the situation of the United States today, it is the Rome of the Republic that is at issue. This is not simply because of the republican constitution that Americans enjoy, but because the power the United States wields overseas is not "imperial" in any sense that takes its cue from the Rome of the Empire. These truths might seem obvious, but contemporary political polemics sometimes obscure them from view.

As to the first point, the domestic political institutions of the Roman Republic and the United States are akin in important respects. The American founding fathers acknowledged as much when they named the upper house of the American Congress the Senate, not to mention that their embrace of a system of checks and balances between three co-equal branches of government reflected their appreciation of the idea of the "mixed" Roman constitutional order, familiar to them above all from the account of the Greek historian Polybius.[3] Both the United States and the Roman Republic came into being through a revolution against a monarchy, and the name of "king" (*rex*) would remain odious to the Roman people over the centuries, even when the reality of it reemerged under the empire. (It is telling that Augustus avoided styling himself king: he was merely *princeps*, first citizen of Rome, and *imperator*, commander of its army.) In the United States in recent years, the greatly expanded reach and power of the office of our chief magistrate has indeed led to periodic denunciations of the "imperial presidency,"[4] but there is little reason to fear that the American people would be willing to tolerate any fundamental aggrandizement of the powers of the president within the constitutional system of the country in even the remotely foreseeable future. This is not to say that the president's dominance in decision-making in crises and war does not remain controversial within the American political class – as, for that matter, was the role of consuls and proconsuls at Rome.

---

[3] Polybius 6. For the reception of Polybius by the American Founders see notably John Adams' *Defence of the Constitutions of Government of the United States of America* (1787); for an account of the influence of the Roman Republic in the revolutionary era see M. N. S. Sellers, *American Republicanism: Roman Ideology in the United States Constitution* (New York: New York University Press, 1994). On Polybius and the idea of Rome as a mixed regime see Kurt von Fritz, *The Theory of the Mixed Constitution in Antiquity* (New York: Columbia University Press, 1954), and Fergus Millar, *The Roman Republic in Political Thought* (Hanover and London: University of New England Press, 2002).

[4] A phrase originally popularized by Arthur M. Schlesinger, Jr., *The Imperial Presidency* (Boston: Houghton Mifflin, 1973).

There is a deeper kinship between the Roman and American systems as well. The Roman political order under the Republic, although conventionally described as an aristocracy, had pronounced democratic features. Writing in the second century BC, Polybius described it as a mixture of aristocratic, popular, and monarchic elements. Modern scholars have tended to dismiss the importance of the popular or democratic component of the Roman order, on the grounds that the hereditary aristocracy, by manipulating the formal institutions that enabled participation in policy-making by the common people, was able to maintain effective control of the regime in the hands of the Senate. In fact, a good case can be made that the sovereignty of the people remained the theory and, in greater or lesser degree, the reality of the political system of the Roman Republic throughout its history.[5] In any case, it is important to remember that the hereditary senatorial order of the early Republic gradually transformed itself in the course of Rome's political development into something it would not be wrong to characterize as an aristocracy "open to talents." From this point of view, Rome differs more in degree than in kind from modern democracies. Even in the United States, not to speak of European countries with lingering aristocratic traditions of government service, the conduct of affairs – particularly national security affairs – is dominated if not entirely monopolized by highly educated meritocratic elites. Rome and the United States resemble each other in this respect more than either resembles the seedbed of democracy, classical Athens.[6]

We have treated in the introduction the question of the sense, if any, in which the United States can be considered an empire or an imperial power. The inappropriateness of any direct comparison between this nation and imperial Rome in its mature phase was argued there and need not be repeated. But if there are indeed useful parallels to be drawn between the international behavior of these two very different states in two radically distinct historical epochs, it is evident that the comparison is not with the Roman Empire properly speaking

---

[5] The conventional scholarly view has been most comprehensively challenged by Fergus Millar; see especially his *The Crowd in Rome in the Late Republic* (Ann Arbor: University of Michigan Press, 1998) and *The Roman Republic in Political Thought*. For a critical assessment of Millar (with comprehensive bibliography), see Karl-J. Hölkeskamp, *Reconstructing the Roman Republic: An Ancient Political Culture and Modern Research*, trans. Henry Heitmann-Gordon (Princeton, NJ: Princeton University Press, 2010).

[6] On Roman political institutions generally see F. W. Walbank, A. E. Astin, M. W. Frederiksen, and R. M. Ogilvie, *The Cambridge Ancient History*, vol. 7, pt. 2 (2nd ed., Cambridge: Cambridge University Press, 1989) (henceforth *CAH* 7.2), 172–212; A. E. Astin, F. W. Walbank, M. W. Fredericksen, and R. M. Ogilvie, *The Cambridge Ancient History*, vol. 8 (2nd ed., Cambridge: Cambridge University Press, 1989) (henceforth *CAH* 8), ch. 6; A. W. Lintott, *The Constitution of the Roman Republic* (Oxford: Oxford University Press, 1999); T. Corey Brennan, "Power and Process under the Republican 'Constitution'," in Harriet I. Flower, ed., *The Cambridge Companion to the Roman Republic* (Cambridge: Cambridge University Press, 2004), ch. 2; John A. North, "The Constitution of the Roman Republic," in Nathan Rosenstein and Robert Morstein-Marx, eds., *A Companion to the Roman Republic* (Oxford: Blackwell, 2006), ch. 12.

but with the Roman Republic – and most particularly with the Republic as it existed from the time of the unification of Italy under Roman rule in the third century BC until the internal crisis of the mid-first century that precipitated its collapse. For it was during this period that Roman expansion was – at least arguably – primarily defensive in nature, responsive to external threats from peer competitors more than to any internal imperial dynamic, and concerned above all with safeguarding the security of Roman Italy and very little with exploiting conquered territories and peoples for Rome's own benefit. It would be going too far to say that Roman policy in these centuries was simply "hegemonial," like that of the United States (as we have maintained) today. But it certainly had an important hegemonial component – particularly with respect to the civilized, urban-centered states of the Greek East. Moreover, as we shall see, there was a significant internal dynamic at work that actually inhibited Rome's expansion overseas.[7]

Precisely what considerations prompted the creation of Rome's first proconsul is not known. The Roman Republic had been at war with various of its neighbors since its founding (in 509 BC, according to tradition), and in certain earlier periods the Romans seem to have vested consular authority in a larger number of military commanders, presumably to deal with multiple contingencies in a particular year, although the details remain obscure.[8] What is clear enough is that the proconsular function at Rome was in its origins a military one. Essentially, it was a device for delegating the prerogative of supreme command (*imperium*) more widely than customary practice in Rome otherwise allowed. Command so understood encompassed some elements of judicial authority, but its core was the command and control of Roman military forces. Over time, however, with the expansion of Rome's power and interests throughout Italy and eventually across the entire Mediterranean, a number of factors combined to increase the scope of proconsular *imperium*, which will be explored in a moment.

The proconsular function cannot be understood except in the light of the consular function in general. We therefore need to look briefly at the role of the consul and other magistrates in the constitutional system of the Republic and above all, the relationship of these magistrates to the Senate.

---

[7] For this argument see especially Ernst Badian, *Roman Imperialism in the Late Republic* (2nd ed., Oxford: Oxford University Press, 1968). The interpretation of Roman behavior in this period remains controversial among historians; for what is probably the dominant view today see above all William V. Harris, *War and Imperialism in Republican Rome, 327–70 B.C.* (Oxford: Clarendon Press, 1970). A useful recent assessment is Arthur M. Eckstein, "Conceptualizing Roman Imperial Expansion under the Republic: An Introduction," in Rosenstein and Morstein-Marx, ch. 26; for a trenchant critique of the Harris school see further Arthur M. Eckstein, *Rome Enters the Greek World: From Anarchy to Hierarchy in the Hellenistic Mediterranean, 230–170 B.C.* (Oxford: Blackwell, 2008). For an overview of the current state of the historiography of the Republic generally: Martin Jehne, "Methods, Models, and Historiography," in Rosenstein and Morstein-Marx, ch. 1.

[8] For these so-called "military tribunes with consular power," see *CAH* 7.2, 192–95.

Reaching the consulship was the pinnacle of achievement for an ambitious Roman. To be eligible for election to it, an individual had to successfully discharge a series of lesser offices, including military service – the famous Roman *cursus honorum*. A consulship brought with it great personal prestige (*auctoritas*), while also adorning the holder's family lineage and increasing the chances that those of his name would attain the office in the future. Indeed, it seems very likely that the disinclination of the early Romans to increase the number of consuls beyond the original two stemmed primarily from a reluctance to dilute the value of the office in the eyes of those who had attained or might aspire to it. Consuls had important political functions in Rome in addition to their military duties outside the city. They had the authority to convene the Senate and the popular assembly, to preside over debates in these bodies, to propose motions, and to draft (with the assistance of a small group of senators) senatorial decrees. They also had certain judicial functions, particularly when on campaign abroad. In the late Republic, the increasingly partisan character of Roman politics enhanced the political importance of the consulship, which became the prize of bitter and sometimes violent factional conflict. In this period, consuls in fact tended to stay in Rome throughout the year to keep watch on the domestic political scene, whereas military command was entrusted to proconsuls.

It is important to emphasize that the consuls were not simply creatures of the Senate: They had to stand for popular election, as was the case even for relatively minor officials. It is possible on a reading of Roman history to form the impression that the consuls were the key locus of power in the Roman system, whereas the Senate played a largely advisory role.[9] The Senate in any case lacked the ability to coerce the consuls – except with the support of the tribunes (on whom more in a moment). A consul of 291 BC is said to have claimed that the Senate did not rule him but he it as long as he held the office. In general, the Senate enjoyed the power of the purse, yet apparently the consuls had great discretionary authority in expending funds allotted to them. The Senate wielded significant power over the consuls through its recognized authority – subject to ratification by the people – to assign the consuls "areas of operations" (*provinciae*) at the beginning of each year.[10] But even here, the choice of which consul would be responsible for which "province" was decided not by the Senate but by lot, or in some cases by mutual agreement of the consuls themselves. On occasion, the popular assembly intervened to assign

---

[9] This was the view of the great German historian of Rome, Theodor Mommsen; cf. Lintott, *Constitution*, ch. 6. It is important to keep in mind that Rome had no "constitution" in the sense of a written constitution or fundamental law, like the United States: Measures of constitutional import could be enacted by simple legislation.

[10] A common error in Roman historiography has been to confuse this original sense of the term *provincia* with its later and familiar meaning as a legally defined administrative unit of the Roman Empire. For a careful analysis see Robert Kallet-Marx, *Hegemony to Empire: The Development of the Roman Imperium in the East from 148 to 62 B.C.* (Berkeley: University of California Press, 1995), ch. 1.

or prolong consular or proconsular commands. This first occurred in the case of Publius Cornelius Scipio ("Africanus"), the conqueror of Carthage in the Second Punic War. It is not altogether surprising that this outstanding figure – one of the Republic's greatest generals and statesmen – should have excited jealousy and opposition in the Senate. The prospect of prolonged command by a popular and capable war hero threatened senatorial prerogatives and – more dangerous yet – the delicate constitutional balance between the Senate and the People. In fact, it was a harbinger of things to come.[11]

In the period we are considering, however, perhaps all that needs to be said is that the consuls tended to function for the most part in what might be described as an organic relationship with the Senate. Not only were they themselves senators, but they were bound intimately to other senators by ties of friendship, kinship, and mutual obligation; more important, all shared the same Roman aristocratic code and religious and patriotic outlook. Precisely because they were seen by their colleagues as peers, they tended to be trusted to do the right thing without detailed instructions or orders.[12] And because they were regarded as peers, their competence in fulfilling required tasks was difficult to question or challenge. This explains, it might be added, the use of the lot in making consular assignments – a practice that could prove hazardous, especially in cases where a consul lacked significant military experience or had shown poor judgment in the past. This problem could and sometimes did spark popular outrage.

Several other important offices should be discussed briefly in this context. The next highest magistracy, the praetorship, also had predominantly military duties, although some praetors were regularly assigned judicial responsibilities as well. By contrast with the consuls, the Romans proved willing to increase the number of praetors several times (from only one originally) to deal with the growing demands of their overseas commitments.[13] At the same time, in the case of praetors, too, the Romans discovered the utility of *prorogatio* (extension or renewal) of their commands after their initial year in office. Proconsuls and propraetors were often used in more or less interchangeable fashion according to their availability for certain missions; propraetors could assist proconsuls, but they frequently had their own independent commands.

---

[11] According to Livy (38.56.12), the people wanted to make Scipio *dictator* for life following his signal victory over the Carthaginians at Zama in 202 BC, though this story may be apocryphal. The dictatorship was an archaic institution that allowed the temporary suspension (specifically, for six months) of normal constitutional procedures in times mainly of external emergency; in the hands of the dynasts Sulla and Caesar, it was used to consolidate their personal control of the state.

[12] Consider the remarks of Arthur M. Eckstein, *Senate and General: Individual Decision Making and Roman Foreign Relations, 264–194 B.C.* (Berkeley and Los Angeles: University of California Press, 1987), 322–24.

[13] The number of praetors was raised from one to two around 242 BC, from two to four in 227 BC to handle the "provinces" of Sicily and Sardinia, and from four to six in 198/7 BC to provide governors for Spain; two more were added by Sulla in 81 BC. Lintott, *Constitution*, 107–09, as well as T. Corey Brennan, *The Praetorship in the Roman Republic*, 2 vols. (New York: Oxford University Press, 2000), I.

Mention should also be made of the office of "tribune of the people."[14] This very curious Roman institution had come into existence under the early Republic as a device for strengthening the political weight of the non-noble majority in their long struggle over political rights with the patricians ("the fathers," *patres*, Rome's original hereditary nobility). The ten tribunes had extraordinary and absolute authority, among other things, to protect individuals threatened with arrest or punishment by the city magistrates, to convene the Senate or the popular assembly and propose motions or legislation, to veto bills in the Senate, and to block certain actions of other magistrates, including the consuls. Potentially, the tribunate provided a power base from which to launch programmatic political reform, as notably in the case of the two Gracchi in the late second century BC – or, for more seditious activity, as in the final crisis of the Republic in the first century.

While the Romans do not seem to have developed a theory of institutional "checks and balances" along the lines of the American founders, their actual practice suggests at least some appreciation of this factor. The tribunate is the obvious case, but the very fact of the double consulship itself is also relevant. There can be little doubt that this institution arose in reaction to the experience of monarchy in early Rome.[15] Accustomed as we are at present to the idea of a unitary chief executive, it is difficult to imagine how such a system can have been anything other than dysfunctional.[16] Evidently, one consul could not prevent the other from acting (except by the awkward expedient of announcing he had seen bad omens), though he could counteract the action afterwards. For all that, friction between the two consuls (at least in the current state of our evidence) seems to have been uncommon, but some cases are recorded. In one egregious instance, C. Cassius Longinus, consul for 171 BC, suddenly decided to leave his assigned province of Cisalpine Gaul to join in the Third Macedonian

---

[14] *Tribunus plebis*, referring to the common people as distinct from the people at large (*populus*); only individuals of plebeian origins could stand for election to the tribunate, though the evolution of a "plebeian" aristocracy in the later Republic would eventually make the office a sought-after stepping stone in a political career. Lintott, ibid., ch. 8.

[15] Against Lintott, *Constitution*, 102–3: "We would be wrong ... to see collegiality in principle as a form of constitutional check: the multiplicity of magistrates was perhaps in origin intended rather as cover for a multiplicity of functions and insurance against the sudden death or disability of a magistrate." This argument seems less than compelling, especially if one keeps in mind that there was originally only one praetor. In the early Republic, as many as six "military tribunes with consular power" replaced consuls in some years, but in 367 BC the Romans discarded this arrangement and returned permanently to the dual consulate. Cf. *CAH* 7.2, 186–90, 192–95.

[16] For instructive contemporary analogies consider France under the Fifth Republic and Russia under the tandem rule of Vladimir Putin and Dmitri Medvedev. A classical parallel is the dual kingship at Sparta. In Aristotle's account of the Spartan kingship (*Politics* 1271a22–26), he notes that the Spartans, lacking trust in the personal integrity of their kings, "repeatedly send them on embassies accompanied by their enemies, and hold that factional conflict between the kings means preservation for the city." The reference to "enemies" is to the Spartan ephors, an institution closely akin to the Roman tribunate; conflict between the two hereditary royal lines was endemic in Spartan politics. If nothing else, this remark shows that the notion of institutional checks and balances was not alien to the ancient mind.

War.[17] There may have been other such cases, because the Romans later felt it necessary to pass a law to the effect that magistrates abroad should not travel or make an expedition outside their provinces without good reason.[18] In general, the Romans seemed to have hit on the practical solution of keeping the consuls separated in space.[19]

Some attention needs to be given to the procedure for creating proconsuls. Initially, the general practice seems to have been for the Senate to propose the prorogation of a consular command and the People to ratify the selection. In the course of the third century, the Senate appears to have gradually assumed sole responsibility for naming proconsuls, although the choice of Scipio in 211 BC was forced on the Senate by the People. At first, only individuals who had served as consul in the previous year had their commands prorogued, but even in relatively early times the Romans observed no hard and fast rules in this respect. Consuls from earlier years were sometimes looked to, and eventually even some who had never held the consulship or even the praetorship. Scipio was in fact the first "private citizen" to be made proconsul, by popular demand. The governors of Spain in the second century were called "proconsuls" even when the office was actually held by a praetor. As regards the duration of proconsulships, the original practice seemed to be to limit tenure of the office to six months, a year, or in some cases the duration of the particular emergency (as in the case of the first proconsul, Q. Publilius Philo). During the Second Punic War, prorogation for two, five, or even seven years can be documented – contrary to a common view that this was a practice only of the late Republic.[20]

The Roman proconsulship, like other Roman political institutions, was a creature of its time and place and displays some features unique to itself. On the other hand, the persistence of the term "proconsul" in later ages – including the present one – suggests that it describes a recurring reality of political governance. The distinguishing property of proconsular rule relative to other forms of delegated political-military governance, to state it simply, is its autonomy relative to the central political authority in decisions on high policy. At Rome, this autonomy was particularly pronounced. Or, perhaps more accurately, it became increasingly pronounced over time, but in accordance with an internal dynamic that was predictable (and was in fact predicted or sensed by some Romans at different junctures in the history of the Republic). It will be useful to give an account of proconsulship in the context of the evolution of Roman imperialism as well as Roman domestic politics down to the end of the

---

[17] Livy 43.1.4–10.

[18] The *lex de provinciis praetoriis* of 100 BC, known only from a recently discovered inscription (Lintott, *Constitution*, 102).

[19] During the Second Punic War, two consular armies operated together in Italy against Hannibal; the consuls alternated in command every day. This experiment was not repeated. Livy 22.41.2–3, 44.5; Lintott, *Constitution*, 99.

[20] On these details see W. M. F. Jashemski, *The Origins and History of the Proconsular and the Propraetorian Imperium to 27 B.C.* (Chicago: University of Chicago Press, 1950), 13ff.

Republic and beyond. First, though, we need to state more fully the various factors that were at work in creating and enhancing proconsular autonomy at Rome.

Perhaps the key point, though one that seems often overlooked, is simply that proconsulship enjoyed great prestige and inherent power by its association with the consulship, the supreme executive authority of the Roman Senate and People. Originally, proconsular authority could only by wielded by ex-consuls, but even when this ceased to be the case, the office itself continued to be seen as partaking of the authority of consular imperium. Proconsuls were not in an administrative chain of command under one or both consuls, though as a matter of custom proconsuls generally deferred to the greater *imperium* of a consul.[21] At the same time, control of consuls and proconsuls alike by the Senate was informal and frequently loose, given the constraints imposed by the size of that body (generally around 300 men), the apparent absence of an established institutional mechanism within the Senate for continuous oversight of the executive magistrates, and the inherent difficulty of communicating with them over the (ever-lengthening) distances separating their areas of operations from Rome. Though subject to approval and, at least theoretically, reversal by the Roman Senate and People, the actions of Rome's proconsuls in the field – even in cases with far-reaching consequences for state policy – were rarely seriously challenged from the earliest times.

A related factor is the nature of consular imperium as it affected Rome's military forces, deriving from the very fact of the dual consulship. Under Rome's ancestral constitutional arrangement, there was in actuality not a single Roman army, but two armies (at any rate when needed in the same year) answering to two equally authoritative commanders. With the advent of the proconsulship, this autonomy of command extended to proconsuls as well. The Roman army under the Republic was in any case wholly non-professional, and had no standing staff or structure to provide continuity between campaigns in succeeding years. All this meant that the bond between the consul or proconsul in command and his soldiers assumed extraordinary importance. The only check on the development of an unhealthy loyalty to the commander on the part of the troops, apart from their traditional patriotic attachment to Rome, was the short tenure of his command. With the practice of prorogation of consular imperium, this check began to break down – with consequences that would prove to be dire for the fate of the Republic.[22]

---

[21] In one famous case, the proconsul Servilius Caepio (a patrician) disobeyed the orders of the consul Mallius Maximus (a non-noble), leading to a Roman military disaster in southern Gaul ca. 105 BC. He was later tried on charges of theft of public funds, though the real transgression was his insubordination.

[22] "It is scarcely too much to say that under the Republic there was no Roman army, but merely detachments of troops stationed in various parts of the Empire. Each army was regarded as belonging to its commander rather than to the state ... This system was of course a dangerous one, and the creation of a central command one of the benefits which the rule of Caesar and Augustus conferred on the world." G. H. Stevenson, *Roman Provincial Administration*

Further compounding this institutional factor was the very frequency of wars in the international environment Rome faced, as well as the martial culture that it helped to create and sustain among the Roman people.[23] The frequency of wars not only enhanced the prestige of military command but gave rise to many situations plainly requiring autonomous decision and action by Roman military commanders. At the same time, the honors to be won in war were instrumental in the advancement of the political careers of Roman aristocrats. The effect was naturally to predispose Roman commanders to aggressive military actions that pushed the envelope of the instructions they received from the Senate. All of this helped to reinforce and sustain an expansive view of the scope of consular imperium and the latitude of consular magistrates in taking actions not specifically authorized by the Senate but likely to gain its approval after the fact, especially in the event of conspicuous battlefield success. In particular, the "provinces" assigned consular officers by the Senate were often ill-defined, and a case could always be made for the hot pursuit of an enemy across a recognized frontier. Caesar's conquest of Gaul is an egregious case, but earlier examples in Italy, Spain, and Macedonia can also be cited.[24]

Rome in Republican times lacked not only a professional army; it lacked a professional diplomatic service – or, for that matter, any permanent diplomatic representation in foreign states. Diplomatic encounters with foreigners were in fact unusual in early Rome except on the margins of military operations. It was therefore natural for consular magistrates to assume a diplomatic role, especially in situations in which military developments might dictate improvised diplomacy toward enemies or potential allies in the course of a campaign at some distance from the city. In the wake of major wars, the Roman commander in the relevant theater of operations was generally looked to to arrange a peace agreement together with wider political measures intended to pacify the area and secure Roman interests for the future, although the Senate typically sought to influence these arrangements by sending a senatorial commission to the region. A notable example is the settlement of Greek affairs by Titus Quinctius Flamininus at the end of the Second Macedonian War (200–197 BC).

Less obvious or remarked on is the sheer ignorance of the non-Roman world on the part of the Roman political class. The Romans lacked not only a permanent diplomatic presence abroad but an organized intelligence service, and many of the enemies they faced were barely literate societies lacking a tradition of historical or other writing that might offer insights into their

(Oxford: Clarendon Press, 1939), 80. See also Paul Erdkamp, "Army and Society," in Rosenstein and Morstein-Marx, ch. 13.

[23] This is the central theme of Harris, *War and Imperialism*. See also Arthur M. Eckstein, *Mediterranean Anarchy, Interstate War, and the Rise of Rome* (Berkeley: University of California Press, 2006).

[24] P. A. Brunt, *The Fall of the Roman Republic and Related Essays* (Oxford: Oxford University Press, 1988), 17–19. On the central role of honor in Roman culture see J. E. Lendon, *Empire of Honour* (Oxford: Oxford University Press, 1997).

behavior.[25] In such circumstances, the intelligence function essentially devolved to the consular magistrates when engaged in military operations abroad, and these magistrates thus acquired considerable latitude in interpreting the intentions of Rome's enemies and in representing them to the Senate.

Finally, a case can be made that the government at Rome simply lacked sufficient interest in its growing overseas empire to monitor closely the actions of its representatives abroad. Roman expansion in Italy had been seen by the Senate and People alike as a matter of supreme importance for the security of the state, given Rome's continuing vulnerability to the predations of the Celtic tribes dwelling north of the Po River. (The city of Rome had been sacked by the Gauls during a massive invasion in 390 BC, an event that remained traumatic in popular memory down to the end of the Republic.) Accordingly, the Senate seems to have paid careful attention to the military and diplomatic realities of the Italian peninsula, and kept a close rein on the Roman military commanders who completed the reduction of the Gallic tribes of northern Italy in the third century (225–222 BC).[26] Especially after Rome began to acquire overseas possessions in the wake of the First Punic War (264–241 BC) against Carthage's maritime empire in the western Mediterranean, however, the great distances separating the conquered territories from the capital as well as competing demands on the attention of Rome's governing elite created more latitude for consular and proconsular decision-making. While the existential threat posed by the Carthaginians (especially Hannibal's invasion of Italy during the Second Punic War) certainly captured senatorial attention, this was much less the case during Rome's initial encounters with the Greek-speaking world, which indeed are reminiscent of the absent-mindedness that was once famously said to accompany Britain's imperial rise.[27] In the upheavals of the late Republic, as the orator-politician Cicero once observed, there was so much of interest going on at Rome that men had no time to think of provincial affairs.[28]

Older studies of the history of the Roman Republic routinely make the confident assumption that Rome had a "foreign policy," devised by a far-sighted and well-informed Senate and carried out scrupulously by its consuls and proconsuls in the field. Those who hold this view tend to understand the Republic as fundamentally aristocratic in character and the Senate as the locus of all important state decisions. As discussed earlier, while this picture is not

[25] On this neglected subject see generally Rose Mary Sheldon, *Intelligence Activities in Ancient Rome* (London: Frank Cass, 2005). Erich S. Gruen, *The Hellenistic World and the Coming of Rome* (Berkeley: University of California Press, 1984), 203–49, effectively debunks the notion that the Romans consciously sought or expected regional "expertise" in Roman commanders, something that seems to have remained true throughout the imperial period, on which see Susan P. Mattern, *Rome and the Enemy: Imperial Strategy in the Principate* (Berkeley: University of California Press, 1999).

[26] Eckstein, *Senate and General*, ch. 2.

[27] See generally Gruen, *The Hellenistic World and the Coming of Rome*, and Eckstein, *Rome Enters the Greek East*.

[28] Cicero, *Pro Plancio* 26.63 (cited in Stevenson, 67).

simply wrong, it seriously understates the role of the democratic or popular component of the Roman political system. But the fact that consular officials were answerable to the People as well as the Senate – and hence in a position to play off these two political masters against one another – cannot but have created more space for autonomous decision and action on their parts. Polybius was correct after all in identifying the consulship as a monarchic element in Rome's "mixed" government. Furthermore, there is good reason to believe that the notion of the Senate as a well-oiled machine for making "policy" relating to war and diplomacy is largely mythical. Unlike certain other aristocracies that managed empires in the spirit of a joint stock company (the Venetians in particular may be mentioned), the Roman aristocracy, obsessed as it was with the pursuit of personal and family honor, was intensely competitive within its own ranks. Its endemic factionalism undoubtedly posed a major challenge to responsible senatorial decision-making – most notoriously in the late Republic, where it was dysfunctional almost beyond belief, but in earlier periods as well.[29] As a result of all this, it is quite unclear to what extent one is entitled to speak of Roman "policy" at all, as distinct from ad hoc reactions to developing events as mediated through the complicated and ever-changing interplay of domestic political forces. At all events, at least given the state of our evidence, there is little reason to suppose the Romans at any period thought systematically or proactively about their security affairs. Even under the Empire, the idea that the Romans had a "grand strategy" for the defense of their territories has to be considered not proven.[30] If one accepts this argument, however, the result once again is to highlight the scope for individual decision and action by Rome's consular and proconsular officers.

All this having been said, it is also important to note that the Romans themselves were far from oblivious to the dangers inherent in unchecked consular authority. In fact, it can be argued that fear of the potential abuse of this authority acted as a brake on Rome's territorial expansion from the Second Punic War until at least the early first century. The example of Scipio Africanus, as mentioned earlier, had already sent a warning to the Senate of the potentially destabilizing effects for the Roman constitutional order of prolonging the *imperium* of a popular consular figure in a major theater of war, and Flamininus' high-handedness in his diplomatic dealings with the Greeks

---

[29] Brunt praises the "remarkable sagacity" the Roman aristocracy showed in acquiring an empire while noting that it plainly never solved the problem of governing it effectively: "[M]utual rivalries and jealousies made the senators ready to entrust mediocrities with the tasks of administration and defence; at the same time they were too partial to their peers . . . to impose effective restraints on their treatment of their subjects" (*Fall of the Roman Republic*, 68–69). Note Brunt's citation of Venice here in connection with his remark that "it is impossible to argue that aristocracies can't run empires."

[30] Edward N. Luttwak, *The Grand Strategy of the Roman Empire* (Baltimore and London: Johns Hopkins University Press, 1976); see the invaluable discussion by Everett L. Wheeler, "Methodological Limits and the Mirage of Roman Strategy," Part I, *Journal of Military History* 57 (January 1993): 7–41, and Part II, *Journal of Military History* 57 (April 1993): 215–40.

shortly thereafter can only have reinforced these concerns. It is almost certainly not accidental that throughout most of the second century BC the Romans decreased their reliance on promagistrates.[31] At the same time, there is reason to think that the Senate was also becoming concerned about the behavior of its officials abroad. As early as 171 BC, it began to hear complaints from Spain about the depredations of Roman governors there, and in 149 BC it established a permanent commission to hear cases of extortion (*repetundae*) against magistrates in the provinces. As one historian puts it: "The excessive powers enjoyed by the holders of *imperium* were bound to corrupt. What is more, they led to an excess of pride and individualism – for which Hellenistic cultural influence often gets the blame. This would make men stand out against the Senate." A number of instances of friction between consular magistrates and the Senate can be documented from this period. Yet the Senate was reluctant to impose harsh discipline on its own, and the problem continued to fester.[32]

In what follows, we survey briefly the evolution of consular and proconsular decision-making in the context of Rome's growing overseas dominions under the later Republic and into the early Empire. It needs to be stated at the outset that much of the evidence underpinning any such discussion is uncertain and often highly contested, and it will be necessary in some cases to adopt without elaborate justification interpretations that remain to some degree outside the mainstream of contemporary historical scholarship.[33] The overall picture, however, seems a reasonably clear one.

The Romans' first venture beyond the confines of Italy proper occurred with the Senate's decision to intervene in the affairs of Sicily in 264 BC, a fateful move that precipitated the First Punic War. For reasons that are unclear, the Senate determined that it was not in Rome's interest to permit the city of Messana, strategically situated on the straits separating Sicily from the toe of Italy, to fall into the hands of a besieging army of Syracusans and their Carthaginian allies. Accordingly, it instructed one of the consuls, Appius Claudius Caudex, to cross into the island and relieve the siege. Contrary to a common view that a state of war between Rome and the two major powers of Sicily already existed and that the expedition was therefore purely military in nature, Claudius clearly understood his instructions as providing him leeway to engage in negotiations with these powers, which he proceeded to do prior to landing any troops near

---

[31] During the years 197–67, less than 40% of the consuls mentioned by Livy had their imperium prorogued, and only 36 of the 128 praetors, though this partly reflected the increase in the number of praetors to 6 at the end of the third century in order to provide for the administration of the Spanish provinces. Jashemski, 47.

[32] Badian, *Roman Imperialism*, 8–9, citing (n. 23) the following instances from Livy's narrative: M. Furius Crassipes (39.3), M. Claudius Marcellus (39.54), A. Manlius Vulso (41.10–11), Q. Fulvius Flaccus (42.3), and M. Popilius Laenas and C. Popilius Laenas (42.7–12, 21, 22).

[33] For the third century, I have relied extensively on Eckstein's *Senate and General*, and for the later Republic, on Kallet-Marx and Badian. See also J. A. Crook, A. Lintott, and E. Rawson, eds., *The Cambridge Ancient History*, vol. 9 (Cambridge: Cambridge University Press, 1994) (*CAH* 9).

the city. When he was rebuffed, he proceeded to cross the straits and may have tried again to achieve a peaceful settlement before launching an attack on the besiegers. None of this was done with further reference to Rome, although the result was to commit Rome to a war that was to last twenty-three years; the Senate seems to have accepted the consul's actions with equanimity.[34]

During the course of the war itself, there were further demonstrations of the leeway Roman commanders enjoyed for independent diplomatic action. The consuls for 263 BC, M'. Valerius Maximus and M'. Otacilius Crassus, both of them assigned to the Sicilian theater, swiftly inflicted a substantial defeat on the Syracusans and leveled a town allied to them. This apparently calculated step had the desired result, as some fifty or sixty cities and towns in the northeastern part of the island soon came over to the Romans without any direct military pressure on them and were accepted on generous terms by the consuls. Shortly thereafter, as they advanced on the city of Syracuse itself, its ruler, Hiero, proposed to open peace negotiations. This was done and a detailed treaty agreed to – without any reference to Rome – which allowed the city to retain its independence and much of its territory and Hiero his own position. Again, however, the Senate and People later ratified these agreements without complaint, and they proved to be wise measures that secured Rome's ascendancy in eastern Sicily for the next forty years.

The Romans were less fortunate in the case of M. Atilius Regulus, who as consul led a Roman army in an invasion of Africa in 256 BC. After decisively defeating the Carthaginians and advancing on the city, he too was approached by enemy envoys seeking peace; but these talks failed, apparently as a result of Regulus' exorbitant demands as well as his own personal arrogance. (The consul later suffered unexpected defeat at the Carthaginians' hands and was himself captured.) At the very end of the war, in 241 BC, terms of peace were worked out in direct negotiations between the local commanders in Sicily. There was some sentiment at Rome that its representative, the proconsul C. Lutatius Catulus, victor in the decisive naval battle of the Aegates Islands, had not driven a hard enough bargain, and ten senators were dispatched to see if better terms could be extracted from the Carthaginians. In the end, however, the Senate accepted the framework of the agreement as negotiated with only a minor modification. Significantly, the peace of 241 came to be called "Lutatius' Peace."[35]

Following the war, however, Carthage remained a formidable rival, and Rome felt it necessary to take advantage of a period of internal turmoil there to seize the islands of Sardinia and Corsica in 238 – a step that virtually guaranteed a renewal of hostilities between the two powers. In 227 BC, Rome in effect acknowledged the permanence of its overseas possessions by creating two new praetorian magistrates to be regularly assigned as civil governors of the "provinces" of Sicily and Sardinia/Corsica. Rome still shared the island of

---

[34] Eckstein, *Senate and General*, ch. 3.
[35] Ibid., ch. 4.

Sicily with independent Syracuse, however, and the defection of that city from the Roman alliance following the death of Hiero ensured that Sicily would again be a theater of war. But the decisive actions of the Second Punic War (218–201 BC) took place in Spain, Italy, and Africa. We will focus here on the role of the war's undisputed hero: Publius Cornelius Scipio Africanus, the vanquisher of Carthage and founder of Roman Spain.

Scipio was a scion of one of Rome's great families. His father, also Publius Cornelius Scipio, was consul in 218, with responsibility (along with his brother Gnaeus) for Roman operations against the Carthaginians and their possessions in Spain. These two Scipios achieved considerable successes over a number of years – not least, by preventing Carthaginian reinforcements from reaching Hannibal's army in Italy as well as solidifying Rome's hold over Spain north of the Ebro; but in 211 their combined forces suffered a disastrous defeat at Ilorca, in southern Spain, near the heart of Carthage's power, and both men were killed. A combination of inadequate intelligence, insufficient Roman forces, treacherous Spanish allies, and defective generalship contributed to this fiasco, which in any case called into question the wisdom of an offensive strategy in this wild and difficult country. Later that year, Scipio the younger, then only twenty-four years old, was given proconsular authority by an unusual vote of the people and assigned Spain as his *provincia* – as noted earlier, the first time this honor had been accorded someone who had not held either of the higher magistracies. Not surprisingly, Scipio set out to reclaim the legacy of the elder Scipios through an aggressive forward policy designed to drive the Carthaginians completely out of the region. In this he succeeded in impressive fashion over the next five years. He did so with modest Roman forces but was supported by a substantial number of Spanish auxiliaries recruited by assiduous personal diplomacy by the charismatic proconsul. His own generalship was consistently brilliant,[36] but his handling of the complex diplomatic situation in the peninsula was equally important for the success of the overall effort. These diplomatic activities, undertaken entirely on his own initiative, served not only immediate wartime purposes but laid a firm groundwork for continuing Roman domination of the country in the future. Scipio's personal ascendancy was so great and his control of Roman policy such that some of the Spanish tribes seem to have been unaware of the very existence of the Senate.[37]

Scipio returned to Rome in 206 BC to great acclaim: Awarded a "triumph," the Republic's highest military honor, he was also elected consul for the year following. It had become quite clear, however, that his successes had proven

---

[36] There remains much of value in the military analysis of B. H. Liddell Hart, *A Greater Than Napoleon: Scipio Africanus* (Edinburgh and London: William Blackwood, 1930). See more generally H. H. Scullard, *Scipio Africanus: Soldier and Politician* (Ithaca, NY: Cornell University Press, 1970).

[37] Eckstein, *Senate and General*, ch. 7. After his daring capture of New Carthage (Cartagena), the main Punic base in southeastern Spain, he was hailed as "king" by some of his Spanish troops. He wisely declined to accept the accolade.

too much for some in the Senate; at the same time, an element of senatorial opinion opposed Scipio's announced plan to take the war to the seat of Carthaginian power in Africa, given the threat still posed by Hannibal's armies within Italy itself – a not completely unreasonable position.[38] The Senate designated Sicily rather than Africa as Scipio's "province," but in a compromise that in fact gave him all that he wanted, it permitted him to cross into Africa if he judged it necessary; this he soon did. In this new theater of operations, Scipio demonstrated again not only his military genius (he was the first Roman general to defeat Hannibal in battle, at Zama) but also his capacity for independent diplomatic action. He neutralized Carthage's local alliance system by creating a Roman client kingdom in Numidia; and when the Carthaginians sued for peace in 203, and then again after Hannibal's return, the renewal of the war, and their final defeat in 202, he negotiated detailed terms with them on his own responsibility.

Political complications persisted, however. The consul for 201, Gnaeus Cornelius Lentulus, sought to block senatorial acceptance of the final peace agreement and the continuation of the war to secure the African command for himself; and there seems to have been wider opposition to the treaty as being too lenient on Carthage. Although this is not certain, there is some reason to believe that Scipio himself was led to favor a peace settlement that left Carthage independent rather than pressing his military advantage to the limit because he feared that any long siege of the city would increase the chances that his political enemies might be able to supersede his command and rob him of the glory of bringing the war to an end.[39] In later years, Scipio remained a powerful figure in Roman politics, reaching the consulship a second time in 194. In spite or rather indeed because of this, he would never again be given a proconsular command. He was, however, able to persuade the Senate to allow him to serve under his brother, Lucius Cornelius Scipio, in the campaign that resulted in the defeat of the Seleucid king Antiochus in Greece and Asia Minor (190), thereby eliminating the last major threat to Roman dominance in the Mediterranean. Africanus' reward was malicious prosecution by his political enemies for mishandling some war booty, and voluntary exile from the city. He died shortly thereafter.[40]

Another important figure from this period of Rome's expansion must also be discussed. Like Scipio, Titus Quinctius Flamininus was elevated to the consulship (198 BC) without having first been a praetor, a sign of his ambition as well as his political connections. Flamininus was chosen (by lot) to deal with the threat posed by Philip V of Macedon, against whom the Romans and various Greek allies had conducted warfare during their struggle with the

[38] The chief spokesman for this view was Quintus Fabius Maximus Cunctator ("the Delayer"), who as general earlier in the war had famously refused to engage his army directly against Hannibal.

[39] Ibid., ch. 8, esp. 255–67.

[40] On this period see Scullard, chs. 10–11.

Carthaginians (nominally allied with Philip) and again after the breakdown of a fragile peace between the parties in 200. With the two men's armies facing off against one another in northwestern Greece, Philip sounded out the Roman commander on possible terms for restoring peace. The Senate had previously made it clear that it expected the Macedonians to disgorge some of their recent conquests, but Flamininus almost certainly had little more specific guidance. While Philip showed a readiness to compromise, Flamininus insisted that he withdraw from all of Greece; Philip refused, and the war continued. After the Romans achieved some tactical gains as well as a major diplomatic success in detaching the Achaean League from its alliance with Philip, negotiations were reopened. But this time Flamininus was more conciliatory – in spite of being in a stronger position to impose terms. The reason for this soon became apparent. Again like Scipio, Flamininus feared that he would be superseded in command by one of the consuls for the new year, and maneuvered accordingly to position himself in a way that would guarantee maximum glory for himself personally whatever action was taken by the Senate. When it turned out that the Senate preferred to assign both consuls to northern Italy in operations against the Celts, Flamininus then intrigued to turn the senators against the very peace he had helped engineer and was prepared to recommend, had his *imperium* in Macedonia prorogued, and continued the war against Philip.[41] The proconsul then went on to win a decisive victory over the Macedonians at Cynoscephalae (197 BC).

This battle shattered Philip's hegemonic position and created a political vacuum at the heart of the Greek world. It was by no means evident what Rome would do at this key juncture. There was considerable sentiment among Flamininus' Greek allies to punish Macedon severely and depose Philip as king, and important strategic issues had been left unresolved, particularly the fate of the "Fetters of Greece" – three fortified places that Philip had now agreed to evacuate.[42] Flamininus appears to have played the critical role in shaping the political settlement that was to follow and securing support for it at home. He declined to break the power of Macedon completely or remove Philip, fearing that this would only open northern Greece to barbarian incursions and unduly aggrandize the Aetolian League, Rome's principal ally. Most importantly, however, he appears to have persuaded the Senate that it lay in Rome's interest to present itself as the champion of Greek "freedom," restoring to the Greek cities the independence they had enjoyed prior to the rise of Macedon and the other successor states to the empire of Alexander the Great. Flamininus' policies met stiff opposition at Rome, including from one of the consuls as well as envoys of the disgruntled Aetolians, but the proconsul managed to carry the day. The Senate approved his settlement and sent a commission of ten senators to

---

[41] For this interpretation of his behavior see especially Livy 32.32.7–8.

[42] The refusal of Philip's envoys to discuss yielding the fortresses of Corinth, Chalcis, and Demetrias had been a key factor in persuading the Senate to continue hostilities in 197. On all this see the detailed account of Eckstein, *Senate and General*, ch. 9.

Greece to oversee its implementation. In a dramatic move, Flamininus' herald read a proclamation announcing Rome's policy to a Panhellenic gathering at the opening of the Isthmian Games at Corinth in 196 BC. The policy promised the complete withdrawal of Roman forces from Greece, including the evacuation of the citadel of Corinth and the other Fetters. The assembled Greeks, surprised and delighted, mobbed Flamininus and hailed him as their savior; they would honor his memory in years to come with public festivals, statues, and even religious cults. The Greeks of his day had much reason to fear and resent the rising power of Rome. Flamininus, it seems fair to say, taught the Roman fathers a lesson that the Greek monarchs had known for generations: the power of Greek public opinion.[43]

Let us now shift our focus from individual proconsuls to the larger question of the evolution of Roman imperialism in the last century or so of the Republic. The significance and impact of Flamininus' settlement of Greek affairs in 197/6 do not seem sufficiently appreciated in this regard. In the short term, it can be accounted a failure, because Rome's withdrawal from Greece only encouraged Antiochus III in alliance with the Aetolians to attempt to fill the resulting vacuum, spurring a further Roman intervention. Nor did it solve the Macedonian problem. This flared again in the late 170s in a Third Macedonian War against Philip's son and successor Perseus and, after Perseus' defeat and the dismantling of the Macedonian kingdom at the hands of another great Roman proconsul, Lucius Aemilius Paullus (168 BC), once more in the 140s with the revolt of the pretender Andriscus. It has been widely assumed that Macedonia was incorporated into the Roman "empire" at this time (148 BC) as a formally constituted "province," and that Greece proper was then added to it in some manner following Rome's defeat of the Achaean League in 146. While the documentary record of the Mediterranean world in the late second century leaves a great deal to be desired, a good case can be made that this was not so. While Rome indeed maintained a permanent military presence in Macedonia thereafter, it did so primarily to stabilize a frontier that was constantly menaced by barbarian tribes descending from the Balkan mountains. Macedonia thus remained a "province" only in its original sense of the term – an area of military operations. Nor, for that matter, was the rest of Greece brought under direct Roman control. Rome maintained no army there, though its commander in Macedonia seems to have had a remit for intervention in Greek affairs if required. As importantly, the traditional city-state (*polis*) remained the primary unit of governance throughout the region, enjoying a large degree of autonomy down to the very end of the Roman Republic. It was not until Pompey's reorganization of Asia in 62 BC following the conclusion of the Mithridatic wars that Roman control in the East can be said to have taken an unambiguously imperial form.[44]

---

[43] Thus Badian, 13; see also his *Titus Quinctius Flamininus: Philhellenism and Realpolitik* (Norman: University of Oklahoma Press, 1973 [1970]), as well as Eckstein, *Rome Enters the Greek East*, ch. 7.

[44] This is the overall argument of Kallet-Marx, *Hegemony to Empire*.

It is worth pausing to reflect briefly on the notion of imperial "control" generally.[45] As discussed above, recent historiography of imperial Britain has emphasized the inadequacy of the traditional view of empires as simply the annexation and direct rule of foreign lands. Economic penetration of foreign markets is an effective instrument of indirect imperial control, as is the exercise of political influence through an array of advisory mechanisms or through cultural or ideological means; colonial settlement is also a noteworthy factor. The conventional historiography of Rome has tended to focus on annexation as the central dynamic of Roman imperialism to the neglect of these other factors. In the original Roman understanding, however, the projection of Roman *imperium* meant not territorial annexations as such but the establishment of Rome's "sway" over others – its ability to compel foreigners to respect its interests and wishes. Many Roman military operations can only be understood in this context, as efforts not to hold territory but to overawe enemies or potential enemies through displays of military prowess as well as through specific psychological measures designed to humiliate or frighten (such as the razing of Carthage and Corinth in 146 BC).[46] Roman diplomacy was an important adjunct to such operations – more important than seems often realized. Rome's demonstrated ability to attract allies is not something that can simply be taken for granted, given the brutality of Roman behavior at times: It reflects Rome's deliberate cultivation of an image of reliability and fair dealing. Rome was also more than ready to collaborate with smaller independent states on the marches of empire where they proved susceptible to its influence, while sparing the Romans the burden of direct rule. Indeed, a pattern of reliance on such client or satellite states as a quasi-integral part of its imperial system was to persist well into the time of the Roman Empire itself.[47]

Already by the late second century BC, however, changes in Rome's domestic politics had begun to alter the trajectory of its imperial development. Two brothers, the tribunes Tiberius and Gaius Gracchus, for the first time posed a serious challenge to the preeminent role of the Senate in policy-making at Rome as champions of the Roman and Italian poor. Tiberius, the first to hold office, attempted to pass agrarian reform legislation benefitting small farmers at the expense of the estates of the nobility.[48] But the Gracchi were given their real opening by an event that occurred abroad: In 133 BC, Rome's long-standing ally Attalus of Pergamum, in Asia Minor, died without an heir, and in his will he bequeathed his entire kingdom to the Roman people. Tiberius Gracchus saw that the enormous riches this legacy would bring Rome could be used to alleviate the economic distress widespread at the time among the common

---

[45] See particularly Arthur M. Eckstein, "Rome in the Middle Republic," in Kagan, ch. 2.

[46] Consider Luttwak's analysis of Roman operations in Judaea during the early Empire: *Grand Strategy of the Roman Empire* (Baltimore: Johns Hopkins University Press, 1976).

[47] A good discussion is in Eckstein, *Rome Enters the Greek East*, ch. 9.

[48] On the Gracchi see *CAH* 9, 1–101, as well as Alvin H. Bernstein, *Tiberius Sempronius Gracchus: Tradition and Apostasy* (Ithaca, NY: Cornell University Press, 1978).

people. Tiberius was eventually murdered by his political opponents, but his brother took up his cause after securing his own election to the tribunate a decade later. Among the most significant measures Gaius proposed and had enacted by the popular assembly were those providing for subsidized grain prices and grants of provincial lands to the poor; at the same time, he took steps to curb the corruption of senators serving as governors in the provinces.[49] Gaius and many of his followers were also killed in further political violence inspired by these measures, and more generally by the threat to senatorial interests and the traditional balance of the Roman constitution that the popular movement inspired by the Gracchi was felt to pose, and an aristocratic backlash ensued. However, the seeds had been sown for a transformation of Rome's relationship to its empire. From being seen primarily as a guarantor of the security of Italy as well as a hunting ground for aristocratic honor, Rome's overseas territories came increasingly to be viewed – by aristocrats and people alike – as a source of plunder.[50]

It will not be necessary to follow in detail the evolution of the empire and the consular and proconsular magistracies in the last years of the Republic. The growth of factionalism and political violence in Rome's domestic politics is the central story of those years, and the primary impetus for the metastasis of these magistracies into instruments for the personal aggrandizement of a few ambitious politicians contending for mastery of the state.[51] But some highlights may be noted.

The end of the second century saw the emergence of another great Roman general, Gaius Marius. A man of relatively humble origins and Gracchan sympathies, Marius managed to have himself elected consul for 106 BC on the strength of his performance in the war against Jugurtha (usurper of Rome's client kingdom of Numidia) and a promise of bringing that troublesome conflict to an end, although the Senate's opposition to his candidacy forced him to recruit his own troops. After achieving success in Africa, he was chosen as consul a second time by the people to meet a new threat to Italy itself posed by two powerful Germanic tribes, the Cimbri and the Teutones. In an unprecedented step, he was elected consul – not proconsul – again in each of the next four years to command Rome's armies for the duration of this difficult war. With this enemy defeated as well, the by-now immensely popular general, supported by several demagogic tribunes, sought to appropriate land to reward his soldiers. This set another evil precedent, laying the groundwork as it did for

---

[49] Specifically, by barring senators from the courts hearing extortion cases in the provinces, the assumption being that they were too sympathetic to or too easily influenced by their peers to judge them impartially.

[50] "It was, basically, Asia that transformed the nature both of the Roman empire and of Roman attitudes toward it." Badian, *Roman Imperialism*, 48.

[51] An outstanding account is Lily Ross Taylor, *Party Politics in the Age of Caesar* (Berkeley: University of California Press, 1966); see also Jürgen von Ungern-Sternberg, "The Crisis of the Republic," in Flower, ch. 4, and W. Jeffrey Tatum, "The Final Crisis, 69–44," in Rosenstein and Morstein-Marx, ch. 9.

the competition by the dynasts of the next century for the loyalty of Rome's legions.[52]

It did not take long for the political struggle between the *optimati* (the aristocratic party) and *populares* (the popular party) at Rome to erupt in full-scale civil war. To forestall a move by the tribunes to deprive him of command in the East, the aristocratic general L. Cornelius Sulla seized Rome in 88 BC with an army he commanded as consul for that year, killing the tribune who had sponsored the legislation and others. Although the city was retaken in the following year by Marius and the consul L. Cornelius Cinna, who proceeded to carry out a large-scale blood purge ("proscription") of the nobility and confiscation of their property, Sulla eventually had the upper hand. Reoccupying Rome in 82, he had himself appointed *dictator* and imposed a sweeping set of legislative reforms intended above all to restore the dominance of the Senate and the aristocracy within the traditional Roman political order. Although his intentions were broadly conservative and arguably patriotic, however, Sulla's actions were revolutionary, and their effect was to legitimize violent and extra-constitutional measures in the hands of a new breed of politician – men like Pompey and Caesar, whose greed for wealth, honor, and power was no longer tempered by the traditional loyalties of a Roman gentleman, and who were able to divert to the service of private ambition the wealth and soldiers of the Roman state.

An incident of 89 BC illustrates the startling decline in the morality and discipline of the leaders of the Republic in this period. In that year the Senate dispatched an embassy to the East, headed by the former consul M'. Aquillius, to persuade the powerful Mithridates, king of Pontus in Asia Minor, to evacuate the territories of two of his neighbors, once client states of Rome. After Mithridates complied, Aquillius forced the newly restored king of Bithynia to plunder Pontic territory to make good on what were essentially promised kickbacks to Aquillius and his colleagues; the predictable result was the First Mithridatic War. This is the first time a major war seems to have been started by a Roman senator – in this case, not even a serving consular magistrate – on his own initiative, though it is unclear whether this was the anticipated effect. As it happened, Aquillius was captured by Mithridates and put to death by having molten gold poured down his throat.[53]

---

[52] For an account of Marius see *CAH* 9, 116–51.

[53] Badian, *Roman Imperialism*, 56–58. Badian draws the contrast between the behavior of Roman aristocrats in the earlier and the late Republic in the following terms: "In their dealings with major powers and civilized states, the representatives of Rome showed, on the whole, a praiseworthy sense of responsibility, and the Senate asserted sufficient control over them, so that outrageous behavior was rare indeed and confined to conditions of special strain.... By 89, many factors had combined to undermine that state of affairs. Above all, Roman nobles had simply become increasingly and excessively arrogant and confident. For one thing, their heads were turned by excessive powers and excessive honors in the provinces. The Roman governor, with his permanent emergency powers, subject to no appeal and *de facto* to no enforceable law, would have had to be more than human to preserve moderation and self-restraint" (55).

The effects of this shift in Roman moral norms are only too apparent in developing Roman attitudes toward empire. In a caricature of Gracchan policy, P. Clodius Pulcher, tribune for 58 BC, caused a law to be passed annexing the rich island of Cyprus (then a dependency of Ptolemaic Egypt) to pay for the distribution of free grain at Rome, primarily to enhance his own political standing. This, one historian remarks, has to count as the "most disgraceful act of Roman imperialism apart from the Gallic War."[54] It was, of course, as proconsul that C. Julius Caesar conducted a virtually unprovoked war against the Gallic tribes outside Rome's orbit, completed the conquest of the country, and proceeded to extend Roman power into Britain, with little if any real direction or oversight from the imperial center. In 55 BC, the consul and triumvir Marcus Crassus took it upon himself to launch an invasion of Parthia, Rome's most formidable remaining rival in the East – leading to one of the worst defeats in the history of the Republic (at the battle of Carrhae in modern Iraq) and his own demise. But an unwarranted arrogance in Roman dealings with the Parthians was already evident in Sulla's encounter with them some years earlier.[55]

Caesar was granted proconsular imperium for a highly unusual five years – in a law that he and his fellow triumvirs connived to pass in 59 BC. Crassus also received a multi-year consulship. This deviation from long-established Roman precedent (under which, as we have seen, consular or proconsular imperium was limited to a year but could be extended), however, should be traced back some ten years earlier to the great commands held by Pompeius Magnus (Pompey). In all these cases, multi-year consulships were voted for specific strategic projects by the People, not the Senate. Pompey's extraordinary naval command against the Cilician pirates, encompassing essentially the entire Mediterranean, and his command of an expansive eastern theater in the war against Mithridates, marked the beginning of the breakdown of traditional constraints on consular imperium in the dimensions of space as well as time. They set the precedent Caesar would later follow in his own strategic project of conquest in northwest Europe.

The final chapter in the history of the Republic begins with Caesar's march on Rome in 49 BC and ends with the victory of his adoptive great-nephew Gaius Octavius (Octavian) over Marcus Antonius (Antony) and Queen Cleopatra of Egypt at the sea battle of Actium in 31 BC. By 44 BC, Caesar had defeated all his rivals and consolidated his hold on power. Having already been appointed by the Senate as *dictator* for ten years to reconstitute the state, he then arranged to be made *dictator* for an indefinite period, as well as – with a nice

[54] Ibid., 77.
[55] Ibid., 55–56, 87–89. Of Caesar, Badian remarks: "The sweet reasonableness of the *Commentaries* cannot disguise the fact that Caesar started a major foreign war and then a civil one – for a variety of reasons, as we all know, but chiefly (as he at times comes close to admitting) for his personal glory and profit" (89). On Caesar see most recently Adrian Goldsworthy, *Caesar: Life of a Colossus* (New Haven, CT: Yale University Press, 2006).

irony – *praefectus morum* (supervisor of morals). His assassination in that year seemed to open the way for a restoration of the Republic, but its champions were disorganized and weak and the senatorial regime was thoroughly discredited. The ascendancy of Octavian, though surely not foreordained, reflected a widespread acceptance of the necessity of a "Caesar" to put an end to Rome's internal strife and to the institutional problems that had increasingly threatened Rome's hold on its empire – now vaster than ever after the final defeat of Mithridates, Caesar's conquests in Gaul and Britain, and the absorption of Egypt following the death of Cleopatra (the last part of the Mediterranean littoral not under Roman control).[56]

Whatever one thinks of his ruthless pursuit and exercise of personal power, Caesar Augustus (as Octavian styled himself after 27 BC) proved to be a statesman of genius, one who endowed the new Roman Empire with sound foundations that would sustain it for another 500 years.[57] He did so in part by avoiding a sharp break with the republican past, above all, by restoring the outward forms of senatorial governance and downplaying his own unique role. Initially, Augustus considered basing his power on the institution of the consulate (in fact, he held this office annually until 23 BC), but decided against it because of the awkwardness of the requirement of an annual election. Instead, he chose to be merely "first citizen" (*princeps*), though endowed with certain tribunician privileges (*tribunicia potestas*: he could not technically be a tribune because he was the adoptive son of his patrician uncle, Julius Caesar), particularly those of initiating and vetoing legislation. After 23, however, he received the power of a consul within Italy, and outside it a special imperium, superior to that of other consuls and proconsuls, styled "greater proconsular command unlimited in time" (*imperium proconsulare maius infinitum*). In effect, this made him the permanent commander in chief of Rome's military forces – or, in short, *imperator*.

Under the Republic, as noted earlier, Rome had never really had a single army, but rather as many armies as it had consuls and proconsuls at a particular time, armies raised for particular campaigns and then dispersed once they were over. Augustus rationalized this unsatisfactory state of affairs both by creating a professional standing army and by assuming overall command of that army. Both steps were necessary to break the personal bond between consular magistrates and their troops, which had proved so problematic for Rome from the time of Marius. But that was not all. Consuls as such no longer served overseas in command of troops. Ex-consuls did go overseas as proconsuls, but Augustus

---

[56] That the dysfunction of Rome's political institutions (specifically, the tribunate and the consular magistracies) rather than, as often assumed, the extent of its empire was the fundamental cause of the collapse of the Republic is cogently argued by Walter Eder, "Republicans and Sinners: The Decline of the Roman Republic and the End of a Provisional Arrangement," in Robert W. Wallace and Edward M. Harris, eds., *Transitions to Empire: Essays in Greco-Roman History, 360–146 BC, in honor of E. Badian* (Norman: University of Oklahoma Press, 1996), ch. 21.

[57] For an account of his rise from a critical point of view see especially Ronald Syme, *The Roman Revolution* (Oxford: Oxford University Press, 1952).

transformed the very nature of the proconsular function by separating it entirely from military command. With only a few exceptions, from Augustus' time on, "proconsul" was the title designating governors of provinces (whether of consular or praetorian rank) that had no assigned Roman military forces, and their tenure in office was carefully restricted (normally to only one year). In this, he was anticipated by none other than Julius Caesar, who during his dictatorship had limited tenure in a proconsular province to two years, and a praetorian to one – evidently, to prevent others from following in his own footsteps. At the same time, Augustus reserved as (in effect) his own *provincia* all those provinces in which Rome kept standing military forces – principally frontier provinces. Governors in these provinces, combining military and civil authority like the consular magistrates of old, were titled "representatives of Augustus in place of a praetor" (*legati Augusti pro praetore*), an office thus markedly inferior to a traditional proconsulate, and were appointed and removed at the discretion of the emperor, with some of them retaining their positions for many years, while proconsuls were chosen by lot (though from a short list of approved candidates) and their selection ratified by the Senate. It has long been believed that the Senate actually exercised significant authority in these "senatorial" provinces as distinguished from the "imperial" provinces directly answerable to the emperor. But these were optics, not reality: The Caesars were undisputed masters of the new Rome.[58]

---

[58] Millar provides a devastating critique of this view. For general discussion see Stevenson, *Roman Provincial Administration*, ch. 4, as well as Frédéric Hurlet, *Le proconsul et le prince d'Auguste à Dioclétien* (Pessac: Ausonius, 2006).

3

Wood in Cuba

> Whatever be the outcome, we must see to it that free Cuba be a reality, a perfect entity, not a hasty experiment bearing within itself the elements of failure.
>
> William McKinley[1]

> The trouble about Cuba is that, although technically a foreign country, practically and morally it occupies an intermediate position, since we have required it to become a part of our political and military system, and to form a part of our lines of exterior defense.
>
> Elihu Root[2]

The explosion that sank the battleship USS *Maine* in Havana Harbor on February 15, 1898, touched off war with Spain and, in its victorious aftermath, a chain of events leading to the emergence of a newly imperial United States of America. As in the case of the "war of choice" launched by the United States against Iraq over a century later, this *casus belli* would turn out to be suspect – the explosion was almost certainly an accident. But America's imperial turn was not an accident. It had deep roots in the nation's early history and political culture. Its progress was furthered by continental expansion and the Union's victory in the Civil War, stimulated by the global imperial "scramble" of the last decades of the nineteenth century and enabled by the development of a modern American navy. Domestic resistance to overseas expansion and a strong federal government and military establishment, largely centered in the Democratic Party (particularly its southern wing, with its fresh memories of Reconstruction), though significant, was waning by the 1890s. It was overwhelmed by a tide of popular support for war with Spain, one that crossed

---

[1] President William McKinley, in a presidential message to the House of Representatives in 1898, as quoted in James H. Hitchman, *Leonard Wood and Cuban Independence 1898–1902* (The Hague: Martinus Nijhoff, 1971), 13.

[2] Philip C. Jessup, *Elihu Root*, 2 vols. (New York: Dodd, Mead, 1938), I, 322.

party and sectional lines. Contrary to a still common view, this war fever was not artificially manufactured by a "yellow press" in response to the destruction of the *Maine*, but reflected widespread humanitarian revulsion at the escalating atrocities committed by the Spanish authorities in their long struggle with the Cuban rebels, coupled with a sense that this situation had become an intolerable affront to the honor of the nation.[3]

At the same time, it is important to keep in proper perspective the meaning of "empire" in the American context. America's "empire of liberty," as Thomas Jefferson (father of the Louisiana Purchase, let it be remembered) had called it, differed in important ways from the overseas colonial empires of the European powers. The continental expansion of the United States during the nineteenth century had occurred over vast territories inhabited only by a small and scattered indigenous population. Whatever view one takes of the treatment of this population at the hands of American settlers and their government or its eventual fate, and of course with the great exception of black slavery in the Old South, it remains the case that the United States was not in the business of conquering or ruling subject peoples. Unlike the European empires, America's continental expansion did not lead to the creation of permanent dependent territories and subjects but rather to new free states on a footing of equality with the original states that had come together to form the federal union.[4]

This is not to deny that the idea of American expansion in the Caribbean and Latin America had been entertained by some from the early days of the Republic. Spanish Florida, after all, had been absorbed by the United States by 1819. But two considerations above all stood in the way of such a development. The first was the complication of American sectional politics prior to the Civil War: It was virtually certain that any further territorial acquisitions in this region would accrue to the slave power. The second was the widespread conviction that the peoples living there were not capable of supporting free political orders, for a complex of reasons relating to race, religion, and social conditions, and hence that their absorption by the United States would pose potential dangers for its republican institutions. By the end of the nineteenth century, the slavery issue was of course off the table, but the second

---

[3] Robert Kagan, *Dangerous Nation: America's Foreign Policy from Its Earliest Days to the Dawn of the Twentieth Century* (New York: Random House, 2006), esp. chs. 11–12, is an outstanding account. On the Cuban struggle for independence see José M. Hernández, *Cuba and the United States: Intervention and Militarism, 1868–1933* (Austin: University of Texas Press, 1993), ch. 1. The insurrection had flared up again in 1895; the brutal policies of the Spanish commander, General Valeriano Weyler, particularly the establishment of concentration camps for Cuban non-combatants, were an important stimulant to the growing anti-Spanish sentiment in the United States in those years.

[4] It is striking, however, that Roosevelt, in defending the American occupation of the Philippines, felt compelled to minimize the differences between that situation and the settling of the American West. See James R. Holmes, *Theodore Roosevelt and World Order: Police Power in International Relations* (Washington, DC: Potomac Books, 2006), 65–68.

consideration remained an important constraint on American imperial temptations – thwarting, for example, the acquisition of Santo Domingo (the Dominican Republic) in the late 1860s and 1870s, in spite of wide support for this step not only in Congress but among the Dominicans themselves.

Nevertheless, several other factors had come into play that forced or encouraged Americans to think more seriously about overseas expansion by the end of the nineteenth century. Foremost among them was security, though economic considerations also played an important role. The last quarter of the century witnessed a race for additional colonial acquisitions by the great European powers, particularly in Africa but also in Asia and the Pacific, and Japan emerged as an important power in East Asia with its decisive victory in the Sino-Japanese War of 1895. Coupled with this was a new emphasis on the role of naval power – thanks in no small measure to the American strategist Alfred Thayer Mahan, whose *The Influence of Sea Power on History* (1890) was an international sensation – and the rapid growth of great power navies in size and technological capability. The Mahanian gospel emphasized the importance of overseas trade for national strength and of navies for protecting the sea lines of communication vital to sustaining trade. Moreover, the transition from sail-driven to coal-fired navies underscored the need to acquire a network of overseas bases of the sort that had proven critical to sustaining Great Britain's global maritime empire – for Mahan, the model to which the United States should aspire. Mahan's influence was strong in a rising generation of American political leaders, in particular, Theodore Roosevelt, the second-ranking civilian in McKinley's Department of the Navy.[5]

In the 1870s, the United States had acquired a naval station in the Pacific in the remote Samoan islands. British and especially German interests in the same place had given rise to a complicated political situation there leading, in the 1880s, to a confrontation between the United States and Germany over the matter that brought home to Americans the seriousness of German colonial ambitions and the potential threat posed by the growing military power of the Reich.[6] Of far greater significance for the nascent American empire, however, were the nation's perceived stakes in the Hawaiian Islands as well as a prospective canal across the Central American isthmus.

As early as the 1840s, consideration was given to offering a protectorate or even full statehood to Hawaii, but the slavery issue mooted this at the time.[7] American-born settlers had become a powerful economic and political force in Hawaii by the 1880s, and the islands' economy was almost entirely dependent on the mainland. Following a protracted political struggle, these settlers overthrew the native Hawaiian monarchy in 1893, established an independent republic (with some military and other support from the United States), and

---

[5] For a brief account see ibid., 74–82.
[6] Kagan, 335–40.
[7] The native Hawaiians themselves proposed joining the Union as a free state, but this option fell afoul of the Missouri Compromise. Kagan, 252–53.

pressed for annexation. Anti-imperialist sentiment in the then-dominant Democratic Party succeeded in blocking this step, but the perception of a growing interest in the islands by other powers, especially Germany and Japan, together with the need to support American military operations against Spain in the Philippines, decided Congress on annexation in 1898.[8]

As for the idea of a transisthmian canal (for which both Panama and Nicaragua were candidates), while it brought obvious economic benefits, its strategic value was the paramount consideration. A canal would allow much easier concentration of the American fleet to meet threats on either of its coasts. But this also meant that defense of the canal by the United States – particularly against a European power staging out of bases in the Caribbean – would be a major preoccupation of American strategy, particularly naval strategy. As we shall see, this concern would strongly color official American attitudes toward Cuba in the aftermath of the war with Spain.

The Spanish-American War has long since receded into the mists of American memory. Indeed, in some ways it seems more remote today than the Civil War or even the Revolution. This is no doubt largely because the cause for which it was fought has lost much of its appeal to a generation or generations whose experience of American entanglements in conflicts in the less developed world has been shaped by Vietnam and Iraq. But there is also an element of the faintly comic in the way the war was fought. While its outcome was never in doubt given the geographical advantages and overall military superiority of the United States and the ineptness of the enemy, the country was nevertheless ill-prepared for it and stumbled badly in various ways. Finally, the aftermath of the war proved problematic, to say the least. American missteps and indecision in the Philippines led to grinding and costly counterinsurgency operations against native rebels, while in Cuba, in spite of initial successes, the United States failed to lay the groundwork for a stable Cuban government over the longer term. At the same time, the war left a legacy of American interventionism in the Caribbean and Central America that continues to burden the nation's relationship with its weaker neighbors to the south.

All this having been said, the response of the American government to the various challenges posed by the Spanish-American War remains an interesting topic, and one of more than passing relevance to contemporary concerns. It has long been the fashion among historians to denigrate the achievements of American leaders during this era and to caricature their abilities and motives, and it has become commonplace to write off their policies as a simple expression of powerful economic interests working behind the scenes in Washington. There can be little question that such a view is seriously misleading. Whatever else can be said about them, the men who were principally responsible for America's imperial turn were intellectually impressive and politically capable, and as American nationalists first and foremost, they were by no means captive

---

[8] George C. Herring, *From Colony to Superpower: U.S. Foreign Relations Since 1776* (New York: Oxford University Press, 2008), 317–18.

to a set of private interests.[9] Recent scholarship has substantially revised the conventional picture of President William McKinley as an earnest but fundamentally confused and indecisive figure who failed to control events on his watch (1897–1901; McKinley was assassinated a year into his second term). To the contrary, McKinley has been called the first truly "modern" American president, in the sense that he was the first to exploit the full range of executive powers and prerogatives usually associated with the two Roosevelts, Wilson, and their more recent successors. More than that, McKinley was a man of considerable political skill who arguably played a masterful game in managing the complexities of international and domestic politics and public opinion to guide the country safely through uncharted waters.[10] If nothing else, he deserves great credit for recruiting as his secretary of war a man who would prove to be one of the outstanding American statesmen of the twentieth century, though he is largely forgotten today – Elihu Root. Root, in turn, along with his friend Theodore Roosevelt, saw to it that the military government of Cuba was entrusted to an obscure army doctor named Leonard Wood, the first of America's proconsuls and soon to prove one of its greatest.

Leonard Wood was born in 1860 on Cape Cod, Massachusetts, to parents both of whom could trace their ancestry to the *Mayflower*. The family had little money, however, and Wood's father, unable to complete an education in his chosen field of medicine, was a professional failure. Serving briefly in the Union army as a hospital orderly during the Civil War, he contracted malaria and permanently damaged his health; he died when Wood was twenty years old. The younger Wood was luckier, acquiring the fundamentals of an education in the classical languages, history, and science, and after his father's death, financial assistance from a Boston philanthrophist that enabled him to attend Harvard Medical School. Wood's ambition and appetite for work were already evident at this stage of his life, but so too were some less attractive features that would become increasingly pronounced as he grew older. After medical school, Wood was hired as an intern at Boston City Hospital, where he chafed at the regimentation and strict limitations under which he was forced to work. Interns were not supposed to operate on patients without supervision unless under emergency circumstances in the middle of the night; Wood stretched this envelope regularly, and was eventually put on probation by the hospital's board of trustees. Ignoring this warning, he was fired shortly thereafter.

With a conventional medical career now virtually closed to him, Wood followed a second time in his father's footsteps and sought to join the Army's medical corps. He did not do quite well enough in a competitive examination

---

[9] For a recent, largely sympathetic account see Warren Zimmerman, *First Great Triumph: How Five Americans Made Their Country a World Power* (New York: Farrar, Straus and Giroux, 2002). The five are Roosevelt, Mahan, Elihu Root, John Hay, and Henry Cabot Lodge. Roosevelt, of course, was the leader of the Progressive wing of the Republican Party, which actively sought to curb the power of the magnates of American business.

[10] See particularly Lewis L. Gould, *The Presidency of William McKinley* (Lawrence: Regents Press of Kansas, 1980).

to gain an officer's commission, but the army offered him instead a temporary contract as acting surgeon with a unit then being formed in Arizona to
pursue the renegade Apache chief Geronimo. Wood seized the opportunity.
In an almost unimaginable campaign that lasted four months and covered
some 3,000 miles (much of it on foot) through the deserts and mountains of
northern Mexico and the American Southwest, Wood demonstrated courage,
endurance, derring-do, and leadership skills beyond anything that could have
been expected from experienced soldiers, let alone a young civilian doctor.
His exploits gained him a reputation as well as an important patron in Major
General Nelson Miles, the operation's overall commander. Although he was
able thereafter to secure a regular commission in the medical corps, for the
next several years Wood's career languished as he was shunted between backwater army posts across the country. But he was eventually able to exploit his
relationship with Miles, by then commanding general of the army, to arrange
to be transferred to Washington, DC – over the strenuous objections of the
army's surgeon general. As one of his biographers puts it, Wood at this critical juncture "got his way by testing the limits of insubordination, learned
a perilous lesson in political manipulation, and made a permanent enemy"
of his immediate superior.[11] It would not be the last time in his unusual
career.

Wood and his wife Louise – who also had important political connections[12] –
moved to the capital in September 1895. In the small-town atmosphere of
Washington in those days, then Captain Wood contrived not only to meet the
president (Grover Cleveland in the last year of his administration) but to play
poker and go fishing with him. With the arrival of McKinley and the Republicans, his fortunes brightened still more. It had been customary for local army
medical personnel to minister to the health of the first family, and Wood quickly
established himself as personal physician and confidant to the new president's
wife Ada, a notorious hypochondriac. Even more important, though, was the

[11] Jack McCallum, *Leonard Wood: Rough Rider, Surgeon, Architect of American Imperialism*
(New York: New York University Press, 2006), 51. The basic account of Wood's life is Hermann Hagedorn, *Leonard Wood: A Biography* (New York: Harper and Brothers, 1931), a
work of lyrical and unstinting admiration of its subject; Jack C. Lane, *Armed Progressive:
Leonard Wood* (San Rafael, CA, and London: Presidio Press, 1978), like McCallum, is more
balanced, though on occasion arguably overcritical. Hitchman's *Leonard Wood and Cuban
Independence* offers a judicious and well-documented appraisal of Wood and the McKinley
administration's Cuban policy. For a defense of Wood more generally against his many contemporary and later critics, see Lewis Gleeck, *The American Governors-General and High
Commissioners in the Philippines: Proconsuls, Nation-Builders, and Politicians* (Quezon City:
New Day Publishers, 1986), ch. 8. See also David F. Healy, *The United States in Cuba 1898–
1902: Generals, Politicians, and the Search for Policy* (Madison: University of Wisconsin Press,
1963).
[12] Louise Wood had been the ward of Stephen Field, a justice of the U.S. Supreme Court and a
prominent Republican, who also lobbied in Washington on Wood's behalf. Neither Miles nor
Field, however, was in good order with the Cleveland administration, an additional political
wrinkle in this situation that further underlines Wood's audacity. McCallum, 48–51.

friendship he developed with Theodore Roosevelt, McKinley's assistant secretary of the navy. With their common love of sports, the West, and what TR liked to call the strenuous life, Wood and Roosevelt quickly became inseparable. When, at the outbreak of the Spanish-American War, it was decided to create several "cowboy regiments" to supplement the regular army, Roosevelt was instrumental in securing Wood's appointment as commanding officer of the First United States Volunteer Cavalry, to be recruited from the American Southwest. Colonel Wood's second-in-command was Lieutenant Colonel Theodore Roosevelt, a man with even less real military experience than Wood himself.[13]

It will not be necessary to follow this story through the actual operations in Cuba, culminating in the iconic American victory at the Battle of San Juan Hill and the capitulation of the Spanish forces in front of Santiago City on July 17, 1898. Though brief, the invasion was by no means a walkover. Wood and Roosevelt both distinguished themselves by their leadership and personal bravery, and Wood was promoted to general on the spot. A few days after the surrender, he was appointed military governor of the city of Santiago. An old friend, Brigadier General Henry Lawton, was made military governor of Santiago (Oriente) province, while overall command rested with Major General William Shafter, both of them Civil War veterans. Santiago de Cuba, the most important city in the eastern part of the island, was a center of mining and agriculture, with a population in 1898 of some 40,000. Though prosperous at one time, the effects of the insurrection and an American naval blockade had left the city starving and near collapse. In addition, it was a sanitary nightmare. "Houses, mottled with black mildew, were built around garden courtyards long since converted to stables, privies, and cesspits. On the odd occasions when sewage was removed, it was heaped in the streets to sink and evaporate. There were no covered drains, little paving, and few sidewalks; only the bravest or poorest traveled on foot. Filth accumulated in the streets until rain and gravity carried the sludge to the harbor's edge to give low tide a pungency that could be appreciated ten miles out to sea."[14] Every summer, hundreds of people routinely died from the dreadful ravages of yellow fever, a disease of unknown origin and at that time having no known cure; typhoid and malaria were also major threats.

In fact, the first crisis facing the American occupiers came not from the remnants of Spain's army or the Cuban *insurrectos* in the hinterland, but from yellow fever, which had broken out among Shafter's troops by the middle of July. Understandably, his senior officers feared that the entire force could be at risk, and requested its evacuation as soon as possible. When this was denied, however, Wood and Roosevelt apparently maneuvered to bring public pressure to bear on Secretary of War Nelson Alger to reconsider this decision, much to

---

[13] For a recent portrait of Roosevelt see Edmund Morris, *Theodore Rex* (New York: Random House, 2001).

[14] McCallum, 111–12.

the annoyance of Alger (already smarting from press criticism of his handling of the war) and McKinley himself, who feared its effect on peace negotiations with the Spaniards.[15] At all events, on assuming control in Santiago, the crisis in public health was front and center among Wood's concerns. Shafter's own instructions were to "maintain order, feed the poor, and do everything possible to facilitate the prompt reestablishment of business," but Wood recognized that improving sanitary conditions also needed to be an immediate priority, enforced by drastic measures if necessary.

And drastic they proved to be. Wood formed hundred-man work crews under the command of his officers to clean up the accumulated filth, using food as an inducement but forcible conscription where that failed, and with no regard whatsoever for social status: those who resisted were publicly horse-whipped. Working twelve to sixteen hours a day, these crews scoured not only the streets but private houses and shops with or without the owners' consent, destroying privies that were considered beyond repair. Bakeries, groceries, and slaughterhouses were either cleaned or closed. And Wood did not hesitate to interfere with time-honored but pernicious local practices such as the lucrative cemetery monopoly of the Catholic Church, which often caused poorer people to abandon the corpses of relatives in sheds behind their houses.[16]

The food and water situation in Santiago was equally dire. The city had virtually no running water, as its supply came from the mountains in pipes that had not been repaired in half a century; all had to be dug up and thousands of leaks repaired. The fertile fields that had formerly surrounded the town had mostly reverted to jungle as a result of the scorched-earth counterinsurgency policies of the former colonial regime. Wood was able to seize food supplies stockpiled by the Spanish for immediate distribution; at the same time, he imposed draconian controls on bakers and other merchants who attempted to take advantage of the situation, while thieves and looters were shot on sight. For the longer term, he developed a strategy for reconstructing Santiago's agricultural hinterland by offering steady employment to farmers in the city while at the same time encouraging them to return to and invest in their rural properties. Aided by the multiple growing seasons of the Cuban year, this strategy began to show important results in a matter of months.

Wood's larger approach to the problems of the local economy is also of much interest, especially in the light of the costly and conspicuous failures of later American economic aid policies in places like Vietnam and Iraq. In the

---

[15] Details of this episode are somewhat unclear, but Roosevelt seems to have taken the lead in drafting a letter for Shafter and his senior officers to send to Washington, at the same time ensuring that it would leak to the press and cause a public furor, as indeed happened; but Wood too was plainly implicated. Ibid., 114–18.

[16] "Cemeteries were owned by the church and grave sites were rented. If the rent was not paid, the corpse was exhumed and the bones, stripped clean by quicklime, were thrown in a communal pit. Wood ordered the priests to perform services regardless of pay and to leave the bodies buried. When they objected, the governor threatened to put them on street cleaning brigades." Ibid., 119.

first instance, Wood specifically avoided creating a dependence on largess from Washington, aiming instead at a locally balanced budget supported by tariffs and fees as well as by drastic reductions in the high government salaries and the bribery and corruption typical of the previous Spanish administration. At the same time, he avoided imposing direct taxes on the people themselves, for sound political as well as economic reasons. This overall approach in fact generated a considerable surplus, all of it reinvested in public works programs that would both improve the city itself and provide income for its residents.[17]

All of this, it is important to emphasize, was essentially owing to the imagination and initiative of one man. No prior planning for the occupation of Cuba had been done in Washington, and Wood had little guidance in the beginning from his own immediate superiors (Shafter was preoccupied with managing the American military presence) or significant direction from the War Department. For all intents and purposes, his authority was at least as absolute as that of General Douglas MacArthur in the early years of the occupation of Japan – if indeed not more so.

Let us now step back and look at the larger political picture. The United States from the beginning treated Cuba differently than its other Spanish conquests. While the fall of the colonial regime in Cuba had put an end to Spanish sovereignty over the island, the United States did not claim sovereignty for itself, as it did in Puerto Rico and eventually the Philippines, merely establishing de facto military control – the result of specific legislation mandating eventual Cuban independence.[18] Of course, this created an acute ambiguity regarding the locus of civil and political authority on the island, as well as the standing of existing Cuban social and political elites in the eyes of the American occupiers. (A similar situation would face the United States following its "liberation" of Saddam Hussein's Iraq.) The revolt against Spain had been led by an uneasy alliance of elements of the largely white professional and business elite and the peasant, largely black army under Generals Máximo Gómez and Calixto García. Assisting the revolutionary movement was a collection of Cuban émigrés based in New York, the so-called Junta, which had raised funds, conducted propaganda for the cause, and lobbied American politicians; its leader was Tomás Estrada Palma, who would become the first president of the Republic of Cuba in 1902. The United States had declined initially to recognize the long-standing provisional rebel government, which in any event was little more than a façade for the caudillo-style sway of General Gómez over the revolutionary movement.[19] Gómez and García, the commander in eastern Cuba, had collaborated more or less enthusiastically with the invading forces,

[17] Leonard Wood, "The Existing Conditions and Needs in Cuba," *North American Review* 168 (May 1899): 593–601; see further McCallum, 122, 126.

[18] This was the so-called Teller Amendment to the Army appropriations bill of 1898, one of several key interventions by the Congress in U.S. Cuban policy.

[19] For the difficult relationship between the civilian and military components of the Cuban revolutionary movement see Hernández, ch. 1. Effective leadership of the movement had essentially passed to Gómez after the death of José Martí in 1895.

and expected to be allowed to occupy areas abandoned by the Spanish and organize them as they saw fit. But this was not to be. García was denied entry into Santiago itself, and although the rebels occupied many towns throughout the island (particularly in its western part, where there were no U.S. forces), it was quickly decided in Washington that there could be no "dual government" in Cuba.[20]

Particularly in light of recent American experience in Iraq, it is tempting to wonder whether this decision was the correct one. A case can certainly be made that the leaders of the rebel army were treated with unnecessary disrespect, and should have been consulted more fully and openly on American activities and plans. On the other hand, it was also clear that the army, though the only significant political force still functioning in the country, was not an appropriate vehicle for reconstituting Cuban politics. It was far from representative of the Cuban population as a whole, many of whom had sided and even fought with the Spanish authorities against it; and it was merely an army, not a political movement. Gómez himself recognized that, though personally popular, he lacked the education and temperament to become president of an independent Cuba. Finally, the Americans were concerned – with some justification – that the army in power might degenerate into a dictatorial regime bent on revenge and oppression of the upper classes. The racial issue also came into play here. The specter of rule by the army, which was perhaps 80 percent black, frightened Americans and Cubans alike in view of the unarguably sorry history of black rule in nearby Haiti.[21]

Though Wood has often been criticized as authoritarian by temper and having little use for his new Cuban charges, this is unfair to him. It should be kept in mind that he could read, write, and speak Spanish fluently from his days on the Mexican frontier. Unlike, for example, MacArthur in Tokyo, he made himself accessible to the Cubans and dealt with them in an open and unpretentious way. Wood's Cuban appointments were generally sagacious, most of them being drawn from the professional elite and chosen in consultation with other prominent citizens; and he sought to devolve authority and responsibility on these officials as quickly as could safely be done. And while Wood personally retained overall control of his administrative apparatus, this control was combined in an unusual fashion with encouragement of personal freedom in the population at large. After Wood replaced the alcoholic Lawton as governor of Oriente Province, he promulgated a list of universal rights modeled closely on the Bill of Rights of the U.S. Constitution. Though conspicuously omitting the right to vote, this document guaranteed freedom of speech and press and freedom of assembly; and Wood in fact allowed the Cubans to hold public meetings whenever they chose and vent their grievances against the occupiers, and generally indulged the Cuban press in spite of its frequent criticisms of the American occupation. This being said, Wood continued to arrogate to himself

[20] The phrase is Shafter's. Ibid., 60.
[21] Ibid.

a wide range of administrative decisions, some of them verging on the petty (he banned bull-fighting, cock-fighting, and the lottery, for example), that seem to have reflected his own Puritan origins more than any settled policy.

The formal transfer of authority in Cuba from Spain to the United States occurred on January 1, 1899. At this time, McKinley appointed General James Brooke, the military governor of Puerto Rico and another Civil War veteran, as commander of the "military department" responsible for Cuba, Puerto Rico, and the Philippines. Brooke installed himself in Havana and took immediate steps to centralize American control of the island – thus confirming the worst fears of Wood, who had lobbied against the appointment. Brooke abrogated Wood's "Santiago Constitution" and restored the Spanish legal code, took control of all revenues and expenditures, and insisted on clearing all civil appointments. The six sub-departments of the island and the city of Havana were headed by American generals, but Brooke also created a powerful cabinet of Cuban officials to oversee the island's civil government. Before long, it was being said that "the American governor reigns but the Cuban secretaries govern." All of this was too much for Wood. He encouraged anti-Brooke agitation in the Santiago papers and then took the fight to Washington. With Roosevelt fully engaged on his behalf,[22] he traveled in person to the capital, receiving a standing ovation at the White House, giving public speeches, and testifying before Congress, all in an effort to replace his superior as governor of the island.

In truth, there could not have been a greater contrast than between Santiago province and the rest of Cuba, though to be sure Santiago under Wood had had a six-month head start. The Havana government itself was a bureaucratic nightmare.

Brooke had overall command of both the civil administration and about 24,000 American troops. Colonel Tasker Bliss ran a customs service staffed partially by American officers and civilians and partially by Cuban civilians. The island's treasurer was an American army officer, but the North American Trust Company of New York was a virtually independent fiscal agent. Senator Mark Hanna's crony Estes Rathbone ran the postal service as a personal bank account. The Quarantine Service was run by the United States Marine Hospital Service and telephones and telegraph were the purview of the Army Signal Corps. Behind all this were the Cuban secretaries and their network of provincial and municipal officials.[23]

This scene would not have been altogether unfamiliar to American observers in Saigon or Baghdad many decades later, but Wood had already demonstrated that it did not have to be so.

Wood's campaign to replace Brooke continued through much of 1899. He took advantage of his wife's contacts in Washington, including the president

---

[22] Roosevelt published a fulsome celebration of Wood's achievements, "General Leonard Wood: A Model American Military Administrator," *Outlook* 61 (January 7, 1899): 19–23 (as cited in McCallum, 135–36).

[23] McCallum, 138.

himself as well as Elihu Root, the new secretary of war; and Wood himself sent McKinley a personal letter touting his own achievements. Roosevelt lent his support again as well. In a letter to Secretary of State John Hay, he wrote:

We need tact and judgment just as much as we need firmness in Cuba now. Wood is a born diplomat, just as he is a born soldier.... He has a peculiar faculty for getting on with the Spaniards and Cubans. They like him, trust him and down in their hearts are afraid of him.... He understands their needs, material and moral, and he also understands their sensitiveness and their spirit of punctilio. Finally, he is able, while showing them entire courtesy and thoughtful consideration, to impress upon them the fact that there can be no opposition when once he has made up his mind.[24]

These efforts prospered, and in December 1899 Wood was awarded his second star and appointed by Root governor-general of Cuba, though only after a prolonged struggle with General James Wilson, another provincial governor who coveted the job and also had allies in Washington.

At this juncture there was a degree of fluidity in American policy. Sentiment was growing in some quarters in the United States for annexation. General Wilson in fact favored a quick American withdrawal and the election of a Cuban government – on the Machiavellian reasoning that this would shortly fail, thus demonstrating the incapacity of the Cubans for self-government and the necessity of permanent annexation, which the Cuban people would then voluntarily embrace. There is considerable evidence that Wood, too, was affected by this line of thinking. In private letters, he referred repeatedly to growing annexationist sentiment among the Cuban elite and expressed doubts about the readiness of the Cubans for self-government in the near term: As he told Root in February 1900, there was "not a sensible man" in the island who thought that the American authorities could leave for a long time, "not measured by months, but by years; several of them at least."[25] In late 1899, rumors circulated in the American and Cuban press that the McKinley administration was contemplating replacing Brooke with a new civilian governor of Cuba, and Wood's name was floated in this connection. This created an uproar among the Cubans, who understandably feared that it signaled a change in American policy and would mean the establishment of a permanent colonial government. While McKinley's ultimate intentions in this regard are somewhat enigmatic, he and Root moved to defuse a potentially dangerous situation by restating the administration's commitment to the congressionally mandated policy of non-annexation and to the existing governing arrangements. Whatever annexationist sentiments he may have harbored privately, Wood loyally supported this program.

[24] Roosevelt to John Hay, July 1, 1899, as cited in Hitchman, 20.
[25] Wood to Root, February 16, 1900, as cited in Healy, 132. In the spring of 1901, he wrote to Root: "My belief is that if encouragement were given, the people of Cuba would with almost one voice ask to become a state in the Union." Wood to Root, April 17, 1901, cited in McCallum, 190.

Wood wasted no time in asserting his own authority in Cuba, and simplifying his reporting chain – it would now go directly to Root.[26] He was particularly careful to exercise oversight of the finances of the occupation and to forestall and root out corruption, and he took the initiative in putting an end to the gross irregularities in the postal service in spite of the dangerous political complications this entailed.[27] In general, the trio of Wood, Root, and McKinley seems to have worked together on Cuban affairs in a spirit of remarkable trust and harmony, and with considerable ultimate success. Key policy decisions were reserved to the president and his secretary of war, but Wood was given considerable latitude both in shaping those decisions and in carrying them out. On some occasions, and in areas beneath Washington's radar screen, his role was fundamental.[28]

What American policy essentially required was the creation of a responsible and reasonably democratic Cuban government, as well as sufficiently stable social, political, and economic conditions to give it at least a decent chance of long-term viability. To what extent all this could be accomplished without a complete remaking of Cuban society and culture was of course the crucial question. The selection of Wood rather than Brooke or Wilson as military governor clearly reflected a choice on the part of Root and McKinley of a more interventionist course in this regard – a choice that seems to have been influenced in significant measure by Wood himself.[29] Root, a lawyer by training, placed top priority on thoroughgoing reform of the Cuban legal and penal system – a reversal of the approach Brooke had taken; Wood's first act in office was a tour of Havana's prisons, which were immediately placed under the direct control of the War Department. Wood also overhauled the courts and the judicial system, introducing basic elements of Anglo-Saxon law such as habeas corpus, the right to legal representation, and trial by jury, and replacing the corruption-prone practice of supporting judges through fees paid by litigants with fixed salaries.

---

[26] Wood abolished the separate military departments on the island, thus not only consolidating his control but removing several generals who could act as rivals to himself; and he eventually succeeded in getting Root's agreement to report directly to him rather than through the adjutant general of the army (for military matters) or the assistant secretary of war (for policy matters), as had initially been the case; and he also managed to have Washington agree that his decisions would be final and not subject to appeal by Cubans to American courts or even the War Department. McCallum, 176–77.

[27] Estes Rathbone, head of the postal office in Havana, was a protégé of the powerful Republican Senator Mark Hanna, who attempted to intervene on his behalf and became a permanent enemy of Wood's thereafter. Wood's timely and vigorous prosecution of Rathbone took the wind out of what the Democrats were prepared to elevate into a major political scandal to tar the administration's Cuban policy as a whole. Ibid., 160–61.

[28] "In Washington, Root set the policy and allowed Wood to work it out; the secretary specifically refrained from directing action at a distance. He received Wood's loyalty in return. Among McKinley, Roosevelt, Root, and Wood, an aura of confidence facilitated the conduct of Cuban affairs." Hitchman, 38.

[29] Cf. Lane, 73–74. Brooke tended to defer to his Cuban advisers; Wilson thought the American role should be limited to keeping order and reforming the agriculture sector of the Cuban economy.

Though not uniformly successful – trial by jury, for example, was soon abandoned in favor of the traditional panel of judges, as Cubans were universally unwilling to convict their fellows – these reforms were radical, and went a long way toward improving the relationship between Cubans as individuals and the state, thus making them more fit for self-government.

Equally sweeping changes were made, largely on Wood's own initiative, in the areas of health care and education. Hospitals, insane asylums, and nursing schools throughout the island were built or rebuilt and adequately staffed. But Wood's greatest achievement here was in combating the infectious diseases that had long been the bane of Cuba and other Caribbean islands, especially yellow fever. A team of pathologists led by Major Walter Reed set out to identify the cause of yellow fever, and succeeded in validating the theory of a Havana physician that it was transmitted by mosquitoes rather than by contagion or unsanitary conditions. Wood's personal contribution to this discovery – he later commented that it alone was "worth the cost of the war" – was to take the considerable political risk of authorizing controlled human experimentation to confirm it beyond a reasonable doubt, and then to take drastic measures to control mosquito populations. By September 1901, yellow fever in Havana had essentially ceased to exist, while the number of malaria fatalities was also greatly reduced by the same measures.[30] With regard to education, prior to the occupation there was not a single building in Cuba devoted solely to primary education, and only 21,000 children attended schools, and not all of them regularly; the rate of illiteracy among adults was more than 65 percent. To make up for the lack of trained teachers, Wood arranged to raise private funds to send 1,450 Cuban women to Harvard for the summer. Beyond that, Wood took it on himself to fire the entire faculty of the University of Havana (some of its professors actually lived in Spain), rebuilding it on the basis of merit and developing a new and modern curriculum. This move seems to have been greeted with satisfaction by the general population.[31]

Wood's view of the Cuban people requires some comment. It is sometimes asserted that the proconsul was contemptuous of Cubans and their ways.[32] He once wrote to the president that the Cubans are at best "impetuous and hot-headed and liable to do many foolish things," and at worst, "stupid and downtrodden." Yet Wood clearly distinguished between the natural abilities of the Cuban people and the deleterious effect on them of centuries of Spanish misrule, particularly the lack of decent education throughout the mass of the population. Moreover, as noted earlier, he made a point of identifying men of talent (as distinguished from mere position) among the educated elite and entrusting them with responsibility, with results that for the most part vindicated his judgment in such matters. The men he appointed to his

[30] Ibid., 166–73.
[31] Ibid., 158–59. For further details on Wood's legal and educational reforms see Hitchman, ch. 3.
[32] Thus Lane, 75.

advisory cabinet on taking over from Brooke combined competence and revolutionary credentials in a way that received almost universal approval in the
Cuban press.[33] It is also true that Wood was frequently exasperated in his
dealings with Cuban politicians. Unfashionable as it may be to say so, however, it would not be easy to make the case that his comment concerning the
impetuous, hot-headed, and foolish or self-destructive tendencies of his Cuban
interlocutors was simply a reflection of his own prejudices and had no basis in
reality.[34] In fact, to the extent that prejudice came into play at all in Wood's
attitudes toward the Cubans, it was rather in his *overestimating* the capacities of the Cuban elite of the day when it came to shouldering the burdens of
self-government.[35]

It was in fact Wood himself who pressed the administration to organize
a constitutional convention in preparation for free elections and the eventual
establishment of a Cuban government. It was this project that consumed most
of his attention for the duration of his tenure in office. During the summer
of 1900, Wood toured the island to take soundings of Cuban opinion and
encourage the selection of delegates to the convention who would act respon-
sibly and in relative harmony with the American authorities. In this, Wood
was largely disappointed. By the time the delegates assembled in November, he
feared for the outcome of the convention, warning Root: "I believe in establishing a government of and by the people of Cuba and a free government,
because we have promised it, but I do not believe in surrendering the present
Government to adventurers who are now in the Convention." He went on: "It
is an extremely delicate situation, both from the sentiment at home which is
that we have got to give these people their independence – a thing which all of
us want to do – and the question whether we are keeping faith with them or
with ourselves if we push them into a condition which we know means their
failure and the ruin of their aspirations." Under these circumstances, Wood
himself seems to have favored prolonging the occupation at least in some form
until a more responsible Cuban political class had emerged. But Washington
had other ideas.

For Root and McKinley, the alternative to a politically unpalatable prolon-
gation of the occupation was an agreement with an eventual Cuban government
that would safeguard the equities of the United States in the country and the
region. In February 1901, the administration persuaded the Senate to add a
rider to the Army appropriations bill for that year defining the future U.S.–
Cuban relationship. This so-called Platt Amendment, at Root's insistence, was

33 McCallum, 152.
34 Consider this description of Wood by a contemporary Cuban: "From the standpoint of Washington, Cuba needed as its head a man more politically minded [than Brooke]; subtle and able
to keep his subtleties concealed from the inquisitive eye; endowed with great force of character
and personal integrity for the management of affairs, yet possessed of a political conscience
reasonably elastic; capable, in the interests of his country, to support as just that which was
expedient and, if need be, to favor might over right." Hagedorn, I, 306–07.
35 Cf. McCallum, 188–91.

to be presented to the convention on a non-negotiable basis and incorporated
in the Cuban constitution. It provided that Cuba make no agreements with foreign powers that would "impair or tend to impair" its independence, that the
government contract no debts it could not pay back out of ordinary revenue,
that the United States would have "the right to intervene for the protection
of Cuban independence," that all acts of the military government were to be
validated and maintained, that current sanitary plans and measures be maintained, and that Cuba would sell or lease naval and coaling stations to the
United States to be agreed upon subsequently. Not surprisingly, these terms
met with a storm of protest from the delegates and Cuban opinion generally.

Wood himself had warned Root earlier that any attempt to codify U.S.–
Cuban relations in the text of the constitution itself would lead to trouble, and
that the Cubans would undoubtedly insist on two entirely separate documents.
In retrospect, Washington's failure to heed this advice seems unfathomable.
The Cubans themselves displayed some flexibility in accommodating American
requirements, and it is difficult to believe that a face-saving approach could
not have been devised that did not so publicly and heavy-handedly flaunt the
superior position of the United States. Root himself authorized Wood to tell the
convention that the intervention clause should not be understood as creating a
new basis for the United States to meddle in Cuban affairs, but merely restated
rights it already possessed under the Monroe Doctrine and the Treaty of Paris
(the peace agreement with Spain). But if that were so, why was it necessary to
advertise it so blatantly?

The answer seems to be that the administration was growing increasingly
concerned over possible German ambitions in the Caribbean and Latin America. Some years later, Root is reported to have remarked: "You cannot understand the Platt Amendment unless you know something about the character
of Kaiser Wilhelm the Second."[36] The Venezuelan debt crisis of 1901–03,
which involved a plausible threat of a naval blockade and possible seizure of
Venezuelan ports by the Germans and the British, showed that this concern
was not altogether misplaced, no matter how exaggerated it may seem in retrospect. American officials worried particularly about the vulnerability of a
future isthmian canal and the sea routes leading to it, which in turn stimulated
their interest in acquiring strategically valuable naval stations along the Cuban
coast. As Root put it: "The trouble about Cuba is that, although technically a
foreign country, practically and morally it occupies an intermediate position,
since we have required it to become a part of our political and military system,
and to form a part of our lines of exterior defense."[37]

It is not clear that Wood was similarly moved by these strategic considerations, or at any rate the overriding priority assigned them by Washington.
In any event, he had the thankless task of forcing the constitutional assembly
to accept the Platt Amendment, on pain of a continuance of the American

---

[36] Philip C. Jessup, *Elihu Root* (New York: Dodd, Meade, 1938), I, 374 (cited in Hitchman, 88).
[37] Ibid., I, 322 (cited in Zimmerman, 374).

occupation. The most unfortunate effect of this was to rule out the option of a national referendum on the new constitution, which would almost certainly have failed. Instead, the text of the constitution and the amendment (as an appendix) were approved only by a closely divided vote of the thirty-one Cuban delegates, whose representative character was itself not above challenge. The constitution itself, modeled heavily on that of the United States (though without a federal element), was unexceptionable from the American point of view. But its legitimacy in Cuban eyes was seriously if not fatally compromised by its association with the amendment. Even Wood was compelled to admit privately that "there is, of course, little or no independence left Cuba under the Platt Amendment."[38]

Wood's last months as military governor were spent in preparations for the transition to Cuban rule as well as in an increasingly desperate effort to improve Cuba's economic prospects by lobbying for an easing of American protective tariffs on Cuban exports, notably sugar. Wood lost this fight (he was eventually ordered to desist by the administration), but a reciprocity agreement would be approved finally by the U.S. Congress in 1903. Unfortunately, the nation's political prospects were less promising. On May 20, 1902, Tomás Estrada Palma was installed as the first president of the Republic of Cuba after an election in which his chief opponent withdrew at the last minute when defeat seemed imminent. In spite of his revolutionary credentials, Estrada Palma had not seen his native country in twenty years (he was in fact an American citizen) and had little rapport with ordinary Cubans. His intransigent personal style and disdain for the military wing of the former revolutionary movement led eventually to armed resistance to his regime and, in 1906, a second intervention by the United States, lasting until 1909.[39]

That Wood should in any way be held responsible for these developments is far from clear,[40] regardless of his preference for rule by Cuba's traditional elite. Indeed, it could be argued that they vindicated his own reservations about Cuban political leadership and the wisdom of immediate independence. Estrada Palma was a maladroit leader in virtually every respect, and he made no effort to bring about a reconciliation of the competing elements of the Cuban liberation movement. On the contrary, by monopolizing political patronage in the hands of his own party (the inaptly named "Moderates") and blatantly manipulating the elections of 1905, he provoked the opposition Liberals into an armed rebellion that brought down the regime. This result was not preordained, but reflected the Cuban president's willful neglect of the role of force in statecraft. Contrary to Machiavelli's classic maxim that every "new prince" should rely on his own arms rather than the arms of others,[41] Estrada Palma was content to look to the United States as the ultimate guarantor not only of Cuban security

[38] Wood to Roosevelt, October 28, 1901 (cited in McCallum, 187).
[39] On this history see notably Hernandez, chs. 5–7.
[40] Consider the comments of McCallum, 195–96.
[41] Machiavelli, *Prince*, ch. 6. See further Lord, *The Modern Prince*, ch. 7.

(as provided under the Platt Amendment) but of his own political position, and had taken no steps to create a proper army loyal to the new Cuban order. In fact, the Roosevelt administration intervened only reluctantly, and when it had done so, quickly determined that it would not be possible to sustain the Estrada Palma regime without facing a serious guerrilla war, with all the political damage that would entail not only in terms of future relations with Cuba but in American domestic politics as well. The American authorities on the island worked thereafter to accommodate the demands of the Liberals and to ease Estrada Palma from the political scene.

Interestingly, Roosevelt considered reappointing Leonard Wood as his Cuban proconsul in 1906, but decided this would be inadvisable. He was apparently concerned that Wood's military connection and autocratic ways might provoke further unrest and lead to violence, which he was determined to avoid. Instead, he chose Charles Magoon, a Nebraska lawyer who had served as governor of the Canal Zone and minister to newly independent Panama. There, as one historian puts it, "he had shown great skill in the art of placating ungovernable people and winning goodwill. But he was essentially a paper-shuffling bureaucrat, a man quite unlike Wood. Instead, Magoon apparently resembled Wood's predecessor, General Brooke, who, as rumor had it, allowed his Cuban secretaries to dominate him."[42] Magoon believed his primary mission was "keeping Cuba quiet" so as not to complicate the prospects of Taft and the Republicans in the presidential election of 1908. In this he was highly successful, but at significant cost to the longer term political health of the Republic of Cuba. The notoriously tight-fisted Estrada Palma had amassed a large surplus in the government's coffers; these funds were liberally dispensed by Magoon in ways that were intended to stimulate economic activity with its attendant political benefits, but also fuelled corruption. Worse, he allowed himself to be captured and manipulated by the Liberals to advance the agenda of their party (and for that matter of factions within it). On the contentious question of a Cuban army, he acquiesced in a compromise solution – the establishment of two entirely independent security forces (the constabulary Rural Guard and a new army) affiliated with Cuba's two major political groupings – that effectively guaranteed the politicization of the country's military and sowed the seeds of future misfortunes.[43] It is impossible to know what Wood would have done in this situation, of course; yet it seems quite likely that he would not have committed these errors.

It will not be to our purpose to follow Wood's later career in detail. His next assignment was to the Philippines, in a relatively subordinate role as military governor of the island of Mindanao, where the Muslim Moro inhabitants continued to resist American authority. The Moros, who practiced piracy and

[42] Hernández, 146.
[43] Magoon acted here over the strenuous objections of some of his own military advisers. See the discussion in Hernández, 151–56, and for the longer term consequences (the sergeants' revolt of September 1933 and the emergence of the Batista dictatorship), 176–79.

slavery and had for centuries refused to recognize the suzerainty of Christian Spain, were an altogether different problem for the United States than the Cubans. While not entirely abandoning the nation-building approach he had followed in Cuba, Wood was inclined to regard the Moros as primarily a military challenge, similar in many ways to the American Indians he had encountered as a young man.[44] Indeed, Wood relished the challenge, professing to be tired of the "administrative work" he had devoted himself to in Cuba and the personal and political squabbling it entailed (an array of Wood's enemies had surfaced in an attempt to block his recent promotion to major general), but it also seems likely that he was eager to burnish his military credentials with the regular army. In any case, Wood applied continuous military pressure against the Moros, in a series of campaigns that were often brutal even by the standards of the day. They were also effective. Within two years, Mindanao was the most prosperous province in the Philippines; the Moros were paying taxes for the first time in their history, and slaving and piracy were much reduced.[45]

In 1905, Wood went to Manila to take charge of the Division of the Philippines, the army's overall command in the islands. In that capacity, he showed great foresight in anticipating the Japanese threat to Hawaii and the Philippines (he was one of the few American officers who predicted Japan's victory in the Russo-Japanese War) and was tireless in pushing for the fortification of the Manila area. America's lack of preparedness for a major war would thereafter become a central preoccupation of Wood's. Wood returned to the United States in 1909, becoming chief of staff of the army in the year following. As such, he was critically positioned to implement the fundamental organizational reforms of the service, set in motion by Root in the Roosevelt administration, that would lay the groundwork for the modern United States Army and for America's participation in World War I.

Wood's later years were marked by a growing political activism, which almost carried him to the Republican nomination for the presidency in 1920. On the outbreak of the war in August 1914, Wood's term as army chief of staff had expired and he was serving as commander of the Division of the East, headquartered at Governor's Island, New York. From this convenient perch, he soon emerged (with Teddy Roosevelt) as among the most influential public advocates of military preparedness – to the understandable irritation of President Woodrow Wilson, who found himself the implicit target of many of his subordinate's jeremiads. This accounts for the fact that Wood, then the most senior general in the army, was passed over in favor of General John

---

44 As he put it: "The situation here is different from the situation in Cuba. There are whole districts containing many people in which it is impossible to find enough intelligent men to form a civil government.... The interior of the island is filled with savage tribes; many live in the trees and others practice human sacrifice and cannibalism. The Moros are treacherous and unreliable, but have one redeeming quality, a certain amount of courage and manliness, out of which we may be able to make something." Wood to Verela Jado, February 3, 1904 (cited in McCallum, 218).

45 See the account of McCallum, ch. 8.

Pershing for the command of the American Expeditionary Force sent to France in 1917.[46] Wood's popularity was scarcely affected by this move, however, and following Roosevelt's death in January of 1919, he became the presumptive front-runner for the presidency on the Republican ticket in the election of the following year. Outmaneuvered in a confused multi-candidate race, he lost on the tenth ballot at the Republican convention to Warren G. Harding.[47]

Yet Wood's proconsular career was not yet finished. In a perhaps inevitable but nevertheless sad coda to that career, he spent his final years (1921–27) in Manila as United States governor-general. We shall encounter him again in due course as we explore the very checkered history of American governance of the Philippines.

[46] Ibid., ch. 9.
[47] Ibid., ch. 10.

4

The Philippines

Politics, when I am in it, makes me sick.
                    William Howard Taft[1]

There is no place for consistency in government.
                    Manuel Quezon[2]

To say that the United States acquired the Philippines in a fit of absent-mindedness would be a serious understatement. Conquest of Spain's Pacific possessions (encompassing Guam as well as the Philippine Islands) was not an American war aim in the Spanish-American War, but the unforeseen result of Commodore (later Admiral) George Dewey's crushing defeat, on May 1, 1898, of a squadron of the Spanish fleet in Manila Bay. When informed by Dewey that the city of Manila could be taken at any time, but that some 5,000 additional American troops would be needed to retain it and "control the islands," President McKinley approved the dispatch of this expedition, but without making clear exactly what the army's mission was to be or what eventual political outcome was desired. Spanish garrison troops in the Philippines at this time amounted to some 10,000 men, but the situation was complicated by the presence of approximately 30,000 Philippine revolutionaries, including a large force then besieging Manila itself. McKinley seems to have assumed initially that the revolutionaries would cooperate with the Americans, but this was quite uncertain, and he soon decided in any case to increase the size of the expedition to 15,000 men. The president's letter of instruction to Major General Wesley Merritt, the expedition's commander, described its mission only as "completing the reduction of the Spanish power" in the islands and maintaining order there while they remained in American hands; nothing was said

---

[1] Henry F. Pringle, *The Life and Times of William Howard Taft: A Biography*, 2 vols. (New York: Farrar and Rinehart, 1939; rpt. Hamden, CT: Archon Books, 1964), I, 290.

[2] Quoted in Peter W. Stanley, *A Nation in the Making: The Philippines and the United States, 1899–1921* (Cambridge, MA: Harvard University Press, 1974), 182–83.

about whether this occupation was to be temporary or permanent, whether it was to be limited to Manila or extend through some or all of the other islands, or what policy should be followed with respect to the Philippine revolutionary movement. General Merritt foresaw conflict with the rebels and took an expansive view of his instructions, while Major General Nelson Miles, commanding general of the army, thought the president had in mind only a temporary occupation of Manila.[3] This inauspicious beginning was to mark the most overtly imperial chapter in the story of America's overseas engagements. Also, however, it establishes what would prove to be a recurring pattern in our history: inattention to American imperial tasks at the center, and a correspondingly greater freedom of action on the part of America's proconsuls on the periphery.

America's most overtly imperial venture, not surprisingly, met with much criticism from Americans at the time, and continues to be in bad odor among historians today.[4] To understand the actions of America's Philippine proconsuls under the occupation (formally ended by the granting of commonwealth status to the Philippines in 1936), it is essential to grasp the strength of the anti-imperial movement in the United States at the beginning of the twentieth century and its role in the partisan domestic politics of the day.[5] The Spanish-American War was fought on a groundswell of popular enthusiasm, but this failed to translate into sustained political support for American overseas expansion. Much has been made by progressive historians of the economic motives driving American imperialism. It is true that great expectations were nurtured in some quarters about the benefits expected for the nation from greater American involvement in the China trade; on the other hand, encouraging agricultural production in Cuba or the Philippines through investment and the lowering of tariff barriers could also bring unwanted competition into domestic markets. Some conservative Republicans favored the acquisition of Hawaii and the Philippines for strategic reasons, but others had grave reservations as to both the strategic value of these territories and the ability of the American polity to assimilate their alien populations. Though a Republican, William Howard Taft was an avowed anti-imperialist when he was pressed by President McKinley

[3] For a succinct account see John Morgan Gates, *Schoolbooks and Krags: The United States Army in the Philippines, 1898–1902* (Westport, CT: Greenwood Press, 1973), ch. 1.
[4] James H. Blount, *The American Occupation of the Philippines, 1898–1912* (New York: G. P. Putnam's, 1913), is a contemporary jeremiad by a former Army officer and judge in the Philippines; in a similar vein are Albert G. Robinson, *The Philippines: The War and the People* (New York: McClure, Philips, 1901), and Moorfield Storey and Marcial P. Lichauco, *The Conquest of the Philippines by the United States, 1898–1925* (New York: G. P. Putnam's, 1926). Of recent critical accounts see notably Stuart C. Miller, *"Benevolent Assimilation": The American Conquest of the Philippines, 1899–1903* (New Haven, CT: Yale University Press, 1982); Stanley Karnow, *In Our Image: America's Empire in the Philippines* (New York: Random House, 1989); and H. W. Brands, *Bound to Empire: The United States and the Philippines* (New York: Oxford University Press, 1992).
[5] See generally Richard E. Welch, Jr., *Response to Imperialism: The United States and the Philippine-American War, 1899–1902* (Chapel Hill: University of North Carolina Press, 1979).

to lead an advisory mission to the Philippines in 1900. Even Theodore Roosevelt would eventually sour on the Philippines because he feared that growing Japanese power in the Far East was making the islands strategically untenable and a liability (as indeed proved to be the case). The Democratic Party and its various constituencies remained vocally hostile to the imperial project. On both ends of the political spectrum, however, there was a fundamental unease regarding both the legitimacy of imperialism given America's founding republican principles and the prospects of success in that enterprise, given the difficulties involved in governing peoples of very different racial and cultural makeup as well as lower levels of social and political development. As a result, while Democrats were consistently critical of the Philippine occupation and advocated granting the territory independence as soon as possible, Republicans were divided and ambivalent. The "retentionists" among them, rather than making forthright arguments for permanent annexation, temporized in the hope that the demonstrated benefits of the occupation over many years as well as the gradual acculturation of the Filipinos to American ways would eventually lead them to accept American overlordship.

During the nearly four decades of direct rule of the Philippines by the United States, the administration was controlled largely by the Republican Party. It is striking, however, that when the Democrats under Woodrow Wilson did come to power (1912–20), the cause of Philippine independence languished in Washington. This was in part because Wilson himself was something less than a staunch anti-imperialist, in part because of the massive distraction of the First World War. But something more fundamental was also involved. In the initial phase of the occupation, there was indeed bitter debate in Congress and in the American press over Philippine policy. Later, however, as one account has it, "the American public became accustomed to the idea of possessing the Philippines and neither it nor Congress paid particular attention to developments there – unless American interests were threatened."[6] During this entire period, oversight of Philippine affairs in Washington (like that of Cuba) was the responsibility of the secretary of war. Strikingly, however, over these forty years the secretary himself visited the territory only five times, and two of these (by Taft) were primarily political occasions; after 1910, there was no secretarial visit for the next twenty years. Within the War Department bureaucracy, moreover, there was usually no more than one relatively junior official (an Army colonel or civilian equivalent) thoroughly familiar with events in the territory. The result was that

American officials in Manila, without significant supervision or inspection, operated under instructions from their superiors in Washington whose basis of information had been sent from their subordinates in Manila. Complaints about abuses in government, when made, were referred to Manila for reply. Since in nearly all cases prestige was involved – and further complicated at times by publicity – the president and secretary of

---

[6] Garel A. Grunder and William E. Livezy, *The Philippines and the United States* (Norman: University of Oklahoma Press, 1951), 69.

war usually backed to the limit the governor-general or his subordinate.... The work of supervision thus remained perfunctory throughout the whole period of American control.[7]

Part of the explanation for this is certainly that the War Department's interest in the islands naturally waned after the decisive if not final defeat of the Philippine insurgency by the Army in 1902. This development also entailed a shift from military to civilian governance in Manila, completed by July 1901, when Taft took over as governor-general. Partly, too, however, it reflects the reality that Washington remained by and large satisfied with its proconsuls in Manila. And the fact of the matter is that these men, faced with a situation that had no real precedent in the American experience and for which they had no significant preparation, did their best to defend American interests in the Philippines both as conveyed in formal instructions (vague though they often were) and as interpreted according to their own lights and the situation on the ground – and managed to do so with what in hindsight can only be considered remarkable success. That the imperial project as a whole did not (and probably could not) succeed should not be allowed to detract from their accomplishments.

Much of the credit for this success must go to one man. William Howard Taft has not been kindly served in American historical memory, but he surely deserves a place in the front rank of American political figures of the early twentieth century. Scion of a political family from Ohio (his father had served in Grant's cabinet and been minister to Vienna and St. Petersburg) and an accomplished lawyer and judge, Taft was selected by McKinley in January 1900 to serve as president of the Second Philippine Commission, the quasi-legislative advisory body assigned the task of organizing a civilian government in the new territory. He was eventually appointed civil governor (later governor-general) of the Philippines in July 1901, remaining there until the end of 1903. Uniquely, Taft went on to serve not only as secretary of war but as chief justice of the Supreme Court and president of the United States (1908–12). What Taft may have lacked in raw political charisma, he made up for in personal charm, tact, and intelligence. His legal mind was never fully comfortable with the political world, but he took on the political tasks assigned him out of a strong sense of patriotic duty and he performed them with competence and complete integrity. Remarkably, although the summit of his ambition was appointment to the Supreme Court, he twice turned down the offer of a judgeship in that body in order to complete what he regarded as his mission in the Philippines.[8]

---

[7] Ibid., 100.

[8] The authoritative biography of Taft remains Pringle's *The Life and Times of William Howard Taft*; for the Philippine years see I, 156–265. For a sympathetic assessment of Taft: Lewis Gleeck, *The American Governors-General and High Commissioners in the Philippines: Proconsuls, Nation-Builders, and Politicians* (Quezon City: New Day Publishers, 1986), ch. 2. Insights into Taft's personality may be found in the letters of Major Archibald Butt, his military aide as president (*Intimate Letters of Archie Butt* [New York: Doubleday Doran, 1930]), though it has to be kept in mind, as the saying goes, that no man is a hero to his valet.

McKinley's offer to Taft came as a complete surprise to him as well as to the president's advisors, and remains something of a mystery. Perhaps the most plausible explanation is that McKinley settled on Taft for the same reason that he chose Elihu Root as secretary of war. When, some months previously, Root was informed by a friend that the president wanted him to take this position, he protested that he knew nothing about war, to which the response was: "President McKinley directs me to say that he is not looking for anyone who knows anything about war or for anyone who knows anything about the army; he has got to have a lawyer to direct the government of these Spanish islands, and you are the lawyer he wants."[9] If this suggestion is correct, it is telling that McKinley so clearly understood that what was required in the Philippines was not so much a competent administrator as someone capable of crafting an entirely new political and legal framework for the governance of the United States' new acquisition. Generals Leonard Wood and Lucius Clay were selected for their proconsular roles primarily because of their demonstrated administrative talents, but in both of these cases the American occupation was assumed on all sides to be a temporary one. The Philippine case was different. In effect, Taft was expected to become the founder of a new Philippine polity.[10]

But there is perhaps another factor that influenced the choice of Taft. McKinley was a shrewder political operator than he is sometimes given credit for, and there can be little doubt that he valued partisan and personal loyalty in his associates. He was fully sensitive to the political vulnerabilities created for the Republican Party and for himself personally by his decision to take the Philippines, particularly when it became clear that this was not going to happen without serious resistance from the Filipinos themselves. Taft was a loyal party man and, like Wood, was readily accepted into the inner circle of the administration's foreign policy establishment. In spite of his later political break with Roosevelt, the two men remained close during most of TR's presidency (Roosevelt succeeded McKinley after the latter's assassination in September 1901), and his rapport with his fellow lawyer Root was excellent from the beginning. The trust and esteem felt for Taft in Washington no doubt contributed importantly to the relatively free rein he enjoyed as proconsul in Manila.

In view of all this, it comes as no surprise that Taft's instructions as president of the Philippine Commission were a joint effort of the secretary of war and Taft himself.[11] It is worth quoting at length from this document, which set the tone for American policy in the Philippines throughout the entire occupation period:

In all the forms of government and administrative provisions which they are authorized to prescribe, the commission should bear in mind that the government which they are establishing is designed not for our satisfaction, or for the expression of our theoretical

9 Philip C. Jessup, *Elihu Root*, 2 vols. (New York: Dodd, Meade, 1938), I, 215–16, cited in Lewis L. Gould, *The Presidency of William McKinley* (Lawrence: The Regents Press of Kansas, 1980), 176–77.
10 Consider Machiavelli's discussion of the "new prince" in a "mixed principality," *Prince*, ch. 3.
11 Pringle, I, 182.

views, but for the happiness, peace, and prosperity of the people of the Philippine Islands, and the measures adopted should be made to conform to their customs, their habits, and even their prejudices, to the fullest extent consistent with the accomplishment of the indispensable requisites of just and effective government.

At the same time the commission should bear in mind, and the people of the islands should be made plainly to understand, that there are certain great principles of government which have been made the basis of our governmental system which we deem essential to the rule of law and the maintenance of individual freedom, and of which they have, unfortunately, been denied the experience possessed by us; that there are also certain practical rules of government which we have found to be essential to the preservation of these great principles of liberty and law, and that these principles and these rules of government must be established and maintained in their islands for the sake of their liberty and happiness, however much they may conflict with the customs or laws of procedure with which they are familiar.

At a more practical level, the instructions specified a list of individual liberties to be guaranteed the Philippine people, including the entire Bill of Rights apart from jury trial and the right to bear arms. Municipal governments were to be established and the Filipinos provided an opportunity "to manage their own local affairs to the fullest extent of which they are capable, and subject to the least degree of supervision and control which a careful study of their capacities and observation of the workings of native control show to be consistent with the maintenance of law, order, and loyalty;" and the principle was laid down that in distributing the powers of government overall, "the presumption is always to be in favor of the smaller subdivision," following the American model of the relationship between the federal government and the states. Filipinos were to be given the responsibility of selecting their own local officials, and Filipinos were to be appointed to other public offices "in preference to any others" as soon as they were found qualified to do so. The commission was entrusted with full legislative power at the national level (executive power being temporarily retained by the existing military authorities) in the areas of taxation and revenues, the expenditure of public funds, the establishment of a civil service, the organization of the courts, and (especially emphasized) the redistribution of lands controlled by the religious orders ("Friars") and public education. Regarding the latter, primary education was to be provided free to all; instruction was to be in the languages spoken by the people, though English was to be taught so as to become eventually a common medium of communication.[12]

Taft arrived in Manila in June 1900. As he later recalled, "the populace that we expected to welcome us was not there, and I cannot describe the coldness of

[12] W. Cameron Forbes, *The Philippine Islands*, 2 vols. (Boston: Houghton Mifflin, 1928), I, 130–34, and for a full text of this document, II, app. VII. The letter, under the president's signature, is dated April 7, 1900. On American educational policy see especially Glenn May, *Social Engineering in the Philippines: The Aims, Execution and Impact of American Colonial Policy, 1900–1913* (Westport, CT: Greenwood, 1980).

the army officers and army men who received us any better than by saying that it somewhat exceeded the coldness of the populace."[13] The military governor of the islands at this time was General Arthur MacArthur, father of the hero of World War II. Unfortunately, McKinley's instruction had failed to delineate clearly the lines of authority in the Philippines, reserving executive authority to the military commander even as it transferred responsibility for legislation to the commission. MacArthur resented the interference of the civilian commission in what he saw as his domain, and tension between Taft and the general persisted until Taft finally engineered his recall by Washington the following July. His assessment of MacArthur senior is worth quoting:

[He was a] very courtly, kindly man; lacking somewhat in a sense of humor; rather fond of profound generalizations on the psychological conditions of the people; politely incredulous, and politely lacking in any great consideration for the views of anyone, as to the real situation, who is a civilian and who has been here only a comparatively short time, and firmly convinced of the necessity for maintaining military etiquette in civil matters and civil government.[14]

The friction between Taft and MacArthur was, however, more than merely personal; the two held divergent views about American policy and strategy. These views were not simply reflections of institutional bias. MacArthur took seriously the extent and intensity of support for the revolutionaries among Filipinos generally; at the same time, he was cautious in the application of military force because he believed that the overriding American objective should be to prepare the natives for early independence. Taft, on the other hand, believed that the overwhelming majority of the people were ready for peace and would accept an American-imposed government were it not for their fear of the *insurrectos*. Taft accepted the need for a cautious approach, but he was also prepared to adopt tougher measures against the revolutionaries because they stood in the way of consolidating a long-term American presence in the islands. When the revolutionary leader Emilio Aguinaldo was captured in a brilliant commando operation in March 1901, MacArthur received him with punctilio in his quarters at Malacanan Palace and pardoned him, in return for taking an oath of allegiance to the United States. Taft, who was not in Manila at the time, was appalled, favoring instead sending Aguinaldo into forced exile on Guam.[15]

A further element of friction between Taft and the army had to do with the frequently arrogant and insensitive behavior of American military personnel toward the native population. Although the army in the Philippines had readily embraced a civil affairs mission, as it had done in Cuba, too many American soldiers displayed racist attitudes, and officers and their wives tended to segregate themselves from Filipino society. Taft would go to great lengths to remedy

13 Pringle, I, 169.
14 Ibid., I, 185.
15 Stanley, 77–79.

this state of affairs as a matter of policy, but he also developed genuinely warm feelings toward the Filipinos. At the same time, Taft did not – to say the least – romanticize them. Here is how he described them in a letter to Root and his wife not long after his arrival:

The population of the islands is made up of a vast mass of ignorant, superstitious people, well-intentioned, light-hearted, temperate, somewhat cruel, domestic and fond of their families, and deeply wedded to the Catholic Church. They are easily influenced by speeches from a small class of educated meztizos, who have acquired a good deal of superficial knowledge of the general principles of free government, who are able to mouth sentences supposed to embody constitutional law, and who like to give the appearance of profound analytical knowledge of the science of government. They are generally lacking in moral character; are with some notable exceptions prone to yield to any pecuniary consideration, and are difficult persons out of whom to make an honest government. We shall have to do the best we can with them. They are born politicians; are as ambitious as Satan, and as jealous as possible of each other's preferment.[16]

The latter half of 1900 saw a marked deterioration in the security situation in the Philippines, particularly in southern and central Luzon, the original center of the insurrection. The revolutionaries, though decisively defeated by MacArthur in conventional battle, became increasingly proficient at guerrilla warfare and political subversion, and their morale was sustained by the hope that the November presidential elections in the United States might retire McKinley and bring to power an avowedly anti-imperialist and pro-independence Democrat, William Jennings Bryan. This further worsened relations between Taft and MacArthur. The Republican strategy for the elections called for keeping the lid on the Philippine situation, while MacArthur (abetted by the pro-Bryan press) rang the alarm bell at rebel gains. With McKinley's reelection, however, the revolutionaries suffered an important psychological reverse, while MacArthur launched a major military offensive in December that marked the beginning of the end of Filipino resistance throughout most of the archipelago. The interplay of the military situation in the theater and the domestic political scene in the United States during this period is strikingly reminiscent of the Vietnam War; the outcome, from the American point of view at least, was a happier one.[17]

[16] Pringle, I, 173–74.

[17] As in the Vietnam case, alleged American atrocities against the revolutionary forces were much exaggerated for political reasons by domestic opponents of the war, though some excesses certainly occurred (most notoriously on Samar at the hands of General Jacob Smith, later dismissed from the Army). At the same time, the approved rules of engagement (based largely on the Civil War–era General Order No. 100) were considerably more permissive than those guiding American troops in Vietnam. See especially Gates, ch. 6, as well as the outstanding recent study by Brian McAllister Linn, *The Philippine War, 1899–1902* (Lawrence: University Press of Kansas, 2000). It is interesting to what extent the debate within the Army at this time between proponents of a "hearts and minds" approach to the insurgency and advocates of the primacy of "kinetic" measures (to use current terminology) echoes debates within the contemporary Army stimulated by the American experience in Iraq and Afghanistan since 2002. See Andrew J. Birtle,

The extent to which the success of the counterinsurgency effort in the Philippines was a function not of American arms but of American stabilization and reconstruction operations (to use the terminology current today) is still not sufficiently appreciated. Even before the arrival of Taft and the commission, the Army itself had initiated ambitious civic action programs in sanitation and public health, legal reform, public works, local government, and, perhaps most significantly, education. In March 1900, a Department of Public Instruction was established; within five months, some 100,000 pupils were enrolled in 1,000 schools, with textbooks and other materials supplied by the U.S. Army.[18] Taft's commission ratified and in some ways radicalized this emphasis on the importance of education for the future of the Philippines. Contrary to the letter of McKinley's instructions (though in conformity with a recommendation by the senior Army education official), Taft established English not only as a subject but as the medium of instruction. Moreover, the commission introduced compulsory vocational training – a measure aimed at breaking down the traditional Spanish-inspired contempt for manual labor.[19] All of this was intended to bring about a secularization of Philippine education that, it was thought, would have a transforming effect on Philippine culture over the longer term.

One religious issue was very much on the immediate agenda of the American occupiers, however. It is difficult to overstate the importance of the Catholic clergy in the Philippines both as a support for central Spanish control in the archipelago's remote provinces and as a component of the agrarian economy. Since the seventeenth century, four orders of Friars had established themselves throughout the Philippines as an authority essentially independent of both the Church and the Spanish governors in Manila, and over time had come to control many thousands of acres of prime farmland and to dominate local government. The rule of the Friars had given rise to many abuses and wide resentment among the native population, and one of the primary objectives of the original insurrection against Spain had been to break their power and, in particular, their control of the land. The army leadership was quick to recognize the problem, but because of the religious sensitivities involved, a solution had proven elusive. It is a sign of the magnitude of this issue that Taft took it on as his personal area of responsibility as president of the Philippine Commission. In 1902, after laying the legislative groundwork in Washington, Taft returned to Manila by way of Rome, where he discussed the issue in a personal audience with the pope. Negotiations with the Vatican proved tortuous, but an eventual settlement was reached to purchase the lands as well as to expel the Friars (a measure necessary in any case for their own protection), who it was

---

US Army Counterinsurgency and Contingency Operations Doctrine, 1860–1941 (Washington, DC: US Army Center of Military History, 1998), ch. 4.

[18] Gates, ch. 4.

[19] Stanley, 84–86. It needs to be kept in mind that many native languages were spoken in the islands, while only some 5% of the population could understand Spanish.

agreed would be replaced by American Catholic priests who were committed to separation of church and state American-style.[20]

The role of the American colonial regime in the economic affairs of the Philippines is a complicated question. As in the case of Cuba, the American authorities recognized that the long-term viability of the newly conquered Spanish territories depended crucially on a reconstruction of their economies and, even more crucially, on a reformation of the socio-economic structures resting on them. Even more than in the case of Cuba, Philippine society was starkly polarized between a large and culturally backward peasant class and a tiny but powerful elite of wealthy proprietors and educated professional men; commerce was underdeveloped, and mostly in the hands of foreigners. Taft pushed hard for American investment in the islands particularly for the building of infrastructure (roads, harbors, and railways) that would promote commercial activity. However, the administration felt constrained in this area by the need to involve Congress, and early attempts to do so would prove frustrating.[21] There was, though, a more fundamental obstacle to economic reform in the Philippines. The economic interests of the Filipino elite were anchored in the social status quo; at the same time, the Americans were highly dependent on this elite to consolidate American colonial governance of the islands. This dilemma was to remain the single greatest obstacle to the American imperial project in the Philippines, one its proconsuls never fully grappled with and were never able to overcome. Taft's own conservative inclinations led him to rely on the Filipino elite as a key partner in the governance of the archipelago. To his credit, however, Taft was never blind to their limitations, and he stressed privately to President Roosevelt the importance of developing more "popular" political institutions that would weaken the oligarchy's political ascendency, requiring a commitment to education of the "densely ignorant masses" and an increase in their political participation.[22]

This brings us to the role of Taft and the commission in reconstituting political order in the Philippines. An important by-product of the administration's early difficulties with Congress over Philippine policy was to convince the administration to allow more leeway to its proconsul. In July 1902, Congress passed the first Philippine organic act, a law extending and giving permanence to the arrangements established by the commission for the governance of the islands. Taft was the principal drafter of this legislation. Its most significant provisions called for a bicameral territorial legislature, with the upper house being constituted by the Philippine commission itself while a lower house of Filipinos was to be elected by the people as soon as the security situation permitted. The governor together with the commissioners would continue to be appointed by the president of the United States, subject to approval by the

[20] See the extended account in Grunder and Livezy, ch. 7, and for the historical background, Stanley, ch. 1.
[21] Ibid., 86–89.
[22] Grunder and Livezy, 99.

Senate. Two resident commissioners to the United States were to be selected by the Philippine legislature. Various economic regulations were also included, particularly pertaining to the disposition of the Friar lands and other public property, but also including a low limit on the amount of land that could be acquired by individuals and corporations; the latter reflected widespread concern in Congress over possible predatory activity by American business interests. Finally, the bill formalized the reporting relationship of the governor to the Bureau of Insular Affairs of the War Department.[23] Taft himself had championed the idea of a native Filipino assembly as soon as possible; he was disappointed that Senator Henry Cabot Lodge, the leading Republican imperialist, had managed to delay this in the course of negotiations over the Cooper Bill. The first Filipino assembly was elected in July 1907 and convened in October of that year, well after Taft's departure. Lodge also saw to it that the bill was silent on the question of Philippine independence.

A political framework encouraging participation by the Filipinos was fine in theory; the test was to make it work in terms of the political realities of the time. Toward the end of 1900, an influential group of upper-class Filipinos came to the conclusion that the United States was going to win the struggle with the *insurrectos*, and therefore that some way had to be found to cooperate with the American authorities that would afford some leverage over American policy while at the same time protect its own economic and social standing. This group, of which the outstanding figure was Trinidad Pardo de Taveras, went on to form a political party, the Federalistas, which by May 1901 had spread throughout the islands and boasted a membership of some 150,000. Pardo was not only a wealthy landowner but a distinguished physician and historian who had spent many years in Europe, developing in the process a somewhat jaundiced view of contemporary Philippine culture and society. He was a firm believer in the need for modernization and argued that the only way this could be realistically achieved was under American tutelage. Initially, the Federalistas favored not only annexation by the United States but eventual statehood, though it soon became clear to them that there was no support for this option among Americans of any political complexion. Taft admired Pardo, though recognizing that Pardo's views were too extreme even for many of his own associates.[24] Particularly given the military exigencies the Americans faced at the time, however, Taft felt he had no choice but to accept

---

[23] In 1903, Roosevelt and Taft discussed the possibility of creating an independent civilian agency (in effect, a colonial office) to administer all of the nation's overseas possessions, but this was thought inadvisable given the continuing need for a substantial military presence in the Philippines. Ibid., 83.

[24] Consider, for example, this passage in a letter from Pardo to General MacArthur: "After peace is established, all our efforts will be directed to Americanising ourselves; to cause a knowledge of the English language to be extended and generalized in the Philippines, in order that through its agency the American spirit may take possession of us and that we may so adopt its principles, its political customs and its peculiar civilization that our redemption may be complete and radical." Stanley, 72.

the Federalistas' embrace, and the party thereafter became a virtual partner in the territorial government. In September 1901, on Taft's urging, Pardo and two associates were added to the Philippine Commission; other Federalistas were appointed to head the new Philippine Supreme Court and the Civil Service. At the same time, Taft refused to recognize officially any native party that called for independence, in the belief that this would only encourage a movement to subvert the basis of American rule. In hindsight, Taft is open to criticism for these moves, sensible as they may have seemed to him at the time.[25]

Taft's immediate successor as governor-general, Luke Wright (1903–06),[26] soon realized that this policy was untenable, given the inability of the Federalistas to appeal to the mainstream Filipino opinion and the rapid rise of competing nationalist parties. Wright moved unilaterally to end the Federalista monopoly of political patronage, appointing instead men independent of party or even nationalists to key positions. Pressed by Pardo and his associates, however, Taft, now secretary of war, engineered a graceful departure for Wright (he was appointed ambassador to Japan) and attempted to turn the clock back, but to no avail. The outcome of the first elections to the Philippine Assembly in 1907 was the handwriting on the wall. The former Federalistas, now styled Progressistas, had sixteen seats, while a Nacionalista coalition took fifty-eight; six went to independents. Two politicians now emerged as charismatic and effective leaders of the nationalists: Sergio Osmena and Manuel Quezon. These men would become at once the principal partners and chief antagonists of the American proconsuls in Manila, in a shifting and complex relationship – a delicate (and sometimes not so delicate) dance – that persisted to the end of the occupation and beyond.[27]

With the appointment of W. Cameron Forbes as governor-general in 1909 (he had already served in an acting role for a year and a half), Washington was finally persuaded that it had to do business with the Philippine nationalists. The only holdover from the Taft era, Forbes nevertheless recognized that, given the changing circumstances, the nationalists had to be accommodated, and he cultivated close personal ties with Osmena and Quezon. Osmena, elected as speaker of the Philippine Assembly in 1907, was elevated to the second ranking officer of the government by Taft himself on Forbes' recommendation, while in 1908 a nationalist chosen by Osmena was added to the Philippine Commission.

---

[25] That Taft in fact erred by over-relying on the Federalistas is admitted by Forbes, I, 146.

[26] Luke Wright, a former Army general and Civil War hero, "may have been the finest man ever to hold the post of governor-general. Taft rose to become president, General Wood was beyond question a man of greatness, Stimson was twice secretary of war and once secretary of state, and there were several others of great spirit and talent, but Wright surpassed them all in moral stature. A man of total integrity unflawed by overweening ambition and without the least trace of arrogance, loyal to his friends and superiors even when they forsook him, a selfless and public-spirited citizen, he was the epitome of the genuine Southern gentleman. Obliged by duty to assume a proconsular role in the Philippines, Wright discharged it without fear of favor and laid it down without regret." Gleeck, 33.

[27] For an overview see Karnow, ch. 9, and for a good sketch of Osmena and Quezon, 231–37.

W. Cameron Forbes, a grandson of Ralph Waldo Emerson and a graduate of Harvard, was a successful businessman in Boston who (mysteriously) abandoned a lucrative career in his family's banking firm to enter public service. Of all American governors-general in the Philippines, he is the only one whose highest ambition was to be a proconsul in the overseas service of the United States. He consciously modeled himself on British colonial officials, particularly Lord Cromer, whom he sought out in London to discuss the finer points of agricultural microfinance in Egypt after a visit to Washington in 1908.[28] Forbes continued to follow Philippine affairs in later years, and wanted to return as governor-general when the Republicans regained the presidency in 1920 (he and Leonard Wood served the new administration on a special advisory commission at this time), but was prevented by chronic ill health. In 1928, he published a massive two-volume work on the islands, defending the general tenor of Republican policies there.[29] Given his own business background and conviction of the fundamental importance of economic improvement for the future of the American imperial project in the Philippines, Forbes distinguished himself by his unrelenting efforts to encourage foreign investment in the territory and to build infrastructure, but lack of full cooperation from the Philippine Assembly limited what he was able to accomplish in this and related areas. Perhaps short-sightedly but understandably, Filipinos were reluctant to welcome investments from American sources, which they feared would only become an additional pressure point for eventual annexation. The private interests of the Filipino elite also continued to complicate and frustrate the most well-intentioned American nation-building schemes.[30]

In spite of Forbes' personal relationship with the Filipino leaders, the internal dynamics of Philippine politics (and movement in American politics as well) led to increasing friction among them. In the period 1909–10, the Progressistas moved to the left to embarrass the Nacionalistas and gain electoral advantage; this coincided with the recapture of the House of Representatives in Washington by the Democrats in the fall of 1910. It became clear to Osmena at this point that his relationship with Forbes was becoming a political liability, and he too moved to the left, calling for a firm commitment to independence and for placing more Filipinos in positions of authority. Quezon proceeded to draft a bill to be proposed in Congress (later known as the "first Jones Bill") calling for an elected upper house, independence within eight years, and an end to an American military presence in twenty years. The Democrats, however, were reluctant to engage on this issue prior to the upcoming presidential elections. The 1912 Democratic platform denounced imperialism and pledged to work for an "immediate declaration of the Nation's purpose to recognize the independence of the Philippine Islands as soon as a stable government can be

---

[28] Gleeck, 108, and for Forbes generally, ch. 6.
[29] W. Cameron Forbes, *The Philippine Islands*, 2 vols. (Boston: Houghton Mifflin, 1928). See especially I, chs. 3–4.
[30] For thematic discussion of this question see Stanley, chs. 4 and 9.

established" – the traditional position of the party. However, Woodrow Wilson, the Democratic presidential candidate, was not a hard-core anti-imperialist (in fact, he had favored annexation of the Philippines in 1899), and in March 1912 he told Quezon, then one of the resident Philippine commissioners in the United States, that the Filipinos lacked sufficient cultural homogeneity to live amicably together and establish a responsible government.[31]

None of this is to suggest that Osmena and Quezon were intransigent ideologues; far from it. They were always prepared to negotiate the best terms for eventual independence achievable at a given time. Indeed, Quezon's flexibility on this issue was so extraordinary that there is reason to believe he was actually ambivalent about it.[32] This became especially clear during the era of Democratic ascendency in Washington, when the new American proconsul in Manila opened the door to the Nacionalistas to an extent they were to find distinctly uncomfortable.

Francis Burton Harrison served as governor-general of the Philippines for the duration of the Wilson administration (1913–20). Harrison was an American blue-blood, a descendant of the Fairfaxes of Virginia and hence of two presidents, a graduate of Yale, and a lawyer. A six-term congressman from New York, he was about to take over the chairmanship of the Ways and Means Committee, one of the most powerful positions in the House and a plausible stepping-stone to the presidency, when he decided instead to throw in his hat to replace Forbes in the Philippines. This strange career move has never been explained, though it is perhaps possible that he saw it as a stage in a new *cursus honorum* on the way to the presidency created by the example of Taft.[33] Harrison had served as a volunteer in the Army during the Spanish-American War and may have developed then a certain taste for imperial adventure.[34] However this may be, even before his departure for Manila he was clearly a man on a mission, and the mission was to succor the cause of Philippine independence

---

[31] Ibid., 179–80.
[32] To Osmena, known for a concern for logical consistency, Quezon once complained: "The trouble with you is that you take this game of politics too seriously. You look far behind you and too far ahead of you. Our people do not understand that. They do not want it. All they want is to have the present problem solved, and solved with the least pain. That is all." Ibid., 182–84.
[33] Gleeck (138) suggests that Harrison's defense of his tenure in Manila, *The Cornerstone of Philippine Independence: A Narrative of Seven Years* (New York: The Century Company, 1922), may have been intended as a campaign book. On Harrison generally see Gleeck, ch. 7, Stanley, ch. 8, Brands, ch. 6, and Michael P. Onorato, "Governor General Francis Burton Harrison and His Administration," *Philippine Studies* (Winter 1970): 178–86.
[34] It is striking that when hostilities broke out between the United States and Mexico in the spring of 1914, Harrison wrote to the secretary of war that he "had for several years cherished the hope that I might be able to take part in the next war which I thought would come with Mexico in the near future," but after receiving his current appointment he concluded he could better serve the administration in the Philippines. All this is more than a little reminiscent of Leonard Wood or Teddy Roosevelt. Gleeck, 149.

in the teeth of all opposition – including opposition from his superiors in the administration and even from the Filipinos themselves.

The great irony of Harrison's tenure as governor-general is that this most anti-imperial of America's Philippine proconsuls actually proved to be the most proconsular of them all in his temperament and actions. Taft and Wood may have had a higher profile and reputation in this regard, but they were restrained by loyalty and a sense of public responsibility to their presidents and the general line hewed to by the Republican Party. Harrison, by contrast, acted as if he had a virtually free hand to pursue an independence agenda that was indeed theoretically subscribed to by the Democrats but in practice cannot be said to have been unambiguously endorsed by the Wilson administration. The governor-general can be excused to some extent by the inattention toward Philippine affairs displayed by the president and his secretary of war, yet he did not hesitate to oppose or indeed simply ignore the views of his immediate superior in the War Department's Bureau of Insular Affairs, the well-informed Frank McIntyre. Another factor was also at work. When the (second) Jones Act finally passed the Congress in 1916, it altered the political framework of the territorial government in a way that actually strengthened the authority of the governor-general, and Harrison took full advantage of this situation to enable him to have his way over resistance in both Washington and Manila.

Although Harrison later claimed the contrary, there is in fact no evidence that he received any specific guidance from Wilson as to the course of action he should follow once in office. It is true that in his inaugural address to Congress in December 1913, Wilson had announced the appointment of a Filipino majority on the commission and described this as part of a process that would lead to self-government. But the pace of that process remained undefined. For Harrison, it was not even enough to let himself be guided by the deep knowledge of the Filipino political scene so clearly possessed by its established leaders. In fact, though he was quick to denounce the racism and condescension toward the natives of his Republican predecessors as well as the American expatriate community in Manila, Harrison seems to have had disdain for the Filipinos and had little to do with them, with the exception of Quezon. Here is Osmena's remarkable account of him:

The chief trouble with Harrison was that he did not follow a fixed policy. He did not have a policy as to the conduct of the government, at any rate did not follow one. One day he gave us complete power and control. The next we could do nothing. Sometimes he refused to assume responsibility; at other times he insisted upon his own views.

Take the matter of appointments. Soon after he arrived, Harrison called me to Mala-canang. He opened a roster of all of the officials of the government and handed it to me. "You people have been clamoring for Filipinization. You want to Filipinize the service, don't you?" "'Yes.'" "Well, here is the official roster. Go right through it. Check those officials whom you wish to have replaced by Filipinos, name the men whom you wish appointed, and it will be done. Take every bureau chief if you wish."

'"But Governor, we want not only a Filipino government, we want good government. We wish to replace Americans with Filipinos only when they can do their work. To make all of these changes immediately would jeopardize the service."'[35]

Nevertheless, Harrison proceeded apace to move Americans out of key jobs and Filipinos into them. In 1918, a major reorganization of the government further consolidated Filipino control by breaking down the separation of the executive and legislative branches, in effect giving the Filipino legislature authority over executive appointments and policy. A new Council of State was created to provide a framework for this new arrangement, with Osmena, still the Assembly speaker, becoming vice president under the governor-general – the equivalent of a prime minister. Elections in 1918 confirmed the Nacionalista ascendency (75 of 90 Assembly seats, 21 of 24 in the Senate). In effect, the territorial government had become a one-party democracy, or perhaps more accurately, an elective oligarchy.

This new state of affairs was not uniformly welcomed by Filipinos themselves. One "intelligent and highly respected" Filipino observer provided this assessment at the time:

When the American flag is lowered, whether it be in one year or in ten years or in a hundred years, I feel that the United States will be remembered in our islands by three principal contributions to our national life: First, by a splendid system of public instruction; secondly, by an excellent judicial system; and thirdly, by an all-pervading system of petty Tammany politics, to the fostering of which the present administration [Harrison's] has very largely contributed. And I feel that the last of these contributions will far outshadow in effect the results of the other two to the everlasting misfortune of my race.[36]

Writing in 1955, a distinguished Filipino judge and industrialist echoed this view:

It may sound ironical, but it is the sad and plain truth that the Philippines has never enjoyed the true essence of democracy except during the transitional period between the military occupation of 1902 and the autonomous regime of 1916. It was only during that glorious period that the people knew or understood, by actual practice and example, the real meaning of the merit system in the public service, equal opportunity for all, freedom of thought and freedom of religion.... But with the advent of the autonomous era of 1916 a new concept or philosophy of government was introduced. Merit or civil service systems must give way to the "tayo-tayo" or spoils system. Public office or positions were, as they still are, among the coveted spoils which rightly belonged to the victors. So were public funds. The more laxity in auditing funds, the better for the new regime.[37]

[35] Interview with Joseph Haydn (1928), cited in ibid., 135 n. 1.
[36] Thomas Lindsey Blayney, "Our Administration of the Philippine Islands," *American Review of Reviews* (January 1916), cited by Lewis Gleeck, *American Institutions in the Philippines, 1898–1941* (Manila: Historical Conservation Society, 1976), 284. Blayney, be it noted, was a supporter and admirer of Woodrow Wilson.
[37] Gleeck, *American Institutions*, 284–85.

A major scandal involving the relationship between the new Filipino political class and the Philippine National Bank dominated much of the last several years of the Harrison era and provided grist for the mill of Republican criticism of administration policy and the desirability of immediate independence for the islands. Harrison resisted efforts by Secretary of War Newton Baker to intervene in this situation.[38] In his later defense of his tenure as governor-general he would state that "no graft, no jobbing, no log-rolling, no cheap politics, no selfish localism, no equivocal opportunism and no hypocrisy is to be charged against the Philippine legislature."[39] This preposterous claim virtually refutes itself, underscoring what can only be described as Harrison's willful ignorance of Filipino political realities.

When the Republicans retook Congress and the presidency in 1920, the time was ripe for a major reassessment of American policy in the Philippines. A commission was duly created under the leadership of Leonard Wood and Cameron Forbes to report on the political situation there and make recommendations for a way ahead. It was tolerably clear at the outset that while independence was off the immediate policy agenda, there was little disposition in the Harding White House to reverse the Jones Bill or Harrison's Filipinization of the territorial government. Not surprisingly, after visiting Manila and the Far East in 1921, Wood and Forbes concluded that the islands were not yet ready for independence, but their report provided few guideposts for judging when they might be. The commission did recommend, however, that the governor-general should "have authority commensurate with the responsibilities of his position," if necessary by overturning all Filipino legislation under the Jones Act that had diminished his role, particularly in appointments of officials.

The commission's recommendations were not based solely on the internal situation in the Philippines. In a diary entry of September 1921 recording a meeting in Peking with Jacob Gould Schurman, the American ambassador there (and former head of McKinley's first Philippine Commission), Wood states that all present agreed that withdrawal from the Philippines "would be very disastrous to American prestige, trade, and the Eastern situation." Japanese ambitions in China and the Pacific were a growing concern, and Wood himself believed that peace in the region depended on the maintenance of an adequate forward-deployed American naval presence.[40]

Wood was a logical choice to succeed Harrison as governor-general of the Philippines, but President Harding probably had another motive as well – to remove from the public eye a potential rival for the Republican presidential nomination in 1924. Wood himself, by now well launched on the national political scene, felt he had to accept the position in spite of more attractive career options at home (he had been offered the presidency of the University

[38] For an extended account see Stanley, ch. 9.
[39] Harrison, 218 (cited in Gleeck, *American Governors-General*, 160).
[40] Hermann Hagedorn, *Leonard Wood: A Biography*, 2 vols. (New York: Harper and Brothers, 1931), II, 394–95 (cited in Grunder and Livezy, 164).

of Pennsylvania). Once in Manila, with no instructions other than what had been on offer from his own commission and in the face of manifest presidential indifference, Wood did his best to undo the damage of the Harrison years, focusing in particular on ending the involvement of the government in business that had grown up during this period while at the same time encouraging private investment in the country's agricultural economy. As usual, the Filipino elite threw up many obstacles here. Generally, though, Wood was given a pass initially by the native leadership, who thought they could wait out what would probably be a short tenure in office. Emboldened by Democratic gains in the 1922 congressional elections, however, they soon declared war on Wood, and relations with them remained antagonistic and embittered until his death in 1927. In July 1923, Quezon engineered a mass resignation of departmental secretaries to discredit Wood in Washington, but the governor-general was firmly supported throughout this difficult period by the secretary of war and the president (who was later put in the position of vetoing a bill passed by the Philippine legislature calling for immediate independence).[41]

It is worth emphasizing the yawning gulf that remains even today between Wood as a popular American hero of his era and Wood in later historical memory. The vilification of Wood that occurred during his own lifetime probably reached its peak during the period of his governor-generalship in Manila, at a time when the general had amassed formidable enemies among partisan Democrats, the press, and even the Army and was seen by the leading Filipino politicians as the primary hindrance to the cause of independence and their own ascendency in the islands. The extent and sophistication of the anti-Wood propaganda mounted by Quezon and associates for the benefit of the domestic American audience should not be underestimated. It ought to be acknowledged that Wood's personality suffered a certain deterioration in the later part of his life, owing no doubt in some measure to the after-effects of a head injury suffered years earlier, but he never became the unfeeling tyrant and bigot so often described by his enemies. Let the last word on Wood be that of the biographer of his distinguished proconsular successor:

Upon many members of his generation, Wood cast a kind of spell impossible not to recognize but at this remove, almost equally impossible to completely comprehend. It may be that what seems now a certain gracelessness of heart and mind was relieved in life by a demonstration of the stoic virtues that were obviously his. It may be that by possessing a degree of sophistication provided by his medical training and as well, something of the moral concern of his native New England, he seemed to demonstrate what his time believed, that the whole duty of man was fulfilled only if the personal virtues were proved in the life of action.[42]

[41] For the trumped-up nature of the charges leveled by Quezon against Wood in the 1923 crisis see Gleeck, *American Governors-General*, 184–87.
[42] Elting E. Morison, *Turmoil and Tradition: The Life and Times of Henry L. Stimson* (Boston: Houghton Mifflin, 1960), 151–52. See particularly the appreciation of Gleeck, *American Governors-General*, ch. 8, citing this passage among other things; also Jack McCallum, *Leonard*

It will not be necessary to follow in detail the careers and roles of the governor-generals and (after 1935) high commissioners of the Philippines up to the outbreak of World War II. Wood was the last to display real independence and initiative, with the exception of the remarkable Paul McNutt at the end of the 1930s. After him, the rules of the game were essentially fixed. In 1922, Quezon had ousted Osmena from the speakership of the lower house, marginalizing him in Philippine politics and cementing his own personal ascendancy. Beginning under the Republicans with Wood's immediate successor, Henry Stimson (1928–29), it was recognized in Washington that there was little to be gained and much potential political damage to be incurred from constant wrangling between the Americans in Manila and the Filipino political establishment, and Quezon in particular. Especially once the Democrats again assumed control under the leadership of Franklin Roosevelt (FDR), it was clear that independence was only a matter of time and that only the details remained for negotiation, thus defusing much of the Filipino nationalist impulse.

At the same time, an evolution occurred in the role of the American proconsuls in Manila. Taft had gone from governor-general to become secretary of war, then president; Wood had been an unsuccessful presidential candidate prior to becoming governor-general. Both of these men were established political figures before their assignment in the Philippines, and neither had sought it as a stepping-stone to the presidency; the same can be said for Stimson (who had already been secretary of war under Taft and did not solicit the position; he of course went on to become secretary of state under both Hoover and FDR). Harrison may well have had the presidency in his sights, as we have seen, though this cannot be proven. After Stimson, however, the Philippine proconsulship came increasingly to take on the flavor of a stage in the presidential *cursus honorum*. Indeed, it seems to have been widely felt that the governor-generalship was now the second most important federal executive office after the presidency itself. FDR's first governor-general, Theodore Roosevelt, Jr. (1932–33), the lightweight son of the great Rough Rider, made no secret of his presidential ambitions, and the same was true of his successor, Frank Murphy (1933–35), former mayor of Detroit and an ardent New Dealer. In both cases, the wily Quezon was able to leverage this knowledge to manipulate, co-opt, and control the Americans, but especially Roosevelt – much to the disgust of the American expatriate community in the islands and even his own staff.[43]

In 1935, in preparation for its conversion to commonwealth status, elections were held in the Philippines for a new president. Quezon defeated the old rebel leader, Emilio Aguinaldo, who briefly contemplated a coup d'état before acquiescing in the people's verdict. At this point, a new American player also appeared on the scene. In what was becoming something of a pattern, General

Wood: Rough Rider, Surgeon, Architect of American Imperialism (New York: New York University Press, 2006), ch. 11.

43 Gleeck, *American Governors-General*, chs. 11 and 12.

Douglas MacArthur had been appointed by FDR commander of the American forces in the islands and "field marshal" in a new Philippine army, largely because the president saw in him a political rival and wanted him out of the country. MacArthur himself had apparently lobbied for the senior civilian position in Manila, now styled high commissioner, but this was not to happen. Under these circumstances, MacArthur found it hard to resist playing political games, ingratiating himself with Quezon at the expense of Frank Murphy. In an episode so absurd it would be impossible to invent, Quezon insisted that at his inauguration in Manila the new president should be honored with a twenty-one gun salute, while the high commissioner should receive only nineteen. Stunningly, MacArthur supported the request in Washington. This dispute was only finally resolved at the level of President Roosevelt himself, who accepted the State Department's recommendation that both receive nineteen guns but that the high commissioner be accorded precedence.[44]

But the most interesting of the high commissioners was Paul V. McNutt (1937–38), a popular former governor from Indiana and a charismatic speaker and able politician. Though entirely forgotten today, McNutt was the leading Democrat in any competition to succeed FDR, and might well have been his vice presidential candidate in 1940 or 1944. FDR's New Deal entourage found the governor too conservative as well as a potential rival, however, and Roosevelt apparently agreed; as was also the case with Frank Murphy, McNutt's Manila assignment was an honorable exile. Unlike Murphy, however, McNutt did not allow himself to be intimidated by this situation; on the contrary, he was forthright not only about his own ambitions but also about asserting American rights and interests under the new commonwealth dispensation. McNutt risked the wrath of Quezon and his supporters by publicly questioning what he bluntly characterized as the president's assumption of dictatorial powers: As he put it in July 1937, "democracy in the Philippines is only a matter of form and not of substance." Yet McNutt, by the force of his personality, also was able to charm Quezon and establish an excellent relationship with him – to the point that Quezon and the rest of the Philippine political establishment became enthusiastic promoters of McNutt's presidential aspirations.

But McNutt also deserves credit for resisting the seemingly inevitable momentum toward Philippine independence given the increasingly dark international scene. In late 1937 and early 1938, a Joint Preparatory Committee was set up in Manila to study the economic dimension of the transition to independence. This committee, a combination of American technical experts and Philippine politicians, focused narrowly on economic issues and drew conclusions largely favoring Philippine positions. To ratchet up the political pressure, Quezon chose this opportunity to issue a call for immediate independence. In a private letter of January 1938 to James Roosevelt, son and aide to the president, McNutt waved off Quezon's posturing: "[T]he whole performance," as

he put it, "reminded me of a nervous woman who threatened to commit suicide in order to get something from her husband." He expressed the opinion
that, "in his heart, Quezon does not want immediate independence and that
he has some doubts about ultimate independence." Most significantly, McNutt
recognized that the Philippine question had a larger strategic dimension that
the committee had entirely ignored:

The Philippine problem is only a part of the great unsolved problem of America's
present and future position in the Orient. On this matter I have reached certain definite
conclusions, unexpressed except in this fashion to the President. America cannot leave
the Orient today without serious loss of prestige and without further endangering world
peace. If she stays in the Orient, she must stay in the Philippines as sovereign.[45]

In fact, McNutt may well have had some influence over Quezon's thinking
in this regard, for in the spring of 1938 he was able to carry to Roosevelt a
message from Quezon suggesting that the best interests of both the Philippines
and the United States might best be served "by an indefinite continuation of the
commonwealth." Reportedly, FDR's response to this was, "If that is what the
Filipinos want, let them say so." It goes virtually without saying that Quezon
felt unable or unwilling for political reasons to repudiate his own full-throated
cries for Philippine independence. In McNutt's assessment:

I am convinced that Quezon hesitates to move because he fears that such a request
would be denied by the present Congress, and that in the event of such denial, he would
lose all political power in the Islands and would lose the respect of the remainder of the
Orient.

In any case, the State Department was adamantly opposed to any reopening
of the political question of the status of the Philippines, and the matter came
to nothing. Nor were McNutt's warnings welcome in the White House. The
persistence of a McNutt for president boomlet in the United States in the end
served only to stir up fratricidal political opposition to him, as anonymous
administration sources leaked defamatory accusations that McNutt was using
confidentially expressed reservations concerning the Joint Preparatory Committee report as an excuse to break publicly with the president and advance his
own candidacy for the office. McNutt realized that his service to the administration was at an end.[46]

Before leaving the Philippine case, something should be said about two other
Americans who, though not proconsuls in any conventional sense, nevertheless
may be said to have played a quasi-proconsular role at two important junctures in the history of the islands. The first is General Douglas MacArthur.
As we have seen, as commander of American forces in the Philippines during

---

[45] Ibid., 331–32.
[46] Ibid., 334–38. McNutt returned to the Philippines as high commissioner, however, in 1946,
after Truman had become president.

the commonwealth period and adviser to the Filipino army, MacArthur was quite familiar with the society and politics of the Philippines and a prominent and influential figure in Manila. Following MacArthur's reconquest of the islands in February 1945, and before his appointment as supreme commander of the American occupation forces in Japan in August of that year, the general was the de facto center of political authority in the Philippines. As such, he made a number of important unilateral decisions that shaped significantly the evolution of Filipino politics in the postwar independence period. MacArthur's extra-military role during the final months of the war has been too frequently neglected; it will be explored in some detail in the chapter dealing with him.

The second figure is Edward Lansdale, probably best remembered today as the supposed inspiration for a character in Graham Greene's novel *The Quiet American*.[47] A sometime Army intelligence officer with a career in the advertising business and an ingratiating manner, Lansdale was recruited in 1942 by the Office of Strategic Services (OSS), forerunner of the clandestine service of the Central Intelligence Agency (CIA). Exactly what he did during the war remains a mystery. After it ended, he returned to duty with the Army and was assigned as an intelligence officer to a command headquartered in Manila, but his flair for public relations and the wide contacts he soon developed among Filipinos brought him before long to the attention of General MacArthur, who continued to follow developments in the islands from his new perch in Tokyo. Thanks to this, Lansdale was quickly promoted and made acting public affairs officer. In 1947, he decided to transfer into the newly created U.S. Air Force and was reassigned to a posting in the United States the following year. In 1949, still in Air Force uniform, he returned to intelligence-related work in Washington in the blandly named Office of Policy Coordination (OPC), a newly formed, highly secret organization for political and psychological warfare that was administratively attached to the CIA but in fact reported jointly to the secretaries of state and defense (it was finally folded into the Agency in 1952). Lansdale's first assignment was to the Philippines.

---

[47] Greene himself would later insist that the figure of Alden Pyle in *The Quiet American* (1955) was not based on Lansdale. But Lansdale was unmistakably portrayed, and in a much more favorable light, in William J. Lederer and Eugene Burdick, *The Ugly American* (1958). Lansdale's own account, *In the Midst of Wars: An American's Mission to Southeast Asia* (New York: Harper and Rowe, 1972), is uninformative if not actively misleading on many matters (particularly his association with the CIA). He was more forthcoming in a series of interviews in the 1980s; see Cecil B. Currey, *Edward Lansdale: The Unquiet American* (Washington, DC: Brassey's, 1998). See also Richard Critchfield, *The Long Charade: Political Subversion in the Vietnam War* (New York: Harcourt, Brace, 1968); Zalin Grant, *Facing the Phoenix* (New York: Norton, 1991); Eva-Lotta E. Hedman, "Late Imperial Romance: Magsaysay, Lansdale, and the Philippine-American 'Special Relationships'," in Richard J. Aldrich et al., eds., *The Clandestine Cold War in Asia, 1945–1965* (Portland, OR: Frank Cass, 2000), 181–94; and Jonathan Nashel, *Edward Lansdale's Cold War* (Amherst: University of Massachusetts Press, 2005).

Then-Lieutenant Colonel Lansdale arrived in Manila in September 1950. He was attached to the U.S. military advisory mission as intelligence advisor to the Philippine army, but this was simply a cover for his real work.[48] His assignment was to help shore up the position of Ramon Magsaysay, the newly appointed defense minister,[49] help Magsaysay deal with the increasingly dangerous Huk insurgency, revitalize the Philippine armed forces, encourage political reform, and prepare the way for an honest legislative election in November 1951. In short order, Lansdale established a personal relationship with Magsaysay, one that grew into a close friendship as the two men virtually lived and worked together for many months in an American military compound in Manila. From Lansdale the defense minister (and through him the Philippine army) learned the essentials of counterinsurgency warfare – with particular emphasis on its political and psychological components, for which the American officer had a unique talent. Magsaysay was an apt pupil, and under his energetic leadership the government as a whole soon began to get the upper hand in the fight against the Huks. Lansdale was also spectacularly successful in ensuring that the 1951 election was fair, giving an important boost to the legitimacy of the fledgling Filipino government.

Lansdale and the OPC were concerned, however, over what they regarded as the incapacity and corruption of the administration of President Elpidio Quirino, and they determined to promote another candidate for the presidency in the upcoming election of 1953. Magsaysay soon emerged as the logical choice. Lansdale then set out energetically to burnish the defense minister's image in the United States as well as in the Philippines through a massive public relations campaign extending over months. Not surprisingly, Quirino became increasingly alarmed at Magsaysay's growing stature and unhappy with Lansdale's relationship with him, but he failed to take action against the American.[50] He did, however, criticize Magsaysay in public, leading to the latter's resignation in February 1953. Lansdale then proceeded to position Magsaysay politically for a presidential run – most crucially, by engineering his switch from Quirino's pro-American Liberal Party to the Nationalist Party and persuading that party's most prominent presidential contenders to offer Magsaysay the top spot on their ticket. This was agreed, and Magsaysay duly received the nomination in April. With Lansdale then acting virtually as his campaign manager and (though he would later deny it) fundraiser, Magsaysay

---

[48] It is indicative of the relationship between the OPC and the CIA at this time that the CIA station chief in Manila was never informed of Lansdale's real mission.

[49] The appointment was itself essentially an OPC-inspired operation.

[50] This is surprising given that on a visit to Washington in early 1953 Quirino learned from CIA Director Allen Dulles the true nature of Lansdale's mission. Yet it may be that the president realized that seeking to expel Lansdale would have been futile given his support at the highest levels of the U.S. government. On the other hand, there is some reason to believe that Quirino's brother may have been behind an assassination attempt against Lansdale in the streets of Manila (Currey, 121–22).

went on to win the election in a landslide, though the candidate also ran a dynamic, American-style populist campaign. (Perhaps inevitably, Lansdale thus acquired the nickname Colonel Landslide.) With his activities becoming a bit overly conspicuous, Lansdale absented himself from the country for six weeks in the run-up to the election. It would not be the last time he visited Saigon.

5

MacArthur in the Far East

In every circle, and truly, at every table there are people who lead armies into Macedonia; who know where the camp ought to be placed; what posts ought to be occupied by troops; when and through what pass that territory should be entered; where magazines should be formed; how provisions should be conveyed by land and sea; and when it is proper to engage the enemy, when to lie quiet.... These are great impediments to those who have the management of affairs ... I am not one of those who think that commanders ought at no time to receive advice; on the contrary, I should deem that man more proud than wise, who regulated every proceeding by the standard of his own single judgment. What then is my opinion? That commanders should be counseled chiefly by persons of known talent ... who are present at the scene of action, who see the country, who see the enemy ... and who, like people embarked in the same ship, are sharers of the danger. If, therefore, anyone thinks himself qualified to give advice respecting the war which I am to conduct ... let him not refuse his assistance to the state but let him come with me into Macedonia. He shall be furnished with a ship, a horse, a tent; even his traveling charges shall be defrayed. But if he thinks this too much trouble, and prefers the repose of a city life ... let him not ... assume the office of a pilot. The city in itself furnishes abundance of topics for conversation; let it confine its passion for talking within its own precincts and rest assured that we shall pay no attention to any councils but such as shall be framed within our camp.

L. Aemilius Paullus[1]

On September 2, 1945, the final chapter of World War II came to a close with the surrender of imperial Japan to the United States and its allies in a formal ceremony on the deck of the battleship USS Missouri in Tokyo Bay. This

---

[1] Livy 44.22, quoting the commander of Roman forces in Greece at the conclusion of the Third Macedonian War. Paullus, the victor of the decisive battle of Pydna (168 BC), went on to preside over the political reconstruction of the Macedonian kingdom. MacArthur kept a framed copy of these words in a conspicuous place on a wall in his office in the Dai-Ichi Building in Tokyo: John Gunther, *The Riddle of MacArthur* (New York: Harper & Brothers, 1950), 55–56.

event also signaled the beginning of a new phase in the history of American involvement in Asia – and in American foreign policy more generally. The occupation of Japan by American military forces ended only in 1952, a period that also witnessed the emergence of a new totalitarian threat to the security of the Western democracies in the form of Soviet and Chinese communism. The United States at this time faced two daunting challenges to its newly won position in Asia and the Pacific. The first was the reconstruction of a shattered Japan and a reorientation of its politics in a way that would put to rest forever – or so it was hoped – Japanese imperial ambitions. The second was to manage the political and military threats posed in the region by the Soviets and, after 1949, by their new Chinese allies. Both involved an unprecedented level of American presence and power in the region. The overall challenge facing the United States – what may be called the reconstruction of the political order of East Asia – was entirely reminiscent of the sorts of challenges that had given rise to the practice of proconsular imperium in the late Roman republic. It is hardly surprising, then, that the United States turned in this situation to a proconsul of its own. This man was, of course, General of the Army Douglas MacArthur.

Douglas MacArthur is one of the most extraordinary figures in the annals of American military history. In his lifetime he was also – and to some extent remains today – a controversial and polarizing figure. Celebrated by many as an American hero and a great man, he was also disliked and distrusted by many of his peers and by others who had observed him closely, as well as by a wide swath of the American Left. There is much in the historical record that can support both assessments. In the words of Japan's postwar prime minister Shigeru Yoshida, the general was "not a simple man." MacArthur was a Victorian (he was born in 1880) of aristocratic temperament and a conservative upbringing; in spite or perhaps in some ways because of this, he craved public acclaim, was adept at cultivating a favorable image in the press, and dabbled – more than dabbled – in domestic politics in an increasingly democratic America. In these respects, he is strongly reminiscent of Leonard Wood – though MacArthur was perhaps less of a natural politician. He was a soldier of strategic vision, yet his strategic judgments were sometimes clouded by extraneous factors. He was capable of great magnanimity and lofty sentiment but could also be arrogant, petty, and manipulative. He was gifted as a public speaker and could be charming in conversation, but he crossed the line easily into bombast and bathos. One of the secrets to MacArthur's success was a pragmatism and flexibility of mind that allowed him to appropriate easily the ideas of others; but he was also slow to give credit and tended to impose a sometimes stultifying conformity on his subordinates. This pragmatism also helps explain what might be described as a certain lack of groundedness in MacArthur's strategic outlook, and to some extent even in his political views.[2]

---

[2] A striking example is MacArthur's semi-endorsement of Philippine President Manuel Quezon's proposal to Washington in early 1942 that it offer the Japanese independence and neutrality for the Philippines in exchange for the evacuation of all foreign troops. As Secretary of War Henry

A British staff officer who encountered MacArthur in Australia in 1943 summed up the man in the following terms: "He is shrewd, selfish, proud, remote, highly strung and vastly vain. He has imagination, self-confidence, physical courage and charm, but no humor about himself, no regard for truth, and is unaware of these defects. He mistakes his emotions and ambitions for principles. With moral depth he would be a great man; as it is he is a near miss which may be worse than a mile."[3]

It is fair to say that MacArthur's star no longer shines as brightly today as it did as late as three decades ago, when William Manchester's hagiographic biography of him appeared.[4] The sour political climate created in the United States by the Vietnam debacle gave rise to a revisionist historiography of the Cold War and of American military history generally that continues to resonate in the academy and beyond. Just as important, however, has been the impact of a continuing stream of fresh documentation of this period from archives and personal memoirs. In the case of MacArthur, the occupation period has come under particularly intense scrutiny by scholars both here and in Japan, given the critical importance of those years in the formation of the contemporary Japanese polity and for U.S.–Japanese relations throughout the postwar era. But much other material has also become available concerning MacArthur's wartime service, in Korea as well as World War II. The overall result is a more nuanced view of the man than previously available. With respect to the occupation, as one scholar has put it, MacArthur has simply "shrunk," as attention has shifted away from him to the role of the occupation bureaucracy, Washington, and the Japanese themselves.[5] More generally, a massive, formidably documented biography by Clayton James has provided an agreed baseline for making sound judgments about MacArthur's actions. A variety of revisionist accounts have used this material to redraw the picture in darker hues. Much of this newer scholarship is indispensable in any serious analysis of MacArthur and his era.[6] At the same time, it is essential not to lose sight of the real accomplishments – indeed, the elements of greatness – in the general's career, or, for

Stimson put it, this was a "wholly unreal message" that took "no account of what the war was for." Michael Schaller, *Douglas MacArthur: The Far Eastern General* (New York: Oxford University Press, 1989), 59–60. After observing the general closely as his labor adviser in Tokyo in 1946–50, the liberal Democrat Theodore Cohen concluded that he was actually a "political primitive with wide open spaces where his reactionary principles were supposed to be." Ibid., 124–25.

3 Lieutenant Colonel Gerald Wilkinson, liaison officer to MacArthur, diary entry, as quoted in Schaller, 74.

4 William Manchester, *American Caesar: Douglas MacArthur 1880–1964* (Boston: Little, Brown, 1978).

5 Carol Gluck, "Entangling Illusions – Japanese and American Views of the Occupation," in Warren I. Cohen, ed., *New Frontiers in American–East Asian Relations: Essays Presented to Dorothy Borg* (New York: Columbia University Press, 1983), ch. 7, 179. For the Japanese perspective see further John W. Dower, *Embracing Defeat: Japan in the Wake of World War II* (New York: W. W. Norton, 1999).

6 D. Clayton James, *The Years of MacArthur*, 3 vols. (Boston: Houghton Mifflin, 1970–85). For assessments of this work see the reviews of volumes 2 and 3 by Brian Loring Villa and Charles M. Dobbs, in William M. Leary, ed., *MacArthur and the American Century: A Reader* (Lincoln:

that matter, of his out-sized impact on the course of events in a pivotal moment in American and world history.

The son of a distinguished Army officer, MacArthur graduated first in his class from West Point in 1903. He saw action later that year in the Philippines, newly captured from the Spanish, where his father Arthur commanded American forces engaged in putting down a native insurrection; it was at this time that he received his first exposure to the Far East, which would become a life-long preoccupation and love. By 1913, he was serving as staff officer to then–Chief of Staff of the Army General Leonard Wood, who had an important influence on him.[7] When the United States entered the First World War, MacArthur served under General John Pershing in the American Expeditionary Forces in France as chief of staff of the 42nd ("Rainbow") Division of the Army National Guard, distinguishing himself by displays of personal bravery as well as by his disciplined and imaginative leadership; he earned many medals and was eventually promoted to brigadier general.

After the war, MacArthur was appointed superintendent of the U.S. Military Academy, where he remained until 1922. At West Point, he urged (not always with great success) sweeping reforms of the curriculum designed to expose the cadets to non-military subjects such as the social sciences, among other things. MacArthur himself read deeply and widely in literature as well as political and military history – not least, that of classical Greece and Rome. He remained convinced of the importance of liberal education in forming a class of officers who would be able to command the respect of an essentially civilian mass army as well as to deal effectively with the political-military challenges frequently encountered at high levels of command. MacArthur's experience of the Army's lack of preparation for its role in the occupation of the Rhineland following the end of hostilities against Germany helped confirm him in this view.[8]

After a series of peacetime assignments in the Philippines and the United States, MacArthur was appointed chief of staff of the Army in 1930 by President Herbert Hoover, a friend and one whose political outlook he largely shared.[9]

University of Nebraska Press, 2001), 471–81. The best overall revisionist account is Schaller's *Douglas MacArthur: The Far Eastern General*. But special mention must be made as well of Richard H. Rovere and Arthur M. Schlesinger, Jr., *The General and the President and the Future of American Foreign Policy* (New York: Farrar, Straus and Young, 1951), a perceptive and engaging account whose judgments stand up well in the light of later evidence. A brief and balanced recent study is Richard B. Frank, *MacArthur: A Biography*, Great Generals Series (New York: Palgrave MacMillan, 2007); see also Geoffrey Perret, *Old Soldiers Never Die: The Life of Douglas MacArthur* (New York: Random House, 1996).

[7] MacArthur "particularly assimilated Wood's skillful manipulation of the press and open dabbling in politics" (Frank, 5); see also James, I, 110–15, 130–31.

[8] The West Point graduate of the future as envisioned by MacArthur must be of "a type possessing all the cardinal military virtues as of yore, but possessing an intimate understanding of his fellows, a comprehensive grasp of world and national affairs, and a liberalization of conception which amounts to a change in his psychology of command." James, I, 264–65. See further Stephen A. Ambrose, "MacArthur as West Point Superintendent," in Leary, 10–29.

[9] See the remarks of Frank, 20.

MacArthur pleaded vigorously for additional manpower for the Army, though to little avail in view of the dire economic situation in the country at the time. As the Depression deepened and Franklin Delano Roosevelt swept into the presidency, MacArthur's conservative views came to seem increasingly out of place in Washington. His role in the unfortunate Bonus Army incident of 1932 (where a demonstration of veterans in the capital seeking promised compensation from the government was forcibly suppressed by the Army) had permanently marked him in the eyes of New Deal liberals as a political enemy, if not as a coup-threatening "man on horseback." When MacArthur's term as chief of staff expired in 1934, Roosevelt reappointed him for only a brief period (apparently, in a maneuver to ensure a favored successor). Roosevelt once famously remarked to an aide that Huey Long, the demagogic governor of Louisiana, was one of the two most dangerous men in America; when asked who the other was, the reply was, "Douglas MacArthur."[10]

At this point in his career, retirement might have seemed the natural option, but MacArthur was not yet finished. In October 1935, he accepted an offer from Manuel Quezon, president of the newly minted "commonwealth" of the Philippines, to take a position as military adviser to his government, with the task of supervising the creation of an indigenous army that could safeguard the security of the islands after they had achieved full independence from the United States, promised for 1946. The assignment was a frustrating one given continuing severe constraints on military spending in Washington throughout these years as well as the assumption – widely shared there – that defense of the Philippines against a determined Japanese assault was essentially hopeless.

Forced to retire from the Army in 1937, MacArthur managed nevertheless to stay on in Manila, in spite of a deteriorating relationship with Quezon and Washington's indifference to his mission there. In July 1941, however, with a clash with Japan becoming increasingly probable, MacArthur was recalled to active duty as a major general and entrusted with overall command of U.S. forces in the Philippines. MacArthur's assurances that he could defend the country from invasion are often assumed to have been instrumental in persuading Washington to send additional resources (notably, several squadrons of B-17s, America's newest bomber), but these assurances proved wholly unrealistic. When the Japanese did strike, on December 8, MacArthur was unable to prevent the destruction of most of his aircraft on the ground and the quick defeat of his ill-equipped ground forces. The question of MacArthur's personal responsibility for this fiasco is still debated today.[11]

It will not be necessary to recapitulate the well-known story of MacArthur's wartime exploits. His tenacious defense of the island fortress of Corregidor in Manila Harbor proved the only bright spot in an otherwise unremitting series of

---

[10] The aide was Rexford Tugwell, as cited in Frank, 25.
[11] For a cogent defense of MacArthur throughout this period see Duncan Anderson, "Douglas MacArthur and the Fall of the Philippines," in Leary, 83–108.

disasters for the Western powers in the Pacific in the war's early days, and made a celebrity of him back home. After his evacuation to Australia, MacArthur was appointed commander of allied forces in what would be known as the Southwest Pacific Area, while Admiral Chester Nimitz was given a parallel command of his own in the Central Pacific. This arrangement, a bureaucratic compromise reflecting the Navy's unwillingness to yield to an Army general the conduct of large-scale naval operations in the Pacific as well as its distrust of MacArthur personally, helped fan what can only be described as a growing paranoia on MacArthur's part toward not only the leadership of the Navy but also Army Chief George Marshall and indeed the president himself. Apart from what MacArthur regarded as FDR's long-standing partiality for the Navy,[12] he believed the national leadership was irresponsibly starving the Pacific theater of the resources needed to defeat the Japanese. MacArthur's criticisms of the Navy and the president's "Europe First" strategy were vocal and widely known. The failure of the Roosevelt administration to rein him in established a fateful pattern of defiance of civilian authority by the military's senior commander that persisted for a decade, culminating in MacArthur's dismissal by President Harry Truman during the Korean War.

As damaging and irresponsible as it appears in retrospect, the behavior of MacArthur's military and civilian superiors is not difficult to understand. During the war itself, MacArthur carefully cultivated his public image and enjoyed universally positive – indeed, adulatory – press coverage as an authentic American hero. Together with his well-known conservative views and critical stance toward FDR, this made him a potentially attractive candidate for president on the Republican ticket; and, in fact, he actively explored this possibility in both the spring of 1944 and the spring of 1948.[13] Roosevelt, perfectly aware of this, not surprisingly feared MacArthur and avoided confrontation with him. Their only meeting during the war, at Pearl Harbor in July of 1944, seems to have been largely a public relations exercise. Roosevelt, by then his party's nominee for an unprecedented fourth term, was content to bask in MacArthur's glory and talk in generalities; contrary to a common assumption, the meeting did little to resolve the ongoing disputes between MacArthur and the Navy concerning the strategy for the liberation of the Philippines. By the same token, MacArthur's superiors in the Army and the War Department tended to appease the general. FDR made it clear to all concerned that he did not want MacArthur made a political martyr.

MacArthur's arduous campaigns against the Japanese in New Guinea and then the Philippines resulted in decisive American victories and also personal vindication, as the general fulfilled his famous vow to return to the Philippines with a dramatic landing on Leyte in October 1944. With the fall of Manila in February 1945, Japan's hold on the Philippines was essentially broken, and

---

[12] Roosevelt had been assistant secretary of the Navy in the Wilson administration.
[13] MacArthur frequently denied it at the time, but the extent of his political intriguing in these years has become ever more apparent. See especially Schaller, chs. 6 and 10.

the way was open for the United States to make preparations for what it was assumed would be the final and decisive campaign of the war, invasion of the Japanese home islands. In April, MacArthur was given command of all American Army and Army Air forces in the Pacific, and the responsibility of leading what would have been the largest amphibious operation in history. This, of course, was to prove unnecessary. On August 6, an American aircraft destroyed the city of Hiroshima with a single atomic bomb; two days later, an equally devastating attack was carried out against Nagasaki. On August 15, the emperor declared in a radio address that Japan would cease resistance. That same day, Harry Truman, the new American president (FDR had died in April), appointed Douglas MacArthur "Supreme Commander" of American occupation forces in Japan.

Most accounts of MacArthur as American proconsul focus exclusively on the occupation period itself.[14] Yet the six months that separate the fall of Manila from MacArthur's assumption of command in Japan are also of considerable interest from this point of view, and have been surprisingly neglected by historians. In important respects, MacArthur's actions during this time prefigure his later behavior under the occupation and after that in the Korean War. Political considerations seem increasingly to have informed the general's conduct of military operations, which also became increasingly unhinged from higher strategy and administration policy. At the same time, MacArthur allowed himself to be drawn into internal Filipino politics in the fluid and chaotic days following the fall of the Japanese-controlled puppet government, in ways that also lacked Washington's sanction and would arguably prove seriously detrimental to American interests.[15]

In assessments of MacArthur's generalship, it has been noticed that the "bypassing" or "enveloping" operational style perfected by him in the conquest of New Guinea (and famously employed again at Inchon during the Korean War) seems to have deserted him during the spring and summer of 1945.[16] Once Manila and the key airfields near it had been secured, there would seem to have been no need to mount more than a minimal effort to contain the Japanese forces still on Luzon and scattered throughout the archipelago. Instead, MacArthur launched a costly campaign, eventually involving four U.S. divisions and stretching into August, in the mountainous jungles of northern Luzon against a large and very capably led Japanese force. More surprisingly, he also issued orders for the liberation of the central and southern Philippines – orders, it should be noted, that were authorized by the Joint Chiefs in Washington only retroactively, though without apparent protest. While arguments could be made on behalf of some of these operations, their strategic value was

[14] But note Rovere and Schlesinger, 80–84.
[15] See particularly Schaller, ch. 7, and Carol M. Petillo, *Douglas MacArthur: The Philippine Years* (Bloomington: Indiana University Press, 1980), ch. 6.
[16] See particularly D. Clayton James, "MacArthur's Lapses from an Envelopment Strategy in 1945," in Leary, 173–79.

close to nil; and they entailed substantial opportunity costs.[17] It seems clear that MacArthur had made up his mind as early as September 1944 that he would liberate the entire Philippines. At the bottom of this decision, evidently, was a mixture of political and personal motives. Recovery of the Philippines had been an obsession of MacArthur's since 1942; it was a matter of personal honor. When it was debated in Washington whether to bypass the Philippines entirely in favor of attacking Formosa, as argued by Nimitz and the Navy, MacArthur adamantly defended the first option, but prevailed only because it was finally determined that the second was not logistically feasible. In addition, MacArthur seems to have thought that this effort was politically necessary to reestablish American prestige and influence in the islands and in the wider region for the future. Though Roosevelt lent some support to this notion, both in public statements and in the Pearl Harbor meeting, it was plainly of much less importance in his wider strategic calculus.[18]

Considerations of this latter kind also appear to explain MacArthur's various initiatives in the wake of the reoccupation of New Guinea aimed at shaping the future political situation in the East Indies. In early 1944, MacArthur took it upon himself to open negotiations in Australia with H. J. van Mook, the lieutenant governor-general of the Netherlands East Indies, regarding future military operations there. Disregarding explicit State Department guidance, MacArthur finally concluded an agreement with van Mook in December that committed the United States to restoring the authority of the Dutch government in the territory with no reference to its eventual political independence. This could perhaps have been justified in the name of military expediency for operations in New Guinea and its immediate vicinity. But MacArthur actually developed ambitious plans, utilizing primarily the Australian troops under his command, to liberate all of the Dutch possessions in the region as well as British North Borneo. In spite of a lack of enthusiasm for this endeavor on the part of the Australians and resistance from the Joint Chiefs, MacArthur succeeded in gaining permission to conduct limited operations against Borneo (the ostensible rationale was to seize its oil resources) in May, June, and July of 1945.[19] Washington showed astonishingly little sensitivity to the policy dimension of MacArthur's actions in either of these cases – not to mention his unmistakable personal freelancing.

---

[17] According to the official Army history, the southern campaigns for the most part had "no strategic importance" but "were designed for the purpose of liberating Filipinos, reestablishing lawful government, and destroying Japanese forces." Robert R. Smith, *Triumph in the Philippines*, vol. 2 of *United States Army in World War II: The War in the Pacific* (Washington, DC: Department of the Army, 1963), 584–85.

[18] James, II, ch. 13.

[19] In fact, analysis done in Washington had by this time completely undermined the oil rationale. MacArthur's original plan included a full-scale assault by the Australians on Java, held strongly by the Japanese; the result could well have been a major bloodbath. The purpose of this operation, as he told the Australian prime minister, was to "restore the Netherlands East Indies authorities to their seat of government." James, II, 468–69, 710–17.

MacArthur's return to the Philippines did not play out quite as he had envisioned it. The Japanese decision to fight to the death in Manila resulted in the virtual destruction of that city and the death of some 100,000 Filipino civilians. The war-weary population of the islands for the most part welcomed its American liberators anyway, but MacArthur's reception was far from the joyous parade through the streets of the capital that he had fondly imagined. In addition, the political situation was complex and uncertain. Much of the political elite of the prewar Philippines had cast their lot more or less firmly with the puppet government the Japanese had established in 1942. MacArthur himself had maintained a steady personal correspondence with former President Manuel Quezon after the latter's exile to Washington, but Quezon's deteriorating health made it impossible for him to reassume the reins of power. His successor, Sergio Osmena, was reinstated as head of a new government at MacArthur's urging shortly after arriving with the general on the beaches of Leyte in October 1944 and formally invested with the sovereignty of the country. Unfortunately, Osmena had no staff, no money, and little ability to shape events; and MacArthur in any case had little regard for him. Many of the immediate tasks facing his government were taken up by Army civil affairs units under MacArthur's command, but these were not adequately prepared for the magnitude of the difficulties they faced and in any case were not accountable to the president. MacArthur thus set up Osmena for political failure.

The general's handling of the sensitive issue of Filipino collaboration with the Japanese, however, was to seal Osmena's fate. In accordance with long-standing U.S. policy, MacArthur had initially decreed that all collaborators would be removed from office and held captive until they could be tried by the Philippine authorities. In March 1945, however, a group of former cabinet members of the deposed government was able to make its way through American lines in northern Luzon; one of these was Manuel Roxas, an officer in the American Army, long-time friend of MacArthur as well as Quezon, Filipino notable, and potential political rival of Osmena's. By excusing Roxas' collaboration on the grounds that his actions had always had the interests of the Philippines at heart and that he had demonstrated his ultimate loyalties through his involvement in guerrilla activity against the Japanese (all true enough), MacArthur succeeded in compromising the entire anti-collaborationist policy. The result was to enable the wartime oligarchy to which Roxas belonged to regain power – a process sealed by Roxas' capture of the Philippine Congress and then his victory over Osmena in the presidential election of April 1946.[20] Moreover, the restoration of the prewar elite to its semi-feudal domination of the Philippine countryside helped fan the discontents that gave rise to the dangerous communist-oriented Huk insurgency later in the decade.[21] Roxas

[20] For a good brief account see H. W. Brands, *Bound to Empire: The United States and the Philippines* (New York: Oxford University Press, 1992), 211–19.

[21] John Benedict Kerkvliet, *The Huk Rebellion: A Study of Peasant Revolt in the Philippines* (Berkeley: University of California Press, 1977).

himself gave a decisive impetus to this development by denying the Huk leadership any role in the political process. But this behavior was fully in keeping with the broadly conservative outlook that Roxas and his followers shared with MacArthur himself.[22]

All of this caused considerable unhappiness in Washington, particularly on the part of the man who was perhaps MacArthur's greatest bureaucratic nemesis: Secretary of the Interior, FDR intimate, and New Dealer extraordinaire Harold Ickes. Even before MacArthur's landing on Leyte, Ickes had supported the idea of creating a "high commissioner" for the Philippines (which prior to its independence fell under his department's jurisdiction), charged with civilian administration of the islands. MacArthur had strongly, and successfully, resisted this. Some very personal history was at work here. In 1900, General Arthur MacArthur had vigorously contested the authority of a civilian commission sent from Washington to oversee the pacification of the Philippines. This commission, headed by future president William Howard Taft, eventually won the day: MacArthur was recalled, and the conciliatory political strategy it favored eventually proved largely successful. Following the death of Roosevelt in April 1945, Ickes tried again, suggesting to Truman that he name as high commissioner none other than the son of the former president, one Charles P. Taft – a move whose pure malignity compels a certain admiration. But Truman also proved unwilling to cross the general. He filled the position – and not with Taft – only after it was clear that MacArthur would be leaving for Tokyo. By this time, the general had lost interest in the Philippines and was looking ahead.[23]

MacArthur arrived in the Japanese capital, then largely in ruins, on August 30, 1945. The general had long considered himself a student of the "oriental mind," and he certainly had a greater familiarity with the Far East than most American officials at the time, but his direct experience of it was confined largely to the Philippines. Indeed, it is striking to what extent the entire American occupation lacked rudimentary expertise on Japanese history or culture. MacArthur himself evidently never read anything about Japan other than intelligence reports, and he never traveled outside of a small part of Tokyo. Moreover, his arrival coincided with a change of the guard in the State Department that displaced the "old Japan hands" – foremost among them former ambassador to Japan Joseph P. Grew, succeeded as under secretary of the department by Dean Acheson in August 1945 – by the "China crowd," including the general's first State Department adviser, George Atcheson, Jr.[24] Compounding all this was the visceral hostility toward and indeed hatred of the Japanese and all

[22] More sinister interpretations of this history are possible though by no means certain. James himself ("MacArthur's Lapses from an Envelopment Strategy in 1945," 175) suggests that MacArthur's operations in the southern Philippines may have been partly intended to aid Roxas politically, as these areas were especially unfriendly toward Osmena.

[23] For all of this see especially Schaller, ch. 7.

[24] See, for example, Dower, 221–24.

their works that understandably persisted in the ranks not only of the armed forces but of the Washington bureaucracy as well, aggravated still further by the ideological animus of New Deal liberals toward Japanese militarism and imperial government. From this perspective, MacArthur's achievement during the occupation period has to be seen as little short of astounding. Particularly as Americans look back from their near-disastrous occupation of Iraq after 2003, the fact that the occupation of Japan met with virtually no violent resistance from remnants of the Japanese armed forces or anyone else is striking; after all, political assassination had become an accepted way of doing business in Japan in the immediate prewar years.[25] This is all the more true considering that the changes MacArthur imposed on the Japanese were much more radical and far-reaching than anything attempted by the Americans in Iraq over half a century later. Mindful of this, MacArthur's SCAP organization carefully monitored the state of Japanese public opinion, and its use of systematic sociological research broke new ground for the American military in its efforts to understand a foreign foe.[26]

It is fashionable today to dismiss as a "heroic myth" the notion that everything the Americans accomplished under the occupation was owing to MacArthur personally. There can be no question that this representation of the general's role – repeated and indeed reinforced in the memoirs of Truman and Atcheson, among others – is at best seriously misleading. It fails in the first place to take due account of the Japanese side, which proved to be adept at maneuvering for subtle advantage and playing off American officials against one another.[27] Second, it fails to take sufficient account of the detailed planning for the occupation that had been going on in Washington since early 1945 or even before.[28] In particular, contrary to what MacArthur himself would occasionally claim, the Japanese constitution in its essentials was a product not of MacArthur's own staff but rather of the State, War, and Navy Coordinating Committee (predecessor of the National Security Council), though his staff famously drafted a version of it in one week.[29] Finally, it ignores or downplays the role of the occupation bureaucracy itself. This organization, SCAP, as it came to be called after MacArthur's own title, Supreme Commander for the Allied Powers, was led by a number of energetic individuals who

---

[25] In fact, there apparently were several underground organizations of former Japanese officers that planned to resist the occupation if its policies proved overly harsh. Ikuhiko Hata, "The Occupation of Japan, 1945–1952," in Lewis, 316.

[26] LTC Michael B. Meyer, USAF, "A History of Socio-Cultural Intelligence and Research Under the Occupation of Japan," *Carlisle Papers in Security Strategy* (Carlisle, PA: U.S. Army War College, April 2009). The effective application of this research was unfortunately limited by the hostility of MacArthur's intelligence chief, General Charles Willoughby.

[27] See notably Koseki Shoichi, *The Birth of Japan's Postwar Constitution*, ed. and trans. Ray A. Moore (Boulder, CO: Westview, 1997).

[28] Hugh Borton, *American Presurrender Planning for Postwar Japan* (New York: Occasional Papers of the East Asian Institute, Columbia University, 1967).

[29] Schaller, 123.

sometimes pushed agendas of their own – notably, of a New Deal flavor – while occasionally operating at cross purposes with each other. To what extent MacArthur fully controlled all that they did remains in fact quite unclear, but it seems likely that he was influenced by them to a greater degree than is usually assumed.[30]

Still, MacArthur needs to be given his due. For all of the general's old-fashioned conservatism, he seems to have been remarkably free of the racism that colored the attitudes of many Americans at the time – including senior officials – toward the Japanese.[31] From the beginning, he displayed a remarkable magnanimity – one that "had not been previously notable in his makeup," in the words of several contemporary observers. "Unlike the merely brisk and efficient commanders of the Lucius Clay type, MacArthur felt that he was performing not one more Army assignment but an exalted historical mission. He communicated a sense of high historical significance to the Japanese, swept them up in the great drama and mystery of reconstruction, and gave them a feeling of spiritual purpose in a moment of unsurpassed national disaster."[32] Essential to the success of this approach was the decision, in which the general played a key part, to retain the institution and person of the Emperor Hirohito as a symbol of the identity of the Japanese people and the formal sovereignty of its government. MacArthur's rule was, unlike Clay's in Germany, an indirect one. Nevertheless, he never let the Japanese forget who was in charge. A widely publicized photograph of his first meeting with the emperor showed a relaxed MacArthur towering over a stiff, timid-looking Hirohito. MacArthur comported himself throughout the occupation in ways that deliberately mimicked the imperial style. Above all, not only did he never travel outside the capital, but he remained remote and inaccessible to all but a few Japanese officials. Criticism of MacArthur or the occupation was off-limits in the Japanese press (and frowned upon as well in visiting American reporters, who not infrequently found themselves expelled from the country). The effect of all this was to establish an unquestioned personal ascendancy among the Japanese people generally that gave occupation administrators enormous leverage to carry out their agenda in his name.

What specific actions of the occupation were owing to MacArthur personally? The general's forceful intervention in the inconclusive Washington debate over the fate of the emperor in the fall of 1945, in view of Washington's divided counsels on this issue, is highly likely if not certain to have been decisive, and

---

[30] Consider Robert E. Ward and Sakamoto Yoshikazu, eds., *Democratizing Japan: The Allied Occupation* (Honolulu: University of Hawaii Press, 1987), esp. ch. 14; also Theodore Cohen, *Remaking Japan: The American Occupation as New Deal* (New York: Free Press, 1987), with the review of Howard Schonberger, "Liberals Look at MacArthur's Japan," *Reviews in American History* 16 (1988): 478–86.

[31] See, for example, Frederick W. Marks III, *Wind Over Sand: The Diplomacy of Franklin Roosevelt* (Athens: University of Georgia Press, 1988), ch. 7.

[32] Rovere and Schlesinger, 86. In retrospect, however, as will be seen shortly, this characterization of Clay is widely off the mark.

helped ensure the smooth functioning of the occupation and the stability of
the Japanese political scene throughout the occupation years and beyond.[33]
Although it has never been widely recognized, in the first months of his tenure
MacArthur acted energetically – indeed, partly in violation of standing Army
policy – to bring emergency medical and food supplies to the Japanese people.
In so doing, he averted a potential demographic disaster that might have fatally
undermined American authority as well as the new Japanese government, perhaps opening the way to a communist takeover of power.[34] Further, though the
matter remains in some dispute, it is generally believed that MacArthur himself was responsible for the renunciation of war clause (the famous Article IX)
in the Japanese constitution of 1946. He certainly took swift and decisive
action to draft a constitution suiting American requirements, preempting competing Japanese efforts while at the same time maneuvering to have the document accepted as an authentic expression of the Japanese government and
people.

Finally, mention should be made of MacArthur's intense interest in the
ideological mission of the occupation. There was a general consensus in Washington at the time that the privileged position of the Shinto religion had to be
ended in view of its role in supporting the Japanese imperial order and the war.
MacArthur's instructions called for making provision for freedom of worship
in the new constitution, which was duly done. But MacArthur went to great
lengths personally to encourage the spread of Christianity in Japan, seeing it
as a strategic necessity to fill what he saw as a spiritual vacuum there and in
particular to forestall the advance of left-wing political ideas. Though mostly
ignored by historians since, this was an important element in MacArthur's
overall strategic vision for the occupation.[35]

However one judges MacArthur's actions in this last area, they point to a
wider pattern of unilateralism in the general's behavior, established early in the
war and increasingly pronounced, as we have seen, as the military endgame
approached. It is worth tracing this pattern through especially the first two
years of the occupation, when MacArthur's influence was at its height and
Washington policy-making was in relative disarray. Underlying many of the
general's divergences from the policy line in Washington, it now seems clear,
were his own political ambitions and the calculations he made regarding a
potential race for the presidency in 1948. The oscillations and even reversals
evident in MacArthur's own positions in the course of these few years can be
explained to some extent by the changing international scene – notably, the
emerging challenge from Soviet and Chinese communism; but the way events

---

[33] Ray A. Moore and Donald L. Robinson, *Partners for Democracy: Crafting the New Japanese State under MacArthur* (Oxford: Oxford University Press, 2002), ch. 2.

[34] Frank, 129–31.

[35] Douglas MacArthur, *Reminiscences* (New York: McGraw Hill, 1964), 309–11; Lawrence S. Wittner, "MacArthur and the Missionaries: God and Man in Occupied Japan," *Pacific Histor-ical Review* 40 (February 1971): 77–98. At the end of the day, it should be added, little came of this.

were playing out in Washington was clearly front and center for him.[36] At the same time, some of these positions also seem to betray what we described earlier as a certain lack of groundedness in MacArthur's strategic outlook.

Toward the end of September 1945, after only a month in Tokyo, MacArthur surprised and angered Washington by preemptively declaring the occupation a success and predicting that this would make possible a drastic cut in the size of American forces in the country. This played havoc with the Truman administration's efforts to slow the pace of demobilization and extend the draft. MacArthur apparently acted out of a suspicion that the administration wanted to maneuver him into a position to take the blame in public opinion for keeping the large numbers of American troops in the region in arms. (At the same time, the general had the audacity to refuse a presidential invitation to return to Washington for a ceremony honoring the victorious commanders of the war, excusing himself by reference to the "extraordinarily dangerous situation in Japan.") In spite of the immediate political motivation, however, this move was broadly congruent with a set of strategic principles that guided MacArthur throughout the occupation years. In the first place, the general remained deeply committed to the "peace constitution" for which he felt largely responsible. He supported the elimination of Japanese military power, and as late as the outbreak of the Korean War opposed efforts by Washington to create a small Japanese defense force, revive military production, and establish permanent American military bases in the country. Second, the security of Japan and American interests in Asia was to be guaranteed instead by a political settlement that would neutralize the Japanese home islands, buttressed by a continuing American military presence in the western Pacific (including Okinawa, which the United States would continue to control). Finally, in spite of his long-standing anti-Communism, MacArthur was not overly concerned with a potential Soviet threat to Japan and believed the Russians would honor Japanese neutrality if U.S. forces were withdrawn. As a corollary to this, he believed the United States could and should move expeditiously to conclude a peace treaty with Japan. Virtually all of these views put him increasingly at odds with the policy consensus in Washington as the Cold War gathered force.[37] Moreover, some of them directly or indirectly undermined MacArthur's political standing with his conservative supporters at home – a fact that helps to explain his frequent verbal inconsistencies and evasions.

---

[36] For a concise overview see Michael Schaller, "MacArthur's Japan: The View from Washington," in Leary, 287–314. As Schaller puts it: "A remarkable opportunism, rather than any consistent political ideology, dictated MacArthur's dazzling policy reversals. At various times between 1945 and the outbreak of the Korean War, he advocated both preserving and dissolving industrial combines, protecting and suppressing organized labor, forbidding and encouraging U.S. military bases, cooperating with and shunning the Soviets in a peace settlement, and ignoring and hiding behind the Allied consulting organs created in 1945. The speed with which he could strike new poses outraged and confused his many critics" (291).

[37] Michael Schaller, *The American Occupation of Japan: The Origins of the Cold War in Asia* (New York: Oxford University Press, 1985), 65–66.

Nothing better illustrates the extent to which MacArthur was willing to defy Washington, however, than his stance – rather, stances – on reform of the Japanese economy. From the outset of his tenure, MacArthur and his senior economic adviser made little effort to disguise their unhappiness with Washington's policies on reparations, anti-monopoly measures, and purging of industrialists. Two special missions were dispatched to Tokyo in November and December 1945 to advance this agenda, but SCAP continued to drag its feet and the administration let the matter drift. At the same time, however, SCAP paid scant attention to Japan's weakened economy and did little to shore up trade and production. By early 1947, it was increasingly clear that the rising threat to the western democracies posed by the Soviet Union and the international Communist movement required a fundamental reassessment of American global policy. With the Truman Doctrine and the Marshall Plan, the United States demonstrated its will not only to resist Soviet expansionist pressures (against Greece and Turkey) but also to counter the appeal of communism in Western Europe through an ambitious program of economic assistance that encompassed former enemies and allies alike. It was obvious that a similar reassessment would need to be made of U.S. policy toward Japan. Faced with this situation, one might think that MacArthur would have leapt at this opportunity to revitalize the Japanese economy while walking back various of the radical New Deal economic policies that Washington had tried to impose on SCAP at the outset. In fact, however, his reaction was the opposite. In a remarkable press conference in Tokyo in March 1947, shortly after Truman had announced the Marshall Plan, MacArthur claimed that no economic progress could be made in Japan until a peace treaty had been concluded and dismissed any initiatives from Washington along such lines. At the same time, in a complete reversal of his earlier position, the general aggressively embraced the cause of dismantling the Japanese system of industrial combines (*zaibatsu*), pressing the Japanese government to enact a law on this controversial issue in spite of political opposition from both right and left.

Although MacArthur succeeded in ramming this legislation through the Diet in the fall of 1947, he had finally overplayed his hand. The political climate in Washington was changing, and MacArthur began to come under attack in the American media for the "socialistic" policies he was said to be pursuing in Tokyo. Although apparently unable to bring themselves to "order" MacArthur to back down on the *zaibatsu* issue, the civilian leadership of the War Department and their allies in Navy and State were becoming increasingly convinced that a radical reorientation of occupation policy in Japan was needed and that MacArthur had to be reined in once and for all. In December 1947, Truman told Secretary of the Army Kenneth Royall that he doubted he could defeat MacArthur for the presidency, and that any public rebuke would only strengthen the general politically. Once the MacArthur bubble had burst in the Republican primaries in April 1948, however, the handwriting was on the wall. A turning point was the visit to Tokyo in March 1948 of George Kennan, director of the newly formed Policy Planning Staff of the State Department and the leading intellectual architect of the administration's nascent "containment" policy. Kennan – who later described the atmosphere of the general's entourage as resembling "nothing more than the latter days of the court of the Empress Catherine II, or possibly the final stages of the regime of Belisarius in Italy" – drew up a lengthy analysis of SCAP's failures and what Washington needed to do to fix them. This document became the basis for an authoritative statement of the administration's Japan policy, blessed by the newly created National Security Council. Following Truman's reelection, the president then sent MacArthur a formal directive ordering him to acknowledge the change in policy and providing additional guidelines for interpreting it. For good measure, a special envoy, the banker Joseph Dodge, was sent to Tokyo to oversee implementation of these guidelines. Although MacArthur initially refused to go along with all this, citing – incredibly – the "international authority" he enjoyed thanks to SCAP's formal reporting relationship to an advisory board of representatives of various allied countries, he had little choice but to comply. This essentially signaled the end of MacArthur's proconsular reign in Japan.[38]

While MacArthur fell into line with the rightward swing of American policy after 1948, however, he remained, to say the least, less than completely reconciled to the Truman administration. Except for the possibility of presiding personally over a Japanese peace conference (which seems to have been a key factor in the general's continuing advocacy of this course), MacArthur saw little scope for action in Japan itself and began to look farther afield. An obvious candidate was China. During the war itself, the United States had supported Chiang Kai-shek and his Nationalist armies against the Japanese, then in occupation of large swaths of mainland China. After 1945, following the dismantlement of Japan's continental empire and the repatriation of its troops, Chiang's control of the mainland was contested by the Chinese Communists under Mao Tse-tung. An American effort to broker a political settlement, spearheaded by MacArthur's old nemesis George Marshall, had failed by early 1947, and the Truman administration at that point declined to invest further in Chiang's waning cause. But others in his administration (particularly in the Department of Defense) as well as in Congress (the Republicans) soon challenged this policy, and MacArthur was unable to resist abetting these efforts, especially during the period of his active interest in the presidency in 1947 and early 1948. Some Republican politicians sounded him out on the possibility of serving as a military adviser to Chiang Kai-shek in a new Republican administration, and the general indicated his interest in this, expressing confidence that within six months he could succeed in expelling the Communists from Manchuria. After the collapse of his candidacy, MacArthur temporarily dropped the China issue, only to return to it after the Nationalists were forced to evacuate the mainland and take refuge on Taiwan (or Formosa, as it was then generally called) in 1949. At this time, he joined forces with Secretary of Defense Louis Johnson in

[38] This account draws primarily on Schaller, *Douglas MacArthur*, ch. 10, and "MacArthur's Japan: The View from Washington."

arguing for keeping Formosa out of communist hands by any means possible, including returning it to Japan – that is, to SCAP's control; and on his own authority he permitted Japanese pilots to travel to Taiwan to provide assistance to the Nationalists' Air Force. Johnson and MacArthur also urged that the United States support anti-Communist Muslim guerrillas in western China and impose a naval blockade on China's northeast. MacArthur continued to intrigue over these matters with the administration's political opponents. In September 1949, he discussed with a visiting Republican senator in Tokyo the idea of naming the general supreme military commander in the Far East. Furthermore, recognizing the political weakness of Chiang Kai-shek, the general in late 1949 initiated efforts to remove him from office (something that had also been considered by others in Washington).

Throughout this period, MacArthur did not simply freelance, but rather sought to maximize his own influence by maneuvering between the State and Defense Departments (and therefore also the president) on a variety of contentious issues dividing them. While siding with Johnson on the defense of Taiwan and other measures against the Communists, he also sided with Secretary of State Acheson over the issue of a Japanese peace settlement. Nevertheless, there can be no question that he remained virtually an independent actor throughout this period, undertaking initiatives of policy significance, if not entirely on his own authority, at least through unofficial and unorthodox channels and often apparently without the knowledge of his superiors. There is reason to believe, for example, that MacArthur entered into secret negotiations with Chiang's government in the late spring of 1950 concerning the possible deployment of Nationalist troops to South Korea in anticipation of an invasion of that country from the North.[39] Shortly following the outbreak of the Korean War on June 25, 1950, MacArthur then took it upon himself to travel to Taiwan for a two-day conference with Chiang and his advisers. Little is known about these meetings – partly because, as MacArthur told his own diplomatic adviser, he had "no intention of providing details" about them to the State Department and indeed failed to do so. In any case, MacArthur's gambit had the effect of significantly strengthening Chiang's position at a time when his removal was still under active consideration in Washington. After MacArthur recommended that jet fighters be sent to Formosa, Truman himself had to remind the general that no one other than himself had the authority to order military action from Taiwan against the Chinese mainland.[40]

It is worth dwelling briefly on MacArthur's attitude toward Korea *before* the communist invasion – an aspect of his proconsular role that has been little noticed. Once the United States had asserted its right, in August 1945, to occupy Korea up to the thirty-eighth parallel in order to forestall a Russian presence throughout the entire peninsula, this area also came under MacArthur's jurisdiction as senior American military commander in the Far East. Like the

---

[39] Schaller, *Douglas MacArthur*, 176–77.
[40] Ibid., 194.

Joint Chiefs in Washington, however, MacArthur from the beginning had little interest in Korea and regarded it as a potential drain on increasingly limited American military resources. In September, he assigned General John R. Hodge with his 24th Corps to represent the authority of SCAP in southern Korea, but Hodge, a man with no political skills or knowledge of the country, was given little guidance by either MacArthur or Washington. The resulting political morass – to which MacArthur contributed by facilitating the return of the nationalist politician Syngman Rhee from his American exile against the advice of the State Department, which considered him reactionary and authoritarian – led to chronic instability and social and political violence. MacArthur's apparent indifference to these developments seems to have reflected not only a dubious assumption about the marginal strategic importance for the United States of maintaining a non-communist buffer regime in the south (quite in contrast to his view of Taiwan), but possibly also a calculation that it was better to leave the State Department holding the bag in an intractable situation that was not likely to enhance his own reputation no matter what the outcome. Finally, although SCAP retained an intelligence presence in Korea after its formal responsibility there lapsed in 1949, MacArthur seems to have been as surprised by the North Korean invasion of June 1950 as anyone in Washington.[41]

The outbreak of the Korean conflict of course gave MacArthur yet another opportunity to take up arms for his country and reap glory for himself – "Mars' last gift to an old warrior," he later called it. The story of MacArthur in Korea is a well-known one and need not be rehearsed here. The operational brilliance of the Inchon landing, reprising MacArthur's New Guinea campaign of the Pacific war, has a secure place in the annals of American military history. It would be overshadowed, however, by the strategic recklessness the general then showed in marching for the Yalu even as it was becoming increasingly likely that this would bring the Chinese communists into the peninsula, as well as the still greater recklessness he displayed in defying the authority of the president by publicly advocating a wider war against mainland China. In April 1951, having tried Truman's patience once too often, MacArthur was finally cashiered.[42] Fortunately for the United States, the general had neither the will nor the ability to march his legions back to the gates of Washington.

---

[41] See the discussion in ibid., 160–63.
[42] Accounts in MacArthur, pt. 9; Rovere and Schlesinger, ch. 3; Schaller, *Douglas MacArthur*, chs. 12–13; and Frank, chs. 13–14.

6

Clay in Germany

Being Military Governor was a pretty heady job. It was the nearest thing to a Roman proconsulship the modern world afforded. You could turn to your secretary and say, "Take a law." The law was there, and you could see its effect in two or three weeks. It was a challenging job to an ambitious man. Benevolent despotism.

John J. McCloy[1]

We cannot win this way. I thought we crossed the Rubicon at London but apparently we sat down in the middle of the stream.

Lucius Clay[2]

As World War II drew to its close in the spring of 1945, it was apparent that the United States would face immense challenges in managing the transition to a new peacetime global order. The thorough defeat inflicted on Nazi Germany by American, British, and Russian arms left many questions unanswered concerning the political vacuum that had now been created in the heart of Europe and the future relationship between the Anglo-Saxon powers and their Soviet ally of convenience. At the same time, the devastation visited on Germany by the allies, coupled with the collapse of the Nazi regime and the virtual disappearance of effective government throughout the country, posed enormous practical problems for the occupying powers. Added to all that, both Britain and the United States faced intense political pressures to reduce their armed forces and bring home the troops. The Anglo-Saxon military presence on the continent was thus a wasting asset. In the Far East, similar challenges existed as the war against Japan entered its final stage.

[1] John J. McCloy, interview of 19 February 1971, as quoted in Jean Edward Smith, *Lucius D. Clay: An American Life* (New York: Henry Holt, 1990) (henceforth Smith), 201.
[2] General Lucius Clay in a cable to Under Secretary of the Army William H. Draper, Jr., 15 June 1948, in Jean Edward Smith, ed., *The Papers of Lucius D. Clay* (Bloomington: Indiana University Press, 1974) (henceforth *Clay Papers*), 678. Clay's concern was apparent backsliding in Washington in response to vacillations in French policy at this juncture: Smith, 488–90.

What is more, this was a time of change and uncertainty at the seat of American power. The death of President Franklin Delano Roosevelt (FDR) in April 1945 marked the end of an era. Under the administration of his untried successor, former senator Harry S. Truman, the influence of the New Deal liberals FDR had installed throughout the government began to wane, while conservative forces in the bureaucracy and Congress gathered strength. The power of the defense establishment – the Joint Chiefs of Staff together with the civilian secretaries of War and Navy – came increasingly under challenge from the State Department, which had been purposely excluded by Roosevelt from the realm of high policy during the war. Both of these developments prepared the way for the gradual shift that was to occur over the next several years in the attitudes of American policy-makers toward the Soviet Union and international communism.

As early as September 1944, FDR's advisers had recommended that he immediately name an American "high commissioner" to manage the occupation of Germany. After much discussion, however, the War Department finally won acceptance of its view that at least in its initial stages, the chief occupation official should be an Army general, reporting to the American commander in the European theater, General Dwight D. Eisenhower. After a delay caused by the failure of the Germans to cooperate (in the form of the Ardennes offensive of December 1944), the search for an occupation head was resumed in the spring of 1945. Although Roosevelt appeared to favor John McCloy, a civilian with a background in business who was then assistant secretary of War, he was prevailed upon to choose a military man instead: General Lucius D. Clay.

At the Yalta Conference of February 1945, Roosevelt, British Prime Minister Winston Churchill, and Soviet leader Josef Stalin agreed, among other things, on a set of arrangements for the occupation of German territory by the three powers. Each power was to have its own exclusive "zone" of control: the British in northwestern Germany, the United States in the south (Bavaria, Hesse, Baden, and Wurttemberg), and the Russians in the east. Later, France was added as an occupying power and given its own zone made up of territories along its border previously assigned to Britain and the United States. General Clay was thus to have sole authority only in the American zone. Within the British zone, the United States exercised joint control of the ports of Bremen and Bremerhaven, to ensure the integrity of its own lines of supply. In addition, all four powers shared control of Berlin, the former German capital, located some 110 miles within the Soviet zone. Quite unlike the situation General Douglas MacArthur would later face in Japan, then, the job of American proconsul in Germany came with a high diplomatic content. In fact, however, no one in Washington seems to have foreseen the political difficulties the occupation would encounter almost from the beginning. Clay was chosen not for any political skills, but because of his reputation as a competent administrator. As things turned out, however, the United States could not have done better. Clay proved to be not only a masterly administrator and an effective diplomat, but also a man of strategic and political vision and indomitable will – at a moment when all of these things would prove to be in short supply. There can be little question that his critical role during this formative period of the Cold War has not been adequately appreciated by historians or Americans generally.[3]

Lucius D. Clay has the distinction of being the only man to reach the rank of four-star general in the United States Army without any combat experience (in spite of his own efforts to remedy this situation). Clay was born in 1898, the son of a three-term United States senator from northern Georgia as well as a direct descendant of the illustrious American statesman Henry Clay. He thus became familiar with the ways of Washington at an early age. Packed off to West Point not long after the death of his father, Clay reacted poorly to the regimentation of Army life and was lucky to graduate; though finishing at the top of his class in English and history, he was a discipline problem. In a twist of fate and quite against his will, he was assigned to the Corps of Engineers on leaving the academy in 1918. In his early assignments, he proved something of a maverick; one of his rating officers went so far as to describe him as a "bolshevik." But his career was made in Washington in the early Depression era, where he served for four years as the Corps' liaison on Capitol Hill. There he worked closely with Roosevelt aide Harry Hopkins to establish the Works Progress Administration and other elements of the New Deal economic recovery program, and he struck up a friendship with Sam Rayburn of Texas, who would be chosen majority leader of the House of Representatives in 1937. Following a brief stint as engineering adviser to MacArthur in the Philippines, Clay returned to the United States to work on various Corps projects, including an emergency airport construction program that vastly expanded the infrastructure of air travel throughout the country just prior to the outbreak of World War II. In the wake of a sweeping reorganization of the War Department in 1942, Clay became the youngest brigadier general in the U.S. Army and was put in charge of Army procurement. Proving himself fully in this position, the general was then (in late 1944) appointed deputy to James F. Byrnes, the

---

[3] Part of the reason for this is that the Army's detailed records of Clay's correspondence remained unavailable until declassified and published by Jean Edward Smith in 1974: see his introductory remarks, *Clay Papers*, xxv–xxxi. But part also reflected Clay's loyalty to the Army and the Roosevelt and Truman administrations, which caused him to downplay publicly his policy disagreements with Washington. Influential early accounts tended to focus heavily on bureaucratic infighting in Washington and to downplay the significance of the occupation government Clay headed in Germany: John Gimbel, *American Occupation Policy in Germany, 1945–1949* (Stanford, CA: Stanford University Press, 1968); John Gimbel, *The Origins of the Marshall Plan* (Stanford, CA: Stanford University Press, 1976); Edward N. Peterson, *The American Occupation of Germany: Retreat to Victory* (Detroit: Wayne State University Press, 1978). In addition to Smith's biography, for a more positive assessment of Clay's role see John H. Backer, *Winds of History: The German Years of Lucius DuBignon Clay* (New York: Van Nostrand, 1983), and especially Wolfgang Krieger, *General Lucius Clay und die amerikanische Deutschlandpolitik 1945–1949* (Stuttgart: Klett-Cotta, 1987). Krieger's exhaustively researched work (with a useful bibliography, 531–52), which is focused on the diplomatic relationships between the occupying powers, claims to address "systematically for the first time" the question of Clay's personal impact on American policy toward occupied Germany – that is, whether the "cliché" of Clay as "proconsul" is actually true (20); though he does not say so in so many words, the answer appears to be a decided yes.

well-connected director of the Office of War Mobilization and Reconversion, with sweeping responsibility for all wartime military production.[4]

This step provoked some criticism of the administration at the time for militarizing defense policy-making in Washington. As Byrnes later told Roosevelt, however, "I... obtained his assignment to my office, because, after dealing with officials of all the departments, I found no man more capable than Clay and no army officer who had as clear an understanding of the point of view of the civilian."[5] Byrnes, soon to be appointed secretary of state, would be a key ally of Clay's as the proconsul set out to navigate the shoals of the Washington bureaucracy. The sentiment was shared by others as well. According to Robert Murphy, Clay's political adviser in Berlin: "Nobody was more devoted to the Army than Clay, but he deliberately organized a predominantly civilian administration in Germany. Of all the Army officers I have worked with, none has matched Clay's respect for the civilian viewpoint, none has revealed more talent for true statesmanship."[6] Though he could be arrogant and opinionated and was a hard man to get to know, as a recent historian has put it, the general's "penetrating intelligence, his cleverness, the brilliant way he had of dealing publicly with difficult questions, his amazing ability to clarify complex connections, his enormous memory for facts and numbers – all this impressed key members of Congress as much as his colleagues, his political opponents, and journalists. There are innumerable written and oral testimonies to this. Hardly anyone was not affected by his intelligence and charm."[7]

Indeed, one of the earliest issues Clay had to grapple with was the relationship of the occupation authority to the Army chain of command in Europe. Clay had to fight to ensure that he would report directly to Eisenhower as an independent deputy rather than through Eisenhower's chief of staff or the Army command reporting to him (Eisenhower himself reported directly to the Secretary of War). This was a particularly sensitive issue because the chief of staff, General Walter Bedell Smith, had coveted Clay's job for himself.[8] Eisenhower fully supported Clay, although tensions between Clay and the Army staff revived and intensified after Eisenhower's departure, ending only when Clay himself took command of American forces in Europe as the first CINCEUR in March 1947 and received his fourth star.[9] The fundamental point, as Clay

---

[4] Smith's recent biography provides an authoritative account of these early years (chs. 1–13), including extensive material from personal interviews with General Clay prior to his death in 1978. It is surprising how little has been written on Clay's life and achievement overall in comparison with other senior military figures of the war such as MacArthur, Marshall, or Eisenhower. Clay's own memoir, *Decision in Germany* (Garden City, NY: Doubleday, 1950), deals only with his time in Germany, after the modest fashion of that era.

[5] Smith, 190.

[6] Robert D. Murphy, *Diplomat Among Warriors* (Garden City, NY: Doubleday, 1964), as quoted in Smith, 223.

[7] Krieger, 21–22.

[8] Smith, 223–29.

[9] Smith, 396–401.

understood and insisted throughout, is that American military government in Germany was in its essence a political undertaking and therefore something entirely distinct from the traditional Army civil affairs function.

It is important to keep this issue in proper perspective. As early as 1942, the question of how the United States should deal with liberated or conquered territories had been addressed at senior levels of the government. The Army, conscious that it had been ill-prepared to handle post-hostilities issues in World War I, gave careful attention to strengthening its civil affairs capabilities and embedding them at every staff echelon; in particular, a large-scale training effort was initiated. This proved controversial, however, as President Roosevelt himself weighed in strongly on the side of handing the military government mission off to civilians at the earliest opportunity. It was widely felt within his administration that military officers would necessarily lack the array of skills – political, social, economic, technical – needed to perform this mission effectively, and that perceived military necessity would for them tend to trump its requirements. As allied forces began to turn the tide of battle in the fall of 1942 and advance into enemy-held territory, the Army itself was eager to divest itself of these responsibilities, but experience was shortly to show that civilian agencies were simply not equipped to function effectively under such conditions and that the Army would have to play a larger role than previously envisioned. This is not to say that Army civil affairs personnel were necessarily lacking in the appropriate skills. Quite contrary to later practice in the American military, many relatively senior officers at this time had entered the Army directly from civilian life and brought with them a wide array of specialized skills; they included academic economists and social scientists, bankers, civil engineers, agronomists, and many others. But only the Army proved capable of providing an organizational framework and culture that enabled these persons to operate effectively in the field. Still, there remained a tension within the Army itself between its own civil affairs personnel and the senior line officers to whom they reported.[10]

There is every reason to think these difficulties could have been minimized by appropriate civilian oversight and political guidance from Washington. Clay's initial problem was that little such guidance or oversight was forthcoming – and what there was he considered unhelpful and even dangerous. As just indicated, the State Department had been largely marginalized by Roosevelt during the war, and it seems never to have occurred to Clay that he needed to consult anyone in the Department on departing to take up his post. By his own account, moreover, State showed virtually no interest in internal German matters over

---

[10] For an authoritative contemporary survey by a distinguished group of American scholars see Carl J. Friedrich, ed., *American Experiences in Military Government in World War II* (New York: Rinehart, 1948); also valuable, though not dealing with the German (or Japanese) case, is Harry L. Coles and Albert K. Weinberg, *Civil Affairs: Soldiers Become Governors, U.S. Army in World War II: Special Studies* (Washington, DC: United States Army Center for Military History, 1964).

the next several years.[11] The sum of Clay's written guidance – given to him as he boarded his flight to Europe – was a War Department directive, JCS/1067, representing a consensus of Washington agencies, including State. This document took a highly vindictive approach to how the Germans were to be dealt with, reflecting the influence in Washington at the time (it was approved in final form in May 1945) of Secretary of the Treasury Henry Morgenthau, who advocated a radical deindustrialization of the country and other punitive measures designed to keep Germany in a weakened state indefinitely.[12] Above all, the document called on the occupation leadership to exercise no controls over the German economy except what might be necessary to serve the needs of the occupying forces and to prevent "disease and unrest" among the population, while specifically enjoining it from taking steps that would raise German living standards above those in neighboring states. Clay immediately protested these instructions and attempted to have them changed, but to no avail. With the encouragement of Secretary of War Henry Stimson, however, Clay from the beginning worked within the letter of JCS/1067 but in direct opposition to its spirit.[13] At the Potsdam Conference in July 1945, the leaders of the three occupying powers agreed on measures that softened these standards to some degree: Steps were to be taken immediately to restore transportation, enlarge coal production, maximize agricultural output, and repair housing and essential utilities. Clay decided under these circumstances that he could live within his mandate, and would not be held to a rigid interpretation of the more punitive elements of the War Department directive.[14]

In fact, reality on the ground rendered most of these strictures academic. The German economy, which in any case had never fully recovered from the aftereffects of World War I, was by mid-1945 a complete wreck. Apart from unimaginable damage to German cities and industry, the loss of a large swath of prewar Germany's eastern breadbasket to Russia and Poland dealt a crippling blow to agricultural production, while millions of displaced Germans fled these territories for the occupied zones. By the spring of 1946, all of Europe was facing a potentially catastrophic food shortage. In Germany, food rationing in some areas dropped to 1,000 calories a day at the beginning of March.[15] At this point, Clay forcefully intervened with Washington, offering his own resignation – for the first of many times in the course of his tenure – if emergency food

[11] Smith, 17–18, 235.
[12] See Henry J. Morgenthau, *Germany Is Our Problem* (New York: Harper & Bros., 1945), and Warren F. Kimball, *Swords or Ploughshares? The Morgenthau Plan for Defeated Germany 1943–1946* (Philadelphia: Lippincott, 1976).
[13] Smith, 234–36. The document is available in *Foreign Relations of the United States, 1945*, vol. 3, 484 ff.
[14] For a detailed account see John Backer, *Priming the German Economy: American Occupation Policies 1945–1948* (Durham, NC: Duke University Press, 1971), ch. 1.
[15] For a graphic account of the situation on the ground from the German perspective see Giles MacDonogh, *After the Reich: The Brutal History of the Allied Occupation* (New York: Basic Books, 2007).

shipments from the United States were not forthcoming. Also for the first time, Clay couched a policy argument with Washington in terms of rivalry with the Soviets, as the economic situation in the Soviet zone at this time was actually better than that of the Western zones. In any event, he prevailed.[16]

Clay's attitude toward the Germans may be said to have reflected a combination of sentiment and calculation. Though Clay's family was not especially sympathetic to the cause of the Confederacy, his upbringing made him aware enough of the excesses of the Reconstruction governments throughout the Old South after the Civil War, and he went out of his way to avoid any such behavior as a matter of policy as well on a personal level, although not all Americans under his command would follow his example.[17] His fundamental decency and humanity shone through on many occasions. He played a significant role in safeguarding German art treasures for the German people, at a time when the Russians were looting them. He resisted efforts to use German prisoners of war as indentured servants in liberated countries, and he opposed – and single-handedly prevented – the appropriation by American authorities of German scientific and commercial information without due compensation, against the desires of both the War and Commerce Departments. He hewed to a policy of non-fraternization with German officials, not for reasons of image and prestige, like MacArthur, but in order not to compromise their future political effectiveness. Also unlike MacArthur, he was reasonably open with the press, and even permitted some criticism of his own actions in the German media. Moreover, he decided early on to communicate between his headquarters in Berlin and military government field representatives in other parts of the American zone by radio, which the Germans could and did listen in to – a strikingly effective psychological measure. In a similar vein, Clay took the decision on his own – indeed, in the teeth of opposition from his own education advisers – to support the creation of the Free University in Berlin.[18]

All of these actions, of course, can and should be seen not just as humanitarian gestures but as part of a calculated agenda, and one that was largely of his own making. Clay saw earlier and more clearly than any other senior

[16] Smith, 356–63. It is telling that Clay suppressed these resignation threats in his own account of these events.
[17] Of the American occupiers George Kennan would write, with his usual puritan animus: "Each time I had come away with a sense of sheer horror at the spectacle of this horde of my compatriots and their dependents camping in luxury amid the ruins of a shattered national community, ignorant of the past, oblivious to the abundant evidences of present tragedy all around them, inhabiting the same sequestered villas that the Gestapo and SS had just abandoned, and enjoying the same privileges, flaunting their silly supermarket luxuries in the face of a veritable ocean of deprivation, hunger, and wretchedness, setting an example of empty materialism and cultural poverty before a people desperately in need of spiritual and intellectual guidance, taking for granted – as though it were their natural due – a disparity of privilege and comfort between themselves and their German neighbors no smaller than those that had once divided lord and peasant in feudal Germany, which it had been our declared purposes in two world wars to destroy." *Memoirs, 1925–1950* (Boston: Little Brown, 1967), 452; see further Peterson, 90–93.
[18] Smith, 309–22, 331–32, 336–37, 375–76.

official in the American government the importance of treating the Germans with forbearance and of fostering the reemergence of a self-respecting German nation in the heart of Europe with a free and strong economy and under democratic governance. Clay very much shared the New Deal spirit of the occupation authority in Tokyo (if not of MacArthur himself) and was convinced that the essentials of the liberal American order could be transplanted to the defeated Axis autocracies. He was also fully sensitive, however, to the paradox of imposing democracy from above. Yet whereas in MacArthur's case American rule was more direct than it seemed, in Clay's case the reverse, if anything, was true. Clay from the beginning took pains to leave the Germans a certain space for choice and decision. He pushed successfully for local and provincial elections on a timetable that some in Washington as well as his own staff regarded as alarming, with the justification that throwing the Germans into the water was the best way to get them to swim, and he later resisted the considerable pressure emanating from the State Department to guide German deliberations on a new constitution.[19]

But Clay's greatest challenge, to say it again, was in the diplomatic arena. Rehabilitating the German nation required the collaboration of the allied powers in establishing a centralized administration throughout the four occupation zones and in managing the German economy as a single entity. In practice, this required the four powers, meeting as the Allied Control Council (ACC) in Berlin, to arrive at consensus decisions on all key issues concerning intra-German policy. This was not to happen. It is natural in retrospect to assume that the Soviets were the odd man out, and that Clay's experience with them was what shaped his hawkish attitudes during the Berlin airlift crisis of 1948–49. In fact, however, this was not the case. While Soviet behavior was not always predictable or helpful, the USSR in the early occupation period did not seem to have a consistent vision or policy concerning the future of Germany, and for the most part it behaved in a reasonably accommodating way. The real problem during these years was instead France.[20]

The French, under the charismatic and prickly General Charles de Gaulle, were late entrants both militarily and politically to the ranks of the allies and felt little commitment to postwar diplomatic arrangements to which they had not been a party. Above all, France had no desire to reconstitute Germany in anything approaching its prewar form, and it opposed from the beginning

---

[19] Smith, 364–65, 538ff.

[20] For an account of this period from the French perspective see John W. Young, *France, the Cold War and the Western Alliance, 1944–49: French Foreign Policy and Post-war Europe* (New York: St. Martin's, 1990), and William I. Hitchcock, *France Restored: Cold War Diplomacy and the Quest for Leadership in Europe, 1944–1954* (Chapel Hill: University of North Carolina Press, 1998), chs. 1–2. The so-called revisionist school of Cold War historiography, in its eagerness to trace the origins of the Cold War to hysterical American attitudes toward the Soviet Union and communism, has grossly understated the problem the French posed to American policy in Europe at the end of the war. Consider the remarks of Gimbel, *The Origins of the Marshall Plan*, ch. 1.

all efforts to treat the occupied areas as a single economic and administrative entity. When he met with Truman in Washington in August 1945, De Gaulle proposed, contrary to what had been agreed at Potsdam in his absence, that the Rhineland and the Ruhr (the industrial heart of the country) be detached from Germany. In the ACC, the French representative refused to approve the establishment of any centralized administrative machinery for Germany until these French claims were accepted, thus creating an impasse. On returning to Washington in November, Clay found that the State Department was not inclined to put pressure on France, largely out of concern for the domestic political situation there (the Socialists and Communists had made a strong showing in elections in October). Back in Berlin, however, Clay took it on himself to tell the ACC that the United States might feel it necessary to proceed with organizing the occupation on a tripartite basis. When the French protested to Washington, they were reassured by Acheson that Clay did not speak for the United States, yet Secretary of State Byrnes sided with the general, his former protégé. This pattern of crossed signals at Foggy Bottom would persist for some time.

De Gaulle resigned abruptly as head of France's provisional government in January 1946, frustrated by the strength of the domestic left, and for a moment it seemed that the Communists might take power, but a coalition government was eventually formed under a moderate Socialist politician, Félix Gouin. The French position on Germany remained unchanged, however; and the State Department continued to press for accommodating their insistence on an internationalization of the Ruhr. In April, increasingly concerned that the German Communists were making political headway by exploiting this situation, Clay proposed to Washington that wheat shipments to the French zone as well as to France itself be halted, and in response to a request from Byrnes, he sent a lengthy memorandum to Washington laying out the case against the French position on the Ruhr.

It is possible, however, to overstate Clay's difficulties with the State Department over French policy. In May, when Clay took the step of ending the dismantlement of plants in the American zone for purposes of reparations, citing the failure of the ACC to agree on a common regime of imports and exports for Germany as mandated at Potsdam, his move has been understood by some scholars as a unilateral measure directed against the French. In reality, however, the Russians were the real target. Clay's action was not only authorized in advance by Secretary Byrnes, but it was actually supported by the French representatives to the ACC in a meeting in late April; the intention, as Byrnes put it at the time, was to "flush out" Soviet resistance to the terms of the Potsdam agreement. This reflected the sharp deterioration in relations between the United States and the USSR in the early spring of 1946, a result of Soviet expansionist pressures against Turkey and Iran and the consolidation of the Soviet grip over Eastern Europe. Byrnes was the key figure here. The Secretary had never been strongly committed to the Potsdam formula of unified four-power control of occupied Germany, and there is reason to believe that by April 1946 he had privately abandoned it as a realistic or indeed desirable objective of American policy. At the same time, it provided valuable political leverage to use against the Soviets. Byrnes thus seems to have played a deep diplomatic game on the whole issue of Potsdam. Indeed, it is not clear that Clay was entirely privy to this game, in spite of his close personal relationship with the Secretary.[21]

The French elections in June, which returned a centrist government under Premier Georges Bidault, changed the dynamic of allied relations. This was not because of any lessening of French intransigeance, but because the Soviets, relieved of any immediate concern over the electoral prospects of the French left, suddenly shifted their line on Germany. In a major speech on July 10, Molotov, the Soviet foreign minister, made a powerful case for a united and prosperous Germany, implicitly criticizing both the French and American proponents of the Morgenthau Plan. The speech was widely reported in Germany and had a dramatic effect on public opinion. Clay immediately recognized that the United States had to respond and, with the encouragement of Byrnes, drafted a new statement of occupation policy that was intended to supersede JCS/1067. This document stressed the importance of German economic recovery, political self-government on democratic lines, and the eventual acceptance of a united Germany in the United Nations, and it openly rejected the French position on the Rhineland and the Ruhr. Although not breaking dramatically with U.S. policy on the ground as interpreted and implemented by Clay, the document was not well received in Washington. Acheson, fearing a united Germany would complicate U.S. relations with France, decided the State Department would do its own study of the question, and Clay was informed that a high-level team would be coming to discuss occupation policy with his staff. In August, Clay received explicit instructions from the War Department that he was not to publish his statement.

Clay bitterly protested these decisions and again toyed with the possibility of resignation. Instead, however, the general decided to play his trump card. Byrnes was then in Paris for ongoing negotiations among the allied foreign ministers; Clay visited him there, made his case, and won the secretary's complete support. What is more, he persuaded Byrnes to make the same case in a major public speech, drafted (as it happens, by John Kenneth Galbraith) and duly delivered at Stuttgart on September 15 with suitable Washington clearance. "It is the view of the American government," Byrnes declared in this speech, "that the German people, throughout Germany and under proper safeguards, should now be given the primary responsibility for the running of their own affairs." At Clay's suggestion, Byrnes added a comment – the general later claimed, no doubt correctly, that it was the most important thing in the speech

---

[21] See on all this Marc Trachtenberg, *A Constructed Peace: The Making of the European Settlement, 1945–1963* (Princeton, NJ: Princeton University Press, 1999), 45–51, against the interpretation of Gimbel, *The American Occupation of Germany*, 57–61, accepted by Smith, 350, among many others.

for its immediate political impact – pledging that American troops would stay in Germany as long as those of any other power. Byrnes was unable to clear this comment with Truman in spite of repeated efforts to reach the president but went ahead with it anyway. The speech was widely publicized and warmly received in Germany and throughout Europe.[22]

But this triumph for Clay hardly ended his problems with the State Department or, for that matter, the Army. Clay was insistent on reviving German political life as soon as feasible, and in the summer and fall of 1946 he pressed the authorities of the German *Länder* (states) in the American zone to draft new constitutions. The Army command in Europe complained to the War Department in this connection that the Germans were showing "increasing disregard for Allied authority" and were lacking in "democratic spirit;" the State Department, on the other hand, on reviewing the proposed texts of these constitutions, sought detailed changes to make them conform more closely to the American political model. Clay refused to impose any such changes by American fiat, insisting that doing so would fatally compromise a process in which the renascent German political elite was by now heavily invested. Clay again carried the day, and by early December the constitutions of the *Länder* were ratified in popular referendums by overwhelming margins.[23]

Clay's difficulties with the Army command in Frankfurt (U.S. Forces in the European Theater, or USFET) to which he was nominally subordinated ceased in March 1947 when the Army, with Eisenhower's strong support, appointed the general overall commander of U.S. forces in Europe (now renamed European Command), awarding him a fourth star in the process. But his problems with the State Department were on the verge of worsening. In January, Secretary Byrnes abruptly resigned when it became clear that he no longer enjoyed Truman's confidence; he was replaced by General George C. Marshall, at the time a special envoy to China. Truman's unhappiness with Byrnes had a large personal and political component, but it also reflected the growing unpopularity in Washington of Byrnes' relatively relaxed view of the possibilities of cooperation with the Soviet Union. Within the State Department itself, Byrnes had clashed repeatedly with senior officials such as Acheson and Kennan over related issues. Moreover, the political winds had shifted with the strong showing of the Republicans in congressional elections in the fall of 1946 (they now controlled both houses). Clay had never been close to Marshall, and the extent of his isolation became apparent in March 1947, when the Secretary arrived in Berlin on his way to a meeting of the foreign ministers of the former allies in Moscow. In Marshall's entourage was John Foster Dulles, Washington lawyer and Republican foreign policy expert (and future secretary of state under Eisenhower), who was brought along to ensure bipartisan support for

---

[22] Smith, 384–89; cf. Krieger, 160–65. As Smith notes, Clay completely omits these internal policy fights in his account of these events in his memoirs.

[23] Smith, 389–92. Clay's nuanced understanding of these complex political issues is apparent from *Clay Papers*, 270–71.

the administration. In the course of discussions between Clay and the delegation, Dulles, echoing the anti-Communist line of congressional Republicans, made a forceful case against a reunited Germany on the grounds that it could not be reliably held for the West and would drive the French into the arms of the Communist Party. In addition, he urged that the United States accede to French wishes and internationalize the Ruhr. Clay responded with some sharpness that it was Germany not France that was critical to the future of Europe, and that failure to proceed with reunification, and above all the detachment of the Ruhr from Germany, would deeply alienate the Germans and risk bringing the Communists to power there. Marshall made clear that he supported Dulles' view. In his eyes, Clay's obstinate defense of quadripartite cooperation was a sign of "localitis" – of a failure to see the larger picture of the global Communist threat.[24]

Clay's confrontation with Dulles and, through him, Marshall and the State Department continued and came to a head in Moscow, where his presence was belatedly requested by Marshall. Clay and Dulles got into a shouting match there when the latter attempted to limit Clay's authority to make commitments on behalf of the United States in a working committee of the four occupation chiefs. Clay did succeed, however, in keeping the issue of internationalization of the Ruhr off the conference agenda. "I was worried," Clay would say later, "that Marshall and Dulles were going to submerge our interests to those of France, and I was determined to prevent it."[25] Had he not done so, the American position in Germany and in Europe more broadly might well have been seriously compromised. In any event, Marshall soon had second thoughts, and the Ruhr issue would remain a dead letter.

The Moscow conference marked a clear shift in overall American policy toward Germany. Clay was afterwards instructed by Marshall to shelve indefinitely the prospect of four-power cooperation and to concentrate instead on working with the British to integrate the economies of the zones controlled by the two allies and increase industrial production. The Anglo-Saxon "bizone" (or Bizonia, as it was sometimes referred to), formally established in the fall of 1946, now took on a greater political coloration, as it became clear that the Ruhr (in the British zone) would not enjoy a special international status but instead would form the core of an embryonic West German state. Clay had by no means opposed the bizonal arrangement and fell readily in step with the new direction of things. In July, the general received a new JCS directive that incorporated his own earlier policy messages to Washington and Byrnes' Stuttgart speech, and made clear that the priority henceforth would be on the revival of Germany's economy. This directive stated that "your authority as Military Governor will be broadly construed" and instructed Clay to take

[24] Smith, 410–18. See also John Foster Dulles, *War or Peace* (New York: MacMillan, 1957), 102–03.
[25] Smith, 418–20.

whatever action he deemed "appropriate or desirable to attain your government's objectives in Germany or to meet military exigencies."

These words notwithstanding, however, Clay's problems with the French and the State Department were not yet done. The general was also told at this time that the agreement on industrial production that he had worked out with his British counterpart, General Brian Robertson, had to be put on hold owing to French sensitivities; it soon emerged that Marshall had personally assured (now Foreign Minister) Bidault that France would have a say in any such measure. Clay's response again was to submit his resignation. The threat was taken seriously in Washington, and Eisenhower intervened personally to convince the general to remain in place. A joint message from Marshall and Secretary of War Kenneth Royall confirmed to Clay that American policy supported the Anglo-American agreement on levels of industry and that no other country would have a vote or veto in the matter. Unfortunately, the State Department neglected to inform the French of this, and when Royall announced the policy publicly during a trip to Berlin at the beginning of August, a diplomatic brouhaha erupted, handing Clay's enemies in the Department yet another opportunity to revisit the issue. The result was a hastily scheduled tripartite conference in London, chaired by Lewis Douglas, the American ambassador to Great Britain. Clay was appalled at the maneuverings of the State Department leadership and resented his status as adviser to Douglas, and agreed to attend only reluctantly. At the five-day meeting, there was palpable tension between Clay and the American diplomats present; as one is reported to have said, "Whenever we go into a conference about Germany, we first have to negotiate a treaty with General Clay."[26] In the end, however, the result was surprisingly favorable to Clay. The Clay–Robertson agreement was essentially reaffirmed, with some face-saving concessions to the French. In fact, the French were able to show new flexibility after the departure of the Communists from the government in May, thus freeing Bidault to indulge more freely his own pro-allied instincts.[27]

By the end of 1947, the break between the three Western allies and the Soviets was virtually complete. At a session of the Council of Foreign Ministers in London in late November and early December, further progress on the future of Germany and Austria proved impossible, and in the face of abusive haranguing by Molotov, Marshall abruptly terminated what would prove to be its final meeting. In December, too, President Truman submitted to Congress the Marshall Plan, signaling the commitment of the United States to rebuilding the shattered economies of Europe as a bulwark against the growing threat posed by international communism. Clay himself accepted this new reality more easily than might be supposed. Indeed, as early as October, at a press conference in Berlin, the general was so outspokenly critical of the Soviets and communism that he was cautioned by his superiors in the Department of

[26] Smith, 441.
[27] Trachtenberg, 72–73.

the Army (as the War Department was now called). In response, Clay stated: "We are engaged in political warfare and we might as well recognize it now. Under these conditions we cannot wait for Washington's approval when our adversaries speak to the German public.... I shall not let Soviet attacks go unanswered and have both our press and the German people believe that we are afraid to answer. Do not worry that I will become a war monger."[28] These remarks were interpreted at the time as indicating a major change in American policy. While denying this, Clay was hardly apologetic. In fact, Clay's sensitivity to the requirements of psychological or political warfare is an underappreciated factor in the success of his proconsular leadership from its earliest days through the great test of the Berlin crisis.

Given Clay's deteriorating relationship with the State Department under Marshall, it is not surprising that senior officials in the department – particularly Robert Lovett, the new under secretary, and George Kennan, director of the Policy Planning Staff – wanted to see him replaced. Marshall himself was unhappy with Clay's independence and his closeness to Eisenhower, then Army chief of staff. Moreover, the secretary had his own candidate: Lieutenant General Walter Bedell Smith, then the American ambassador to Russia. Smith, perhaps Marshall's closest friend in the Army, was tired of Moscow and had long coveted Clay's job and the fourth star it would bring him. In January 1948, it was announced in Washington that the State Department would take over responsibility for the occupation of Germany in June, while Bedell Smith would be installed as the new military governor. Clay was taken totally by surprise by this move, which he first learned about through press accounts. Clay himself had repeatedly offered to turn over his responsibilities to the State Department, but the way in which the matter was handled was humiliating, suggesting as it did that he had actually been fired. Ever the loyal soldier, however, Clay did not protest and began to pack for his return to Washington. Fate intervened, however, in the form of James Byrnes, the former secretary of state and wily political operative, who – entirely without Clay's knowledge – used his considerable clout in the Senate to lobby against the confirmation of Bedell Smith as Clay's replacement. Marshall, who apparently did not realize that the position was subject to senatorial confirmation, declined to fight for Smith and eventually reversed course on the State Department's occupation role as well.[29] Instead, Clay was to remain as military governor for the indefinite future and would continue reporting through Army channels.

This obscure Washington intrigue may well have affected the course of the entire Cold War. It ensured that Clay would remain at the helm in Germany at just the time when the Soviets began to put pressure on the anomalous allied presence in Berlin, thus initiating a crisis of monumental proportions that carried a very real threat of military hostilities and even full-scale war

---

[28] *Clay Papers*, 459–60, 463–64.
[29] Smith, 455–60. All of this was a well-kept secret at the time; Clay himself only became aware of it in the course of discussions with Byrnes in the 1950s.

between the USSR and the Western powers. That Clay's leadership during the Berlin crisis was decisive in ensuring its successful outcome seems a virtual certainty. It was unarguably his finest hour.[30]

The Berlin crisis of 1948–49 was a direct consequence of the breakdown of four-power cooperation over German issues at the end of 1947, and resulting moves by the Western allies thereafter to proceed with the establishment of a friendly German government in the three western zones. This outcome was by no means a foregone conclusion, however, as the French continued to dither over the terms of joining the Anglo-American bizone, and the Soviets decided to take advantage of this situation to sow further dissension among the Western powers and thereby prevent or delay the emergence of a West German state. Accordingly, as early as January 1948, they began to interfere with the free movement of rail traffic between the American and British zones and the western sectors of Berlin, in what amounted to a campaign of prolonged psychological warfare.

The allied presence in Berlin was, to say the least, precarious. A small garrison of some 15,000 troops provided a symbolic military presence, but was surrounded by superior Soviet forces and dependent on Soviet goodwill for access to local supplies of food, water, fuel, and other essentials, as indeed were the 2.2 million Germans living in the western part of the city. Unfettered access to Berlin for the Western powers by air had been formally granted by the Soviets in September 1945, but access by road and rail rested only on an oral agreement between Clay and his Soviet counterpart of June of that year; Clay himself later admitted he had made a mistake in not insisting on a written document.[31] In any case, the Soviets had honored the agreement in practice in the past, and it was only too clear that even apparently minor or technical changes in their behavior in this regard were politically motivated and constituted a serious challenge. For that matter, the Soviets signaled their intentions through an escalating propaganda war, first in their diplomatic dealings with the Western powers in Germany (in the Allied Control Council and the Kommandatura, the four-power headquarters in Berlin) and then in the Soviet-controlled press. Alarmist speculation about the situation soon began to appear in the wider European and American press, threatening to force the Western governments to play out what seemed an increasingly weak hand.

Clay and his political adviser, Robert Murphy, had warned Washington repeatedly of the likelihood of increased Soviet pressure on Berlin and sought to stiffen what they perceived as a lack of resolve on the part of the Truman

---

[30] For the Berlin crisis as a whole see Krieger, 345–400, as well as Avi Shlaim, *The United States and the Berlin Blockade, 1948–1949: A Study in Crisis Decisionmaking* (Berkeley: University of California Press, 1983).

[31] On the other hand, it is far from clear that the Soviets would have agreed to formalizing such an understanding in writing. See the detailed discussion of this episode in Daniel J. Nelson, *Wartime Origins of the Berlin Dilemma* (University: University of Alabama Press, 1978), 130–35.

administration to stand firm on the issue. Clay himself consistently viewed Soviet actions as directed not against Berlin as such but against the Western (and more particularly American) position in Europe. In his eyes, the threat was a political rather than a military one, and he was convinced that the Russians neither wanted nor expected the crisis to lead to war and would back down if effectively challenged. Others in Washington were not so sure, and eventual withdrawal from Berlin began to seem to some the inevitable course of action. In mid-March, responding to congressional inquiries, General J. Lawton Collins, the Army vice chief of staff, sought Clay's opinion of a possible withdrawal of military dependents from the city. Clay forcefully argued that such a move, though perhaps justifiable from a military point of view, would be catastrophic in its political impact, particularly on the Germans living in the western sector.[32]

It needs to be remembered that Clay at this point not only headed the occupation but was commander in chief of the American military forces in Germany and throughout Europe. Although (to say it again) he did not consider the outbreak of war with the Soviet Union at all likely,[33] some contingency planning was only prudent, and the general seems to have operated here without particular reference to Washington. As early as the last week in March, Colonel Frank Howley, commandant of the Berlin garrison, drew up his own plan for emergency actions to be taken in the event of a Soviet blockade, while Clay's air commander, the redoubtable Lieutenant General Curtis LeMay (later to be head of the Strategic Air Command), took steps to reduce the vulnerability of the principal U.S. supply line through the port of Bremerhaven. Remarkably, LeMay apparently worked out an informal – indeed, virtually clandestine – arrangement with the chiefs of the French and Belgian air forces for the use of airfields in their own territory, safely removed from the Soviets' reach. There can be little question that Clay authorized these measures, in spite of ongoing diplomatic difficulties with the French, and it seems that no one in Washington was ever informed of them. LeMay later called it his "private little NATO"– a precursor to what within a year would become a full-fledged military alliance between the United States and Western Europe.[34]

---

[32] Smith, 468–70.

[33] Clay did not help himself with his Washington superiors, however, when he said the following in a cable to Lieutenant General Stephen L. Chamberlin, head of Army intelligence, on March 5: "For many months, based on logical analysis, I have felt and held that war was unlikely for at least ten years. Within the last few weeks, I have felt a subtle change in Soviet attitude which I cannot define but which now gives me a feeling that it may come with dramatic suddenness." *Clay Papers*, 568–69. This was immediately leaked to the press and had a significant impact on American public opinion as well as on the thinking of the military itself, especially then Army chief of staff General Omar Bradley; and it features prominently in many accounts of the origins of the Cold War. In fact, however, the statement was disingenuous: In a rare fit of poor judgment, Clay had allowed himself to be used in a bureaucratic maneuver to help the Army persuade Congress to reinstitute the draft. For the entire episode see Smith, 466–68.

[34] Curtis E. LeMay, *Mission with LeMay: My Story* (New York: Doubleday, 1965), 412–13, cited in Shlaim, 120–21.

The Berlin situation worsened markedly at the end of March, when the Soviets announced a new set of regulations affecting military rail traffic to Berlin, including notably a right of Soviet inspectors to board allied trains. Clay secured agreement from the Army leadership that all trains should proceed at his discretion and that the Soviets should under no circumstances be permitted to board them, but he chafed at instructions that he was not to increase the number of armed guards or allow them to open fire unless fired upon. On April 1, the Russians made good on these threats, stopping trains from both the American and British sectors when their commanders refused to allow inspectors on board. At this juncture, Bradley and Royall again raised the issue of evacuation of dependents from the city. In a lengthy teleconference, Clay again strongly opposed such a move. But Clay's position on the matter was nuanced. Reduction of American personnel in Berlin made sense in several respects – it meant fewer mouths to feed in the event of a blockade, and many of the jobs supporting the Allied Control Commission were becoming superfluous in any case. Nor would it do to compel dependents to remain if they felt in danger, in effect making them hostages to Soviet misbehavior and gravely damaging morale. The general's solution was to allow any dependents who wished to depart but require that spouses accompany them. (Not surprisingly, as it turned out, no one left.) At the same time, Clay did nothing to stop the normal rotation of personnel from Berlin back to the American zone, and new assignments to Berlin were limited to officers without dependents. This approach, a combination of firmness and flexibility, was characteristic of Clay's leadership throughout. But it was not enough to reassure Washington.[35]

Indeed, the full extent of the queasiness in Washington was only apparent in another teleconference with Bradley on April 10, following a further escalation in Soviet pressure on rail traffic into Berlin the day before. Bradley told Clay: "We doubt whether our people are prepared to start a war in order to maintain our position in Berlin and Vienna," and suggested that the United States announce a unilateral withdrawal rather than allow itself to be forced out, so as to "minimize the loss of prestige." Clay's response deserves to be quoted at length:

We have lost Czechoslovakia. We have lost Finland. Norway is threatened. We retreat from Berlin.... There is no saving of prestige by setting up in Frankfurt that is not already discounted. After Berlin will come western Germany, and our position there is relatively no greater and our position no more tenable than Berlin. If we mean to hold Europe against communism, we must not budge. We can take humiliation and pressure short of war in Berlin without losing face. If we move, our position in Europe is threatened. If America does not know this, does not believe that the issue is cast now, then it never will and communism will run rampant."[36]

---

35 In a move that is perhaps understandable but does little credit to him, Bradley quietly arranged for his own son-in-law, an Air Force officer then stationed in Berlin, to be transferred to a desk job in the Pentagon. Smith, 475.

36 *Clay Papers*, 621–25.

Clay's stand seems to have had a temporary calming effect, but several weeks later it was the State Department's turn. At the behest of Secretary Marshall (following a suggestion of Kennan), Bedell Smith on May 4 approached Molotov in Moscow with the conciliatory message that "as far as the U.S.A. is concerned, the door is wide open for full discussion and the composing of our differences." In response, the Soviets provided the press an edited version of the statement that gave the impression the United States was proposing new high-level talks. The apparent weakness on display in all this enraged Clay and produced a storm of protest from the West Europeans, who had not been consulted.[37]

The position of the British and French at this juncture was critical, as the principal target of Soviet actions in Berlin was less the United States than allied unity on German issues, and above all their emerging intention to create a West German government. Throughout this period, Clay enjoyed the strong support of British foreign minister Ernest Bevin, and it was actually Bevin who delivered, in a speech in early May, the first clear statement by any allied leader of the emerging hard line on Berlin. But the French were still a problem. Improbably, given his own frequently rocky relationship with their political leadership, it was Clay himself who achieved the decisive breakthrough on this front. In early April, he met informally in Berlin with Maurice Couve de Murville, the senior French diplomat handling German issues, at the latter's suggestion, to review the state of play in ongoing allied negotiations over the future of Germany. Cutting through the minutiae that had bogged down these discussions, Clay got Couve de Murville to agree to a brief, eight-point statement of principles, including the election of a constituent assembly no later than the beginning of September, the drafting of a West German constitution by that assembly, and the election of a new government following ratification of the constitution. Pending all that, French occupation policies in their zone would be brought into line with those of the bizone, particularly in the area of currency reform and export–import policy. Couve de Murville sold this document to his government on his return to Paris, and it became the basis for the final communiqué of the London conference on June 6.[38]

But that was not quite the end of the story. The London agreements had to be ratified by the French National Assembly, and it was clear the vote there was going to be close, with both the Communists and the Gaullists being in vocal opposition. The Socialist-led Bidault government therefore engaged in some eleventh-hour maneuvering to soften the terms of the agreements for public consumption. Bevin resisted all such concessions and, indeed, used his influence within the international labor movement to bring pressure to bear on the French Socialists to go along, but Washington again appeared to develop cold feet – thus prompting Clay's jibe about crossing the Rubicon. In the end, though, the Bidault government survived – if narrowly (by fourteen votes) – a no-confidence

37 Smith, 476–78; Shlaim, 144–46.
38 Smith, 478–80.

motion on the issue, and Clay was able to secure French cooperation on the immediate issue of currency reform in separate discussions in Berlin.

Currency reform in the three western sectors took effect on June 21. Clay had foreseen for some time that this move would escalate matters with the Soviets, and he was right. Berlin had not been included in the allied move, on the hope that a single currency under quadripartite control could still be agreed upon there, but the Soviets made it known at once that they planned to introduce a single currency for Berlin under their own control. This step was rejected by the allies, who were supported in this by the Berliners themselves (courageously, the City Assembly voted on the matter at a site within the Soviet zone and in the teeth of physical intimidation by the Russians); it would have made the allied position in Berlin completely untenable. Clay himself then (June 23) took the final step of placing the new West Mark in circulation in the three western sectors.[39] On the morning of June 24, the Soviets responded by cutting the last rail link to the city. Shortly thereafter, they shut down all road and canal traffic. Thus began the Berlin blockade proper.

While the Soviet move was certainly not a complete surprise, the United States was not adequately prepared for it, and no coherent response had been worked out at the top levels of the administration. As George Kennan later put it, "No one was sure, as yet, how the Russian move could be countered or whether it could be successfully countered at all. The situation was dark and full of danger."[40] The Russians, for their part, grasped for the psychological advantage by launching an immediate diplomatic overture calling for a return to quadripartite control of Germany, the formation of a German government, a peace treaty, and the withdrawal of all foreign forces from Germany soon thereafter. By contrast, the Washington bureaucracy could do no better at the outset than a temporizing "no comment." It was therefore left to Clay, or rather to Clay and his intemperate subordinate, Colonel Frank ("Howling Mad") Howley, to deliver the first public response to the Soviet moves. In a radio broadcast on the afternoon of the 24th, the commander of the Berlin garrison stated baldly: "We are not getting out of Berlin.... The American people will not stand by and allow the German people to starve." Speaking directly to the Russians, the colonel then added: "We have heard a lot about your military intentions.... If you do try to come into our sector, you better be well prepared. We are ready for you."[41] Later that day, Clay himself told

---

[39] Clay was supported fully in this by Robertson, but the French only reluctantly acquiesced. Clay failed to clear this very important decision with Washington – probably because he feared that the right answer would not be immediately forthcoming. Shlaim, 158–61.

[40] Kennan, 421.

[41] Howley later admitted his comments were off the reservation but justified them by saying: "when you are faced with a long-planned attempt to create absolute chaos you can't wait until the issue goes all the way up to Pennsylvania Avenue for a decision. You have got to make an appraisal of the determination of the American people yourself." Frank Howley, *Berlin Command* (New York: Putnam's, 1950), 200. There is little reason to suppose Clay himself would have seriously disagreed with this sentiment.

reporters that the Soviets "cannot drive us out by an action short of war as far as we are concerned." Since no decision had in fact been made to stay in Berlin, Washington was surprised at press reports of these remarks and disturbed particularly by the general's reference to the possibility of war. It is difficult to believe that these public interventions were not carefully calculated on Clay's part.[42]

Clay's initial preferred response to the blockade was to challenge the Soviets on the ground by sending a significant American armored force to convoy a column of supply trucks into the city. This was an idea he had floated to Bradley as early as the beginning of April.[43] Clay thought such a move would call what he was convinced was a bluff: He continued to believe the Soviets were not looking to start a war, and he was surely on strong ground given the apparent absence of intelligence indicating any serious Soviet preparations for combat in the Soviet zone or elsewhere in the theater. Nevertheless, it was felt – not only in Washington but by the otherwise hawkish British – that the risks of such a move were simply too great, and moreover that it would be too easy to counter by various forms of obstruction short of an armed confrontation. There was, however, another alternative. Resupply of Berlin from the air was not only firmly established as an allied right, but it would be difficult or impossible for the Soviets to counter by passive measures.[44]

Clay has of course been immortalized by the airlift that was to sustain the western sectors of Berlin for almost eighteen months and force the Soviets to admit defeat at a crucial juncture of the Cold War. In fact, though, the idea of the airlift was not Clay's; it originated with the British. General Robertson, the military governor of the British zone, had arranged for the Royal Air Force to begin delivering supplies to the British garrison on June 25, and quickly persuaded Clay that a large-scale resupply operation was in fact feasible. In spite of the limited number of American transport planes then available in the theater (mostly vintage C-47s, with a capacity of only two and a half tons), Clay ordered General LeMay to devote them entirely to the Berlin mission, and the first arrived with food supplies for the civilian population on the morning of June 26. Clay's first order of business was to convince the Berliners themselves that an airlift would work. Calling in the mayor of Berlin, Ernst Reuter, Clay made clear to him that while he was confident that sufficient food could be provided for the population, there would undoubtedly be shortages of fuel and electricity, and he needed to know whether the Berliners could tolerate this sort of hardship. Reuter responded: "General, I can assure you, and I do assure you, that the Berliners will take it."[45]

[42] *Clay Papers*, 701; Shlaim, 199–200.

[43] Ibid., 607.

[44] Some concerns were expressed in the Pentagon over the possibility of the Soviets using barrage balloons to interfere with the safe operation of aircraft flying into the city. Clay was actually instructed at one point not to shoot down such balloons, but he refused to agree and the matter was dropped (Smith, 510).

[45] Smith, 501–02.

It is altogether characteristic of Clay that he was more concerned with the Germans at this moment than with the American government. Clay's decision to go ahead with the airlift was in fact taken without any consultation with Washington. And the reason for this was plainly not that Clay thought the support of his superiors in Washington could be taken for granted; quite the opposite. This is evident in the revealing response he gave to a reporter who asked whether it was true that Washington had told him he could have as many planes as he needed. Clay said: "I don't doubt that someone in Washington would have said something of the sort to me. But I didn't ask Washington. I acted first. I began the airlift with what I had, because I had to first prove to Washington that it was possible. Once I'd proved it, it was no longer hard to get help."[46] In fact, Washington remained cautious and irresolute for several more days, in spite of public and diplomatic pressure from Bevin and the British. On June 28, President Truman himself had to intervene in a meeting with his senior advisers to quell further talk of withdrawal and affirm an American commitment to remaining in Berlin.[47]

Even then, Clay's path was hardly smooth. Pessimism prevailed in official Washington over the prospects for success of the airlift. In July, the National Security Council was informed that the Air Force believed the airlift was "doomed to failure," a view shared by Under Secretary of State Robert Lovett as well as James Forrestal, the new Secretary of Defense, who sought to have the president revisit the issue. A renewed effort by Clay to gain permission to send an armored convoy into Berlin was once again rebuffed by Marshall, supported in this by the president. Even Robertson, inspirer of the airlift idea, became convinced the airlift could not be sustained through the winter – much to the disgust of Bevin, who remained Clay's only stalwart ally. In this atmosphere, the idea of a renewal of negotiations with the Soviets gathered momentum, in spite of resistance from Clay and Bevin, and at the beginning of August representatives of the three Western powers opened talks with Stalin in Moscow.

Stalin told this delegation that the Soviets were prepared to lift the blockade provided the three powers accepted the use of Soviet currency in Berlin. Walter Bedell Smith, the American representative, indicated willingness to accept this deal, but without insisting on any form of Western control over this currency. When Clay and Bevin vociferously objected, the delegation backed away from this position, and the Soviets eventually withdrew their initial offer. Although these talks dragged on through the end of August, it was evident that the Soviets were playing for time, and that they too were convinced that the airlift could not supply Berlin over the winter. Finally, the allies reached an agreement in principle with Moscow concerning quadripartite control of a currency regime for Berlin, but attempts to work out details of this agreement by Clay and his counterparts in further talks in Berlin proved futile.[48]

[46] Curt Riess, *The Berlin Story* (New York: Dial Press, 1952), 164–65, cited in Shlaim, 206.
[47] For a detailed account see Shlaim, 207–22.
[48] Smith, 512–18.

Washington and Moscow alike misjudged the situation in two key respects: They underestimated the potential of the airlift itself, and they ignored the critical contribution of the Berliners themselves and their will to resist Soviet domination. In order to expand the capacity of the air terminals in the western sectors, Clay organized an army of 30,000 German volunteers to construct a new airport from scratch in a mere two months (the current international airport for Berlin at Tegel). Further evidence of the mood of the population appeared when a crowd of some 300,000 gathered near the Brandenburg Gate to listen to speeches by Reuter and other political leaders denouncing Soviet behavior; part of the crowd later entered the Soviet sector and burned a Russian flag, and several demonstrators were killed when Soviet guards opened fire on them.[49] As for the airlift itself, Clay, with the U.S. Air Force and support from the British, performed virtually unimaginable feats of logistic and operational virtuosity.[50] Yet a key obstacle remained. The success of the airlift depended on the availability of modern transport aircraft more capable than the C-47, particularly the C-54 (DC-4). Clay had received a handful of these; but the Air Force was reluctant to release the sixty or so it held as a strategic reserve in the event of a new war. Clay made his case at a National Security Council meeting in Washington in October, but he received no support from those at the table, above all the Air Force. Fortunately for the general, he had persuaded the one man who mattered: Truman intervened on the spot to overrule the unanimous view of his civilian and military advisers.[51] As Truman later put it in describing this moment: "General Clay placed before us an account not only of the technical achievement of the airlift but also of the effect our action in Berlin had on the German people. They had closed ranks and applied to the task of reconstruction with a new vigor. It had turned them sharply against communism. Germany, which had been waiting passively to see where it should cast its lot for the future, was veering toward the cause of the Western nations."[52]

Even without the C-54s, however, it was increasingly clear by October that the airlift was succeeding. Clay had told Bradley that with these planes he could deliver a satisfactory level of 5,200 tons of supplies per day; yet already on September 18 LeMay and the British were able to land some 7,000 tons in the city. (By March 1949, the daily average was 8,000 tons.) A public opinion poll taken in October showed that 83 percent of Berliners thought the city could be supplied by air for the foreseeable future (as opposed to only

---

[49] Ibid., 517, 522.

[50] For the flavor of these operations from a British perspective see Robert Rodrigo, *Berlin Airlift* (London: Cassell, 1960); a colorful recent account is Richard Reeves, *Daring Young Men: The Heroism and Triumph of the Berlin Airlift, June 1948–May 1949* (New York: Simon & Schuster, 2010).

[51] See Smith, 503–5, for Clay's account of this episode.

[52] Harry Truman, *Years of Trial and Hope* (Garden City, NY: Doubleday, 1956), 130, quoted in Smith, 524.

45 percent in July). On November 1, in a characteristic flourish of psychological warfare, Clay announced that food rations in Berlin would be increased by 20 percent, to a level of 2,000 calories – more than anywhere else in Germany. Increasingly, these facts on the ground were recognized in the American press and began to be acknowledged in official Washington.

All of this notwithstanding, Western policy toward Germany seemed dangerously adrift by early 1949. Not only were the French still dragging their feet on integration of the French zone with the Anglo-American bizone, but Washington itself appeared suddenly unsure of whether it wanted to proceed with the creation of a separate West German government. In November, George Kennan's Policy Planning Staff at the State Department had issued a document, "Program for Germany," that argued against a West German government and advocated a neutralized Germany with all foreign troops removed.[53] This reversal of view on the part of Kennan seems in retrospect little short of bizarre: Both he and Clay had now come to embrace the positions each had criticized in 1947.[54] Nevertheless, Kennan's view gained purchase for a time when Marshall was replaced by Dean Acheson as secretary of state at the beginning of Truman's second administration. But the Pentagon was solidly behind Clay this time, and effectively killed the Kennan proposal by leaking a copy of his memorandum to the *New York Times*. Acheson was subsequently brought around to Clay's view by Robert Murphy, who returned to Washington to head an interdepartmental committee tasked with drafting a new statement of the administration's German policy.

The statement emerging from Murphy's committee in early April was entirely acceptable to the general, and in effect marked the end of the long-running and not infrequently bitter feud between Clay and the State Department. Under Acheson's decisive leadership, the French – the general's other old nemesis – were also brought into line, and agreement on a trizonal arrangement and occupation statute was finally achieved at a meeting of the three Western foreign ministers later that month in London, which also saw the signing of the North American Treaty formalizing the defense relationship between the United States and the democracies of Western Europe.

With the success of the airlift and the demonstrated commitment of the three Western powers to a free West Germany, the blockade of Berlin by the Soviets lost its fundamental purpose, and its termination was only a matter of time. In fact, secret diplomatic contacts between the two sides had been initiated

---

[53] For the text of this document see *Foreign Relations of the United States, 1948*, vol. 2, 1325–38.

[54] Kennan admits there was little sympathy for what came to be called "Plan A" even elsewhere in the State Department. For his perspective on German affairs generally and this episode in particular see *Memoirs*, ch. 18; note especially his retrospective confession of error, 447–48, which (tacitly) acknowledges the superior insight of Clay. At the same time, he allows himself to speak of a "military occupational establishment which I regarded as both politically illiterate and corrupted by the misleading discipline of its own experience" (447).

as early as March 1949, and on May 5 a four-power statement announcing the end of the blockade was released simultaneously in Washington, Paris, London, and Moscow. Ten days later, to an emotional sendoff from a crowd of thousands of Berliners lining his route to the airport, Clay left the city for the United States and an honorable retirement.

7

Vietnam

The ill-starred American intervention in Southeast Asia at the height of the Cold War continues to fade into history as the generation that fought or lived through it departs from the scene. As a parable of the crimes and follies of "imperialism" American-style, though, it retains much of its emotional power in ongoing debates over American intervention in the Middle East and Southwest Asia today, and has to feature prominently in any account of the foreign policy of the United States after World War II. At first sight, however, the war in Vietnam seems a singularly unpromising candidate for a case study in neo-imperial proconsulship. Over the course of the two decades of American engagement in Southeast Asia (1954–75), many senior officials labored in a variety of locations on behalf of a number of U.S. government entities to counter communist advances there, but no single man on the spot ever enjoyed authority over the entire American effort. These included diplomats, military commanders of advisory and later combat units, and a variety of other officials operating out of not only Saigon (South Vietnam) but Vientiane (Laos), Bangkok (Thailand), and Honolulu (headquarters of the U.S. Pacific Command). At times these officials collaborated closely; at other times they operated virtually independently; not infrequently, they fought each other bitterly for control of policy on the ground. Furthermore, it would not be misleading to say that the Vietnam War was for all practical purposes waged directly from Washington – that is to say, that it was micromanaged to a degree that is probably unique in the annals of America's overseas conflicts. Unfortunately, the problems that prevented effective cooperation among different government

---

[1] Signed editorial in the English-language *Times of Vietnam* in August 1963 on the occasion of the appointment of Henry Cabot Lodge as U.S. ambassador to South Vietnam. Anne E. Blair, *Lodge in Vietnam: A Patriot Abroad* (New Haven, CT: Yale University Press, 1995), 22.

agencies in the field were largely replicated at the center – and in fact were fatally aggravated by weak and divided leadership there.

This having been said, closer inspection of the history of the war will show that proconsular leadership was not simply absent. Washington was incapable of managing the war on a day-to-day basis, and considerable initiative if not independent decision was retained by the men on the spot over the course of the conflict. It is rather that such leadership existed in partial or fragmented form, and more in certain periods than others, reflecting changing circumstances and personalities. There was the awkward fact that the military chain of command subordinated the commander of U.S. forces in Vietnam (a three- or four-star Army general) to the commander in chief of the U.S. Pacific Command (a four-star admiral) based in Hawaii, who also controlled air and naval assets that played a direct part in the war. But fragmented leadership was most in evidence at the level of the ambassador and the military commander, the two most senior American officials in the country, whose respective roles and relationship were never clearly established. Some ambassadors barely communicated with their military counterparts, notably Ambassador Henry Cabot Lodge, whose tenure in office at a critical juncture (August 1963 to May 1964) certainly represents the closest approach to a proconsular moment in the history of America's involvement in Vietnam – with results that were to prove little short of calamitous.

Less obvious but not less important were three other factors that further fragmented the American effort in Southeast Asia, at least through its first dozen or so years. The first of these was the split between conventional military operations and the "other war," as it came to be called – the pacification program and the paramilitary, civic, and economic aid and development measures that accompanied it. Only in 1967–68 was the divided command of these two dimensions of the war finally overcome. The second was the fragmentation of diplomatic leadership in the region. The American ambassador in Saigon exercised no control over American policy or operations in Laos, Cambodia, or Thailand, all of which had a significant impact on the course of the war in Vietnam itself. In Laos, the ambassador and the Central Intelligence Agency (CIA) ran their own "secret war" over many years.[2] The international settlement of the three-way Laotian civil war in 1962 – the diplomacy of which was largely driven by a special presidential envoy (Averill Harriman) in the teeth of intense bureaucratic resistance from many quarters in the Departments of State and Defense as well as in the theater – was a disastrous error, contributing perhaps more than anything else to the American failure in Vietnam.[3] Finally, there is the issue of the role of the CIA and its representatives in Saigon. While

---

[2] See notably Jane Hamilton-Merritt, *Tragic Mountains: The Hmong, the Americans, and the Secret Wars for Laos, 1942–1992* (Bloomington: Indiana University Press, 1993).

[3] For this argument see, for example, Norman B. Hannah, *The Key to Failure: Laos and the Vietnam War* (Lanham, MD: Madison Books, 1987), and C. Dale Walton, *The Myth of Inevitable US Defeat in Vietnam* (London: Frank Cass, 2002), ch. 4.

a very great deal is known today about the inner workings of the American bureaucratic machine during the Vietnam era, this is less the case with the CIA, whose official records of those years remain closed. What is reasonably clear at present is that the agency played a very significant operational role in the elite politics of South Vietnam, particularly in the period before the overthrow of President Ngo Dinh Diem in 1963. Of particular interest for our purposes is the part played by the extraordinary Edward Lansdale in the creation of the Diem regime in 1954–55.

The Vietnam War has been the subject of a vast literature and remains in some respects intensely controversial among historians. To survey this literature adequately is not possible here, and it is unnecessary in any case for the purposes of this study, but several points may be made. The dominant narrative in the literature continues to hold that the war was fundamentally unwinnable by the American side, and that American involvement in Vietnam was therefore misguided no matter how strong the rationale behind it – if not from the beginning, certainly with the introduction of U.S. combat forces in 1965. It holds further that the rationale for intervention was in fact weak. American decision-makers, according to this line of argument, were driven by an anti-Communist ideology that blinded them to the realities of the situation and the region, especially the political strength of Vietnamese "nationalism," the indigenous character of the insurgency in the south, the deep unpopularity and lack of effectiveness of the South Vietnamese government, and the historical animosity between Vietnam and China. The strategic stakes at play in Southeast Asia were marginal in any case, yet the American government also grossly exaggerated the communist threat to the region as a whole (the "domino theory").[4]

Both elements of this narrative are questionable. Indeed, they have been questioned increasingly in recent scholarship, reflecting, among other things, much new information deriving from communist sources.[5] As for the strategic stakes at issue, a good case can be made that they were substantial, and that the domino theory was in fact entirely plausible.[6] But leaving aside the question of

---

[4] The following recent studies may be taken as representative of this view: David L. Anderson, *The Vietnam War* (New York: Palgrave Macmillan, 2005); Robert Buzzanco, *Vietnam and the Transformation of American Life* (Malden, MA: Blackwell, 1999); David E. Kaiser, *American Tragedy: Kennedy, Johnson, and the Origins of the Vietnam War* (Cambridge, MA: Harvard University Press, 2000); Frederick Logevall, *Choosing War: The Lost Chance for Peace and the Escalation of the War in Vietnam* (Berkeley: University of California Press, 1999); Robert D. Schulzinger, *A Time for War: The United States and Vietnam, 1941–1975* (New York: Oxford University Press, 1997).

[5] For a review of these debates and the relevant scholarship see Marc Jason Gilbert, ed., *Why the North Won the Vietnam War* (New York: Palgrave Macmillan, 2002), 1–45, and Mark Moyar, *Triumph Forsaken: The Vietnam War, 1954–1965* (Cambridge: Cambridge University Press, 2006), preface.

[6] On the domino theory, see notably Moyar, *Triumph Forsaken*, 375–91. Moyar's work is the most original, detailed, and far-reaching of the "revisionist" accounts of the war. See further William Colby, *Lost Victory: A Firsthand Account of America's Sixteen Year Involvement in*

the rationale for the war, or whether it was worth the cost in blood and treasure, was it really unwinnable? Can it reasonably be maintained that the decisions of individual American officials made and could have made no significant difference in the end in determining the course or outcome of the war?

The massive difficulty with such a view is the fact that American fortunes on the battlefield actually improved dramatically in the latter part of the war. And they did so thanks in substantial part to a change in proconsular leadership in South Vietnam itself. When Ambassador Ellsworth Bunker and General Creighton Abrams assumed the reins of the American effort there in 1967–68, they inaugurated a new era of civil–military partnership and operational competence (much like that in Iraq during the recent Crocker–Petraeus era) and by 1970 had clearly reversed the war's momentum in favor of the United States and its South Vietnamese ally. Indeed, an excellent case can be made that the war was by many measures virtually won by 1973. The final collapse of 1975 is not a reflection on U.S. or South Vietnamese leadership in the field, but rather the result of the domestic political crisis in Washington that led to the implosion of the Nixon administration and the abrupt cutoff of American military assistance to Saigon by the U.S. Congress, which permitted Hanoi to launch a full-scale conventional assault on the South without fear of further American intervention.[7]

It is remarkable to what extent this final period of the Vietnam War has been simply ignored in many historical accounts, which tend to focus primarily on the events leading up to the commitment of substantial American ground forces in May 1965. But if American failure was not preordained in 1973, is there reason to think it was preordained in 1960, 1963, or 1965? In fact, the thesis of the inevitability of American defeat in Vietnam is almost surely wrong. As a compelling recent analysis of the overall American war strategy puts it: "[O]nce Washington decided to enter the conflict, it required numerous major errors on the part of the United States to make Hanoi's conquest of South Vietnam feasible;" "even a minimally competent strategy would have prevented the conquest of South Vietnam;" "there were numerous roads to victory, but Washington chose none of them."[8]

If this is indeed the case, it underlines the importance of trying to understand the genesis of these errors in the American decision-making process. Not surprisingly, there has been a great deal of discussion in the literature of the details of high-level American decision-making on Vietnam during the Kennedy and Johnson administrations. Most of this has focused, however, on Washington-level bureaucratic players. We are interested instead in the role of American

Vietnam (Chicago: Contemporary Books, 1979); Phillip B. Davidson, *Vietnam at War: The History, 1945–1975* (Novato, CA: Presidio Press, 1988); and Guenter Lewy, *America and Vietnam* (New York: Oxford University Press, 1978).

[7] On all this see especially Lewis Sorley, *A Better War: The Unexamined Victories and Final Tragedy of America's Last Years in Vietnam* (New York: Harcourt Brace, 1999).

[8] Walton, 4–5.

officials in South Vietnam itself and their various contributions to generating or abetting the policy errors that were made, as well as (above all in the latter part of the war) the extent of their responsibility for American successes.

Many histories of the Vietnam War neglect not only the post-1968 period but also the early years of American involvement in the country. Yet it is impossible to understand the difficulties the United States faced (including those of its own creation) in the 1960s without some understanding of this very formative time. It is also important to realize that the United States had a significant presence in Vietnam for a full decade prior to the introduction of American combat forces there. While it is obvious that Vietnam was not a high priority of American foreign policy during most of this period, it is not true, as has so often been asserted by critics of the war, that the United States was grossly ignorant of Vietnam's political history or its society and culture. The CIA had an active station in Saigon at this time. The French-speaking American operative Lucien Conein had actually been in the country since 1945, and was extraordinarily well-connected in elite Vietnamese political and military circles. Rufus Phillips (also originally with the agency) played a key part over many years in the pacification effort in South Vietnam and was generally regarded as perhaps the most knowledgeable American about the country as a whole. And then there was Lansdale.

Ed Lansdale's first exposure to Vietnam was in the summer of 1953, when he was included in an American military delegation headed by General John "Iron Mike" O'Daniel, later to become head of the American Military Assistance and Advisory Group (MAAG) in Saigon. At this time, the French, acting in the name of the semi-fictitious regime of the Emperor Bao Dai (then residing on the French Riviera), were attempting to bring an end to their drawn-out struggle against the Vietnamese communists led by Ho Chi Minh. While the report submitted by O'Daniel was relatively upbeat, Lansdale was pessimistic, and in a separate memorandum through CIA channels he presciently predicted a long guerrilla war and argued that the French were unprepared for this. In Washington, the Vietnam situation had the attention of the highest levels of the U.S. government. In a National Security Council meeting in January 1954, President Eisenhower made clear his unwillingness to commit ground forces in support of the French, but there was a consensus that something had to be done. CIA Director Allen Dulles and his brother, Secretary of State John Foster Dulles, impressed with Lansdale's success with Magsaysay in the Philippines, raised the possibility of a similar role for him in Vietnam. At a meeting later that month with the Dulles brothers as well as Admiral Arthur Radford, chairman of the Joint Chiefs of Staff, Lansdale was told to go to Saigon "to do what you did in the Philippines." That was the extent of his instructions.[9]

---

[9] Cecil B. Currey, *Edward Lansdale: The Unquiet American* (Washington, DC: Brassey's, 1998), 135–37. Lansdale later liked to claim that these words were spoken by the secretary of state, but apparently they were an instruction from his boss, Allen Dulles. Jonathan Nashel, *Edward Lansdale's Cold War* (Amherst: University of Massachusetts Press, 2005), 78.

Lansdale arrived in Saigon on June 1, 1954, three weeks after the catastrophic defeat of a large French force by the Viet Minh at Dien Bien Phu,
which led the French finally to abandon hope of retaining their former colony.
Though officially only the assistant air attaché, his true assignment was to
head up the "Saigon Military Mission" – in reality, a second CIA station with
a special mandate to conduct unconventional warfare and a direct line to Allen
Dulles. Predictably, this arrangement was resisted by the chief of the primary
CIA station in the capital, forcing Lansdale to have him recalled to Washington;
but Lansdale was welcomed and his mission fully supported both by General
O'Daniel and Ambassador Donald Heath. Lansdale then set out to assemble
his team and begin to learn something about Vietnam.

He did not have long to wait, though, to seize his great opportunity. Toward
the end of June, Ngo Dinh Diem arrived in Saigon, having been appointed by
Bao Dai prime minister of a new non-communist government to be established
in southern Vietnam under an agreement negotiated at an international conference in Geneva. Diem, an austere and rather shy personality and, like many of
his countrymen, a Catholic, came from a long line of Vietnamese Mandarins.
He had served as a provincial governor before the war, but since 1950 had
lived in Europe and the United States (at a monastery in New York) and lacked
any real political base in the country. Lansdale, who was not shy, paid a call on
the prime minister in his office the following day, introduced himself, offered
to help, and laid on Diem's desk some notes with suggestions for organizing his
government. Within a matter of weeks, Lansdale had become a close adviser,
often spending hours alone with the prime minister at his palace in the middle
of the night; and it was not long before he was brought into Diem's inner
circle. The most important of these figures were Diem's brother Ngo Dinh Nhu
and Nhu's formidable wife, who was to become a political force in her own
right.

How did he do it? "Ed was more Asian than the Asians," a colleague would
later say. Unlike many American officials in dealings with their Vietnamese
counterparts, he was receptive, non-confrontational, sensitive to the importance of "face," and perhaps above all, patient. He was certainly free with his
advice, but always seemed to know the right moment to offer it. With Diem,
who enjoyed talking literally for hours on end, all this was crucial. As a result,
as another colleague attested, "Diem trusted Lansdale about as much as he
trusted any foreigner."[10]

The situation facing Diem was grim. The government was still largely staffed
and led by French officials, and French troops continued to provide essential
security to the country; but the French would be gone within months, and in
any case they were not happy with Diem's appointment. Indeed, the French
soon came to view Diem as an American puppet and to scheme actively for his
removal. Not only was Diem's own position not secure; his effective control
barely extended beyond the neighborhood of his own palace. Saigon itself was

[10] Ibid., 152–54.

dominated by the Binh Xuyen, a quasi-criminal gang that controlled gambling, prostitution, opium dens, and the local police force, while acting as paymaster to the playboy emperor. In adjoining provinces, powerful religious sects – the Hoa Hao and Cao Dai – controlled armies of upwards of 15,000 men each. Though they had fought with the French against the Viet Minh, the loyalty of these sects to the new regime was by no means certain. The country had no organized political parties, and no political class that was not tainted by service in the colonial bureaucracy. Indeed, to understand the course of later events in Vietnam – and above all the domestic policies of Diem and his supporters – it is essential to understand the extent to which political life altogether had been suppressed or driven underground under the rule of the French. There is an important parallel in this respect between the political culture of South Vietnam in the early years of its independence and the political culture of Iraq following the overthrow of Saddam Hussein. The weakness of political institutions puts a premium on personal, family, and religious loyalties; at the same time, it encouraged conspiratorial behavior and political violence.[11]

In the dominant narrative of the Vietnam War, Diem has been portrayed as a deeply flawed leader. Though a man of undoubted intelligence and integrity, he is seen as indecisive, authoritarian, clannishly attached to his own family and co-religionists, concerned more with the loyalty of his subordinates than their competence, and too often unreceptive to constructive American advice. That there is something to all this may be accepted, but a case can certainly be made that it has been much exaggerated, especially by those personally invested in the decision to remove him from power in the fall of 1963. As the saying goes, sometimes paranoids really do have enemies, and the Diem regime had more than its share. Lansdale himself was well aware of these criticisms, which he called "pretty mean caricatures." "When others talked about him I would look at them in wonder. You can't see that there are other qualities in him? He's not like that."[12] No American was in a better position to know.

Diem's personal and political insecurities certainly help make sense of what has often been seen as an attachment to his younger brother that borders on the irrational. The fact of the matter is that Nhu was from early days the intelligence and security arm of the regime. He controlled the political police, and later a special paramilitary unit (it was trained by CIA) whose main function was

---

[11] "In his travels into Hanoi and Haiphong, Lansdale spoke also with members of two prominent nationalist political parties, the Dai Viet and the Vietnam Quoc Dan Dang (VNQDD).... Secrecy for both groups was a way of life. French rule had prevented the formation of open political parties because *any* political activity by the Vietnamese seemed a threat to colonial authority. Those who had defied this understanding had been arrested, imprisoned, murdered, or exiled. When Lansdale suggested that now was the time for them to come out in the open, they were leery and refused even to admit that they were members of Dai Viet or VNQDD. They were afraid of open politics, more comfortable with membership in clandestine and revolutionary activities. Part of small cells, under strict discipline and led by a secret directorate, they had little faith in Lansdale's promises that a new era was beginning." Ibid., 146–47.

[12] Ibid., 151.

regime protection. As such, it was absolutely vital that his personal loyalty to Diem be above suspicion, and it was. In understanding the Diem–Lansdale relationship, it is also important to keep in mind the relationship that developed between Lansdale and Nhu – one that was inherited and nurtured by the CIA station up to the end, though it remains very imperfectly known. At the same time, it would be a mistake to suppose that Diem was driven only by a desire to remain in power. He was a proud figure and a patriot. He felt keenly his growing dependence on American assistance, and it is hardly surprising that he could be prickly in dealing with his well-meaning if often arrogant and ignorant patrons.[13]

Diem's first crisis came quickly enough, as his relationship with his army chief of staff, Nguyen Van Hinh, deteriorated and the latter began to challenge his authority, abetted by the French. O'Daniel, Heath, and Lansdale intervened personally to foil coup attempts by Hinh in September and October 1954. Eventually, Diem succeeded in forcing him to leave the country. Lansdale also undertook negotiations with the Binh Xuyen and Cao Dai that relieved some of the tension in Diem's relations with these groups, and the Cao Dai agreed to provide a security force to protect the Doc Lap palace in Saigon.[14] But this only postponed the showdown with the sects.

The picture was suddenly complicated in November by the arrival in Saigon of a second American proconsul. Eisenhower and Dulles decided that at this critical moment the United States needed a more high-powered ambassador in South Vietnam, and settled on the person of General J. Lawton ("Lightning Joe") Collins, who had recently stepped down as Army chief of staff. Collins was to go on a temporary basis but with a broad mandate to take a fresh look at the situation in South Vietnam, help stabilize the new Diem government, and recommend a program of military and economic assistance to shore it up. On paper, he received "broad authority to direct, utilize and control all agencies and resources of the U.S. government with respect to Vietnam." As it happened, his tour would last six months. Far from imparting unity of effort to the American presence in Saigon, however, Collins if anything undermined it, above all by his eventual decision to oppose continuing reliance by the United States on Diem – thus setting himself at odds with Lansdale in particular, who thought the general had no real understanding of conditions in Vietnam.[15] Collins' judgment of Diem's character and potential was initially somewhat ambivalent, but when a new crisis flared in March 1955 over the sects,[16] he concluded that Diem could not be a reliable partner, and that the United States

[13] For a cogent defense of Diem's actions during this period see Moyar, *Triumph Forsaken*, ch. 2.
[14] Currey, 167–69.
[15] For Lansdale's view of Collins see ibid., 169–71. Lansdale apparently walked out of the first country team meeting held by the general.
[16] This was triggered by Diem's attempt to liquidate their private militias by enrolling some in the regular army and disbanding the rest. The three sects then joined forces in a "National Front," called openly for the overthrow of the Diem government, and briefly assaulted government troops and facilities in Saigon until restrained by the French.

should either look elsewhere or withdraw from the country. On returning to Washington in April, he very nearly succeeded in selling this view. Eisenhower and Dulles were remarkably ready to defer to Collins' judgment in the matter, and the general eventually overrode opposition within the bureaucracy: On April 27, a detailed cable was sent from the State Department to the embassy instructing it to withdraw support from Diem and seek to replace him and his brother with two politicians believed more popular in the country.[17]

In the meantime, however, the situation in Saigon had changed dramatically. Ignoring pressure from Collins and the French, Diem decided to launch an attack on the Binh Xuyen stronghold in the Cholon section of Saigon. As reports of this move filtered back to Washington, Dulles decided to countermand the cable he had sent six hours previously. At a National Security Council (NSC) meeting the following day, attended by Collins as well as the president and the secretary of state, the door was left open to removing Diem; yet the apparent success of the operation, as well as pressure from influential Diem supporters in the Senate, soon succeeded in inducing second thoughts in the State Department. By May 2, Dulles was describing Diem as a "popular hero."

But there is almost certainly more to this story.[18] While rumors of an effort to unseat the prime minister were circulating widely in Saigon, it seems virtually certain that Diem was tipped off about events in Washington and moved deliberately to preempt the Dulles cable. In his memoirs, Lansdale asserts that he learned only from Diem himself of the decision to remove him, but other evidence suggests that the colonel was in active communication with Washington and may in fact have been instrumental in persuading State to rescind the cable.[19] Collins would later claim that Lansdale was receiving private instructions through his CIA channel.[20] It seems highly likely in any case that Lansdale was aware of the situation in Washington and alerted Diem to it – whether under instructions or not. Indeed, it is not unthinkable that Lansdale actually inspired Diem's move against the Binh Xuyen.[21] If so, this would have to count as perhaps the most brilliant psychological operation of his career.

At this juncture, Diem had to fend off a challenge from another quarter, as Bao Dai attempted to come to the rescue of the Binh Xuyen by summoning

---

[17] Accounts of the Collins mission: J. Lawton Collins, *Lightning Joe: An Autobiography* (Baton Rouge: Louisiana State University Press, 1979), ch. 19; Ronald H. Spector, *United States Army in Vietnam: Advice and Support, the Early Years, 1941–1960* (Washington, DC: U.S. Army Center of Military History, 1983), ch. 13; David L. Anderson, *Trapped by Success: The Eisenhower Administration and Vietnam, 1953–1961* (New York: Columbia University Press, 1991), ch. 5.

[18] See especially the account in Anderson, 110–15.

[19] Lansdale, 282–84.

[20] "The big mistake made frankly with respect to Lansdale and me," he said in a later interview, "was that there were two people supposedly representing the United States government. I [was] getting instructions from the president of the United States, and this guy Lansdale, who had no authority as far as I was concerned, [was] getting instructions from the CIA." Anderson, 112.

[21] Bao Dai later charged that MAAG officers under Lansdale's direction actually "prepared the operation" (Anderson, 113), though he can hardly be considered a reliable source.

Diem to France and appointing an ally, General Nguyen Van Vy, as commander of the South Vietnamese armed forces, with a mandate to end all hostilities. The French now openly injected themselves into the situation, with Prime
Minister Edgar Faure declaring at a press conference in Paris that the Diem
government was finished and endorsing Bao Dai's move. Diem ignored them,
redoubled his effort to eliminate the Binh Xuyen, rallied senior military leaders, and forced General Vy out of the country. Over the next several months,
by an adroit combination of military pressure, bribery, and diplomacy, Diem
succeeded in fracturing further the coalition of the sects and consolidating his
position. Eventually, he was strong enough to go on the political offensive, and
held a nation-wide referendum to determine whether he or Bao Dai would be
the supreme authority in the nation. This was duly done to the accompani-
ment of a sophisticated political and propaganda campaign that was evidently
orchestrated by Lansdale and Nhu. Diem won in October in another "landslide," abolished the imperial office, and took supreme power as president of
the Republic of Vietnam.

    Though his methods were not always laudable, it is difficult not to be
impressed with Lansdale and his contribution to the founding of the South
Vietnamese state, which if anything has probably been significantly under-
rated. William Colby, Saigon station chief in the early 1960s and later CIA
director, would call him one of the ten best intelligence operatives in American
history.[22] But Lansdale was flawed in some ways, and the result of his activities
in Indochina plainly fell short of what he had accomplished in the Philippines.
This was not entirely his fault. Diem was not as malleable an instrument as
Magsaysay. In particular, he was not as responsive to Lansdale's efforts to
remake him as an American-style politician. For it is a mistake to see Lansdale
simply as a Machiavellian manipulator. He was an American patriot and pas-
sionate democrat who believed Americans had forgotten the lessons of their
own revolution – the very model of the psychological-political "revolutionary
warfare" Lansdale constantly preached as the only antidote to contemporary
communism. Whatever the merits of this model, it held limited appeal for Asian
elites and ultimately hurt his effectiveness in dealing with the Ngos.[23] This having been said, it remains true that Lansdale forged a relationship with Diem
closer than that of any other American, one that endured even after Lansdale
had been out of the country for several years. From this point of view, he may
fairly be said to offer a model for proconsular relations with foreign allied
leaders and elites that has continuing relevance today.[24] Oddly, however, the
virtues Lansdale displayed in his relations with foreigners too often deserted

---

[22] Richard Widdington, *Almanac of Adventure* (New York: Rand McNally, 1982), 165.
[23] Currey, 182–84. Lansdale apparently made a serious effort to persuade Diem to expand his
    political base and curb his authoritarian inclinations; in this regard, his outlook differed little
    from most other senior American advisers in the country. See Nashel, ch. 5.
[24] Consider notably the close relationship between (Afghan-American) Zalmay Khalilzdad and
    Afghan president Hamid Karzai when the former served as U.S. ambassador in Kabul.

him when dealing with Americans. Though he could be very effective bureaucratically, he could also be outspoken, impatient, and even insulting with those who got in his way, and he did not suffer fools gladly. His reputation as a maverick and hothead did not serve him well in later years.

Still, Lansdale was capable of inspiring great admiration and loyalty in those who worked with him. Conein, Phillips, and many others in Lansdale's Saigon Military Mission were his disciples and defenders. General Samuel ("Hanging Sam") Williams, who replaced O'Daniel as head of the Military Assistance and Advisory Group (MAAG), was particularly close to Lansdale and would later emulate him by establishing the sort of friendship with Diem that Lansdale had enjoyed. Lansdale also got along well with George Frederick Reinhardt, who succeeded Collins as ambassador. Unfortunately, Reinhardt's successor, Ambassador Elbridge Durbrow, who arrived in Saigon in March 1957 (Lansdale had departed toward the end of 1956), was cut from a different cloth. Durbrow was the authentic "ugly American."[25] Having tried and failed to assert his authority over the MAAG, Durbrow had from the beginning a poor relationship with Williams. He displayed open contempt for the Vietnamese generally and was confrontational in his relations with Diem, routinely threatening to cut U.S. aid as a way to generate pressure for reform. More than that, he connived with political opponents of the regime and may in fact have helped inspire a coup attempt against Diem in November 1960, although this cannot be proven.[26] All this was an evil harbinger of things to come.

During the waning years of the Eisenhower administration, Lansdale was back in Washington but remained in close touch with developments in Southeast Asia as a Defense Department liaison officer with the intelligence community. In 1960, he was promoted to brigadier general. In 1959 and again in 1961, he returned to Vietnam for brief visits and met with Diem each time. The report he prepared on the second occasion was more pessimistic than the official line emanating from Saigon and lamented the lack of progress on the counterinsurgency front. It quickly found its way to the newly inaugurated president, John F. Kennedy. JFK was impressed by this memorandum as well as by the extent of the problems it depicted. Among other things, Lansdale had recommended that the president replace Durbrow as ambassador to Saigon with someone "who can work with real skill, with great sensitivity to Vietnamese feelings, and with a fine sense of the dangerous limits of Vietnamese national security in a time of emergency." Quite clearly, he had himself in mind. The president would soon come to agree. On January 28, Lansdale was invited to a meeting in the White House Cabinet Room with the president's national security team. Lansdale's memorandum was on the table. After soliciting the general's view

[25] In fact, Lederer and Burdick begin their book with a withering portrait of the American ambassador to "Sarkhan," a fictional country in Southeast Asia. Lansdale once said that Durbrow was "better suited to be the senior salesman in a ladies' shoe store" than U.S. ambassador to South Vietnam (Moyar, *Triumph Forsaken*, 69).

[26] Ibid., 67–68, 105–15.

of the situation in Vietnam, JFK remarked somewhat casually that he wanted Lansdale to "go over there as the new ambassador."

Incomprehensibly, yet fatefully, Lansdale failed to seize this moment. He replied that he was a serving military officer and didn't think his "place was in diplomacy," whereupon the president let the matter drop. While Kennedy had by no means given up the idea, Lansdale's hesitation opened a window for his enemies in Washington to mobilize against the appointment. The new secretary of state, Dean Rusk, was surprised and annoyed by the president's offer, and opposition surfaced in the military as well. Rusk eventually threatened to resign if Lansdale was made ambassador to Saigon. JFK then contacted Admiral Arleigh Burke, chairman of the Joint Chiefs, and suggested that Lansdale be promoted to lieutenant general and sent back to Vietnam as chief of the MAAG. This idea was not well received either, to put it mildly, and only helped stir the anti-Lansdale hornets' nest in the Pentagon. As Colby later summed it up: "I think the bureaucracy couldn't handle Ed. He made them very uncomfortable and . . . cut across their lines of command." Unfortunately, the president failed to stick to his guns. It would not be the last time.[27]

As it turned out, however, the new ambassador to Saigon, Frederick ("Fritz") Nolting, would prove a follower of the Lansdale rather than the Durbrow model and set out to restore Diem's confidence in the United States and its ambassador. Fluent in French and with a PhD in philosophy, Nolting was a distinguished career diplomat as well as "a man of rare strength and character," in the words of White House aide Walt Rostow, who knew him well. Like Lansdale and Williams, he succeeded in developing a genuine friendship with Diem.[28] Lansdale himself would continue to have some influence over Vietnam policy in his capacity as special adviser to the new deputy secretary of Defense, Ros Gilpatric, on intelligence and unconventional warfare and as executive director of a newly created interagency Vietnam Task Force that Gilpatric chaired. This arrangement could have served as an effective substitute for a proconsular role for Lansdale in the theater. But Lansdale misplayed this hand as well, and as a result found himself increasingly walled off from Vietnamese affairs over the course of the year. When Kennedy decided on a major expansion of the American commitment to Vietnam in the spring of 1961, Nolting, acting under instructions from the State Department, presented Diem with a list of American demands as the price of this increased aid, including giving the United States an institutionalized voice in South Vietnamese government decision-making. Predictably, the president's response was: "Vietnam does not want to be a protectorate."[29] It was clear that Lansdale's influence had by this point virtually evaporated.

[27] See the account of Currey, 226–29.
[28] Moyar, *Triumph Forsaken*, 130. For the ambassador's own perspective see *From Trust to Tragedy: The Political Memoirs of Frederick Nolting, Kennedy's Ambassador to Diem's Vietnam* (New York: Praeger, 1988). Apart from his sensitive handling of Diem, Nolting also had the foresight to favor a partition of Laos.
[29] Moyar, *Triumph Forsaken*, 142–44.

Following the Bay of Pigs debacle in April, Lansdale was asked by the president to lead an effort to organize the overthrow of the Castro regime in Cuba by unconventional means; this would occupy him fully for some time. Apart from a brief visit in October 1961 (during which Diem unsuccessfully pressed for a permanent Lansdale presence in Saigon), the general would not return to Vietnam until 1965 – in a surprising partnership with Henry Cabot Lodge.

Before discussing the pivotal Lodge proconsulship, however, something must be said about the state of the war and the condition of the South Vietnamese government at this juncture. According to the dominant narrative of the Vietnam War, the performance of the Diem regime declined precipitously with the stepping up of communist military activity in the South beginning in the fall of 1961, and no recovery was realistically possible without a change in the South Vietnamese leadership. Yet this view is questionable in the extreme, reflecting as it does the outsized influence of the reporting of contemporary American journalists, especially David Halberstam of the *New York Times* and Neil Sheehan of United Press International.[30] In part, their influence can be explained by the complete inadequacy of the public relations efforts of the U.S. and South Vietnamese governments in this period. With the advent of the Kennedy administration, moreover, pressure was increasingly exerted from the highest reaches of the administration to downplay or suppress negative news from Vietnam for reasons of domestic politics.[31] In this atmosphere, it is understandable that reporters would develop an adversarial attitude toward American or Vietnamese officialdom and a muckracking style of journalism. But Halberstam, Sheehan, and others went further, allowing themselves to be used by unreliable sources[32] and developing strong biases and agendas of their own. Halberstam in particular waged what can only be described as a political campaign against the South Vietnamese government and military and the Ngo family in particular – one consciously designed to encourage the overthrow of the Diem regime. President Kennedy himself became increasingly disgusted with Halberstam's slanted and highly damaging reporting, and at one point went so far as to personally ask the editor of the *New York Times* to reassign him.[33]

---

[30] See particularly the discussion in ibid., 169 ff.

[31] For example, the president, asked in a press conference in April 1961 whether U.S. troops were involved in combat in Vietnam, answered with a categorical denial; yet American pilots were in fact flying combat missions in disguised aircraft, while three weeks previously the U.S. army lost its first soldier in ground combat. Such misrepresentations would be virtually unthinkable today. Ibid., 148–51.

[32] The most notorious case was Army Lieutenant Colonel and ARVN adviser John Paul Vann, a major source for Sheehan's book *A Bright Shining Lie*. On him see ibid., 172–77.

[33] Ironically, a decision had already been made to recall Halberstam from Vietnam, but the move was put on hold so as not to seem a capitulation by the paper to White House pressure. Ibid., 253. It should be noted that the reportage of Halberstam et al. was sharply criticized by other journalists at the time. See notably Richard Tregaskis, *Vietnam Diary* (New York: Holt, Rinehart and Winston, 1963).

In fact, the deterioration of the situation in Vietnam over the course of 1961 was largely arrested in the following year, thanks not only to a large infusion of American weaponry and advisers but also to vigorous prosecution of the war by the South Vietnamese themselves, both at the conventional level and in the pacification arena, where Diem's "strategic hamlet" program scored impressive gains. It is another common misconception that Diem and the South Vietnamese military were incapable of recognizing the importance of the unconventional dimension of the war, or of waging it effectively.[34] According to an official communist history, South Vietnamese leaders "obstinately continued to strengthen their forces and wage an increasingly fierce 'special war' against our people in the South" through the end of 1962.[35] Indeed, the security situation in the South continued to improve through the first half of 1963.[36]

It was at the political level that things began to unravel for the Diem regime during these months. The catalyst was political unrest among militant Buddhist opponents of the Saigon government, and the government's violent response to a militant demonstration in the northern city of Hue on May 8 in which some twenty-three people were killed, though the exact circumstances remain murky. While the Buddhists claimed they were only reacting to official persecution and favoritism toward Catholics, it seems reasonably clear that they were in fact engaged in a concerted campaign to bring down the Diem regime.[37] Their most effective weapons proved to be the self-immolation of Buddhist monks, and the favorable coverage of these actions and their movement generally by American journalists, and again particularly David Halberstam. The reaction of the government was conciliatory, but the Buddhist leadership remained intransigent. Washington became increasingly alarmed by these developments, and the mood in the State Department became increasingly hostile to Diem. After the first Buddhist suicide on June 8, Averill Harriman (then assistant secretary for Far Eastern affairs) and Roger Hilsman (head of the Bureau of Intelligence and Research) delivered an ultimatum to Diem to meet all of the Buddhist demands immediately or face public denunciation by the United States. President Kennedy learned of this ultimatum on the same day it appeared in a story in the *New York Times*. Understandably upset, he instructed the department to make no further threats without his personal approval, yet Harriman and Hilsman persisted in pressing Diem for far-reaching and potentially damaging

---

[34] It is often said that the strategic hamlet program was the brainchild of Sir Robert Thompson, based on his experience in the British counterinsurgency campaign in Malaya in the early 1950s; in fact, the initiative came from Diem himself. In the early years of his own rule, Diem was quite aware of the communist political infrastructure within South Vietnam and in fact effectively suppressed much of it. See Moyar, *Triumph Forsaken*, 56–59, as well as Mark Moyar, *Phoenix and the Birds of Prey: Counterinsurgency and Counterterrorism in Vietnam* (Lincoln: University of Nebraska Press, 2007 [1997]), chs. 1–4.

[35] Cited in Moyar, *Triumph Forsaken*, 183.

[36] Ibid., 206–11.

[37] This was clearly recognized in one CIA report at the time: ibid., 223.

concessions to the Buddhists. As Diem and Nhu strongly suspected (but the Americans on the spot apparently refused to believe), communist influence within the Buddhist movement was substantial. It is now known that several of Halberstam's most important sources among the Buddhists were actually agents of Hanoi. There are good grounds for believing the same may have been true of their leading spokesman, Tri Quang, who continued to make trouble for every South Vietnamese government until he was finally sent into internal exile in 1967.[38]

Having had enough, Diem finally moved against the Buddhists on August 21, declaring martial law and sending troops into Buddhist pagodas across the country. This move succeeded in short order in quieting the militants, and (like Diem's forceful measures against the sects some years earlier) actually increased the prestige of the regime. Unfortunately, false stories of massacres by the government retailed by Halberstam inflamed public opinion in the United States and further hardened official views of the regime.[39] It was in this atmosphere that a new U.S. ambassador arrived in Saigon.

Henry Cabot Lodge was a descendent of several of America's most distinguished families.[40] His grandfather of the same name had served in the U.S. Senate and was leader of the isolationist opposition to Wilson's League of Nations. Lodge himself was elected to the Senate from Massachusetts in 1936, at the young age of thirty-four. A reservist in the Army, he took leave from Congress at the outbreak of World War II and eventually resigned his seat to join the regular Army (the first senator since the Civil War to do so); afterwards he returned to the reserves and eventually rose to the rank of major general. He was reelected to the Senate in 1946 but lost his seat in 1952 to John F. Kennedy. Lodge aspired to be secretary of state under Eisenhower but had to settle instead for U.S. ambassador to the United Nations, where he would prove an effective spokesman in the public relations wars with the Soviets. (Lodge was in fact less conservative and more of an internationalist than his famous namesake.) In 1960, he ran as the vice-presidential candidate on the Republican ticket with Richard Nixon, once again against Kennedy. After Nixon's narrow defeat, Lodge let it be known at the White House that he would be interested in a diplomatic assignment and apparently suggested the Saigon post. Lodge

[38] Ibid., 214–18.

[39] Ibid., 233–36. Halberstam was also instrumental in spreading the politically mischievous but in fact false report that the pagoda raids had been masterminded by Nhu; in fact, the senior leadership of the military approved them and they were largely conducted by the military, not just the paramilitary force controlled by Nhu. This canard would tip the scales very significantly against the regime in the eyes of Washington.

[40] Surprisingly, Lodge has for the most part escaped attention from biographers. Anne E. Blair, *Lodge in Vietnam*, is an authoritative account utilizing interviews and extensive material from Lodge's personal papers that have never been published, including a lengthy "Vietnam Memoir" (see her comments on this, ix–xi). Lodge himself published almost nothing on his two tours in Vietnam – for reasons it is not difficult to guess. A very brief account may be found in Henry Cabot Lodge, *The Storm Has Many Eyes: A Personal Narrative* (New York: W. W. Norton, 1973), 205–19.

had no expertise in Asian affairs, but he did speak French, and he seems to have been intrigued by the military dimension of the challenge in Southeast Asia. Moreover, it seems quite likely that he regarded the Saigon assignment as a significant credential supporting a run for the presidency in 1964.

The political aspect of the Lodge appointment deserves particular comment. JFK clearly saw the move as politically advantageous. It underlined the bipartisan support that the administration enjoyed for its Vietnam policies and inhibited Republican criticism in the future. An aide later recalled that when Rusk had suggested that Lodge go to Saigon, the president said that he had approved the appointment "because the idea of getting Lodge mixed up in such a hopeless mess as Vietnam was irresistible."[41] JFK may well have felt that the appointment would hurt rather than help Lodge's prospects as a presidential rival. What no one appears to have foreseen, however, is that this political dynamic would provide Lodge great leverage in his proconsular role. Lodge himself was in any case something of a lone wolf.[42] Coupled with the fact that he was not beholden either to the bureaucracy or to the party controlling the White House, Lodge had great scope for conducting policy his own way, and any effort by Washington to rein him in threatened to make a martyr of him and generate political ammunition for the 1964 elections. Like MacArthur, Lodge could use his presidential prospects to maximize his own proconsular freedom of action. Although there is no real evidence that he would do so consciously, this fear definitely shaped the way he was handled by the administration.

Lodge's one meeting with the president prior to his departure for Southeast Asia occurred the day following the first Buddhist suicide, which was extensively covered in the American press. Expressing his concern over the deteriorating situation in Vietnam, Kennedy spoke of the bad relations between the embassy in Saigon and the press, and added: "I wish you, personally, would take charge of press relations." The president also stated that the Diem government was "entering its terminal phase." However, neither JFK nor Rusk apparently provided Lodge any guidance regarding Diem or his government or any indication that they were contemplating a change in U.S. policy. Rusk himself strikingly told Lodge: "[W]e need an ambassador out there who is tough; who can act as a catalyst; who will take responsibility and make decisions and not refer many detailed questions to Washington. We want to make the political side of things go as well as the military side has been going."[43] It is far from clear that other senior figures in Washington would have endorsed

---

[41] Blair, 13; cf. Arthur Schlesinger, Jr., *A Thousand Days: John F. Kennedy in the White House* (Boston: Houghton Mifflin, 1965), 989.

[42] Blair aptly describes Lodge as "a man of immense authority and charm, motivated by personal loyalties and his conception of duty, impatient of detail, and inclined to move on once a solution to a problem appeared to have been found. He was in some ways a nineteenth century figure functioning in modern professional structures of whose workings he remained splendidly unconscious" (xi).

[43] Ibid., 14–15.

this statement – so different from the general tenor of the administration's demonstrated approach to Southeast Asian affairs.

It is also striking that neither Rusk nor Lodge raised the issue of the authority of the ambassador over U.S. military personnel and activities in South Vietnam. A perennial source of bureaucratic difficulty, this issue had become even more pressing after the MAAG was replaced in 1961 by the Military Assistance Command–Vietnam (MACV), an operational military command headed by a four-star general.[44] Fritz Nolting had sought clarification of his authority from Washington at this time; told by McNamara that a full general could not be expected to report through an ambassador, he let the matter drop. Lodge, apparently, was given to understand by Rusk and Harriman that his authority would be absolute, but neither he nor anyone else sought to have this confirmed by the Pentagon or the president or put in writing.[45]

In fact, this was symptomatic of a larger problem. In looking back on this period, Nolting would later write: "In twenty-two years of public service, I never saw anything resembling the confusion, vacillation, and lack of coordination in the U.S. government. While I had sympathy for President Kennedy in his dilemma, one cannot admire his failure to take control. The Harriman–Lodge axis seemed too strong for him."[46] Much of the problem can be traced to the very significant structural changes made by the new administration to the national security decision-making machinery. Reflecting the structure of military staffs, the National Security Council (NSC) in the Eisenhower years had relied on two distinct interagency instruments, a Planning Board (chaired by the president's national security adviser), and an Operations Coordinating Board (chaired by the under secretary of state). This system, much criticized at the time as too ponderous and inflexible, was abolished at the outset of the Kennedy administration in favor of a more informal and ad hoc approach. Kennedy's national security adviser, former Harvard dean McGeorge Bundy, assumed for the first time a role as an independent and active player in the national security policy process, along with his small but high-powered personal staff. The president himself disliked hierarchical structure and scripted meetings, and did not hesitate to deal directly with Bundy's staff or indeed subcabinet officials in other agencies. In meetings, he encouraged free-form discussion from all participants regardless of rank or position, and often left unclear what decisions if any were being made or who was being tasked to implement them. Nor did Bundy or his staff exert themselves to impose discipline on the process. The information flow was often casual and incomplete,

[44] Military advisory group leaders were part of the embassy "country team" and thus subordinate to the ambassador, at least in theory, but an operational military command in the country normally fell outside his authority. The "country team" concept was formalized by President Kennedy in a directive of May 1961.
[45] Ibid., 19–20.
[46] Nolting, 132.

and by that fact also vulnerable to bureaucratic manipulation (as we shall see in a moment).[47]

Something also should be said about the president's relationship with the other national security agencies. Consonant with his desire to play a more operational role in foreign policy-making, Kennedy also sought to limit the power of the secretary of state, appointing to the position, in the person of Dean Rusk, a man who was expected to be exceptionally deferential to presidential wishes. Like many other presidents, he soon became dissatisfied with the quality and responsiveness of the department's work as well as with Rusk personally, and as a result increasingly relied on direct dealings with lower ranked officials there, particularly Averill Harriman. At the Defense Department, Kennedy's appointment of Robert S. McNamara would also have fateful consequences. Chosen for his management skills rather than expertise in military or national security affairs, McNamara and his civilian subordinates (the so-called Whiz Kids) deeply antagonized the uniformed military by their undisguised arrogance and contempt for professional military advice. Their reliance on quantitative methods of analysis and game-theoretical approaches to military conflict rather than traditional military strategy would become notorious – with toxic results for the management of the war in Vietnam. As for the uniformed military itself, Kennedy was deeply unhappy with the failure of the Joint Chiefs of Staff to warn him of the impending disaster of the Bay of Pigs episode, and his confidence in them never fully recovered. He was also convinced – and for good reason – that the Army's approach to Vietnam was overly conventional, and took steps to strengthen the military's special operations forces and unconventional capabilities, though with only limited success.[48]

Even before Lodge's arrival in Saigon, it had become clear (though possibly not to the president himself) that there was a serious split within the administration over Vietnam. In Washington, Harriman, Hilsman, and Under Secretary George Ball at the State Department and Michael Forrestal of the NSC staff essentially endorsed the Halberstam line and favored a change of regime; generally supportive of Diem, on the other hand, were McNamara, the Joint Chiefs, CIA Director John McCone, his Vietnam expert Bill Colby, and Vice President Lyndon Johnson, who had been impressed by him during a visit

---

[47] As General Maxwell Taylor, Kennedy's White House military adviser, later put it: "I was shocked at the disorderly and careless ways of the new White House. I found that I could walk into any office, request and receive a sheaf of top secret papers, and depart without signing a receipt or making any record of transaction. There was little perceptible method in the assignment of duties within the staff." Maxwell D. Taylor, *Swords and Plowshares* (New York: Da Capo, 1972), 198. For a recent account see Andrew Preston, *The War Council: McGeorge Bundy, the NSC, and Vietnam* (Cambridge, MA: Harvard University Press, 2006), ch. 2; and see more generally Carnes Lord, *The Presidency and the Management of National Security* (New York: Free Press, 1988).

[48] A good account is Dale R. Herspring, *The Pentagon and the Presidency: Civil–Military Relations from FDR to George W. Bush* (Lawrence: University Press of Kansas, 2005), ch. 5. See also Andrew F. Krepinevich, Jr., *The Army and Vietnam* (Baltimore: Johns Hopkins University Press, 1986).

to Saigon; Rusk and Bundy were relatively non-committal. In Saigon, Nolting, Harkins, and CIA Station Chief John Richardson all supported Diem. With the departure of Nolting and the worsening of the Buddhist crisis, however, the anti-Diem group saw an opportunity. On August 24, Harriman and Hilsman drafted a cable to the embassy in Saigon stating that the U.S. government could no longer tolerate Nhu's presence in the government, that Diem should be asked to remove him, and that if he did not do so and make other concessions to the Buddhists, the United States would withdraw its support for him and look for alternative leadership.

August 24 was a Saturday, and much of official Washington was on vacation. Harriman and Hilsman reached the president by telephone on Cape Cod and read the message to him; he agreed to approve it on the condition that they obtain the agreement of Rusk and the Defense Department. Rusk, also out of town, was then contacted and told simply that Kennedy had approved the message, whereupon he gave his own approval. Ros Gilpatrick, standing in for McNamara, was called next and given the impression that Kennedy and Rusk had already signed off on the cable; he too agreed. Neither was told that the president's approval was to be conditional on theirs. By this remarkable maneuver, the Harriman faction momentarily seized the helm of U.S. Vietnam policy and executed an abrupt change of course. Though they would not long maintain their hold on it, the move nevertheless had a lasting impact. This was in part owing to a news broadcast by the Voice of America, apparently inspired by Hilsman, openly criticizing Nhu's supposed role in the pagoda raids and threatening a cutoff of U.S. aid if Diem did not take action against him. But the decisive factor was the new ambassador. Lodge quickly embraced the recommendations of the State cable and, indeed, was eager to go further. Virtually Lodge's first order of business in Saigon was to invite Halberstam and Sheehan to dinner and mend relations with them; indeed, he would eventually come to rely more on them for information about the political situation in the country than on his own embassy team, and essentially accepted their analysis of it. Remarkably, the ambassador did not ask Washington for clarification of the intent of the August 24 cable, nor did he call a meeting of his country team to discuss its implications and coordinate follow-up.[49] Instead, Lodge immediately asked the department to modify the instructions so as to encourage the generals to remove Nhu at once without asking Diem – and then decide among themselves whether to remove Diem as well. Ball approved this on the twenty-fifth, apparently without further clearance or coordination, and the next morning Lodge instructed the CIA station to transmit the message to the generals who might be disposed to cooperate. Up to this point, the high command had been largely united in wanting to keep Diem in power. Lodge's

---

[49] Maxwell Taylor later claimed he would have sought such clarification (*Swords and Plowshares*, 292). Lodge was specifically instructed to hold a country team meeting on the August 24 cable (Blair, 44).

message as well as the Voice of America warning "promptly transformed many of the generals into conspirators."[50]

When news of what had happened circulated in Washington, McNamara, McCone, and Taylor were outraged; even the president was (uncharacteristically) furious. Yet when he polled these key advisers as to whether the new policy should be overturned, they demurred, on the grounds that an abrupt turnaround in policy would cause the United States to lose credibility. When word came back from Saigon that the generals were prepared to launch a coup within a week, therefore, Kennedy's chief concern was whether the coup would succeed – not whether the administration should be in the coup business at all. At this juncture, Lodge wired the following message to Washington: "We are launched on a course from which there is no respectable turning back: the overthrow of the Diem government. There is no turning back in part because U.S. prestige is already publicly committed to this end in large measure and will become more so as the facts leak out. In a more fundamental sense, there is no turning back because there is no possibility, in my view, that the war can be won under a Diem administration."[51] In fact, the coup rapidly fizzled out owing to the uncertain loyalties of key military units and commanders and a loss of heart by the generals once news of the plot came to the attention of Nhu. But Lodge was not about to give up.

No doubt sobered by the new American attitude, Diem and Nhu took a conciliatory line, with Nhu even promising he would remove himself from the government and free Buddhist prisoners as requested by the ambassador; Madame Nhu actually left the country, though she continued her public criticisms of U.S. actions. Lodge ignored these promising signs, and for the first time directly insisted to Diem on Nhu's departure while repeating the threat of an aid cutoff. Yet this heavy-handed approach only caused Diem to dig in his heels on the matter of Nhu, which had now become a question of face. Frustrated, Lodge cabled Washington again on September 11 once again advocating a coup. When it appeared that Washington had no appetite for this, Lodge promptly began to explore the possibility of launching one on his own. McCone, who learned of this through the Saigon CIA station, informed Kennedy; the State Department was then compelled to rein the ambassador in. This in turn prompted Lodge to declare war on John Richardson, the station chief, who continued to be supportive of Diem and to maintain personal contact with Nhu. In a direct message to Rusk he requested Richardson's removal – and the appointment of Lansdale in his place, who, he was given to understand,

50 Moyar, *Triumph Forsaken*, 240. As Blair pointedly notes: "Within two days of Lodge's arrival in Saigon, he had made judgments with far-reaching implications on the basis of testimony from informants with vested interests of which he could know little" (47). Colby (147) remarks on the curious absence of serious analysis in Washington of the Vietnamese generals who might potentially succeed Diem. Lodge habitually referred to Vietnam as "Confucian," but "nowhere in his writings did he reveal any appreciation that professional soldiers had always commanded little esteem in a Confucian society" (Blair, 47).
51 Moyar, *Triumph Forsaken*, 242.

could serve as a good "coup manager."[52] McCone refused. At the beginning of October, however, an article appeared in the American press accusing the CIA Saigon station of refusing to carry out Lodge's instructions and making Richardson's name public – thus blowing his cover and forcing McCone to recall him.[53] Evidently, this information emanated from Harriman or Lodge himself.

In late September, the president sent McNamara and Taylor to Saigon to reassess the situation there. This whirlwind mission was an important turning point, for it brought McNamara around to the view that Diem had to go.[54] On returning to Washington on October 2, the two reported that the war was going very well but that the political front needed renewed attention. They recommended that the United States cut its aid enough to force Diem to undertake various reforms yet not so much as to disrupt the war effort, and that he should be given two to four months to comply before the United States should consider supporting a coup against him. JFK quickly embraced these views, ordering the cut in aid and directing Lodge to avoid giving active encouragement to a coup, while at the same time authorizing him through CIA channels to seek out and build contacts with possible alternative leaders.[55] Lodge proceeded to take advantage of the contradictory character of these instructions. When General Minh, one of the leading potential conspirators, asked Conein to seek assurances from the U.S. government that it would not attempt to thwart a coup and would continue to provide aid afterwards, Lodge asked the president (through a direct reporting channel established at JFK's request) to authorize him to provide these assurances. The president's reply recapitulated at greater length the confusion of the original instructions: While stressing that "we did not wish to leave the impression that the U.S. would thwart a change of government or deny economic and military assistance to a new regime," he also made clear that no specific assurances could be given Minh without "detailed information clearly indicating that Minh's plans offer a high prospect of success." Lodge, essentially ignoring the second part of this message, had Conein tell the generals (on October 10) that the United States would not "thwart a change of government or deny economic or military

---

52 In the words of Rufus Phillips, who was himself playing a game here: Phillips did not tell Lodge that Lansdale remained sympathetic to Diem, because he thought Lansdale's presence would in fact be a way of saving Diem while ousting Nhu. Ibid., 251.

53 The journalist was Richard Starnes of Scripps-Howard; the story was then picked up in a Halberstam piece in the *New York Times*, October 3, 1963 (though Halberstam omitted the false charge that Richardson had behaved insubordinately – the station was in fact under strict orders to carry out Lodge's wishes).

54 Apparently, McNamara was particularly swayed by a private meeting with South Vietnamese Defense Minister Nguyen Dinh Thuan, during which the latter argued that Diem had lost his capacity to lead. Since Lodge hoped that Thuan might succeed Diem, this assessment might well have been self-serving; it was certainly treacherous. Lodge also arranged for Vice-President Nguyen Ngoc Tho to tell the visitors that the strategic hamlet program was not working – a highly misleading assessment. Blair, 61–62.

55 Moyar, *Triumph Forsaken*, 253–55; Blair, 60–63.

assistance to a new regime if it appears capable of increasing the effectiveness of the military effort." (Fully aware that he was violating the president's order, Lodge did not report this back to the White House.) The generals got the message. The coup was set for October 26.

Now, however, a complication arose. At a cocktail party at the British Embassy on October 22, Harkins, the MACV commander, took aside one of the Vietnamese generals involved in the plot and told him he opposed a coup. This caused the generals to postpone the attempt and to seek further clarification of the situation from Lou Conein. Conein subsequently told them that Harkins did not represent official policy. As a result, the date of the coup was moved up to November 2. At the same time, assuming that Harkins would be reporting on this encounter through his own channels, Lodge was forced to inform the president of his communications with the generals. At this point, Kennedy realized the magnitude of his Lodge problem. In a White House meeting on October 25 with McNamara and others, he complained about the ambassador's amateurish and insubordinate plotting with the generals and the need to provide him more direction, though he also stated that whatever reservations they all shared about Lodge's conduct, "he's there, and because he's there we can't fire him." Evidently, political considerations dictated this attitude. But Kennedy did have Bundy send Lodge a sharp message expressing "considerable concern" over the Conein contacts, emphasizing the need for evidence of whether a coup could succeed, and repeating previous guidance against the stimulation of a coup. In reply, Lodge essentially ignored these admonitions and repeated his arguments in favor of a coup.[56]

Two days later, Lodge had an extended encounter with Diem, at the latter's hilltop retreat at Dalat. Just minutes before departing with him from the Saigon airport, however, Lodge met briefly with General Tran Van Don, one of the principal conspirators – and confirmed to him that Conein had indeed been speaking for him and the U.S. government regarding the planned coup. Contrary to Lodge's own account of these events, this deal was sealed before, not after, the meeting with Diem and had nothing to do with the president's recalcitrant behavior at that time; indeed, Diem once again was conciliatory.

In Washington, Kennedy called his advisers together for another meeting on October 29. Colby began by briefing on the political loyalties of the South Vietnamese military leadership. According to him, pro- and anti-coup forces in the Saigon area were about evenly balanced. Harriman and Rusk then spoke in favor of removing Diem. At this point, Attorney General Robert Kennedy interjected: "I just don't see that this makes any sense on the face of it. If it's a failure, I would think Diem is just going to tell us to get the hell out of the country.... We're just going down the road to disaster." Taylor and

---

[56] Incredibly, Lodge could write: "[W]henever we thwart attempts at a coup, as we have done in the past, we are incurring very long lasting resentments, we are assuming an undue responsibility for keeping the incumbents in office, and in general are setting ourselves in judgment over the affairs of Vietnam." Moyar, *Triumph Forsaken*, 260.

McCone concurred with the president's brother. In McCone's words: "We think that an unsuccessful coup would be disastrous. A successful coup, in our opinion, would create a period of political confusion that would seriously affect [the situation] for a period of time which is not possible to estimate. It might be disastrous." This assessment, of course, would prove to be correct. The president then asked to review the instructions Lodge had been given. McNamara said: "We have, rightly or wrongly, led him to believe that we would support a coup, or at least would keep hands off." Kennedy then pointed out that if pro- and anti-coup forces were evenly balanced, a coup would in fact be unwise. It was eventually decided that Bundy would cable Lodge to notify the generals at once that the coup plans were not seen as sufficiently promising and to hold off until he, Harkins, and the CIA could do a new assessment. In responding to this message, Lodge argued that the coup could not be stopped short of betraying the plotters to Diem, which could lead to the decimation of his army's top leadership, and he brushed off any concerns about the prospects of success; nor did Lodge ever instruct Conein to deliver the president's message to the generals. Later that night, following the receipt of several cables from Harkins objecting to Lodge's policy and defending Diem, the president, obviously uneasy about the direction of events, sent Lodge a further message including the pointed comment: "We do not accept as a basis for U.S. policy that we have no power to delay or discourage a coup." He stopped short, however, of ordering the ambassador to desist, but instead authorized him to make the final decision based on his own judgment of the coup's viability. With that, Lodge had won the day.

In a final meeting on November 1, Diem asked Lodge to meet with Nolting and Colby when he returned to Washington to discuss the matter of Nhu. He then added: "Please tell President Kennedy that I am a good and frank ally, that I would rather be frank and settle questions now than talk about them after we have lost everything. Tell President Kennedy that I take all his suggestions very seriously and wish to carry them out but it is a question of timing." Lodge deliberately delayed the cable in which he reported on this conversation: It reached Washington some hours after news of the coup against Diem had begun to arrive there.[57]

It will not be necessary to follow the details of the generals' coup or the brutal murder of the Ngo brothers as they were being held in the back of an armored personnel carrier. It is difficult to improve on the following summary assessment of these events:

While South Vietnam's President was ousted and killed by certain of his countrymen, ultimate responsibility for his fate belonged to Henry Cabot Lodge, to the President who appointed and refused to fire Lodge, and to the individuals who were giving Lodge information and advice on the political situation – a few State Department officials in Saigon and Washington and a handful of resident journalists. Lodge had overridden a much larger and better informed group of Americans who had opposed a coup,

[57] Ibid., 263–66.

including most of Kennedy's top advisers, the top CIA and military officials in Vietnam, and veteran American journalists, and he had disregarded orders against encouraging a coup from President Kennedy, who himself was torn by serious doubts about removing Diem. Hiding his actions from Washington, Lodge pushed South Vietnamese generals into launching a coup they had not wanted to undertake in the first place and were hesitant to undertake until the very end.... Although Kennedy eventually discovered his ambassador's conniving, Lodge's potential role in the 1964 election dissuaded the President from firing him and led the President instead to try, in vain, to steer Lodge and the plotters away from the coup.[58]

In a further twist of fate, of course, just three weeks later, in Dallas, Texas, Kennedy himself would fall to an assassin's bullet.

The new president, Lyndon Baines Johnson, was very unhappy with the role Lodge had played in the coup against Diem, but like Kennedy, he was reluctant to dismiss him because of his probable presidential candidacy in the coming year; indeed, he ordered that all of Lodge's requests be met, so as not to give him a pretext for resigning.[59] LBJ did, however, fire Roger Hilsman and exile Harriman; and he instructed Lodge not to push the new government to undertake reforms in the American image. In fact, some liberalizing measures initially taken by the military junta under General Duong Van Minh were in any case soon abandoned as the government spiraled into chaos. What is surprising about Lodge's behavior during this period is the almost total lack of interest he showed in helping to shape the new regime. The generals lacked political experience, and the hybrid civil–military structure they cobbled together initially soon proved unworkable, but Lodge made no effort to advise them on the mechanics of government and signally failed to encourage their attempt to broaden the base of the regime by creating a "Council of Notables" broadly representative of the country.[60] Nor did Lodge intervene to halt the extensive purges of South Vietnamese provincial commanders and officials by the new junta, which would prove extremely damaging to the government's ability to wage war against the Communists over the next several years.[61]

At the same time, Lodge remained unwilling to relinquish what he regarded as his overall authority over the American governmental presence in South Vietnam, and in particular continued to be at odds with Harkins. Eventually, LBJ decided that something had to be done to improve interagency cooperation in Saigon and dispatched David Nes, an experienced foreign service

---

[58] Ibid., 273. A good case can be made that Lodge in fact bears personal responsibility for the killing of the Ngo brothers through his failure to arrange for their safe departure from the country (ibid., 271–72).

[59] Blair, 96–98. After the coup, though, Kennedy did ask his brother to find a way to remove Lodge.

[60] See ibid., 78–81. Blair rightly remarks: "Another ambassador might have viewed the immediate post-coup period, bound to be fluid, as no less important to US foreign policy interests, if not more so, than the pre-coup period," but Lodge remained oddly detached; indeed, he seemed to feel his mission was over (78).

[61] Moyar, *Triumph Forsaken*, 281–82.

officer, as the new deputy chief of mission with a virtually explicit mandate to perform the role of administrative coordinator of the embassy's country team that Lodge had shown himself incapable of. Predictably, Lodge refused to give Nes any authority, or even full access to cables from the State Department. Then General William Westmoreland, who became Harkins' deputy at MACV in January (and would succeed him in June) of 1964, invited Nes to act as vice-chair under himself of a new interagency Pacification Committee. This committee succeeded in restoring a measure of order to the overall American effort, but when Lodge realized that it was effectively cutting him out of the direction of the war, he had it disbanded after only four weeks of operation. In the meantime, Lodge's political supporters in the United States were busy orchestrating his presidential run, whose prospects were in fact enhanced by the death of Kennedy. In March, Lodge won an overwhelming victory in the New Hampshire Republican primary as a write-in candidate. But Lodge's unwillingness to campaign doomed his candidacy, as had also happened with Douglas MacArthur. After his defeat in the Oregon primary in May, Lodge announced his withdrawal from the race. In June, he also submitted his resignation as ambassador to South Vietnam.

The departure of Lodge and the advent of Westmoreland in 1964 marked a sea change in the management of the war. In Washington, McNamara and the Defense Department displaced State as the epicenter of Vietnam policy. At the same time, MACV under Westmoreland soon became the dominant player in Saigon. The appointment of JCS chairman General Maxwell Taylor as Lodge's replacement further highlights what may fairly be called the militarization of the U.S. effort at this juncture. It would be a mistake, however, to assume that this was necessarily a bad thing. Harkins' political judgment, after all, had been unarguably superior to Lodge's. Indeed, this new alignment of the players constituted an important opportunity to fix the broken Vietnam policy process, and in particular the civil–military disconnect in Saigon itself. Taylor brought four stars and great prestige to bear as the new ambassador to South Vietnam. If anyone was in a position to exercise proconsular-style authority there over the course of U.S. engagement in Southeast Asia, it was Taylor, not Lodge. And Taylor was in fact able to extract from LBJ a writ of authority more sweeping than that of any of his predecessors – in particular, control of the American military effort in Vietnam.[62] Yet, for reasons that are not entirely

---

[62] "As you take charge of the American effort in South Vietnam, I want you to have this formal expression not only of my confidence, but of my desire that you have and exercise full responsibility for the effort of the United States Government in Vietnam. In general terms this authority is parallel to that set forth in President Kennedy's letter of May 29, 1961, to all American ambassadors; specifically, I wish it clearly understood that this overall responsibility includes the whole military effort in South Vietnam and authorizes the degree of command and control that you consider appropriate." This language was apparently drafted by Taylor himself. In a forwarding note to the president for his signature, McGeorge Bundy said of this document: "What it does is to give Max full control over everything in South Vietnam. This is something the military never let the ambassador have before, and now that we have a man whom the

clear, he failed to take full advantage of this mandate. Part of the reason for this may have been that Taylor did not care to force the issue of his role in the military chain of command, which posed a basic challenge to the authority of Admiral Ulysses S. Grant Sharp, the theater commander in Honolulu.[63] But his relationship with Westmoreland also seems to have been problematic. Although the two generals got along personally, it soon became clear that they had rather different approaches to the conduct of the war. Taylor favored a program of air strikes against North Vietnam while resisting significant increases in the number of American troops on the ground in the south that threatened to escalate U.S. involvement in the conflict. Westmoreland, on the other hand, pressed consistently for more U.S. ground forces, including combat forces; and his view eventually carried the day with the Pentagon and the president. When American combat units deployed in South Vietnam beginning in March 1965, Taylor was therefore effectively marginalized as a player in the military arena. His influence in Washington apparently also suffered from a perception that he had failed to cope effectively with the chaotic ("revolving door") political scene in Saigon during this period, though this may not have been altogether fair.[64] In any event, Taylor's position was probably seriously compromised at the outset by his stated intention to leave his post after a single year, thus making him something of a lame duck.

There can be little question that the period of Taylor's tenure as ambassador was marked by extraordinary indecision and confusion in American policy-making on Vietnam generally. It is therefore difficult to isolate his own contribution to this state of affairs. One is tempted to think nevertheless that the general missed a real opportunity to provide strategic leadership to the American effort at this critical juncture. At a time when the Joint Chiefs were effectively marginalized by McNamara and LBJ, while civilian officials in Washington lacked strategic focus, the men on the spot had an opening. Yet Taylor and Westmoreland seemed to lose sight of the bigger picture. Arguments between Saigon and Washington over desired force levels too often failed to

---

military cannot refuse, it is time to establish the principle." John M. Taylor, *General Maxwell Taylor: The Sword and the Pen* (New York: Doubleday, 1989), 298–99.

[63] Taylor himself claims this was not a problem, saying he discussed the directive with both Sharp and Westmoreland and made clear he "had no intention of getting into MAC/V's day-to-day business," but only wanted to be sure that Westmoreland cleared all policy cables through himself (Taylor, 316); but this seems misleading. See McMaster, 171–72.

[64] In December 1965, Taylor administered a tongue-lashing to four of South Vietnam's leading generals and subsequently pressured then–Prime Minister General Nguyen Khanh to resign, at which point the ambassador came close to being declared *persona non grata* and asked to leave the country. Moyar, *Triumph Forsaken*, 343–47. Taylor acted in this manner at least partly because he himself had been pressured by LBJ to straighten out South Vietnamese politics. Nevertheless, this incident seems to have shaken Washington's confidence in the general. In a memorandum to the president in early March, Bundy would write: "McNamara and I, if the decision were ours to make, would bring Taylor back.... Max has been gallant, determined and honorable to a fault, but he has been rigid, remote, and sometimes abrupt." Cited in John M. Taylor, 311–12.

come to grips with the question of just what these new American units would be expected to do. Perhaps most tellingly, Taylor seems not to have intervened in or otherwise reacted to Westmoreland's decision in March 1965 to reject a plan to insert a five-division force across the 17th Parallel to block the Laotian infiltration routes. This operation might well have changed the entire course of the war.[65]

Taylor was replaced as ambassador in July 1965 by none other than Henry Cabot Lodge. This move is surprising and the reasons for it unclear, but a political calculation of some kind may well have been involved.[66] Yet still more surprising is that Lansdale, too, had a second act in Vietnam at this time. This was largely owing to the intervention with Lodge of Vice President Hubert Humphrey, to whom Lansdale had managed to open a channel. Lansdale went to Saigon as the ambassador's special assistant for pacification. This arrangement was doomed from the start. This time, Lansdale lacked an institutional base in the CIA, while Lodge proved unwilling to give him strong hands-on support. Without any direct control over programs or money, Lansdale inevitably came into competition with the established agencies – including the State Department itself, as Deputy Ambassador William Porter was formally charged with coordinating the pacification effort. Lansdale tried with some success to recreate a web of personal relationships with the new South Vietnamese leadership, which was finally stabilizing under the joint rule of Generals Nguyen Van Thieu and Nguyen Cao Ky. But these efforts attracted the enmity of Lodge's political officer Philip Habib, who set out to undermine and thwart Lansdale at every turn. Nevertheless, the general hung on through Lodge's tour and well into the Bunker era, departing Saigon for the last time in June 1968.[67]

The pacification question gained increasing attention in Washington during this period, not least from the president himself. In March 1966, LBJ decided

---

[65] Ibid., 368–69. Rufus Phillips describes General Taylor in the following terms: "Taylor had previously exhibited only the most conventional approach to Vietnam, looking on it mainly as a military and geopolitical problem. Although he had a reputation as an intellectual, at heart he was a very traditional and often rigid military thinker, imbued with the formal hierarchy of command and wanting always to be in control.... As ambassador he would exhibit an extreme inability to understand or adapt to the constantly shifting dynamics of the Vietnamese side of the war. He was a big-picture man whose vision was unable to focus on the nuances of Vietnamese politics, which constantly surprised him." *Why Vietnam Matters: An Eyewitness Account of Lessons Not Learned* (Annapolis: Naval Institute Press, 2008), 235.

[66] Of LBJ's reappointment of Lodge, Fritz Nolting says: "I have never understood why. I know that Vice President Johnson disapproved of much of Lodge's advice and many of his actions under Kennedy in 1963. Why, then, did he reappoint him? I can only speculate, but I suspect that Johnson, like Kennedy, wanted a thick piece of Republican asbestos out there to shield him from the heat." Nolting, 135. In fact, though, Bundy apparently supported the appointment because he thought Lodge would give more attention to pacification. See Richard A. Hunt, *Pacification: The American Struggle for Vietnam's Hearts and Minds* (Boulder, CO: Westview, 1995), 66–67.

[67] See the account in Currey, ch. 13.

to create a pacification "czar" in the White House to improve interagency planning and implementation of the variety of programs falling under this general rubric, and appointed to the new position Robert Komer, a former CIA officer then on the National Security Council staff. Komer, famously nicknamed "Blowtorch Bob," was a hard-charging bureaucratic warrior who had the president's trust and full support in this project. But the Saigon end would remain problematic, given the administrative ineptitude of Ambassador Lodge. For the next eight months, various options for strengthening and consolidating the management of pacification in the field were wrestled over. The key issues were establishing clear operational authority over the pacification effort and the role the military should play in it. Komer, McNamara, and eventually the president came to favor a solution that in effect embedded pacification within the MACV chain of command, but the civilian agencies resisted this idea. In November, it was provisionally decided to retain civilian control of pacification but to create a new operational entity, the Office of Civilian Operations, headed by Deputy Ambassador Porter and staffed by some 1,000 officials seconded from various agencies. Porter, however, was burdened by his other responsibilities in managing the embassy, while Lodge and Westmoreland were unable or unwilling to solve at their level the problem of integrating the military and civilian sides of the war.

Frustrated by this situation, LBJ cast about in early 1967 for a new solution. For a time, he considered the radical alternative of making Westmoreland the U.S. ambassador while retaining command of MACV – that is, something like a true proconsul. Westmoreland was to have assistance from an "Ambassador at Large, assuming responsibility for our political policy," and Johnson identified for this role the senior and highly respected career diplomat Ellsworth Bunker. Neither Bunker nor Westmoreland welcomed this arrangement, however, and it was also opposed by McNamara and Rusk. It is possible that the president put forward this scheme for tactical reasons; at all events, he quickly backed off and opted for what may have been his preference all along – a civilian-led pacification organization located within the MACV structure.[68] Thus was born what would be known as CORDS – Civil Operations and Revolutionary Development Support. In May, LBJ officially authorized this new organization and appointed Bob Komer as its first director, with the rank of ambassador.[69] At the same time, Johnson selected General Creighton W. Abrams as deputy (and expected successor) to Westmoreland, with the specific task of improving the performance of the South Vietnamese armed forces.

The CORDS experiment was a unique one in the annals of America's small wars. Komer served as Westmoreland's deputy commander for the military as well as civilian aspects of pacification, and CORDS itself was a hybrid organization, with military as well as civilian officers at every level, including

---

[68] Hunt, 86–87.
[69] See Komer's own account in Robert W. Komer, *Bureaucracy at War: U.S. Performance in the Vietnam Conflict* (Boulder, CO: Westview, 1986).

field officers in military regions, provinces, and districts. Komer himself had a two-star Army general as his own deputy; senior civilians usually had a military deputy, and vice versa. Indeed, integration went so far that senior civilians were actually able to write performance evaluations of their military subordinates, and the same held for senior officers and their civilian subordinates. CORDS commanded and controlled U.S. Army civil affairs units and took over responsibility for supplying, equipping, and advising the Regional Forces and Popular Forces – the South Vietnamese paramilitary elements that were the front lines of pacification in the countryside. This latter was probably the most important organizational change for the eventual course of the pacification effort. It also took control from the CIA of programs for identifying and targeting the Viet Cong "infrastructure" or secret government throughout South Vietnam.[70]

Robert McNamara surely ranks as the worst secretary of defense in the short history of that office, though he has some competition. Lyndon Baines Johnson was the worst American war president at least since Woodrow Wilson. Both men had little use for professional military advice and went to considerable lengths to cut the military leadership out of national-level decision-making on Vietnam. Both were fundamentally astrategic in their approach to the war. Both failed to take the measure of the enemy. They paid little attention to intelligence, and instead tended to project American ways of thinking on the Vietnamese communists.[71] Both grossly misjudged the danger of Soviet or Chinese intervention on the side of the North Vietnamese – indeed, they failed to subject this critical issue to serious analysis or testing;[72] this in turn reinforced their misguided approach to using force in a highly limited fashion to convey political or diplomatic messages rather than for actual strategic effect. Furthermore, there can be no question that Johnson's handling of the war was influenced by domestic political considerations to a degree that in retrospect is little short of scandalous.[73] This, it should be added, is what largely explains LBJ's failure (with some limited exceptions) to correct the dysfunctionality of the national security decision-making machinery he inherited from his predecessor.

Given all this, it is hardly surprising that the dominant narrative of the Vietnam War places most of the blame for the debacle on the leadership in Washington, and in particular the senior civilian leadership. Within the U.S. military itself, it remains an article of faith that the war was lost fundamentally as a result of unwarranted and incompetent interference by civilians in Washington in matters that were properly the responsibility of the military.[74]

---

[70] Authoritatively discussed in Moyar, *Phoenix*.
[71] CIA director John McCone resigned in disgust in April 1965, citing his lack of access to the president and the administration's "apparent disinterest in intelligence" generally. McMaster, 257.
[72] See the discussion in Walton, ch. 6.
[73] This is thoroughly documented by McMaster in particular. See also Herspring, ch. 6.
[74] Colonel Harry Summers' treatise *On Strategy: A Critical Analysis of the Vietnam War* (Novato, CA: Presidio, 1982) remains the bible of this faith.

Nevertheless, there is a strong case to be made that the military leadership cannot entirely escape blame. In Washington, the Joint Chiefs were passive and
ineffective to a fault. And in Saigon, there is the question of the role of General
Westmoreland.

It is certainly possible to mount a plausible defense of Westmoreland. His
conduct of the war was clearly hampered by constraints of both policy and
resources over which he had little control. At the end of the day, however, he
was simply the wrong man for the job.[75] The general's first fundamental error,
paradoxically, was that he was a good soldier – that is to say, he refused to
play proconsular politics. He was too ready simply to accept the parameters
of his situation instead of challenging them, in the manner of a MacArthur or
Clay. Johnson himself was mindful of this possibility and might well have been
decisively swayed at various junctures by political pressure generated by Westmoreland, whether through private threats of resignation (the preferred style
of Clay) or more or less open politicking (the MacArthur mode). At the least,
Westmoreland could have pressed Washington to elevate his command to the
level of a regional CINC for all of Southeast Asia and called for greater authority to conduct operations in Laos and Cambodia.[76] Or he could have pressed
for the creation of a unified command that would include the armed forces
of South Vietnam and the other allies.[77] Instead, he wasted his limited clout
on repeated calls for troop increases that he should have known were difficult
or impossible to get approval for in the deteriorating political environment of
Washington.

Westmoreland's second fundamental error – in this case bearing directly on
his competence as a military professional – was his flawed strategy. It would
perhaps be better to use the term "operational concept," for it is doubtful
that Westmoreland had what can be considered a strategy in any meaningful
sense. This concept, variously described as "attrition," "search and destroy,"
or the "war of the big battalions," reflected a deeply conventional approach to
contemporary warfare, one that made little sense in the context of the highly
political and irregular battlefield that was Vietnam. To what extent Westmoreland himself was responsible for driving this approach is difficult to say.[78]
There were certainly some in the Army leadership who had reservations about
it. At the very least, one would have to conclude that he did not question it
sufficiently, particularly as evidence accumulated that it was not effective. This

---

[75] For the general's own story see William C. Westmoreland, *A Soldier Reports* (Garden City, NY:
Doubleday, 1976). See also Samuel Zaffiri, *Westmoreland: A Biography of William C. Westmoreland* (New York: William Morrow, 1994), and especially Lewis Sorley, *Westmoreland:
The General Who Lost Vietnam* (Boston: Houghton Mifflin Harcourt, 2011), an understated
yet authoritative – and devastating – account.

[76] Eventually, he did come around to appreciate the need for action against Laos and Cambodia,
but by this point Washington had become paralyzed by the fear of a wider war.

[77] Walton, 59–61.

[78] See especially Krepinevich, ch. 6 ("A Strategy of Tactics"), who emphasizes the extent to which
Westmoreland's approach was culturally rooted in traditional Army doctrine and practice.

is not to say, as some have argued, that the Vietnam War could have been won by pacification measures alone, for the war was finally lost to the "big battalions" of Hanoi. What was wrong with the concept, most fundamentally, was that the enemy could simply not be "attrited" without steps to stop continuing infiltration of troops from the North via the Ho Chi Minh Trail. Indeed, if anyone was being attrited, it was the American side, in the sense of erosion of support for the war on the home front.

There were three pillars of a successful allied strategy in South Vietnam. The first was the employment of America's "big battalions" to hold the ring against large concentrations of North Vietnamese conventional forces; the second was pacification; and the third was training, equipping and advising the South Vietnamese military. Of these, only the first was a priority for Westmoreland. As noted earlier, it is to LBJ's credit that he recognized a problem here and took steps to strengthen both the pacification and training/advising pillars. But it was only after Westmoreland's departure that all three pillars were welded together in a single coherent whole by the new and more effective proconsular team that Johnson – again to his credit – put in place.

It will not be necessary to follow developments in the Bunker/Abrams era in any detail, but several points should be made. The most dramatic single event in the war was of course the Tet Offensive of January 1968. This uprising of Vietcong cadres across the breadth of South Vietnam took the allies by surprise and led to several months of bloody fighting. It was a turning point in the war in several senses. Most obvious at the time was the shock it administered to American public opinion and to the credibility of the U.S. military leadership and the Johnson administration as a whole. At the same time, Tet was a military and strategic disaster of the first magnitude for the Communists themselves, though this only became clear over time. Apart from the enormous number of casualties inflicted on them (some 240,000 killed or wounded), in the aftermath of Tet the Vietcong essentially ceased to exist as an independent military and political actor. This was an important precondition for the turnaround in the pacification effort in South Vietnam that was to occur in the coming years. But the pacification effort itself was also greatly improved under Komer's successor as head of CORDS, the very able Bill Colby.

What one might call the proconsular triad of Abrams, Bunker, and Colby fundamentally altered the course of the Vietnam War, shifting the political and military momentum increasingly to the side of the allies while at the same time overseeing an impressive buildup of South Vietnamese military and governing capacity and the relatively smooth functioning of the Saigon regime. Their contributions in this regard have never been adequately recognized. This is so largely because this achievement so obviously undermines the orthodox narrative of the Vietnam War, and also because it was overshadowed at the time by the advent of the Nixon administration and its early embrace of a new strategy for the war that became known as "Vietnamization." In fact, however, as we have seen, the seeds of this strategy were sown in the final years of the Johnson administration and were beginning to bear fruit well before

Nixon and his secretary of defense, Melvin Laird, unrolled the Vietnamization policy in the spring of 1969. The real change that occurred under the new administration was rather a shift from a strategy of victory over Hanoi to one of negotiating with the Communists for the best deal that would permit a graceful U.S. withdrawal from the country. Their achievement is all the more impressive in this debilitating psychological environment.

What did the triad do differently? It is sometimes claimed or assumed that little in fact changed in the actual prosecution of the war in the Abrams era. Abrams never promulgated a document describing and mandating a different approach to the use of the military instrument, and he seems to have allowed considerable freedom to his subordinate commanders to conduct large-scale operations as in the past.[79] While it is true that he generally was able to break his forces down into smaller units, this reflected in considerable part the damage inflicted on the enemy during the Tet offensive. Yet it needs to be kept in mind that Westmoreland remained very much in the picture at this time, having been promoted to Army chief of staff after departing Saigon. It is natural to suppose that Abrams would have wanted to downplay any differences with his boss and avoid any public or written criticism of his performance at MACV. In private and in person, by contrast, Abrams constantly emphasized to his staff and commanders that the United States was now fighting "only one war," of which pacification and the improvement of South Vietnamese capabilities were both integral aspects; and the overriding objective of that war was to be securing the population, not merely killing large numbers of the enemy. "Search and destroy" would henceforth yield to "clear and hold."[80] Moreover, the new warfighting approach rested on a very different operational concept from one based on attrition: destruction of the enemy's logistics and supplies. Capture of rice sacks, not body counts, would be the metric for this concept.[81] This could only be understood as a fundamental repudiation of the Westmoreland way of war. Also worth emphasizing is the new emphasis Abrams brought to intelligence. Intelligence became a centerpiece of his own way of war and scored impressive successes, above all in understanding and targeting North Vietnamese military traffic on the Ho Chi Minh Trail. At the same time, offensive military operations were able to engage the enemy's maneuver units in better planned, more efficient, and more lethal

---

[79] See, for example, ibid., 252–57. Krepinevich quotes Komer himself as denying that Abrams effected any change in U.S. strategy, but he is hardly a reliable source: Abrams disliked Komer and eventually arranged his relief. Sorley, 61–63. At all events, there is now plentiful evidence of Abrams' real thinking with the recent publication of transcripts of tapes of the general's weekly staff meetings: Lewis Sorley, ed., *Vietnam Chronicles: The Abrams Tapes, 1968–1972* (Lubbock: Texas Tech University Press, 2004). This marvelous work provides in effect an extended window on day-to-day proconsular decision-making generally. See also Sorley's earlier biography, *Thunderbolt: General Creighton Abrams and the Army of His Times* (New York: Simon & Schuster, 1992).

[80] Cf. ibid., 29–30.

[81] Sorley, *A Better War*, chs. 1–2.

encounters.[82] Finally, the new emphasis on Vietnamization resulted in a few short years in a quantum improvement in the quality and quantity of the South Vietnamese armed forces, though some serious shortcomings remained.[83]

On the pacification front, Colby oversaw an enormous buildup in the Popular Forces, Regional Forces, and People's Self-Defense Forces (part-time local militia) as well as dramatic improvements in their equipment, while forging an effective partnership between CORDS and a parallel structure within the South Vietnamese government, which retained primary responsibility for the overall effort. Colby's (unfairly maligned) "Phoenix" program coordinated intelligence collection on the so-called Viet Cong Infrastructure (VCI), the secret communist apparatus throughout the country, thus permitting a sharp increase in the effectiveness of police and paramilitary action at the political level of the war. Other programs sought to empower local officials and villagers, help them economically, and strengthen their loyalty to the government. Perhaps the most important of these was the "Land to the Tiller" land reform effort launched by the South Vietnamese in 1970. Contrary to the received wisdom, the South Vietnamese government was increasingly popular in the countryside during this period as a result of these demonstrated successes.[84]

As for the ambassador, Bunker can best be understood as a return to the Lansdale model of interaction with the South Vietnamese leadership. Though faced with difficulties and reverses on that front (particularly Thieu's unopposed presidential candidacy in 1971), Bunker deserves much credit for his quiet but persistent efforts to move the South Vietnamese in the direction of constitutional government and at least a semblance of popular participation in the regime.[85] His relationships with Washington were similarly smooth, and the ambassador was respected and listened to by both of the presidents he served.[86] Bunker saw eye to eye with Abrams, sharing with him a very broad or holistic view of the war. Both followed closely not only political and

---

[82] Ibid., ch. 3. Only recently has the story of signals intelligence during the Vietnam War been told: Robert J. Hanyok, *Spartans in Darkness: American SIGINT and the Indochina War, 1945–1975* (Fort Meade, MD: Center for Cryptologic History, National Security Agency, 2002); this originally top-secret study was declassified in 2008 and can be accessed at http://www.fas.org/irp/nsa/spartans/index.html.

[83] Notably, in the area of leadership, as became apparent in the rapid collapse of the ARVN in 1975. See James H. Wilbanks, *Abandoning Vietnam: How America Left and South Vietnam Lost Its War* (Lawrence: University Press of Kansas, 2004), 277–88.

[84] See especially Moyar, *Phoenix*, chs. 20–26, 29, as well as Colby's own account in *Lost Victory*, especially chs. 15–17.

[85] Howard B. Schaffer, *Ellsworth Bunker: Global Troubleshooter, Vietnam Hawk* (Chapel Hill: University of North Carolina Press, 2003), 181–88. Bunker's dispatches to Washington (like Lodge, he communicated directly with the president) are an important historical resource: Douglas Pike, ed., *The Bunker Papers: Reports to the President from Vietnam, 1967–1973*, 2 vols. (Berkeley: Institute of East Asian Studies, University of California at Berkeley, 1990).

[86] Perhaps the most noteworthy example of what might be termed proconsular independence on Bunker's part was his successful opposition to the efforts of Clark Clifford, Johnson's new secretary of defense, to move the president toward an early ending of the war. Schaffer, 209–11.

economic as well as military developments in Vietnam itself but also events in the larger theater, and Bunker supported Abrams in arguing for taking the war into Laos and Cambodia. In this respect, they can be seen as proconsuls not just for Vietnam but for the "paramountcy" of Southeast Asia, even when their ability to act outside the country itself was severely constrained. In all these respects, they offer a model that has continuing relevance for the present day.

8

Clark in the Balkans

Never ask "Mother, may I," unless you know the answer.

General Wesley K. Clark[1]

Toward the end of the Clinton administration, in a series of widely noticed articles later expanded into a book, *Washington Post* correspondent Dana Priest called attention to what she claimed to be a novel feature of the post–Cold War era: the growth in the prestige, power, scope of activity, and relative independence of the United States' regional military "commanders in chief" (CINCs).[2] Since that time, the notion that the regional CINCs are in effect the "proconsuls" of a new American "empire" has become a standard trope in the contemporary literature on American foreign policy. They have become Exhibit A in the larger argument – which has proponents on many points of the political compass – that American foreign policy since the end of the Cold War has taken a turn toward unilateral and military solutions to international problems and, in particular, the forceful imposition of democratic governments on unfriendly autocracies around the world.[3] What is one to make of all this?

---

[1] Dana Priest, "A Four-Star Foreign Policy? U.S. Commanders Wield Rising Clout," *Washington Post*, September 28, 2000.

[2] In addition to the article just cited, see Dana Priest, "Free of Oversight, U.S. Military Trains Foreign Troops," *Washington Post*, July 12, 1998; "Standing Up to State and Congress," *Washington Post*, September 28, 2000; "An Engagement in Ten Time Zones; Zinni Crosses Central Asia, Holding Hands, Building Trust," *Washington Post*, September 29, 2000; and *The Mission: Waging War and Keeping Peace with America's Military* (New York: W. W. Norton, 2003).

[3] See notably Andrew J. Bacevich, *American Empire: The Realities and Consequences of U.S. Diplomacy* (Cambridge, MA: Harvard University Press, 2002), esp. ch. 7 ("Rise of the Proconsuls"), as well as *The New American Militarism: How Americans are Seduced by War* (Oxford: Oxford University Press, 2005). (Bacevich is a retired Army colonel.) See also Chalmers Johnson, *The Sorrows of Empire: Militarism, Secrecy, and the End of the Republic* (New York: Henry Holt and Co., 2004). Johnson tells us: "Leaving foreign policy in the hands of regional proconsuls advances militarism because they inevitably turn to military assets to achieve foreign policy objectives" (126).

The origins of the current system of regional CINCs – or as they are now called, combatant commanders[4] – go back to the immediate aftermath of World War II. In effect, the first CINC was General Dwight Eisenhower, who in June 1945 was given command of a new organization, U.S. Forces in the European Theater (USFET), headquartered in Stuttgart and later encompassing General Lucius Clay's military government command in Germany as well as regular army and air units throughout Western Europe. This would eventually become U.S. European Command (USEUCOM or simply EUCOM). Its commander (styled USCINCEUR or simply CINCEUR) would later be "dual-hatted" as the senior North Atlantic Treaty Organization (NATO) military officer, or Supreme Allied Commander in Europe (SACEUR), a position that ever since has been occupied by an American four-star general officer. But the impetus behind the creation of a comprehensive worldwide system of CINCs actually came from the Navy, which remained deeply unhappy over FDR's decision to create a separate theater command for General Douglas MacArthur in the Southwest Pacific during World War II. After much interservice wrangling, a plan was agreed upon and approved by President Truman in December 1946. Eventually known as the Unified Command Plan (UCP), this "interim measure for the immediate postwar period" would become a founding document of today's American military, while being altered some twenty times in the intervening years to reflect new strategic realities and requirements.[5]

By far the most important of the regional unified commands over the years have been EUCOM and the Pacific command (PACOM), headquartered in Honolulu, Hawaii. Today, EUCOM's "area of responsibility" (AOR) encompasses all of Europe, Russia, Ukraine, the Caucasus, Turkey, and Israel, as well as the Mediterranean, Black, and Caspian Seas and a large swath of the Atlantic Ocean. PACOM covers East, Southeast, and South Asia and large parts of the Pacific and Indian Oceans as well as the Antarctic. There are currently four other regional commands: NORTHCOM (North America), SOUTHCOM (South and Central America and the Caribbean), CENTCOM (the Middle East and Central and Southwest Asia), and AFRICOM (Africa less Egypt). None of these have their primary headquarters in the region itself. SOUTHCOM was transferred from the Panama Canal Zone to Miami in 1979; CENTCOM's primary headquarters is in Tampa, though there is a small forward headquarters in Qatar in the Persian Gulf. The recently (2007) established AFRICOM remains collocated with its parent organization EUCOM in Stuttgart, Germany, though a move to some African venue is a possibility in the future.

4 The name change was mandated in October 2002 by then–Secretary of Defense Donald Rumsfeld, in order to underline the overall constitutional authority of the president as "commander in chief" of the American armed forces. It was part of a larger effort by Rumsfeld to reassert civilian control of the U.S. military.
5 For an overview see Gregg Garbesi, "U.S. Unified Command Plan," in Derek S. Reveron, ed., *America's Viceroys: The Military and U.S. Foreign Policy* (New York: Palgrave Macmillan, 2004), ch. 2, and for a detailed and authoritative account see *The History of the Unified Command Plan, 1946–1993* (Washington, DC: Joint History Office, 1995).

Typically, the CINCs commanding each region are from the service that is most engaged in that region; this is especially true of PACOM, which has always been headed by an admiral, and EUCOM, usually an Army general (the current occupant, though, is Admiral James Stavridis).

The primary function of the unified commands is to provide a mechanism to ensure the unified action of all U.S. military services in a theater, including both the planning and conduct of operations. Prior to World War II, there was no such mechanism. The secretary of war and the Army chief of staff controlled all Army and Army air forces, while the secretary of the Navy and the Chief of Naval Operations controlled the forces of the Navy and Marine Corps; the two service chiefs also owned war planning. Cooperation between them in war or peace was ad hoc and subject to negotiation. The combatant commanders are supported by a "joint staff" manned by personnel of all the services, of whom the most important are the "component commanders," the senior representatives of each service.[6] A key variable in the evolution of the unified commands is the nature of their relationships to the services and the service chiefs. Originally, the service chiefs – after 1942 constituted as a single body, the Joint Chiefs of Staff (JCS) – essentially controlled the CINCs, both administratively and operationally. One of the service chiefs was at first informally designated as "executive agent" for each unified command, a practice that was formalized by the Key West Agreement signed and issued by President Truman in April 1948. President Eisenhower was dissatisfied with this arrangement and the power it gave the service chiefs, however, and in the course of his administration moved to strengthen the role of the secretary of defense (created by the National Security Act of 1947) and his immediate staff, the Office of the Secretary of Defense (OSD), as well as that of the president himself in relation to the chiefs. An act of 1958 transferred authority from the JCS to the president to establish and disestablish unified commands, to assign them missions, and to determine their force structure. Most importantly, to reduce the influence of the services over the CINC component commands, this law made the CINCs directly responsible to the president and secretary of defense and gave them full operational command over all forces assigned to the theater. For various reasons, however, the actual impact of these changes would be relatively marginal.

As we have seen, the 1960s were a time of considerable tension in civil–military relations in the United States. Presidents Kennedy and Johnson both lacked confidence in the senior military leadership and tended to ignore their professional advice when it proved inconvenient, and the same was true of the civilian leadership of the Pentagon – above all, Secretary of Defense Robert McNamara himself. Under these circumstances, little was or could be done to further strengthen and institutionalize civilian control of the military command chain linking Washington and the field. Indeed, in some ways the chiefs

---

[6] There is also a component commander for the U.S. Special Operations Command, which in this and other respects functions much like a separate service.

benefited from this state of affairs; at any rate, their informal influence over the CINCs remained very considerable. Nevertheless, accumulating evidence of poor interservice cooperation in a number of contingency operations in the 1970s and 1980s – particularly the fiasco of "Desert One," the failed effort to rescue U.S. hostages in Iran in 1980 – led to increasing calls for additional reform legislation to enhance "jointness" throughout the military. The proponents of reform eventually won an extended debate on this subject, and in 1986 the U.S. Congress passed the Goldwater–Nichols Department of Defense Reorganization Act, a landmark piece of legislation that would substantially reshape the organization and functioning of the American military after the Cold War.[7]

The Goldwater–Nichols bill made explicit and emphatic that the operational chain of command extends from the president to the secretary of defense and from the secretary directly to the unified commands, thus bypassing the Joint Chiefs. On the other hand, one of its most important effects was to strengthen the power of the chairman of the JCS relative to the other chiefs by authorizing him to provide independent advice to the president and the secretary of defense. Specifically, it empowered the chairman to solicit program and budget recommendations directly from the CINCs rather than from the services only, their traditional providers of personnel and weaponry. The intent of this provision was to strengthen the link between the war planning traditionally conducted at the various commands and Washington-level decision-making on military policy and force structure. And in fact this is now routinely done. As a recent observer has said, these changes have "served to empower the combatant commanders to the point where many now perceive that combatant commanders are aggressively setting the agenda instead of acting as passive recipients of what the Services offer."[8] In practice, of course, the service chiefs cannot simply be bypassed by the chairman or the civilian leadership, and retain much of their former influence over military policy and strategy. But the new legislation has nevertheless given the CINCs an unprecedented degree of independence as well as, for the first time, a seat at the policy table.

But this enhanced role in military decision-making is only one aspect of the increased power and responsibilities of the combatant commanders today, and the least remarked on. Those who worry about the proconsular proclivities of our CINCs are concerned primarily over their diplomatic role. Contrary to the view taken by Dana Priest and others, however, there is nothing especially new, surprising, or inappropriate in such a role. It seems to have evolved in a more or less unplanned fashion to support the global military presence that the United States has maintained ever since the end of World War II. Yet it is fair enough to say that there has been a gradual shift in recent years in the nature

---

[7] For this history see the authoritative inside account of James R. Locher III, *Victory on the Potomac: The Goldwater–Nichols Act Unifies the Pentagon* (College Station: Texas A&M University Press, 2002).

[8] Garbesi, 40.

of this role. With the exception of the European case, where the American CINC from the beginning served in an inherently multinational and diplomatic role as SACEUR, contacts between senior American military officers and their foreign counterparts were for the most part limited to matters such as military sales, security assistance, basing arrangements, and the like, though even here the State Department also had a major role to play. Today, the CINCs and other senior military officials frequently perform diplomatic tasks of a much higher order, tasks that in the past would have been exclusively the province of elected officials, senior political appointees, or foreign service officers (FSOs), often dealing directly with the senior leadership of a foreign country. It is probably also fair to say that they show more initiative and enterprise in doing so than might have been considered proper in the past.

There are several reasons for this. Perhaps the most obvious one is that the unified commands are rich in resources, while the State Department is typically cash-strapped. Each regional combatant commander, for example, has the use of a personal aircraft to tour his AOR.[9] But the decisive advantage enjoyed by the CINC is the fact that he has no State Department counterpart in the region. Though theoretically outranked by an ambassador, in practice – and understandably – the CINC tends to be looked to by the countries in his region as *the* authoritative voice of the United States there on national security matters broadly conceived. Theoretically, the CINC receives any foreign policy guidance he requires from the corresponding regional bureau at the State Department by way of his senior political adviser (POLAD), an ambassadorial-rank FSO. In practice, the matter is more complicated than that. POLADs rank relatively low in the pecking order at Foggy Bottom; there is also the lamentable fact that State's regional bureaus do not correspond in any neat way to the CINCs' AORs as set out in the Unified Command Plan. But even more important is the fact that the State Department itself has a culture that is deeply bilateral in character: What matters most are the interactions between embassies and individual "country desks" in Washington; regional perspectives are an afterthought. Finally, State simply lacks depth of expertise in the complex array of security issues that face the unified commands on a day-to-day basis, and its cumbersome internal processes often mean that policy guidance is late, inadequate, or indeed non-existent.[10]

---

[9] This is a major theme of the Priest critique. She claims that the combined budgets of the unified commands amounted to some $380 million in 2000, an increase of some 35% adjusting for inflation over the 1990 figure, and notes that SOUTHCOM, the smallest of the commands, employs some 1,100 people, more than those working on Latin American matters at the Pentagon and the Departments of State, Commerce, Treasury, and Agriculture combined. Priest, 71–77.

[10] For the limitations of today's State Department see, for example, Hart–Rudman Commission, *Road Map for National Security: Imperative for Change* (Washington, DC: U.S. Commission for National Security/21st Century, 2001), and Newt Gingrich, "Rogue State Department," *Foreign Policy* (July–August 2003): 42–48.

There are other factors to be considered as well. It is not often enough remarked that today's flag and general officers are much better educated on the whole than, say, their predecessors in the 1950s or 1960s. Most have attended a war college, where much of the curriculum consists of the study of history and contemporary international affairs rather than narrowly military topics, and many also hold advanced degrees from civilian universities (General David Petraeus, for example, is a Princeton PhD). It is therefore difficult to argue that they are somehow fundamentally ill-prepared or unsuited to play a diplomatic role. Moreover, it is also the case that they can enjoy certain advantages in that role when compared with civilian officials. Foreign leaders who are active or retired military officers are likely to feel more comfortable with them and more inclined to listen to them than to their civilian colleagues, particularly in times of crisis or war. It should also be remembered that foreign military officers in many parts of the world have great influence on and access to their own political leadership. Finally, it is relevant to note that the post-9/11 American military has given a new emphasis to the study of foreign languages and cultures.

At one level, the growing role of the combatant commanders in regional diplomacy can be understood simply as a reflection of the nature of the post–Cold War era. During the Cold War, it was generally understood that the over-riding responsibility of the unified commands had to be planning for global war with the Soviet Union. When the forerunner of CENTCOM, the Rapid Deployment Joint Task Force, was created in March 1980, it was in response to a perceived Soviet threat to Iran and the oil resources of the Persian Gulf following the overthrow of the Shah and the Soviet occupation of Afghanistan in 1979, not to any local threat or requirement. With the Soviet menace gone, the regional unified commands might well have been abolished, as was apparently envisioned in the first UCP. Yet they had proved over time their utility for regional "engagement," and this now became for most practical purposes their primary mission. The Clinton administration's *Quadrennial Defense Review* white paper of 1997 in fact stressed this mission and introduced a new term for it – "shaping," suggesting a more robust and deliberate approach to developing and maintaining relationships with regional friends and allies and influencing the perceptions of potential adversaries.[11] The regional CINCs of the day embraced the mission enthusiastically. In the case of SOUTHCOM, after the demise of a communist threat to Central America in the 1980s, the command was redirected by Marine General Charles Wilhelm to focus on drug trafficking and the associated narco-guerrilla threat to friendly nations, especially Colombia; and Wilhelm himself was largely responsible for selling this new policy to the Pentagon and Congress.[12] Another Marine officer, General Anthony Zinni, a notably bluff and energetic CINCCENT, played an important role in

---

[11] Derek Reveron, ed., *Shaping the Security Environment*, Newport Paper 29 (Newport: Naval War College, September 2007).

[12] Priest, ch. 9, and Dean A. Cook, "U.S. Southern Command: General Charles E. Wilhelm and the Shaping of U.S. Military Engagement in Colombia, 1997–2000," in Reveron, ch. 6.

solidifying American ties to the newly independent nations of Central Asia in the late 1990s, in spite – or because – of the scant attention given this region in Washington.[13] Admirals Joseph Prueher and Dennis Blair were forceful proponents of engagement in the PACOM AOR.[14] AFRICOM was created in 2007 in response not to a conventional military threat but rather to the growth of transnational terrorism on the continent and the opportunities afforded to it by failed states like Somalia. Strikingly, the United States has gone out of its way to reassure Africans about the benign intentions guiding the formation of the command, emphasizing the extent to which it is being organized as a hybrid civilian/military entity with an ambassador as deputy to the CINC, and putting on the shelf the original plan to locate it somewhere in the region.[15]

Have the CINCs grossly overstepped the bounds of their authority, thus succeeding in "militarizing" American foreign policy? Priest's tendentious account provides very little real evidence for this. One can certainly agree that on certain occasions they pushed the envelope, but it is difficult to distinguish this from the behavior of any aggressive civilian bureaucrat. Even when they did so, however, it was not necessarily to privilege military over diplomatic approaches or solutions.[16] Indeed, it could be argued that CINCs have good institutional reasons for favoring and promoting greater civilian and interagency involvement in the theater.[17] On the other hand, it does seem to be the case that proconsular status brings with it a tendency to intemperate speech. On one occasion, General Zinni blasted the administration's support of certain Iraqi exiles in testimony before a Senate committee and was told by a senior Pentagon official accompanying him to be more nuanced henceforth in such settings. (Zinni's response: "Nuanced? I'm a marine!"[18]) In more recent years, Admiral William J. "Fox" Fallon, a newly anointed CINCCENT, was cashiered by Defense Secretary Robert M. Gates[19] for making pronouncements at odds with American policy toward Iran. In reality, however, these lapses say more about the culture of the military today than they do about the combatant commanders as such. They are indeed suggestive of ongoing civil–military pathologies but in no way

---

[13] Priest, ch. 5, and James S. Robbins, "U.S. Central Command: Where History is Made," in Reveron, ch. 7.

[14] Priest, ch. 10. See also Joseph W. Prueher, "Warfighting CINCs in a New Era," *Joint Force Quarterly* 13 (Autumn 1996): 48–52.

[15] For contrasting views of the advantages and disadvantages of AFRICOM see Edward Marks, "Why USAFRICOM?" and Mary C. Yates, "U.S. Africa Command: Value Added," *Joint Force Quarterly* 52 (1st Quarter 2009): 148–51, 152–55. Both writers are U.S. ambassadors.

[16] In fact, Admirals Prueher and Blair both attracted criticism from some quarters with their forceful advocacy of greater "engagement" with the People's Republic of China; General Zinni would become an outspoken critic of the war in Iraq.

[17] A particularly forward-leaning expression of this is Admiral James G. Stavridis, *Partnership for the Americas: Western Hemisphere Strategy and U.S. Southern Command* (Washington, DC: National Defense University Press, 2010).

[18] Priest, 97–98.

[19] Sara Carter, "Warriors Welcome Resignation," *Washington Post*, March 13, 2008. Fallon too was more "dovish" on Iran than many in the administration.

can be taken as proof that civilians have lost control of the American military. In fact, the way these incidents were handled points rather in the opposite direction.[20]

Proconsular misbehavior should be relatively difficult to conceal, particularly from the non-military side of the American national security establishment. What do senior State Department officials have to say about the matter? Former Assistant Secretary of State Lincoln Bloomfield claims he "could probably give 100 cases where the combatant commander has accomplished something we needed to get done. One, he's on the scene. Two, the power to get something done may have been in a foreign military rather than a foreign ministry." He adds: The "flow of information from State to embassies to commanders . . . is not as isolated as it once was." Elizabeth Jones, former assistant secretary for European and Eurasian affairs, recalls: "I'm always on the phone with the EUCOM commander, coordinating our approach to the region." Former Under Secretary of State for Political Affairs Marc Grossman, then the third-ranking official in the department, says that "in six years in Turkey as [deputy chief of mission] and ambassador, there was never a single conflict. Now, I'm dealing with Colombia; I've made five of my six visits with SOUTHCOM's commander. We do everything together. Yes, someone could goof. But the system works wonderfully – the [regional CINCs] are some of the finest America has to offer. . . . I'm a complete believer." Even Ambassador Robert Gelbard, who crossed swords with Admiral Dennis Blair, commander of PACOM, in one of the few clear cases of a CINC circumventing an ambassador, blames the episode on a failure of coordination in Washington rather than any impropriety on Blair's part.[21]

The strongest case for proconsular freelancing in recent years is without doubt General Wesley K. Clark, during his tenure as SACEUR in the late 1990s. Especially during NATO's brief war with Serbia over Kosovo in 1999,[22] Clark aggressively "pushed the envelope" (his own phrase) by pressing Washington to intensify the air war and prepare for ground operations if necessary. This put him increasingly at odds with the stated policy of the Clinton administration and created strained relations with both Secretary of Defense William Cohen and the Joint Chiefs, particularly the chairman, General Hugh Shelton. It is important, however, to appreciate the political context of this episode, which

[20] It is undeniable that recent trends in the civil–military relationship have raised legitimate concerns, but the offending officers have more frequently been retired senior generals or even Chiefs rather than CINCs. See Martin Cook, "Revolt of the Generals: A Case Study in Professional Ethics," *Parameters* (Spring 2008): 4–15.
[21] Personal interviews conducted by then–Air Force Colonel Howard D. Belote, "Proconsuls, Pretenders, or Professionals? The Political Role of Regional Combatant Commanders," in *Essays 2004: Chairman of the Joint Chiefs of Staff Strategy Essay Competition* (Washington, DC: National Defense University Press, 2004), 1–20. Gelbard had tried to block Blair's access to certain Indonesian generals implicated in human rights abuses.
[22] For a detailed history and assessment see Ivo. H. Daalder and Michael E. O'Hanlon, *Winning Ugly: NATO's War to Save Kosovo* (Washington, DC: Brookings Institution, 2000).

was more than a little reminiscent of the Kennedy administration's handling of Vietnam. The administration was seriously divided on its policy toward the former Yugoslavia. Secretary of State Madeleine Albright was hawkish on the subject, the Pentagon skittish, and the White House distracted by scandal and the specter of a presidential impeachment. At the same time, Clark had another master as well – the military and political leaders of NATO's nineteen nations. Clark "worked for" NATO formally and literally in his capacity as SACEUR, not merely for Washington as the commander of EUCOM. This necessarily gave him an independence of Washington and freedom of maneuver exceptional for a CINC, but it also put him in a delicate and difficult position. For the most part, Clark navigated these dangerous waters adroitly, but in the end Washington was unhappy with his performance. In what can only be interpreted as a deliberate slap administered by the secretary of defense, Clark's tour was not only not extended but abruptly and prematurely terminated once the war was over.[23]

The breakup of the former Yugoslavia in 1990 brought war to Europe for the first time since 1945. The eventual intervention of NATO in the Balkans – in Bosnia in 1995 and then in Kosovo in 1999 – was thus the first test of the NATO alliance under conditions of actual warfare. It was in particular the first real-world test of the NATO decision-making and command structure. But the circumstances the alliance faced were altogether different from the kind of conflict it had anticipated and for which it was organized and trained – a massive Soviet ground invasion of West Germany through the armor-friendly Fulda Gap. Rather than an apocalyptic World War III, the alliance had to deal instead with something more like the Vietnam War – an intensely political struggle using limited and precise applications of force to coerce the adversary and prepare the way for a negotiated settlement. Because this was so, however, the day-to-day direction of the war on the ground could not be divorced from the conduct of diplomacy, both with the Serbian strongman Slobodan Milosevic and other interested parties (notably Russia) and within the alliance itself. But this meant that SACEUR was unavoidably engaged in the diplomacy of the war in a major way. It is clear that this fact was never sufficiently appreciated in Washington. Also not fully appreciated there was the importance of the war politically for NATO and America's European allies. The objective stakes in the wars of the Yugoslav succession were low, certainly lower than those in Southeast Asia in earlier decades. Serbia was in no way a military threat to any of the NATO countries. But in another sense, the stakes were high, since the fundamental credibility of the NATO alliance – indeed, its very survival – was widely believed to depend on a successful outcome to these conflicts.

---

[23] See Derek S. Reveron, "U.S. European Command: General Wesley Clark and the War for Kosovo," in Reveron, ch. 5, as well as General Wesley K. Clark, *Waging Modern War: Bosnia, Kosovo, and the Future of Combat* (New York: Public Affairs, 2002 [2001]). Clark's memoir is detailed and frank in describing these matters, if frequently difficult to verify. (Cohen in particular has produced no account of this period.)

Clark himself understood this well, and it explains the lengths to which he was prepared to go to accommodate the political requirements of the Europeans and avoid measures that might jeopardize the unity of the alliance, even though these might not find favor in Washington. In this respect, Clark arguably brought a longer perspective and a strategic clarity to bear on the Balkan situation that were not always in evidence among his superiors in Washington. That he championed this perspective and vision even at manifest risk to his own career does him great credit.

Wes Clark was born in Chicago, the son of a lawyer and (interestingly, in view of Clark's later run for the presidency) local politician affiliated with the Democratic Party. After graduating from West Point in 1966, he spent two years at Oxford as a Rhodes Scholar. As a young captain, he commanded a mechanized infantry company in Vietnam, where he was wounded and received a Purple Heart. Following a stint teaching economics and political philosophy at West Point, Clark then went to Washington to serve as a special assistant to the director of the Office of Management and Budget as a White House fellow, a prestigious assignment. His first exposure to NATO was as a special assistant to General Alexander M. Haig when he was the Supreme Allied Commander. By the time Clark finished first in his class at the Army Command and Staff College, he had already attracted the attention of the Army's top brass. In 1986, he put on his first star and was made commander of the National Training Center; following that, he took command of the First Cavalry Division with a second star. In 1993, he became the Director of Plans and Policy (the J-5) on the Joint Staff, another plum assignment, and another star. In theory, at least, this made him the senior strategist supporting the Joint Chiefs of Staff, and also injected him into the ongoing crisis in the former Yugoslavia. His first trip to Bosnia-Herzegovina was in August 1994, during which he had an opportunity to meet many of the key players on all sides. In the year following, he became deeply immersed in the efforts of a negotiating team led by Richard Holbrooke of the State Department to resolve the Bosnia problem through a political agreement among the contending parties and the introduction of a peacekeeping force from several NATO nations but also with Russian participation, culminating in an extended and intense negotiating session among all parties in Dayton, Ohio. In March 1996, Clark acquired his fourth star on becoming CINC of the U.S. Southern Command. When the position of SACEUR became available in the summer of 1997, however, Clark was a logical candidate and won the assignment, though CINCs are normally expected to remain in place for at least two years. His rise had been little short of spectacular.

Important for understanding the bureaucratic obstacles Clark had to confront are the actual political-military structures within NATO. On the civilian side, the senior NATO official is the secretary general, a position always held by a European; at this time it was occupied by a former Spanish socialist politician, Javier Solana. The secretary general in turn is answerable to the North Atlantic Council (NAC), which consists of the ambassadors to the organization from its component member states. Also subordinate to the NAC is a NATO

Military Committee, consisting of representatives of the defense ministries of the various members; its chairman at this time was the German General Klaus Naumann. These two NATO officials were the functional equivalent of the U.S. National Command Authority, which resides in the president and the secretary of defense, and Clark answered directly to them both. Concerning this overall structure, Clark makes the following observation: "Thus the foreign ministries had the upper hand and the last word in working the issues. This was doubly the case for the United States, where the White House and Secretary of State seemed to place a higher priority on NATO's requirements and responsibilities than did the Defense Department. It was perhaps for this reason that Secretary General Solana seemed to speak more often with the White House and the Secretary of State than with the Secretary of Defense." Clark continues: "For me, then, I was torn between the guidance and perspective I gained from NATO, heavily influenced by the Department of State and the White House, and what I would hear in my U.S. military chain reporting to the Pentagon.... Many times, I had to set my own compass and follow it."[24]

The overriding theme of *Waging Modern War*, Clark's excellent memoir of his experiences in the Balkans, is the changed nature of the contemporary battlefield compared to the Cold War or to the largely Cold War–inspired campaign against Iraq in 1991. This directly affected and shaped the general's personal engagement in events on the ground in the former Yugoslavia. "I remained deeply involved in the Bosnia mission, because every day's activities had strategic impact. This wasn't like some textbook campaign, where the top commander waves his hand over a map and then sits back patiently for a few days to await results. The way I saw it, each action or decision involved four elements: the political, the strategic, the operational, and the tactical. This was a function of modern communications and the media – actions that were relatively small could have potentially large political impact, and therefore affect the course of an entire campaign.... In military doctrine, we recognized that the strategic, operational, and tactical levels of war had been compressed, and their distinctions blurred."[25] And all this was true from the very beginning of Clark's tour, in July of 1997, as NATO's Stabilization Force (SFOR) struggled to uphold the terms of the Dayton accords while Milosevic and the Bosnian Serbs did all they could to undermine and evade them. This was a struggle waged primarily in the local and international media, but it also required good intelligence, aggressive maneuvering on the ground, agile communications, and close coordination among all national contingents as well as with the civil authorities.

Perhaps most noteworthy was Clark's decision to push for an active NATO effort to identify and arrest Bosnian Serbs for war crimes as arguably provided by Dayton, though prior to his arrival the American commanders had regarded this as beyond their mandate. In this and other respects, Clark was determined

[24] Ibid., xliii.
[25] Ibid., 85–86.

to undo the psychological atmosphere created by the weak and confused leadership of the United Nations Peacekeeping Force (UNPROFOR) during the
years preceding Dayton, which continued to color Serbian perceptions of the
political will of the Europeans and Americans.[26] In doing so, he was acting in
broad agreement with Solana that NATO's military forces needed to support
more directly the political reconstruction of Bosnia. But Clark was clearly a
driving force in selling this approach and aggressively implementing it. As it
turned out, operations against individual Serb officials, by allied as well as
American special operations units, were well-planned, effective, and discreet.[27]
    Unfortunately, not all of this was fully appreciated in Washington. The first
sign of trouble occurred when the general briefed Secretary Cohen in the Pentagon on his initial operations. Clark noticed at one point that the secretary's
"body language shifted abruptly"; he paused and said: "Sir, I am within your
intent, aren't I?" Cohen's unnerving response was: "Just barely." But the secretary failed to provide the general with any explanation or alternative guidance.
Some weeks later, in the course of a complicated series of deliberations in Washington and Brussels over the parameters of NATO strategy in Bosnia, Clark
would discover that the American military representative had received instructions from the Pentagon to announce to the Military Committee that Clark's
recommendations on this issue exceeded his "political guidance." When Clark
called General Hugh Shelton, Chairman of the Joint Chiefs, to ask what was
going on, there was no clear response; but the cable was not rescinded, and the
general suffered the embarrassment of what was in effect a public reprimand
by his own government (delivered by a three-star general, no less), without
any warning or explanation. In the end, NATO endorsed the more aggressive
approach favored by SACEUR.[28]
    In the spring of 1998, signs of a new crisis in NATO's relations with Serbia
began to appear. The southernmost Serbian province of Kosovo had been the
core of the medieval Serbian kingdom as well as the site of the most famous
military victory in the nation's history, at Kosovo Pole against the Ottoman
Turks in 1389. As such, it held great symbolic importance for the Milosevic
regime, which now depended on Serbian nationalism as a critical prop of its
legitimacy – a fact not widely appreciated at the time. The problem was that
the population of Kosovo was now less than 10 percent Serbian; the rest were
ethnically Albanian. The Albanians had long suffered neglect and discrimina-
tion by the government in Belgrade, and an armed Albanian resistance against

---

[26] It needs to be recalled that some NATO countries, especially France and the UK, tended to
    be relatively friendly toward the Serbs because of their long history of military collaboration
    in the two world wars. The commander of UNPROFOR (the United Nations peacekeeping
    organization in Bosnia) in 1993–95, the British General Sir Michael Rose, had indulged the
    Serbs at the expense of the Bosnian Muslims to a degree that was almost absurd. See on this
    period notably Richard Sale, *Clinton's Secret Wars: The Evolution of a Commander in Chief*
    (New York: St. Martin's, 2009), chs. 13–14.
[27] Ibid., ch. 41.
[28] Clark, 105.

Serbian domination had recently sprung up. Determined to suppress this movement, which became known as the Kosovo Liberation Army (KLA), Milosevic initiated a major buildup of Serbian military and police forces in the province and began launching punitive raids against Kosovar villages in areas where the KLA was active.

Clark was quick to realize the potential danger presented by the Kosovo situation to NATO's Balkan mission, and in a memorandum to Cohen and Shelton laid out the case for a forceful démarche to Milosevic threatening a NATO response to continued Serbian military action against the Kosovars. This initiative was not well received at the Pentagon. Clark was told by General Joseph Ralston, the vice chief, that the Pentagon had "too much on its plate" to take on any more problems, adding that the secretary was concerned "that Madeleine Albright might get a copy of this." Shelton, who had been out of town, was annoyed that Cohen had seen the paper before he had, and was also unreceptive. In Brussels, however, Solana fully shared Clark's concerns, and a subsequent NATO foreign ministers' meeting registered similar sentiments, including remarks by Secretary of State Albright, although no specific measures were agreed on.[29] Meanwhile, the Pentagon's priority seemed simply to be keeping Clark in his lane.[30]

Part of the Pentagon's reluctance to support Clark, as the general came to realize, was the fundamental shift in its priorities that had resulted from the ending of the Cold War. With the disappearance of a Soviet threat to NATO, Europe was no longer a critical theater of potential war for the United States. Instead, the military's newly revised doctrine called for shaping its (shrunken) force structure to focus on countering the "medium regional contingencies" the U.S. would most likely face – in the Korean Peninsula and the Persian Gulf.[31] These conflicting perspectives would become increasingly important once Clark began making concrete requests for American air and naval assets to support coercive air operations against Serbia – and even more so when he pushed for the planning of a possible ground campaign. The latter would finally exhaust the Pentagon's patience with the general.

In June 1998, however, in another Washington trip, Clark managed to persuade Shelton, Cohen, and (with their blessing) National Security Adviser Sandy Berger to pursue a strategy of "carrot and stick" designed to draw Milosevic to the negotiating table by threatening the Serbs with NATO air strikes. This attempted fusion of the military and diplomatic tracks would be the

---

[29] Ibid., 108–12.

[30] In a bizarre episode at around this time, Cohen called Clark to complain that the general had overstepped by providing "military advice" to Richard Holbrook, then in private business but a U.S. government consultant who had been asked to meet with Milosevic in Belgrade. It turned out that Cohen had somehow obtained a copy of a report on the Kosovo situation by the leader of the Bosnian Muslims given to Holbrook by Clark, mistaking its authorship. Clark rightly remarks on the absurdity of being forbidden to share "military advice" informally with senior American civilian officials traveling in the region. Ibid., 112–13.

[31] Ibid., 46–47.

first time the United States or NATO had actually developed a comprehensive strategy for dealing with Milosevic. Still, the Pentagon remained nervous about having actually to carry out an air campaign if the threat by itself failed to work, or about escalating the conflict to include ground operations, and dragged its feet.[32] Back in Washington in September, Clark enlisted Under Secretary of Defense Walt Slocombe to support the idea of an ultimatum to Milosevic concerning the deteriorating situation in Kosovo, and Cohen appears to have been persuaded; in any case, with Pentagon acquiescence, the United States helped engineer a UN resolution on September 23 calling for a halt to hostilities and demanding immediate steps to avert a "humanitarian catastrophe" in Kosovo and seeking a political settlement and the withdrawal of Serbian security forces from the province. This resolution implicitly authorized the use of military force to ensure compliance. On the same day, at a meeting in Portugal of the NATO defense ministers, the stiffened American position as well as the lobbying of Clark, Solana, and Naumann helped overcome widespread reluctance to committing to an air option. Serious planning for this contingency now began in Brussels and Washington.

At the same time, diplomatic pressure was ratcheted up on Milosevic. After lengthy negotiating sessions with American envoy Richard Holbrooke as well as the NATO triumvirate in October, the Serbian leader finally acquiesced to the demand that he withdraw the security forces that had been newly introduced into Kosovo. But he successfully resisted any NATO presence on the ground. Instead, it was agreed there would be unarmed observers from the Organization for Security and Cooperation in Europe (OSCE) on the ground, supported by NATO reconnaissance aircraft, to verify compliance with his pledges. But the Serbs continued to play games. In January 1999, however, a seismic shift occurred in the political landscape when it was discovered that Serbian forces had executed some forty Albanian civilians near the village of Racak. Milosevic refused to allow an investigation of the incident by an official of the International Criminal Tribunal on Yugoslavia and otherwise remained unrepentant and uncooperative; indeed, he initiated a new buildup of Serbian forces in the province. This accelerated NATO action on both the military and the diplomatic tracks. Efforts were intensified to insert NATO ground forces into neighboring Macedonia in anticipation of an agreement to allow them into Kosovo as a peacekeeping force. At the same time, a new round of negotiations was begun in mid-February at a chateau near Rambouillet, outside Paris.

With the failure of the Rambouillet talks in mid-March, the military track came to the fore. On March 20, the OSCE verifiers were withdrawn from Kosovo in preparation for the planned air campaign; the Serbs then proceeded to launch an ethnic cleansing campaign on a scale larger than anything they had previously attempted. At this point, the die was cast. NATO's war on Serbia commenced on the evening of March 24.

It might be thought that once actual hostilities were underway, Clark's task would have been simplified and clarified; after all, as Supreme Allied

---

[32] Ibid., 118–19.

Commander of all NATO forces he might have been expected to have considerable latitude to make day-to-day decisions. In fact, this was far from the case. The political complications of the situation continued to dominate military decision-making, in Washington as well as with the Europeans. Targeting issues were preeminent. While the original plans had envisioned that SACEUR would have the authority to strike targets within overall categories specified by NATO's political leadership, Washington insisted that targets had to be approved on an individual basis. As in the case of Vietnam, final approval authority would rest with the president himself. But the NATO allies also got into the act. Missions flown by aircraft based in the UK were subject to review by lawyers. The Dutch attempted to prevent a strike against a residence of Milosevic by noting that it housed a Rembrandt painting. (Hearing this, Klaus Naumann famously remarked: "It's not a very good Rembrandt.") Clark himself from early on favored punishing strikes against high-value targets in Belgrade, fearful of falling into a Vietnam-style bombing campaign so burdened with political restrictions that its strategic impact was largely dissipated. But Clark also sought to bring NATO's air power to bear against Serbian military and police units in Kosovo itself, which continued to wreak havoc on the population there. The centerpiece of this aspect of the campaign was to be American Apache assault helicopters, flying out of bases in Macedonia or Albania. Clark succeeded in convincing Shelton of the merits of this, but the Army leadership strongly resisted. Eventually, their objections were overcome, and the Apaches appeared in Albania, but Clark was never authorized to use them.

On the night NATO's bombing campaign began, President Bill Clinton addressed the nation on television from the Oval Office. In the course of his remarks, he said emphatically: "I do not intend to put our troops in Kosovo to fight a war." While this may have been only simple realism considering the lack of enthusiasm for the war in the Pentagon as well as in Congress, it took the allies by surprise and greatly complicated Clark's later efforts to force NATO and the Pentagon to plan for – and, if necessary, execute – a ground operation in Kosovo. It is by no means clear that it reflected the president's real sentiments.[33] But it created a political reality that under any circumstances would have been difficult to walk back. Nevertheless, Clark eventually succeeded in persuading Cohen and the Chiefs that NATO needed to commence planning for a ground offensive.

As it turned out, 1999 was the fiftieth anniversary of the birth of NATO, and a summit meeting was scheduled for April 23 in Washington in celebration of it. This offered an important opportunity for a demonstration of alliance solidarity and resolve, and for a serious alliance-wide discussion of next steps in

---

[33] In fact, a staffing glitch was involved. The original text of Clinton's statement said only that he had no "plans" to introduce American ground forces; the word was dropped in favor of "intention" on the advice of a consultant to the NSC Staff, on the grounds that the announcement suggested that the administration's planners had not done their jobs. The change was made by Sandy Berger, apparently without approval from Secretary Albright, who almost certainly would have objected. Sale, 355–56.

the Balkans. It also became the occasion of a further clash between Clark and his superiors in the Pentagon. In a telephone conversation with General Shelton on April 19, Clark stressed the importance of working the ground troops issue at the summit and offered to help personally with this, whereupon Shelton asked in apparent alarm, "You're not coming to the summit, are you?" Clark replied that SACEURs had always attended these gatherings, that the entire Military Committee, of which he was a non-voting member, would be in attendance, and that he would be expected to brief NATO's current operations to the heads of state. "We had finally come head-to-head," as Clark recounts the episode,

about the responsibilities of my command. In his view, perhaps, I was just a subordinate who should take military orders and leave the policy to the civilians. But in NATO it could never work that way. At the senior levels military action and policy making were totally intertwined, and I had to participate in both worlds. The summit was going to be the key location on the strategic battlefield, both for the policies and for the military plans. It was the decisive point. . . . But if the SACEUR wasn't present at the decisive point, it would be taken as an indication of problems within the command or worse, problems with the strategy and results of the operation. Further, the Europeans were aware of Washington's ambivalence about Operation Allied Force, and they were becoming increasingly aware of problems within the U.S. command channel. My presence at the summit could help correct that. And whatever needed to be done at the summit, I believed that I could help.

Shelton dropped the subject and the conversation ended, but a few minutes later Clark was called by Solana, who had been contacted by Sandy Berger with the message that Secretary Cohen was "uncomfortable" with Clark's presence at the summit. After speaking directly with Cohen, Solana called again and told the general: "He does not want you to come to the summit. He feels you are too busy here to be spared. I have told him that you are the Supreme Commander, that I would relay his views, and that I will support whatever you decide." Clark replied that he felt he needed to go. As he explains: "Because I was coming in my NATO capacity, Washington apparently didn't feel it could simply order me not to attend. Had they done so, I would have had no choice but to remain in Belgium. . . . I was loyal to Cohen and Shelton. But at this point, caught up in the middle of an operation whose outcome was still in doubt, I had been given a choice. I was at the very fulcrum of the policies, the strategy, and the operations. If for no other reason, I had to go back to see people in Washington and at the summit face-to-face and hear and understand what people there wanted, and to explain my assessment and recommendations in a very fluid, evolving situation."[34] This is probably the clearest case of Clark flouting, if not a direct order, certainly the express will of his chain of command.[35]

---

[34] Clark, 261–63.

[35] Clark further explains: "As a U.S. commander, I would have to regard the hesitations of my superiors as implicit orders, but in NATO, I could not always accept them as such. Instead I was bound to continue pushing the strategy until instructed otherwise." Ibid., 453.

At the summit itself, the ground troops issue was apparently the topic of a "stormy discussion" between President Clinton and British Prime Minister Tony Blair, as a result of which there would be no further discussion of the matter there, though Solana did release a press statement authorizing NATO to do an "assessment" of a ground intervention. In a private meeting, Cohen made clear to Clark that he was not to raise the subject, and Clark quickly agreed. The rest of the summit proceeded without incident. Several days later, after the general had returned to Brussels, he gave a press conference recapping his Washington briefing on NATO operations in the Balkans. In response to a question about the efficacy of air attacks against Serbian forces on the ground, Clark said something to the effect that it was hard to tell because Milosevic continued to send reinforcements into Kosovo. The next morning's *New York Times* carried the headline: "NATO Chief Admits Bombs Fail to Stem Serb Operations." Later that day, he received a call from the chairman. Shelton said: "Wes, at the White House meeting today there was a lot of discussion about your press conference. The Secretary of Defense asked me to give you some verbatim guidance, so here it is: 'Get your f – g face off the TV. No more briefings, period. That's it.' I just wanted to give it to you like he said it. Do you have any questions?" Though Clark doesn't say so, Cohen's anger no doubt reflected a belief that the general's comment was another effort to further his own ground campaign agenda. At any rate, this must have been part of the White House discussion, as the president himself apparently read the offending article and remarked that the actual story did not support the headline.[36]

It will not be necessary to recount the endgame of the Kosovo war. Milosevic was finally persuaded that he had to yield to NATO's terms, withdraw his forces from the province, and allow the entry of NATO as well as Russian peacekeepers. The involvement of the Russians, who had been highly supportive of the Serbs, was important for the diplomacy of this phase of the war, though it led to a mini-crisis when a Russian airborne unit unexpectedly headed toward the airport at Pristina, the Kosovo capital. In a dramatic scene, Clark asked the commander of KFOR, the ground peacekeeping force, to get to the airport ahead of the Russians and block the runways. The commander, British Lieutenant General Mike Jackson, refused the order, saying "Sir, I'm not starting World War III for you." London and Washington would end agreeing with Jackson.[37]

The struggle for Kosovo was indeed a "strange little war."[38] It is surely odd that it should be used to support the thesis that the regional combatant commanders, America's "proconsuls," wield unprecedented power and authority

[36] Ibid., 268–73.

[37] Jackson asked Clark on whose authority he was issuing the order; Clark replied, "By my authority as SACEUR." Jackson responded: "You don't have that authority," and as Clark seems to admit though doesn't state, Jackson was correct. Ibid., 391–400.

[38] The title of the introduction to Andrew J. Bacevich and Eliot A. Cohen, *War Over Kosovo: Politics and Strategy in a Global Age* (New York: Columbia University Press, 2001).

today and have contributed to a dangerous militarization of American foreign policy in recent years.[39] General Wesley Clark was in fact remarkably sensitive to the larger political and diplomatic context of the Kosovo war, and understood perfectly well the constraints on his own authority as EUCOM commander and SACEUR. As far as one can tell from his own account, he seems to have been careful to observe most if not all bureaucratic redlines, even as his driving personality so clearly made his superiors nervous. Clark's aggressiveness was in any case always about more than personality. As with all officers of his generation, Clark's fundamental outlook toward the use of force was shaped by the American experience in Vietnam. He was determined not to repeat the errors the United States made in that conflict – above all, in waging a highly constrained air campaign against North Vietnam. NATO had to maintain "escalation dominance" over the Serbs, even if it meant an eventual transition to ground force operations. If it failed to do so, as the United States had failed in Vietnam, Clark rightly foresaw that NATO's will to continue the conflict could quickly collapse. And he shared with Secretary General Solana, though apparently not with his superiors in the Pentagon, the conviction that a NATO defeat in the Balkans would have devastating political consequences for the alliance and for American interests in Europe if not beyond.

But the deepest reason for the – in retrospect astonishing and appalling – tensions between Clark and the Pentagon was the strategic vacuum that persisted in Washington over the course of the war, a vacuum that Clark inevitably had to try to fill. This in turn reflected continuing deficiencies in national security organization at the center. Clark makes clear that he believes the war showed that the Goldwater–Nichols reforms in fact made little difference in strengthening the role of the CINCs relative to the Joint Chiefs, one of its key intended purposes. Throughout the conflict, the Army and its chief, General Dennis Reimer, were less than supportive of Clark, and the chairman, another Army general, was never a forceful proponent of his CINC, as the legislation had also envisioned. Indeed, both General Shelton and his boss, Bill Cohen, seemed more interested in protecting the equities of the Department of Defense than in actively helping Clark to shape and sell a comprehensive American strategy for victory. As Clark argues: "Military organizations and their leaders must be agile enough to deal with the actual and changing requirements of battle as war unfolds. This was why the Goldwater–Nichols legislation sought to strengthen the hand of the CINC. I never saw any indication that war was threatened in any other theater. We could have afforded to do whatever might prove necessary to succeed. Nor should the Services place their long-term plans above success in the operation at hand. When nations commit their military forces to combat, the operations have to succeed. The Services knew this well (this was why they always seemed to fear that the air campaign would lead to

[39] Note Bacevich's comment on retelling the story of Clark's confrontation with Jackson over the Russians: "As a gauge of Clark's impoverished standing as SACEUR, a more telling incident could scarcely be conceived. The proconsul had been hung out to dry." *American Empire*, 191.

a ground effort), but some seemed to resist their obligation to win. And some in political positions, perhaps inevitably, viewed military advice primarily as a political problem to be managed rather than a resource to be developed and used. There was also within the Pentagon a reluctance to allow the regional commanders to engage fully along the broader political-military axes necessary to do their jobs."[40]

In some ways, Wes Clark is reminiscent of Lucius Clay. Both generals held jobs that were intensely political in nature and involved a complex set of diplomatic relationships that could not easily be managed from Washington. Both men were strong personalities and not afraid to "push the envelope" to advance a coherent strategic approach that the Washington agencies frequently failed to provide, while remaining properly deferential to the appropriate authority. It is a sad commentary on the American defense establishment of recent years that Clark's major fights were with the Defense Department (including his own Army brethren) rather than the diplomats who bedeviled Clay, while the latter was for the most part solidly and competently supported by the Pentagon of his era.

---

[40] Clark, 455. Strikingly, he says at one point of a conversation with Shelton: "But as I listened to him, I realized that I had little idea, and never had during the entire crisis, how the Commander in Chief or the Secretary of Defense were making their decisions. Wouldn't they have been able to make better decisions, and have them better implemented, I thought, if they brought the commander into the high-level discussions occasionally?" (341).

9

Bremer in Iraq

It is one thing if you make mistakes when you are pushing the envelope. It's another thing if you make mistakes walking to work.

Donald M. Rumsfeld[1]

The four years separating NATO's intervention in Kosovo from the American-led invasion of Iraq in the spring of 2003 were eventful ones indeed for the United States, marking as they did the emergence of a new global strategic environment in the wake of the terrorist attacks on New York and Washington on September 11, 2001. The strategic stakes for the United States and its allies in the Balkans were marginal, and the Clinton administration as a whole would prove a reluctant warrior in committing American prestige and resources in a war of "choice" waged overridingly for humanitarian purposes. The events of 9/11 represented the first time United States territory had been attacked since Pearl Harbor, and deeply shocked the nation. The administration of George W. Bush quickly realized that a new enemy had appeared on the international stage in the form of radical Islamism, a fanatical and elusive enemy that posed a threat of unknowable but potentially grave damage to the American homeland and required a fundamental rethinking of American national security policy. The administration acknowledged that these attacks were in fact acts of "war," not simply acts of terrorist criminality, and that the United States would have to take this war to its source, rather than simply attempting to defend itself against this new foe. Quite unlike the conflicts the nation had been involved in since the end of the Cold War, this "global war on terror" would be a war not of "choice" but of "necessity."

Much would remain uncertain about the nature and intentions of the foe, but 9/11 did seem to establish some clarifying certainties. Sympathy for the United States around the world was virtually universal, and for the first time since its founding, NATO declared its readiness to help defend one of its

---

[1] Bob Woodward, *State of Denial* (New York: Simon & Schuster, 2006), 37.

members under the terms of Article V of the North Atlantic Treaty. It was generally accepted that terrorism could no longer be treated as a nuisance to be dealt with primarily by the tools of law enforcement, but needed to be seen as a threat of global reach and potentially of mass destructiveness, to be addressed by all means up to and including the military instrument. New emphasis was placed on the problem of state sponsorship of terrorism and the importance of preventing terrorists from acquiring so-called weapons of mass destruction (WMDs), especially nuclear or radiological weapons. And it was widely understood that the United States and its allies would need to pay much greater attention and commit greater resources to homeland security than had been done at any time in the past.

Unfortunately, it would not take long for these certainties to begin to blur. Initial American retaliation against Al Qaeda, the organizer of the 9/11 attacks, and its ally and protector, the Taliban regime in Afghanistan, was for the most part favorably received. Some critics in the United States and elsewhere warned, however, that it would not be wise for the nation to become embroiled in a country famous as "the graveyard of empires," and slow progress in the early stages of the conflict reinforced fears of a repeat of the Vietnam experience. These fears were dispelled for the time being by the surprisingly quick victory over the Taliban achieved by rival Afghan forces aided by U.S. airpower and a limited contingent of intelligence operatives and special forces on the ground in late 2001. A year later, however, when the United States decided to invade Iraq to overthrow the regime of Saddam Hussein, it depleted much of the good will it had garnered as a result of the 9/11 attacks and raised large question marks concerning the real intentions of the United States in the Middle East and indeed globally. One result was the emergence of the narrative of "American Empire" that would become a dominant theme of discussions of American foreign policy over the coming half-decade and more.

This is not the place to rehearse the heated debates in this country and elsewhere concerning the rationale for the second Iraq war and the motives of the United States in launching it. Whether the invasion of Iraq and subsequent occupation of that nation, and the toll it exacted in blood and treasure, will prove wise or disastrous in historical insight is still impossible to say. If the U.S. government had realized at the time that the idea that Iraq possessed actual stockpiles of weapons of mass destruction was a phantom construct of American (and allied) intelligence deliberately encouraged by Saddam himself, it seems highly unlikely that the invasion would have occurred. Whatever its other shortcomings, it is certainly a misrepresentation of the Bush administration to suppose that it ever considered invading Iraq or any other place simply to impose American-style democracy and thereby expand a putative "American Empire." The democracy rationale was emphasized by the administration largely because of the eventual failure of the WMD rationale.[2]

---

[2] See the discussion in Douglas J. Feith, *War and Decision: Inside the Pentagon at the Dawn of the War on Terrorism* (New York: Harper, 2008), 470–77. For the origins and course of the Iraq

However all this may be, there can be little question that the United States badly botched its Iraq venture. Not unlike the case of Vietnam in the Kennedy era, the blame for this can be shared by a dysfunctional national security bureaucracy in Washington, an uncertain presidential hand, and flawed proconsular leadership in Iraq itself. But here, too, the extent to which proconsular leadership proved an independent – and malign – variable in this equation is still not sufficiently recognized.

Even more than in the case of Vietnam, the United States lacked a good understanding of its Iraqi adversary. In spite of its earlier encounter with the Iraqi military in the Gulf War of 1991 and in the intervening years, when the United States and its allies maintained "no fly zones" in the northern and southern parts of the country to protect the Kurds and Shi'ites from retaliation from Baghdad for their disloyalty in the wake of the American attack, American intelligence on the state of Iraqi politics and government, society, and the economy ranged from marginal to actively misinformed.[3] There were several reasons for this. Iraq under the rule of Saddam Hussein and his Baath Party was a brutal tyranny having many features in common with modern totalitarian regimes, especially in the area of domestic security and counterintelligence. As such, it was an exceptionally difficult target for American and other intelligence services. It nurtured high levels of distrust and fear within its own ranks that discouraged conspiratorial behavior or contact with foreigners; and it specialized in deception and disinformation, as became painfully clear when Saddam's WMD hoax was exposed. Moreover, Iraq's international isolation following the Gulf War and the regime of UN sanctions imposed on it led to a gradual hollowing out of Iraq's state institutions and deterioration of its economy and infrastructure that only became fully visible once coalition forces had toppled the Baathist regime. All of this would gravely complicate the subsequent American occupation of the country.[4]

Furthermore, and even more importantly, the United States harbored unrealistic expectations about the reactions of the Iraqi people themselves to Saddam's overthrow. It was widely anticipated in Washington that the Iraqis would welcome their American "liberators" and cooperate willingly in the political and material reconstruction of the nation, thus allowing a rapid withdrawal of U.S.

war see also Williamson Murray and Robert H. Scales, Jr., *The Iraq War: A Military History* (Cambridge, MA: Harvard University Press, 2003); Bob Woodward, *Plan of Attack* (New York: Simon & Schuster, 2004); Michael R. Gordon and Bernard E. Trainor, *Cobra II: The Inside Story of the Invasion and Occupation of Iraq* (New York: Pantheon, 2006); Thomas E. Ricks, *Fiasco: The American Military Adventure in Iraq* (New York: Penguin, 2006); and Ali A. Allawi, *The Occupation of Iraq: Winning the War, Losing the Peace* (New Haven, CT: Yale University Press, 2007).
[3] For a succinct catalogue of the CIA's errors about Iraq see Feith, 517–18.
[4] It seems likely, too, that American officials were misled by the apparent historical parallels of postwar Germany and Japan as well as the aftermath of the fall of communist regimes in Eastern Europe at the end of the Cold War, where state bureaucracies largely survived their collapsed regimes.

forces. This was indeed true of the Kurdish minority in the north, but the bulk of the population was another story. The Sunni Arabs, some 20 percent of the population, had formed the backbone of the Saddam regime, virtually monopolizing senior positions in the government, the military, and the party. Because of a misfire in the original American invasion plan, however – namely, the last-minute refusal of the Turkish government to permit the 4th Infantry Division to invade northern Iraq through its territory – the heartland of the Sunni areas of the country had seen virtually no coalition troops prior to the taking of Baghdad and the fall of Saddam. It is thus hardly surprising that the Sunnis were not easily reconciled to defeat. This is especially so because it quickly became apparent that any new regime the Americans would install in Baghdad would empower the despised Shia Arab majority (some 60 percent of all Iraqis) at the expense of the Sunnis. As for the Shia themselves, while they welcomed this radical improvement in their political position in the country, their attitudes toward the American invasion were ambivalent at best. Many remained distrustful of the United States because of its failure to support their rebellion against Saddam at the close of the 1991 war. Others – notably the followers of the charismatic cleric Moqtada al-Sadr – were vehemently anti-American or had close ties with the regime of the ayatollahs in Shiite Iran. All Iraqis had ready access to weapons.

It would be wrong to suppose that no efforts were made in Washington to anticipate problems the United States might encounter after invading Iraq. State, Defense, and CIA all cultivated contacts in the Iraqi exile world. The State Department organized in 2002 a major study by exiles and other experts on the country of various challenges of a postwar period. CENTCOM planners had the primary responsibility for drawing up plans for so-called Phase Four or stability and reconstruction operations as part of an overall Iraq-centered war plan. An "Iraq Political-Military Cell" within the Joint Staff studied postwar issues. Substantial efforts were mounted at the Army War College and the National Defense University. When an Office of Reconstruction and Humanitarian Assistance (ORHA) was established in early 2003 under the leadership of retired Army Lieutenant General Jay Garner, postconflict planning at last had a single home. But this improvised organization was poorly supported by the Defense Department, and there was not sufficient time to integrate usable products of the other planning exercises into its work prior to the invasion. The fact remains that no systematic, authoritative, operationally oriented planning for the aftermath of the invasion was undertaken by any U.S. government entity. This includes CENTCOM as well as the State Department's "Future of Iraq" project, which – contrary to some accounts – was a series of think-pieces more than a single actionable plan.[5]

[5] Ricks, 78–81; Gordon and Trainor, 138–63; Feith, 274–98, 375–78. An authoritative account of ORHA and these precursor planning efforts is now available: Gordon W. Rudd, *Reconstructing Iraq: Regime Change, Jay Garner, and the ORHA Story* (Lawrence: University Press of Kansas, 2011).

The proximate responsibility for this state of affairs lies with then–Secretary of Defense Donald Rumsfeld. While Rumsfeld involved himself in the details of the operations plan for Iraq to an extent that exasperated the Joint Chiefs and the CENTCOM staff, he showed little interest or sense of urgency when it came to the Phase Four component. The reason for this is evidently that Rumsfeld did not expect or want a lengthy occupation; and although he fought hard to achieve primacy for his own department in postwar Iraq, he was reluctant to have the Pentagon saddled with what he considered at the end of the day an essentially civilian responsibility.[6] The problem, though, was larger than this. CENTCOM's Phase Four planning was half-hearted and thin at best, and both General Tommy Franks and his subordinate in Iraq, Lieutenant General David McKiernan, were too preoccupied with preparations for the invasion to give these (largely non-military) issues serious attention. At the same time, little direction was forthcoming from the White House, reflecting what had become by this point in the Bush administration a broken interagency process, marked by open hostility between the State and Defense Departments, the inability of National Security Adviser Condoleeza ("Condi") Rice to overcome it (and, in particular, to discipline an often uncooperative Rumsfeld), and the unaccountable toleration of this situation by President George W. Bush.[7]

At the end of World War II, as has been seen, there was also uncertainty and hesitation in the White House over the role of the military in the occupation of Germany and Japan. At the end of the day, however, FDR was persuaded that occupation government had to be "military government." The occupation authorities would naturally include detailees from civilian agencies or civilians in temporary uniforms, but they would be embedded in a military chain of command. At the same time, it was also accepted that occupation policy would be formulated primarily in Washington, even though some scope would necessarily remain for improvisation on the ground. It turned out, of course, that the scope for decision-making on the ground proved to be greater than anticipated, given both the circumstances of the day and the independent-mindedness of two strong proconsuls. Nevertheless, it was clear who "owned" the occupation.

In Iraq, by contrast, this was never really clear. ORHA was a hybrid civil–military organization that reported directly to the CENTCOM commander, General Tommy Franks – in itself an awkward arrangement, because it cut out the coalition military commander in Iraq proper, Lieutenant General

---

[6] For a full-scale biography of the secretary of defense, see Bradley Graham, *By His Own Rules: The Ambitions, Successes, and Ultimate Failures of Donald Rumsfeld* (New York: Public Affairs, 2009). The secretary's own account has recently appeared: Donald Rumsfeld, *Known and Unknown: A Memoir* (New York: Sentinel, 2011). For some (generally representative) assessments of this work see Adam Garfinkle, "Wrestling with History," *National Review*, April 4, 2011, 42–46; Bob Woodward, "How Rumsfeld misleads and ducks responsibility in his new book," www.ricks.foreignpolicy.com/posts/2011/03/01; and Peggy Noonan, "The Defense Secretary Who Let Bin Laden Get Away," *Wall Street Journal*, March 12, 2011, 15.

[7] Consider his own comments on the matter: George W. Bush, *Decision Points* (New York: Crown, 2010), 87–90.

McKiernan; this problem was fixed, but only at the last minute.[8] ORHA received intermittent policy guidance from Douglas J. Feith, Undersecretary of Defense for Policy and third-ranking official in the Pentagon, but neither Franks nor any Washington entity took responsibility for providing it personnel, funding, or clear operational direction. In April 2003, ORHA was folded into a larger and more civilian-oriented organization, the Coalition Provisional Authority (CPA). Initially, General Franks nominally headed this, too, but the Pentagon felt that a senior civilian administrator with a political or diplomatic background would eventually be needed to run it, particularly for the delicate task of reconstituting a governing structure for the country. Former ambassador L. Paul ("Jerry") Bremer was recruited for this assignment, taking over from Franks as director of the CPA (and thereby essentially superseding Garner as well) on May 13. In a meeting with Bush a few days before his departure for Baghdad, the president agreed that Bremer would act as a "presidential envoy" in Iraq with "full authority to bring all the resources of the American government to bear on Iraq's reconstruction." This provided Bremer an opening he was quick to seize, though it was some time before this became fully apparent to the players involved. With an audacity that in retrospect is breathtaking, Bremer began to insist that he really "worked for" the president, though reporting to him "through" Rumsfeld; and he established a pattern of direct and often daily communication with National Security Adviser Rice as well as with Secretary of State Colin Powell. At the same time, he was able to use his Pentagon affiliation to protect himself from unwanted scrutiny by the interagency process presided over by Rice. In this way, he succeeded in carving out a highly autonomous role as American proconsul in Iraq. It did not take long for the consequences of this development to make themselves felt.[9]

Jerry Bremer was not an obvious choice to serve as American proconsul in Iraq. A career Foreign Service officer, Bremer had served as an assistant to Secretary of State Henry Kissinger in the mid-1970s, as deputy chief of mission in Norway, and as ambassador to the Netherlands (1983–86). He had no background in the Middle East, did not know Arabic, had never been in the military, and had never run a large organization. He did, however, have special expertise in terrorism and counterterrorism, having served as ambassador-at-large for counterterrorism before retiring from the Foreign Service; he had also chaired a bipartisan National Commission on Terrorism in 2000. In the interim, he had been managing director of Kissinger Associates, the former secretary's consulting firm. Perhaps Bremer's most salient qualification was simply that he had not worked in the Clinton administration. He was certainly not a prominent Republican foreign policy adviser, but politically he was a

---

[8] The transfer was made on April 6, three days before Baghdad was secured. Rudd, 192.

[9] For a generally sympathetic view of the CPA and Bremer in particular see James Dobbins, Seth G. Jones, Benjamin Runkle, and Siddharth Mohandas, *Occupying Iraq: A History of the Coalition Provisional Authority* (Santa Monica, CA: RAND, 2009). Allawi's scathing account is probably more representative of the published literature.

reassuring figure from the perspective of the Bush people. Surprisingly, given Rumsfeld's poor relationship with the State Department, it was the secretary of defense who proposed Bremer for the job.[10]

Bremer's appointment was arranged hastily, and little seems to have been done to provide him considered guidance from across the Washington agencies that would have some relationship to the CPA's mission and in fact enable its success. Nor was any clarification sought concerning protocols for managing the Washington–Baghdad channel. In the crucial early months of the CPA's existence, the Pentagon failed to circulate Bremer's correspondence to other agencies or to the White House. At the same time, it sought to discourage non-military staff of the CPA from developing independent reporting channels to their home agencies. Within the Pentagon, Bremer was keen to avoid the appearance and still less the reality of "working for" Feith (or his immediate superior, Deputy Secretary Paul Wolfowitz) and soon ceased communicating with him or anyone else in the department below the level of the secretary himself. One of the great mysteries of this period is why Rumsfeld himself so long tolerated such organizational dysfunctionality. At first the secretary seemed highly supportive of Bremer and willing to give him wide latitude to handle the situation in Baghdad as he saw fit. Later, one is strongly tempted to think that Rumsfeld deliberately sought to distance himself and the department from what looked increasingly like a trainwreck in progress.[11]

In large part, the failure to create any real interagency framework in Washington for (to use the term of art) "backstopping" Bremer's operation until much later in 2003 reflected continuing infighting between the Department of State and the CIA on the one side and the Pentagon on the other concerning postwar U.S. policy toward Iraq, and in particular the possible role of Iraqi exiles in an interim Iraq government. State and the CIA had developed a special aversion toward one of the most prominent of these figures, Ahmad Chalabi of the Iraqi National Congress, who had cultivated and been cultivated by senior officials in the Defense Department. They feared that any move by the United States to engineer a quick turnover of political authority in Iraq from the American military to the Iraqis would inevitably empower the "externals" in general and Chalabi in particular, thereby fatally undermining the perceived legitimacy of such a government in the eyes of the Iraqi people and further destabilizing the situation. The Pentagon, on the other hand, feared the consequences of an extended occupation of Iraq and pushed for the most rapid possible transition of authority consistent with the maintenance of order and security and the reconstitution of Iraqi governing capacity. The ins and outs of this question continue to be hotly debated and cannot be fully adjudicated

[10] Rumsfeld later found it expedient to downplay his own role in the selection of Bremer: Woodward, 173–74. Feith says that the secretary told him that one of his motives for this choice was "to make it easier for Defense and State officials to work together" (422). In his memoir (504), Rumsfeld says he believes he was "one of the first" to put Bremer's name forward.

[11] Cf. Graham, 436–38.

here. Feith, in his carefully argued and well-documented memoir, has laid out the Pentagon's side of the story and provided a persuasive defense. Beyond denying that he or his superiors ever had the intention of installing Chalabi as regent in Baghdad, Feith provides a detailed account of the high-level debates occurring in Washington in March–April 2003 over the establishment of an "Interim Iraqi Authority" (IIA), which makes clear among other things that the Pentagon's concept for the transition had been briefed to and approved by the president himself at a National Security Council meeting on March 10.[12]

The key elements of this concept were as follows. The IIA should be formed "as soon as possible after liberation" and include internals, Kurds, and exiles, the internals to be fully represented; a division of responsibilities between the United States and the IIA should be decided by agreement; the IIA would serve only for an interim period, until a more fully representative government could be established through elections; and the United States and the IIA would work together on appointing ministry officials and each ministry should be transferred to full Iraqi control as soon as possible. It was to be emphasized to the Iraqi people that the IIA would not be a military occupation government, but rather an Iraqi "government in formation" that would exert increasing authority over the Iraqi government and provide a framework for the process of building democratic institutions. According to Feith, Bremer was extensively briefed on all of this by his Pentagon staff. "As far as we knew, he agreed with the policy and intended to put the IIA plan into practice."[13] And yet – it never happened.

Bremer has been widely and harshly criticized for two momentous decisions announced by him within weeks of his arrival in Baghdad. The first, "CPA Order No. 1," dealt with so-called de-Baathification. As in the occupation of Germany following World War II, it was clear that some effort needed to be made to disestablish the ruling party of Iraq and eliminate its hold on the government and security services of the country. In contrast with the Nazi Party in Germany, though, the Baath Party was not really an ideologically based political organ so much as it was a mechanism of administrative control operating on behalf not only of Saddam Hussein but of Iraq's ruling Sunni minority generally. Moreover, as most senior administrative and command positions throughout Iraq's bureaucracy were held by Baathists who were in some way compromised by their service to Saddam's regime, their wholesale removal threatened to immobilize the operations of any Iraqi government. Naturally, Bremer's sudden decree caused great consternation in Iraq (though it was also welcomed by many who had suffered under the former regime), and it startled much of official Washington. As Feith makes clear in his memoir, Bremer was promulgating a policy that had been developed and cleared

---

[12] On Chalabi and the exiles generally see Feith, 239–45, 252–57. Oddly, Bush, in his recent memoir, seems to suggest he had opposed a leading role for the externals: George W. Bush, *Decision Points* (New York: Crown, 2010), 249.

[13] Feith, 423–24.

within the Department of Defense, but the matter had never been discussed in any interagency forum. The policy itself was relatively lenient. No one would face punishment merely for belonging to the Baath Party; only the top one percent of Baathist officials (some 25,000 individuals) would be affected at all; and exceptions could be granted in particular cases. Nevertheless, the ban reached many individuals who were only nominal Baathists but played vital roles in the government bureaucracy.[14] Garner and CIA station chief Charlie Sidell immediately protested the decision to Bremer and asked him to soften it; Bremer refused, claiming he was acting under instructions. Sidell told him: "If you implement this, you will have between 30,000 and 50,000 Baathists go underground by sundown." Bremer himself admits that a serious mistake was made in handing off implementation of the policy to a special committee headed by Ahmad Chalabi – a Shi'ite who took to the task with gusto – rather than establishing a special judicial tribunal with a more impartial face.

The second and more problematic decision, handed down in "CPA Order No. 2," involved dissolution of the Iraqi army and Iraqi intelligence and security organizations. Originally, the Pentagon seems to have gone along with Jay Garner's plan to retain and make use of the existing Iraqi military for reconstruction tasks as well as security. The Pentagon had already addressed the issue of disbanding the intelligence service and the elite Republican Guard, but Bremer in short order persuaded Feith and Rumsfeld that it would be better to make a clean break with the past with respect to the regular Iraqi army as well.[15] He argued in the first place that the regular army had virtually disbanded itself after the end of the fighting: The bulk of it – Shi'ite enlisted men who tended to be badly treated by their Sunni officers – had simply gone home. Second, he claimed (not very credibly) that Kurdish leaders had "made it clear" to him that any recall of the army would have led to the secession of the Kurdish regions from Iraq and probably civil war. Bremer was able to sell his approach initially by leaving the impression that the dissolution of the

---

[14] Specifically, the order banned all who had held the top four ranks in the party from future employment in the public sector, and also those with any Baathist affiliation who had held positions in the top three ranks in the government. "The senior two positions in Iraq were normally political appointments, but the third rank, while political in stature, was frequently held by senior bureaucrats or technocrats, who were most needed to get the Iraqi government back on its feet. Despite their party rank, in practice many directors general were only nominal party members but of great importance to their respective ministries." Rudd, 312.

[15] It is not altogether clear what role Rumsfeld himself actually had in the decision. Feith (433) assumes the secretary approved the final order, but did not see anything from him in writing; Rumsfeld himself says only that Bremer "briefed" him on the plan on May 19, adding that the decision, "particularly its specifics, did not receive the full interagency discussion it merited" (517). Rumsfeld further adds: "Later I revived the question of whether it might be desirable or possible to reassemble units of the old Iraqi army and bring them into service in some form. I asked General Abizaid for an assessment. But Bremer strenuously objected to this idea, apparently on the grounds that Iraqis would not want any remnants of the old army reconstituted. Whether or not disbanding the Iraqi army was ultimately a good idea, the failure to reform and reconstitute it quickly was costly" (518).

regular army would be a largely symbolic and temporary measure, and that much of this force would be recalled in a matter of months. This seems to have been disingenuous. It soon became evident that the real plan of Bremer and his senior defense adviser, Walt Slocombe, called for the creation over a period of as long as two years of a "New Iraqi Corps" of three divisions or some 40,000 troops, primarily for external defense of the country; a division-sized force of light infantry was to be in the field by the end of 2003. Again, Garner protested Bremer's order, to no avail. Abizaid, at CENTCOM, was not only not consulted but was deliberately misled about the Slocombe plan, and was understandably livid.[16]

It seems clear that the consequences of this move were simply not well thought through.[17] The dissolution of the army and security services affected some 400,000 Iraqis. The move was indeed popular with the Kurds, but much less so among most of the population. Former Iraqi Defense Minister Ali Allawi, an exceptionally incisive critic of the American occupation, argues that the Army (though not the security services) had always been considered a "noble institution," and that even the Shia were reluctant to see it displaced by a very small force that would only have a defensive capability. Furthermore, when it was shortly made clear that the formidable Kurdish militia (the *peshmerga*) would be exempted from the order, suspicions were aroused about ulterior American motives in effecting a permanent change in the internal balance of power in the country. All of this seemed to confirm fears that the United States intended a protracted occupation. And once again the effect was compounded by serious errors on the CPA's part in implementing the policy – particularly the failure to provide reassurance at the outset that stipends would continue to be paid, and then a lengthy delay in actually beginning these payments.[18] Again, there were many complaints in Washington about Bremer's move. Apart from Rumsfeld, none of the National Security Council principals, including the chairman of the Joint Chiefs and the director of the CIA, were informed of it ahead of time, let alone given an opportunity to analyze and weigh in on the issue.[19]

Bremer seems to have insisted on such quick action on these weighty matters in large part for a personal reason – to put a Bremer stamp on the CPA and establish his own authority among the Iraqi people. No one seems to have

---

[16] See especially Rudd, 365–67.

[17] Beginning with the name itself. The acronym for the force turned out to be a particularly obscene expression in Arabic; it was quickly restyled "New Iraqi Army." Ibid., 434.

[18] Allawi, 155–59.

[19] According to Rumsfeld's account, "Apparently Bremer felt he was blamed unfairly for the decision, and in truth, it wasn't all Bremer's fault. I was told of Bremer's decision and possibly [!] could have stopped it. Members of the NSC had been informed of his decision before Bremer announced it, and not one participant registered an objection" (517). In fact, this is simply wrong. An NSC staffer present at the video-teleconference where Bremer announced his signing of the order to the NSC principals has stated that neither Rice nor Powell had had any previous knowledge of it, but rather registered "stunned silence and shock" (Rudd, 332).

given particular thought to the optics of the situation more broadly. As Allawi observes, the Americans were now ruling by decree – just like Saddam Hussein.[20] The dictatorial style was not obviously necessary; at the least, Bremer might have tried to find himself some local political cover by at least feigning consultation with key figures on the Iraqi political scene, but he seems to have had little use for them. But above all, there was a disastrous failure to assess adequately the likely impact of these two actions on the Sunnis, the prime support of the former regime. The affront to Sunni honor, the material deprivations, and the loss of societal and political power were bound to be traumatic for Sunnis of all political inclinations. Hundreds of thousands of former Iraqi officers and troops were now on the streets, angry and well-armed. It was eminently predictable that the conditions were being created for an Iraqi insurgency; and the first signs of this were in fact already evident in the spring of 2003.

Bremer's autocratic style was displayed in his dealings not only with Iraqis but with his own countrymen as well. In staff meetings, he did not invite discussion or tolerate challenge. According to James Stephenson, the mission director in Iraq of the U.S. Agency for International Development (USAID), "it became evident early on that Ambassador Bremer was not receptive to advice and was actively hostile to any that went against his own judgment. Perhaps he took it from others, but he rarely did from me. That was his prerogative, but it was not good leadership."[21] In fact, Stephenson disagreed fundamentally with the CPA's overall approach to Iraqi reconstruction. "I was deeply concerned," he says, "at the heavy concentration of large infrastructure projects that would be slow to develop, generate little employment, and be largely invisible to the average Iraqi in spite of CPA promises to the contrary. The whole approach ignored the lessons learned during a half century of foreign assistance, particularly with regard to postconflict transitions. I found virtually no funding for reforms in agriculture, economic policy, health, education, public administration, or rule of law and inadequate funding for democracy activities across the board, including election support." But Stephenson was unable to persuade Bremer. It took the vigorous intervention of Major General Peter Chiarelli, commander of the 1st Cavalry Division, the American unit then in charge of Baghdad, to move the CPA in this direction.[22]

As a rule, though, Bremer's relationship with the U.S. military leadership in the country was no better than his relationship with civilian officials like Stephenson. Bremer and Lieutenant General Ricardo Sanchez, commander of all U.S. forces in Iraq, did not collaborate closely, to say the least, and there was

---

[20] "In a June 2003 public notice, the CPA exempted itself, the military, and foreign contractors from coming under the jurisdiction of Iraqi laws. Most Iraqis could not miss the irony that the CPA had replaced Saddam's rule by decree with yet another form of arbitrary authority, albeit apparently sanctioned by international law and mostly benign in its intent." Allawi, 160.

[21] James Stephenson, *Losing the Golden Hour: An Insider's View of Iraq's Reconstruction* (Washington, DC: Potomac Books, 2007), 19.

[22] Ibid., 30, 59–65.

constant friction at the staff level. Sanchez seems to have feared that Bremer was trying to establish de facto control of the American military presence in the country. A study conducted in May 2004 by the Center for Army Lessons Learned offered the following general assessment of the CPA's performance from the military's point of view:

The common perception throughout the theater is that a roadmap for the rebuilding of Iraq does not exist. There is not a plan that outlines priorities with short, medium and long-term objectives. If such a national plan exists with the CPA, it has not been communicated adequately to Coalition forces. Task force staffs at all levels of command have reiterated that there is no clear guidance coming from Baghdad. The inability to develop or articulate a plan contributes to a lack of unity of effort between the Coalition and CPA. . . . Coalition commanders and staff view the CPA as understaffed, sluggish, hesitant to make a decision, and often detached from the true situation on the ground. With CPA officials on 90-day rotations, much time is required for replacements to become knowledgeable with the specific issues and players they are facing. . . . Whether rooted in the lack of staffing or security concerns, there appears to be an inability of CPA Headquarters (Baghdad) to get the needed "eyes on" what is happening. Subsequently, CPA directives appear to be out of synch with the current situation.[23]

When Bremer accepted the president's offer of the CPA assignment, a condition he stipulated, and to which the president at once agreed, was that he would be the sole "presidential envoy" to Iraq. This meant that the White House had to abruptly terminate the assignment of Zalmay Khalilzad, an Afghan-American who had been serving on the staff of the National Security Council, as a "presidential envoy" to the Iraqi political opposition (Khalilzad was subsequently appointed U.S. ambassador to Afghanistan). This was a move that may well have had fateful consequences. The contrast between Bremer and Khalilzad is more than a little reminiscent of that between Elbridge Durbrow and Ed Lansdale in Vietnam. Khalilzad, a Muslim himself, was thoroughly comfortable with Arabs and had an instinctive feel for their culture and operating style. In Afghanistan, he would establish a relationship with President Hamid Karzai that recalled Lansdale's relationships with Magsaysay and Diem; and he had proven very effective in dealing with the exiles and other political figures in Iraq. Bremer, on the other hand, was the "ugly American." From the beginning he made it clear that he thought little of these personages and was highly skeptical of their ability to govern the country effectively. In his first meetings with the "externals" in Baghdad, he was more interested in impressing them with his own standing and toughness ("I was exerting the authority President Bush had granted me, 'putting down the hammer'") than in soliciting their opinions or reassuring them about American intentions. It is hard to overstate the importance of these attitudes in shaping the subsequent course of events during Bremer's reign.[24]

---

[23] Cited in Ricks, 212.

[24] Pointedly noted by Feith, who collects examples from Bremer's memoir of the disparaging language he used of the Iraqi leaders (444–45).

Where exactly the CPA train went off the rails remains something of a mystery, but it may well have occurred even before Bremer arrived in Baghdad. Feith's careful sifting of the record at the Washington end points to an NSC Principals' Committee of May 8, attended by Khalilzad and Bremer as well as Powell and Rice (Feith represented the Pentagon), as the point at which consensus on the IIA concept approved by the NSC and the president in March began to come apart. Powell in particular claimed that the president "wants us to take our time," and suggested that a decision on the timetable should be left to Bremer on the ground (contrary to the previously approved position that the IIA should be formed "as soon as possible after liberation"). He also spoke of the sovereignty issue as an either–or proposition, thus implicitly questioning the hybrid character of the IIA as clearly envisioned in March. Rice appeared to accept this notion, suggesting that the IIA might have a purely technocratic advisory character but no executive authority. Interestingly, Bremer spoke up at this point and said that the Iraqi leaders might "choose to stay back and not play" if the IIA were merely technocratic in character – as indeed almost certainly happened on his own watch. Feith commented that in retrospect he was "struck by the mixed nature of the signals Bremer received from Administration officials all over town" but did not suspect at the time that Bremer was heading down the avenue apparently favored by Powell and Rice. In his own memoir, Bremer recalls hearing Garner on the radio in early May announcing that a transfer of power to an "Iraqi government" would occur on May 15 and reacting with shock: "I knew it would take careful work to disabuse both the Iraqi and American proponents of this reckless fantasy – what some in the administration were calling 'early transfer' of power." According to Feith, Bremer never told him this was his thinking, nor did the two ever discuss the possible risks of an extended occupation government.[25] In fact, Bremer's behavior should not have been altogether surprising given the State Department's long-standing preference for a more extended transition period. To what extent Bremer was actually responding to behind-the-scenes guidance from the senior leadership at Foggy Bottom, rather than relying on his personal assessment of the situation in Iraq – a question not often asked – is quite unclear.

A few days after arriving in Baghdad, Bremer made it clear that, unlike Jay Garner, he was not in a hurry to establish an interim Iraqi government. Meeting with the Iraqi Leadership Council or G-7, a group of seven Iraqis Garner had been working with to advance the political process, Bremer told them that power could only be transferred to a body "representative" of the country as a whole, and that the Council itself, of whom six (including Chalabi) were externals, was not such a body. Over the coming months, Bremer

---

[25] Ibid., 438–40. Khalilzad himself, at the May 8 meeting, may also have contributed to the mixed signals Bremer was receiving by presenting a paper that seemed to reopen issues regarding the IIA that had seemed settled in March.

ull Iraqi sovereignty," including such formidable hurdles as the writing of
new constitution and national elections; for the interim period, the CPA
vould continue to govern the country, without serious reference to the Iraqi
Governing Council or any other indigenous political structure. This was a
tunning move. As a result of it, Feith tells us, "Rumsfeld had to rethink his
elationship with Bremer. The article, in effect, mocked the idea that Bremer
vorked for him." Rumsfeld declined to confront Bremer directly, fearing that
his firing or resignation could compromise the entire American position in
raq, while Bremer seems to have quickly enlisted Powell in support of the new
policy.[27] But the magnitude of the administration's Bremer problem had now
come into focus.[28]

The Pentagon's response was to conduct an intensive high-level review of
raq policy overall, at first without and then with Bremer present. The main
outcome of this review was to establish the principle that the primary goal of
the occupation authorities should be preparing Iraqis to assume responsibility
for managing their own affairs, not running the country for them or planning
a new constitution. In particular, higher priority had to be given to rapidly
creating Iraqi security forces to bring the mounting insurgency under control.
Bremer was continuing to insist that the new Iraqi military *not* be used for
nternal security.) But the critical realization was that the only way a rapid
transition to Iraqi sovereignty was going to happen was by insisting on an
early termination of the CPA. In protracted discussions with Bremer, Rumsfeld
and his team eventually prevailed upon him to accept this idea in principle.
Bremer pushed for a date of December 2004; Wolfowitz and Feith favored
April. Eventually, June 30 was settled on. This solution was then blessed by the
president at a National Security Council meeting on October 29, 2003. Back
n Baghdad, Bremer quickly wrapped up an agreement with the IGC along
these lines on November 15.[29] Contrary to Bremer's repeated warnings, the
government of Prime Minister Iyad Allawi that replaced the CPA and IGC at

---

[27] The secretary in fact traveled to Baghdad in mid-September and told the IGC that it was
"absolutely essential" that "governmental legitimacy rest on a constitutional basis leading to
elections" and that "giving sovereignty" to the Governing Council was "entirely unacceptable."
Feith, 459. Feith notes that he did not know whether Bremer's piece had been seen prior to its
publication by anyone else in Washington; one is certainly entitled to speculate about this.

[28] Woodward (*State of Denial*, 250–53) recounts a private dinner convened at the initiative of
Rumsfeld confidant Steve Herbits with Paul Wolfowitz and former Speaker of the House Newt
Gingrich on September 30 to discuss Bremer and the probable impact of failure in Iraq on
the president's reelection prospects. Gingrich is supposed to have remarked in the course of
this discussion: "Bremer is the largest single disaster in American foreign policy in modern
times.... The most dangerous thing in the world is a confident, smart person with the wrong
model because they have enormous enthusiasm in pursuing the wrong model. Bremer arrives
thinking he was MacArthur in Japan and that we should have an American-centric system."
Apparently, it was Herbits who on this occasion first suggested a termination date for the CPA
of June 30, 2004, with an eye primarily to the presidential calendar.

[29] Ibid., 457–66. As Feith points out, Bremer's own account of these events (167) is seriously
misleading.

increasingly emphasized that the appropriate political process was one
through the development of a new constitution, popular ratification
document, national elections, and the installation of a representativ
cratic Iraqi government – a process the CPA envisioned taking as lon
years. While sustaining the impression that he still adhered to the conc
interim Iraqi administration in which Iraqis would share real power
was determined to minimize the extent of that power. A complica
tor, however, was that United Nations Resolution 1483 authorizing t
adopted on May 22, specifically directed that the political future of
to be sorted out under the guidance of the CPA and a special UN r
tative. Chosen to serve in this role was the Brazilian diplomat Serg
de Mello, then the UN High Commissioner for Refugees. De Mello a
Baghdad on June 2 and immediately let it be known that he favorec
normalization of the political situation and the return of sovereign
Iraqi people. In the negotiations that ensued over the formation of a la
more representative Iraqi interlocutor, the Iraqi Governing Council (IC
mer was forced to moderate his preferred course and accept that the
would be granted some real powers, notably that of naming and supe
twenty-five–person cabinet. The CPA, however, retained complete con
financial and security issues, and the question of the actual locus of so
was left ambiguous. The Iraqi Governing Council (which included th
well as eighteen other members) met for the first time on July 13, 20c

Not surprisingly, the IGC was widely regarded as simply a pupp
CPA, in spite of the persistent efforts of at least some of its members to
themselves from the occupation, and its relationship with the CPA w
constant friction. De Mello's presence might have helped overcome th
culties and create an IGC in the spirit of the Pentagon's original IIA
Tragically, however, de Mello was killed along with twenty-one ot
massive truck bombing of the United Nations headquarters in Bag
August 19, thus effectively ending the UN presence and role in the
(One of the many puzzles of this period is why the rapidly deteriorat
rity situation in the country, and above all in Baghdad itself, did not r
alarm bells in Washington or even within the Green Zone. On Septe
Aqila al-Hashemi, a senior diplomat and prominent female member o
and a vociferous champion of the Council, was attacked and killed ou
house by nine assailants as she was preparing to attend the annual m
the UN General Assembly. The CPA evidently did nothing to provide
security to these exposed individuals until after this event.[26])

On September 8, any doubts about the Bremer agenda for the
reconstruction of Iraq were dispelled by an opinion piece under the pr
name appearing in the *Washington Post*. This piece, which was not c
even seen by anyone in the Pentagon, laid out seven steps "on the

[26] Allawi, 163–67.

increasingly emphasized that the appropriate political process was one that led through the development of a new constitution, popular ratification of that document, national elections, and the installation of a representative democratic Iraqi government – a process the CPA envisioned taking as long as two years. While sustaining the impression that he still adhered to the concept of an interim Iraqi administration in which Iraqis would share real power, Bremer was determined to minimize the extent of that power. A complicating factor, however, was that United Nations Resolution 1483 authorizing the CPA, adopted on May 22, specifically directed that the political future of Iraq was to be sorted out under the guidance of the CPA and a special UN representative. Chosen to serve in this role was the Brazilian diplomat Sergio Vieira de Mello, then the UN High Commissioner for Refugees. De Mello arrived in Baghdad on June 2 and immediately let it be known that he favored a rapid normalization of the political situation and the return of sovereignty to the Iraqi people. In the negotiations that ensued over the formation of a larger and more representative Iraqi interlocutor, the Iraqi Governing Council (IGC), Bremer was forced to moderate his preferred course and accept that the Council would be granted some real powers, notably that of naming and supervising a twenty-five–person cabinet. The CPA, however, retained complete control over financial and security issues, and the question of the actual locus of sovereignty was left ambiguous. The Iraqi Governing Council (which included the G-7 as well as eighteen other members) met for the first time on July 13, 2003.

Not surprisingly, the IGC was widely regarded as simply a puppet of the CPA, in spite of the persistent efforts of at least some of its members to distance themselves from the occupation, and its relationship with the CPA was one of constant friction. De Mello's presence might have helped overcome these difficulties and create an IGC in the spirit of the Pentagon's original IIA concept. Tragically, however, de Mello was killed along with twenty-one others in a massive truck bombing of the United Nations headquarters in Baghdad on August 19, thus effectively ending the UN presence and role in the country. (One of the many puzzles of this period is why the rapidly deteriorating security situation in the country, and above all in Baghdad itself, did not ring more alarm bells in Washington or even within the Green Zone. On September 20, Aqila al-Hashemi, a senior diplomat and prominent female member of the IGC and a vociferous champion of the Council, was attacked and killed outside her house by nine assailants as she was preparing to attend the annual meeting of the UN General Assembly. The CPA evidently did nothing to provide physical security to these exposed individuals until after this event.[26])

On September 8, any doubts about the Bremer agenda for the political reconstruction of Iraq were dispelled by an opinion piece under the proconsul's name appearing in the *Washington Post*. This piece, which was not cleared or even seen by anyone in the Pentagon, laid out seven steps "on the path to

[26] Allawi, 163–67.

full Iraqi sovereignty," including such formidable hurdles as the writing of a new constitution and national elections; for the interim period, the CPA would continue to govern the country, without serious reference to the Iraqi Governing Council or any other indigenous political structure. This was a stunning move. As a result of it, Feith tells us, "Rumsfeld had to rethink his relationship with Bremer. The article, in effect, mocked the idea that Bremer worked for him." Rumsfeld declined to confront Bremer directly, fearing that his firing or resignation could compromise the entire American position in Iraq, while Bremer seems to have quickly enlisted Powell in support of the new policy.[27] But the magnitude of the administration's Bremer problem had now come into focus.[28]

The Pentagon's response was to conduct an intensive high-level review of Iraq policy overall, at first without and then with Bremer present. The main outcome of this review was to establish the principle that the primary goal of the occupation authorities should be preparing Iraqis to assume responsibility for managing their own affairs, not running the country for them or planning a new constitution. In particular, higher priority had to be given to rapidly creating Iraqi security forces to bring the mounting insurgency under control. (Bremer was continuing to insist that the new Iraqi military *not* be used for internal security.) But the critical realization was that the only way a rapid transition to Iraqi sovereignty was going to happen was by insisting on an early termination of the CPA. In protracted discussions with Bremer, Rumsfeld and his team eventually prevailed upon him to accept this idea in principle. Bremer pushed for a date of December 2004; Wolfowitz and Feith favored April. Eventually, June 30 was settled on. This solution was then blessed by the president at a National Security Council meeting on October 29, 2003. Back in Baghdad, Bremer quickly wrapped up an agreement with the IGC along these lines on November 15.[29] Contrary to Bremer's repeated warnings, the government of Prime Minister Iyad Allawi that replaced the CPA and IGC at

---

[27] The secretary in fact traveled to Baghdad in mid-September and told the IGC that it was "absolutely essential" that "governmental legitimacy rest on a constitutional basis leading to elections" and that "giving sovereignty" to the Governing Council was "entirely unacceptable." Feith, 459. Feith notes that he did not know whether Bremer's piece had been seen prior to its publication by anyone else in Washington; one is certainly entitled to speculate about this.

[28] Woodward (*State of Denial*, 250–53) recounts a private dinner convened at the initiative of Rumsfeld confidant Steve Herbits with Paul Wolfowitz and former Speaker of the House Newt Gingrich on September 30 to discuss Bremer and the probable impact of failure in Iraq on the president's reelection prospects. Gingrich is supposed to have remarked in the course of this discussion: "Bremer is the largest single disaster in American foreign policy in modern times.... The most dangerous thing in the world is a confident, smart person with the wrong model because they have enormous enthusiasm in pursuing the wrong model. Bremer arrives thinking he was MacArthur in Japan and that we should have an American-centric system." Apparently, it was Herbits who on this occasion first suggested a termination date for the CPA of June 30, 2004, with an eye primarily to the presidential calendar.

[29] Ibid., 457–66. As Feith points out, Bremer's own account of these events (167) is seriously misleading.

the end of June, though entirely appointive, did not seem to have any problem getting its legitimacy accepted by the Iraqi people.[30]

By September, it was already evident to the White House that Bremer was veering out of control and that Rumsfeld seemed unable or unwilling to do anything about the situation.[31] In a memorandum of October 2, National Security Adviser Rice announced the creation of an "Iraq Stabilization Group" that would strengthen interagency support to both the Pentagon and the CPA. There were to be four "cells" to this group, chaired by members of her own staff, in the areas of politics or governance, counterterrorism, economics, and media or strategic communications.[32] This move was a surprise to the Pentagon and greatly annoyed the secretary. Rumsfeld complained to White House Chief of Staff Andy Card that he had not been consulted, and recommended that any such group should report to the State Department rather than the NSC staff, which lacked the capabilities to perform this task; at the same time, he pressed for the formal transfer of Bremer's reporting chain from Defense to State. For reasons that are unclear, this was rejected, and the basic organizational problem persisted through the end of the proconsul's tenure.[33]

Any comprehensive assessment of Bremer and the CPA would have to acknowledge their positive achievements, especially given the many adverse circumstances they had to contend with. One such analysis makes the claim that in the course of the CPA's fourteen-month existence it had:

restored Iraq's essential public services to near or beyond their prewar level, instituted reforms in the Iraqi judiciary and penal systems, dramatically reduced inflation, promoted rapid economic growth, put in place barriers to corruption, began reform of the civil service, promoted the development of the most liberal constitution in the Middle East, and set the stage for a series of free elections. All this was accomplished without the benefit of prior planning or major infusions of U.S. aid. Measured against progress registered over a similar period in more than 20 other American-, NATO-, and UN-led postconflict reconstruction missions, these accomplishments rank quite high.[34]

This judgment can be questioned, but all of these achievements were in any case put in jeopardy by the CPA's blunders relating to the security situation and

---

[30] Rightly noted by Feith, 468. It had proved impossible to organize elections for this interim government in the time available; nonetheless, Bremer's dogged insistence on providing it some electoral "legitimacy" led him to engage in a pointless quarrel with Ayatollah Sistani, the preeminent Shi'ite religious leader, over the option of organizing local "caucuses" as opposed to a full-fledged national ballot – thus gratuitously placing the United States government in the position of opposing democratic elections.

[31] "Rice had been growing profoundly frustrated with Bremer.... She had been receiving so little information from him that summer that, in order to assess the real state of events at the CPA and in Iraq, she began reading the diplomatic reports that the British embassy in Washington passed to her staff." Rice apparently became convinced at this time that "the long-term occupation the administrator contemplated wasn't viable." Ricks, 254–55.

[32] Woodward, *State of Denial*, 240–42, 248–49.

[33] Ibid., 469–70.

[34] Dobbins et al., xxxviii.

governance of the country. While the CPA did not have primary responsibility for security, there can be little question that Bremer's hasty decision to disband the Iraqi military without a thorough consideration of its consequences and possible alternative courses of action did more than anything else to fuel the insurgency. The effects of this error were compounded by the inadequate levels of American troops in the country, the failure to take immediate steps to halt looting and other forms of lawlessness, and – what may have been the single most consequential CPA mistake – the failure to prioritize the training and equipping of Iraqi security forces in large numbers. In all of these respects, to be sure, much of the blame rests with Washington and with Rumsfeld in particular, as well as CENTCOM and the military commanders in Iraq.[35] But Bremer never seems to have realized that the very credibility of the CPA as *the* governing authority in Iraq was fundamentally compromised by the American inability to stabilize the security situation, and that he needed to push relentlessly in Washington and within the theater to focus on the seriousness of this issue.

But it is in the matter of governance that Bremer's performance was to prove most problematic and damaging. It seems reasonably clear that Bremer arrived in Baghdad determined to walk back the administration's established policy concerning an early transition to Iraqi sovereignty. This entailed, however, an American occupation of Iraq lasting – so Bremer seems to have expected – many years, along the lines of the postwar occupations of Germany and Japan. It should have escaped no one that the Iraqis would deeply resent being placed, whether formally or otherwise, in a status similar to that of the Palestinians in the territories "occupied" by Israel.[36] Arguably, however, the real analogy for the occupation of Iraq is not Germany or Japan, but rather the Philippines, at any rate from the time it was clear the United States would eventually grant the country its independence and leave.[37] In the later stages of the American presence in the Philippines, the United States was not (or no longer) interested in a massive reconstruction effort, but had the more modest goals of ensuring

[35] Consider Woodward, *State of Denial*, 308–10, where Wolfowitz is said to have prodded Rumsfeld repeatedly but unsuccessfully to ramp up training for Iraqi forces. "Wolfowitz told close associates it was not just neglect but that Rumsfeld had blocked efforts to get the training up and running earlier. 'I can't understand it,' Wolfowitz told one associate."

[36] Under the UN Security Council Resolution establishing the CPA, the United States and Britain were formally designated "occupying powers." This reflected State Department concerns over several legal issues, particularly the CPA's ability to expend Iraqi funds; Bremer was not responsible for it.

[37] Peter Rodman, then–Assistant Secretary of Defense for International Security Affairs, wrote a memorandum to the secretary of defense arguing that a better historical analogy for the occupation of Iraq than Germany or Japan is France in 1944. An allied "military government" had originally been planned for France as well as Germany, Rodman observes, but the reception of General Charles de Gaulle by the French people after liberation persuaded Roosevelt and Churchill to abandon this idea – fortunately for the allies, as it would very likely have led in short order to a communist takeover of the country. Memorandum for the Secretary of Defense, August 15, 2002, declassified and reprinted in Feith, Appendix 7, 546–47.

security, nurturing economic progress, and developing a political class capable eventually of running the country on its own. For Bremer, the Iraqi politicians he dealt with were essentially a nuisance to be tolerated and if necessary worked around. Instead, they should have been seen as a valuable resource to be encouraged, cultivated, and mentored.

It is still not completely clear what motives drove Bremer in all this. Perhaps he really did model himself on MacArthur.[38] But it is difficult to dismiss the suspicion that much of what lay behind Bremer's virtual contempt for the Iraqi leadership was, not merely a belief that the externals lacked legitimacy in the eyes of their countrymen, but a conviction that one external in particular had to be prevented at all costs from assuming a leadership role. This, of course, was Ahmad Chalabi. The most telling indication of this is that in June 2004 Bremer was willing to turn over Iraqi sovereignty to an interim government not very different from the Iraqi Governing Council – with one major exception, Chalabi's absence.[39] And from this time forward, the entire issue of the supposed illegitimacy of the exiles slipped from view, in Washington as well as Baghdad. Evidently, no voices were raised at State or the CIA (or whispered to the newspapers) that the new interim government lacked legitimacy and was headed toward disaster. If the notorious animus of senior officials in these agencies toward Chalabi was the real driver of Bremer's handling of the Iraqi political scene, it would be quite extraordinary indeed. For the fact of the matter is that none of the various allegations against Chalabi, including the most damaging – that he passed classified information on U.S. forces in Iraq to the Iranians – was ever proved. More than that, however, the director of the CPA's own governance team later said that without Chalabi's help, the CPA would not have achieved many of its successes; and none other than Bremer himself called Chalabi "one of the very few Iraqis whom I met in my time there, in government or outside, who actually understands a modern economy."[40]

At the heart of the failure of the Bremer enterprise in retrospect was a massive strategic error: the failure to align ends with means. Bremer seems to have

---

[38] "My new assignment did combine some of the viceregal responsibilities of General Douglas MacArthur, de facto ruler of Imperial Japan after World War II, and of General Lucius Clay, who led the American occupation of defeated Nazi Germany." Bremer, 36.

[39] On the "marginalization" of Chalabi at this time see Allawi, 281–83.

[40] Feith, 487. The successes included the law on direct foreign investment, the flat individual and corporate income tax, the November 15 agreement, and the interim constitution. Feith also reports that Robert Blackwill, Rice's deputy for Iraq, told Rumsfeld that he found Chalabi "far and away the most competent Iraqi official" and was "amazed at the relentless attacks on Chalabi by various U.S. government officials and others." Oddly, both opponents and champions of Chalabi seem to have taken for granted that a government of externals would necessarily be controlled by him, while political logic should have suggested that a troika leadership arrangement – Shi'ite, Sunni, Kurd – would have been both possible and more defensible in terms of legitimacy as well as checks and balances. It is also worth revisiting the question of whether it would not have been better to create an Iraqi exile "provisional government" even prior to the invasion of the country, as discussed in an internal Defense Department memorandum of October 10, 2002 (Feith, Appendix 8, 549–51.)

believed his assignment was to bring about a fundamental reconstruction not only of the Iraqi economy and infrastructure but in an important sense as well of the political, cultural, and intellectual habits of the Iraqi people – much in the way the great postwar proconsuls approached the challenge of reconstructing and rehabilitating Germany and Japan. Hence, notably, the emphasis on extirpating Baathist "ideology" and, later on, promoting the virtues of a free market economy. But the instrument available to him was completely inadequate for these tasks. The CPA was an organization assembled and run in haphazard fashion, staffed inadequately in quality as well as numbers, poorly supported in Washington, and subject to crippling operational limitations in the theater. Because of its problematic relationship with the American military command structure in Iraq, it had little presence outside the Green Zone and thus insufficient access to current information and intelligence. In spite of its frenetic level of activity and the manic energies of Bremer himself, the CPA was set up for failure.

But the limitations of the CPA were not only material and organizational. Because the ends it pursued were not unambiguously endorsed at the policy levels of the government, at the end of the day the CPA operated under substantial political constraints, causing it to settle for halfway measures in many areas – measures that usually had unwanted side effects. For example, it would have been better either to leave de-Baathification entirely to the Iraqis themselves (though perhaps under a different organizational arrangement), or to do it in a more controlled and systematic way under the CPA aegis. Government ministries were never simply taken over and run by the CPA, yet Iraqis were given insufficient authority (particularly over funding) to manage them on their own; the result was much continuing cronyism, corruption, lack of initiative, sectarianism, and general ineffectiveness.[41] Economic reform was in some areas too rigidly free-market in orientation and in others, not enough (a particularly interesting case: the continuing shortfalls in the electric power supply, caused less by infrastructure problems than by a failure to raise subsidized utility rates in the face of increasing demand).[42]

What key lessons can be drawn from this history? Leaving aside Washington-level issues, perhaps the most important avoidable error was the establishment of the Coalition Provisional Authority as a free-standing civilian entity with unclear reporting channels and a problematic relationship with the military

---

[41] For the perspective of one CPA adviser (to the Education ministry), see John Agresto, *Mugged by Reality: The Liberation of Iraq and the Failure of Good Intentions* (New York: Encounter, 2007). Agresto emphasizes especially the failure of the CPA and the Americans generally to gauge the depth of religious sectarianism among the Iraqi people and, perhaps more interestingly, their failure to grasp elemental human realities that have been obscured by our own liberal political culture.

[42] Particularly on the economic policy issues see the detailed discussion in Allawi, 196–202, 249–65, 348–69. (It should be kept in mind that Allawi served as finance minister in the government of Ibrahim al-Jaffari.)

command structure in Iraq and the theater. The CPA should have been a separate military command reporting to CENTCOM and (for policy matters) to the Office of the Secretary of Defense, or perhaps better, a component of a single military command for Iraq. Both models can be seen in operation under Clay during the occupation of Germany. In spite of continuing and probably unavoidable frictions with civilians in the State Department (in the era before the introduction of the NSC system), both worked tolerably well there. The advantages of such a model are simply that the military framework in a postconflict environment is more conducive to strategic thinking, coherent planning, and disciplined operational execution. Finally, given the constricted time-frame, the CPA (and ORHA before it) should in any case never have been built from scratch; it should have been created out of a standing military headquarters or task force with a capability for rapid and sustainable deployment.[43]

An important corollary of this, however, is that it also matters what sort of individual is in charge of the organization. One can argue that Bremer should never have been chosen to head the CPA because of his lack of military and administrative experience and unfamiliarity with the region. At the same time, it needs to be recognized that the military chain of command also bears considerable responsibility for identifying the appropriate senior officer to fill an important political-military assignment of this sort. This was another area in which the Bush administration came up short. The Pentagon failed to ensure that General Franks undertook serious Phase Four postconflict planning for Iraq in spite of his obvious lack of interest in it. The appointment of Lieutenant General Ricardo Sanchez as commander of U.S. forces after the invasion was a signal mistake, one that greatly compounded the CPA's problems. Sanchez was the youngest three-star general in the Army and had never commanded more than a single division; in particular, he had no significant political-military experience, and indeed was a very conventional and tactically oriented officer. In addition, he seems to have had personality and leadership shortcomings that made him even less suitable for such an assignment. It is an indictment of the Army personnel system that he was chosen, but perhaps even more, it is indicative of the inadequacy of strategic leadership at the combatant command level as well as the higher reaches of the administration (and in the Senate for that matter) that the appointment was approved without objection.[44]

Bob Woodward reports an exchange touching on this issue in an interview with Secretary Rumsfeld that is highly revealing and worth quoting at length.

Woodward: "I quoted former Secretary of Defense Robert McNamara, 'Any military commander who is honest with you will say he's made mistakes that have cost lives.' Is that correct?" Rumsfeld: "I don't know. I suppose that a

---

43 For an extensive and sensible discussion of these organizational issues see Rudd, 381–400.

44 Consider the comments of Rumsfeld, 500–02. Sanchez' headquarters was badly understaffed – another failing in the military chain of command. Rumsfeld himself claims he does not recall "being made aware of the Army's decision to move General Sanchez into the top position" (!).

military commander – " Woodward: "'Which you are,' I interrupted." Rumsfeld: "No, I'm not." Woodward: "Yes, sir." Rumsfeld: "No, no. Well..."
Woodward: "'Yes. Yes.' I said, raising my hand in the air and ticking off the
hierarchy. 'It's commander in chief, secretary of defense, combatant commander.'" Rumsfeld: "I can see a military commander in a uniform who is engaged
in a conflict having to make decisions that result in people living or dying and
that that would be a truth. And certainly if you go up the chain to the civilian side to the president and me, you could by indirection, two or three steps
removed, make the case."[45]

Woodward, of course, is correct. The president and the secretary of defense
constitute the "National Command Authority" and are empowered by law
(unlike the uniformed Chiefs) to exercise direct command authority over the
combatant commanders. As he goes on to remark, it is "inexplicable" that
Rumsfeld would say this, given his insistence in the run-up to the Iraq war on
his right to provide guidance to and second-guess General Franks and his field
commanders. But it seems rather to point to a fundamental misapprehension
on Rumsfeld's part of the proper role of the secretary of defense. Rumsfeld
prided himself on challenging conventional military wisdom and encouraging
the uniformed military to "think outside the box," and he was willing to be
aggressive to the point of rudeness in doing so. At the same time, he was oddly
reluctant to provide clear guidance, issue instructions when necessary, or (quite
unlike his successor, Robert Gates) relieve underperforming officers for cause.[46]
Yet as the example of Abraham Lincoln if nothing else so clearly demonstrates,
the hiring and firing of military commanders is one of the most fundamental
strategic functions and prerogatives of the president (and, derivatively, the
secretary of defense), above all in wartime. It is only an apparent paradox that
the "National Command Authority" is made up of two civilians. For it is here
that the civilian–military distinction blurs and in fact becomes meaningless –
in fact, it is precisely this that in the last analysis enables civilian control of the
military in a democracy.[47]

The demise of the CPA and the reestablishment of an American embassy in
Baghdad in July 2004 soon proved a major improvement in the management
of the Iraq conflict as far as the civilian side was concerned.[48] The security
situation in the country, however, became increasingly dire over the next several
years, although Washington was slow to recognize this. On the military side,
the key story of this period has to do not so much with proconsular leadership

---

[45] Woodward, *State of Denial*, 487.
[46] The secretary did, however, insert himself fairly aggressively in the process of selection and
promotion of senior officers: Rumsfeld, 299–301.
[47] On Lincoln and more generally, see Eliot A. Cohen, *Supreme Command: Soldiers, Statesmen,
and Leadership in Wartime* (New York: Free Press, 2002).
[48] According to Deputy Secretary of State Richard Armitage: "As soon as we got [Ambassador
John] Negroponte out there, and got State involved, everything changed. We had reporting,
it was orderly, things started to run... we started getting reams of reporting, so we got the
texture of society, we got the debate of society, we got all of it." Ricks, 391.

properly speaking as with a struggle within the Army – highly reminiscent of the later Vietnam War – between proponents of counterinsurgency and more conventionally minded officers. Standard-bearer of the former was, of course, General David Petraeus. As commander of all U.S. forces in Iraq in 2006–08, Petraeus devised a new and more effective strategy for handling the Iraq conflict, and in tandem with the very effective Ambassador Ryan Crocker, effected a decisive shift in American fortunes in the country.

10

Petraeus in the Middle East

American: "Do you want to kill me?" Iraqi: "Yes. But not today."
                                         Thomas E. Ricks[1]

Tell me how this ends.
   General David Petraeus[2]

It is worth emphasizing again that Iraq in the summer of 2003 differed in fundamental ways from Germany or Japan in the fall of 1945. Both Germany and Japan prior to their defeat at the hands of the United States and its allies had been advanced modern states with populations that were almost completely homogeneous, in ethnic if not religious terms. At the end of the war, the Nazi and imperial Japanese regimes had been comprehensively defeated and were by and large discredited in the eyes of their people; in spite of some fears to the contrary, in neither country did former regime elements or sympathizers attempt to wage guerrilla warfare against the victorious occupiers. The primary tasks facing the occupation authorities were therefore political and economic reconstruction, rather than the provision or maintenance of security. And these tasks were themselves greatly facilitated by the institutional structures that were available for salvage from the wreckage of the relatively developed German and Japanese states and economies.

In the case of Iraq, by contrast, what had once been one of the most advanced countries of the Arab Middle East had been devastated and rendered virtually dysfunctional by some forty years of tyrannical and incompetent government. Much more damage was done by Saddam Hussein to his own country during this time than by all coalition military operations from 1991 to 2003. Furthermore, Iraq was far from being a homogeneous nation. Cobbled together

[1] Thomas E. Ricks, *The Gamble: General David Petraeus and the American Military Adventure in Iraq, 2006–2008* (New York: Penguin Press, 2009), 207.
[2] Rick Atkinson, *In the Company of Soldiers: A Chronicle of Combat* (New York: Henry Holt, 2004), 6.

originally by the British out of three provinces of the old Ottoman Empire, Iraq had profound ethnic cleavages – notably, between Arabs and the large Kurdish minority in the north. Most critically, however, it was religiously divided between Sunni and Shi'ite Muslims, the latter making up some 60 percent of the population – a fact of paramount political importance given the fact that Saddam's regime had been sustained largely by the support of the Sunni Arab minority. The Sunni–Shia split was also a profound one, with its roots in an antagonism going back to the first century of the Muslim faith. Finally, it is also important to note the persisting role in Iraqi society and politics of tribal groupings. As we shall see, a belated grasp of the role of the tribes, particularly in the Sunni Arab rural areas, by American military commanders contributed in a decisive way to the turnaround in American fortunes in Iraq on the watch of General David Petraeus.

Predictably (although few predicted it), the American occupation of Iraq would prove to be something other than an occupation in the traditional sense of the term. It was in fact a war – a continuation in some ways of the initial struggle, in other ways a morphing of that struggle into a complex multi-player unconventional conflict, and one that could not be countered effectively short of the continuing application of military force by the United States.[3] Whether the invasion of Iraq could have been considered a front in the "global war on terror" at the time it occurred, as asserted by some, there can be little question but that it soon became one. The American presence in Iraq turned the country into a magnet for aspiring jihadists from all corners of the Muslim world, under the sponsorship and general direction of a franchise of Osama bin Laden that came to be called Al Qaeda in Iraq (AQI). What might have been a manageable problem if the United States had at the outset taken appropriate steps to secure Iraq's borders quickly became unmanageable as it failed completely to do this – the result of inadequate American troop levels from the beginning of the conflict coupled with the disastrous decision to disband the Iraqi army.[4]

Initially, the security problem that loomed largest for the United States was unrest among the Sunni population, particularly in the rural areas north and west of Baghdad that had seen little if any coalition military presence. Saddam Hussein's home town, Tikrit, was in this area, which was also home to many experienced military and security officers of the former regime. Armed resistance there gathered steam in the summer of 2004, centered on Fallujah and Ramadi, the major cities in the sprawling Anbar Province in the west. It was not long, however, before AQI established itself in the relative sanctuary offered by Anbar, to support and stiffen the Sunni tribes as well as to funnel foreign fighters infiltrating across the nearby Syrian border into the rest of

[3] See Heather S. Gregg, Hy S. Rothstein, and John Arquilla, *The Three Circles of War: Understanding the Dynamics of Conflict in Iraq* (Washington, DC: Potomac Books, 2010).

[4] On the later part of the Iraq "war" see especially Ricks, *The Gamble*, Bob Woodward, *The War Within: A Secret White House History 2006–2008* (New York: Simon & Schuster, 2008); Linda Robinson, *Tell Me How This Ends: General David Petraeus and the Search for a Way Out of Iraq* (New York: Public Affairs, 2008); and Bing West, *The Strongest Tribe: War, Politics, and the Endgame in Iraq* (New York: Random House, 2008).

Iraq. In November and December, a major campaign was waged by U.S. forces in Fallujah, killing 70 Americans and more than 2,000 insurgents in bitter house-to-house fighting.

It was already clear by this time, however, that the Sunnis and Al Qaeda (also Sunni in orientation) were not the Americans' only problem. In August, the brash and charismatic Shi'ite cleric Moqtada al-Sadr attempted to tighten the hold of his militia, the Jaish al-Mahdi (JAM), on central and southern Iraq and establish himself as the leader of a nationalistic Shi'ite movement hostile to the interim government and the American presence. Supplied by the Iranians with funds, weapons, and (according to some reports) actual fighters, Sadr infiltrated the city of Najaf and seized the shrine of Imam Ali, one of the holiest sites of Shia Islam. In concert with the government of Iyad Allawi, a secular Shi'ite, U.S. forces moved to put down the revolt and arrest Sadr, but this effort was frustrated by a last-minute intervention by Ayatollah Sistani, the leading and widely revered Shi'ite cleric who resided in Najaf. Among other things, this episode fatally damaged Allawi politically, smoothing the way for an elected government dominated by a more religiously oriented and sectarian Shi'ite leadership. Sunnis largely boycotted the national elections of January 2005, the effect of which was to give the Shia an even more overwhelming dominance in the new legislature and effective control of the government. This was a government prepared not only to tolerate but in varying degrees actually to collude with JAM and other Shia militias, in a sustained campaign to consolidate Shia control of the country. Failure to suppress the Sadrist movement in the early stages of the American occupation was a cardinal error. It made civil war between the Shia and Sunni virtually inevitable and handed the Iranians an invaluable tool that enabled them to manipulate Iraqi politics and at the same time bleed and otherwise weaken the Americans now on their doorstep.[5]

The second Iraq war was one the United States was forced to wage, then, on multiple fronts. It faced both a Sunni insurgency, mostly in the north and west and (mainly west) Baghdad, and a Shia insurgency, mostly in the south and east and (mainly east) Baghdad. The Sunni insurgency became increasingly lethal due to the support and involvement of AQI, an amalgam of foreign and native Iraqi jihadists. The Shia insurgency, while less threatening to U.S. forces, was nevertheless difficult to deal with because of the tendency of the government to shelter it and the virtual sanctuary it enjoyed as a result in Sadr City, the

---

[5] In this instance, Bremer and the CPA deserve credit for recognizing the seriousness of the Sadr problem in the summer of 2003 and urging his arrest (there was strong evidence implicating him in the murder of another cleric); this step was resisted by American military commanders in Iraq and senior levels of the Pentagon. According to Lieutenant General Ricardo Sanchez: "When my staff and I evaluated the situation, we agreed with the Marines, who didn't like the idea of trying to arrest al-Sadr. They were three weeks away from going home and they didn't want to create any instability." Abizaid, the CENTCOM commander, also concurred. See the account in Ali A. Allawi, *Occupying Iraq: A History of the Coalition Provisional Authority* (Santa Monica, CA: RAND, 2009), 297–307.

large Shi'ite slum in eastern Baghdad; from this convenient staging area, the Sadrists could regularly rocket coalition headquarters in the Green Zone at the center of the city with little fear of retaliation. At the same time, it, too, became increasingly lethal thanks to material support and training provided by the Iranians, including particularly highly effective anti-armor munitions. Iranian involvement also raised the possibility of an escalation of hostilities to the level of an interstate war. For the most part, though, whether rightly or not, the United States seems to have ignored what often appeared to be Iran's intentionally provocative behavior.[6]

But the situation was still more complicated. The United States was certainly fortunate that the two insurgencies never fused into one, as the Sunni and Shia remained distrustful and mutually antagonistic. What it did not anticipate was that this antagonism would explode into a virtual (if relatively low-level) civil war. Driving this development were two factors. First, not only were the jihadists viscerally anti-Shia, but they realized that the best way to increase pressure on the coalition to end the occupation was to ratchet up the level of violence and general chaos throughout Iraq. The simplest way to accomplish this was to conduct a campaign of sectarian terror against Shi'ite civilians, in the expectation that this would lead to retaliation by them against the Sunnis – as indeed proved to be the case. Second, the Shia themselves, far from seeking reconciliation with their former Sunni masters, were intent on taking advantage of the political situation created by the overthrow of Saddam to consolidate their control of the state and in particular to cement their hold on the capital. This they proceeded to do by a systematic campaign of terror and ethnic cleansing in the Sunni and mixed neighborhoods in (mostly west) Baghdad, spearheaded by JAM but with the tacit and sometimes even open support of the Shia-dominated national police.

There can be little question that the American effort in Iraq was faltering badly during 2005–06. Anbar had for all intents and purposes been lost. In Baghdad, violence was pervasive, public services had largely broken down, and much of the population had fled. JAM and other militias controlled much of the Shi'ite south, including Basra, Iraq's third largest city, whose British garrison eventually abandoned it for the relative safety of the airport. General George Casey, the American military commander, seconded by General John Abizaid at CENTCOM, saw no solution to the deteriorating situation other than keeping American troops as much as possible out of the crossfire and accelerating the training of Iraqi security forces. This general view was also shared by the civilian leadership at the Pentagon as well as the Joint Chiefs. Incredible as it seems in retrospect, General Casey continued to assure Washington that progress in expanding the Iraqi armed forces would enable the United States to begin drawing down American combat units in the relatively near term.

In the last half of 2006, there was a dawning realization in several places in the American national security establishment, however, that this position was

[6] Cf. West, 323–25, 349–51.

no longer sustainable. The White House was not the least of these places. The president himself was becoming increasingly concerned about the dysfunctional relationships among his senior advisers, and in particular the apparent drift of the Pentagon under Donald Rumsfeld. Earlier in the year, Rumsfeld had come under withering public attack for his handling of Iraq from a number of retired Army and Marine Corps generals, a clear reflection of the widespread unhappiness with the Secretary that pervaded the active duty military. President Bush later claimed he was prepared to replace Rumsfeld as secretary of defense at this time, but he decided against it on the grounds that he could not be perceived as giving in to the generals' protest, a step he (with some justification) thought would undermine the principle of civilian control of the military. He has also said he did not want to be seen as making a personnel move that might be interpreted as a political calculation prior to the November 2006 congressional elections. In any case, Rumsfeld was asked by the president to leave the administration shortly after the elections, the results of which in any case were widely interpreted as a repudiation of the administration's Iraq policy.[7]

At the president's request, the National Security Council staff had already begun to explore alternative military options in the summer of 2006. Within the military chain of command, Casey was telling his superiors by July that he no longer supported a drawdown and might indeed have to request additional forces. In Washington, the chairman of the Joint Chiefs, Marine General Peter Pace, ordered a quiet review of the Iraq situation by a special "Council of Colonels." Meanwhile, in an extraordinary development, General Jack Keane, recently retired as Army vice-chief of staff, became sufficiently alarmed by the trend of events that he took it upon himself to launch a major effort outside of official channels to make the case for a major increase in U.S. combat forces in Iraq. Thus was laid the groundwork for what can only be called the spectacular turnaround in American fortunes in the Middle East that would unfold over the coming year or so.

The shorthand way of referencing this turnaround is "the surge." This term has been used to describe primarily the president's decision in early 2007 to increase the U.S. Army presence in Iraq by five combat brigades. However, much more was involved than a mere increase in numbers of troops. The entire American approach to the war changed, at the tactical, operational, strategic, and political levels. Several hands can claim some responsibility for this dramatic development. No one was more critical in assuring its success than General David H. Petraeus.

David Petraeus was born in Cornwall, New York, in 1952, a town in the shadow of West Point.[8] He attended the U.S. Military Academy, graduating in

---

[7] George W. Bush, *Decision Points* (New York: Crown, 2010), 87–94.
[8] For Petraeus' earlier career see Robinson as well as David Cloud and Greg Jaffe, *The Fourth Star: Four Generals and the Epic Struggle for the Future of the United States Army* (New York: Crown, 2009).

the class of 1974; in the same year he married the daughter of the Superintendent, Major General William Knowlton. Knowlton, a military diplomat who spoke six languages fluently, had served in Vietnam as a top official in the Civil Operations and Revolutionary Development Support (CORDS) program and would go on to retire after a distinguished career with four stars. The general was an important influence on Petraeus, convincing him of the importance of historical study for effective officership, and may well have sparked his later interest in counterinsurgency at a time when this topic had become profoundly unfashionable in the Army. In the 1980s, Petraeus would go on to write a PhD dissertation at Princeton on the influence of the Vietnam War on the next generation of officers. This substantial piece of work was never published, no doubt in part "out of a wish not to gouge the current senior leadership in public." Nevertheless, Petraeus' considered view, that the United States could not afford simply to turn its back on limited or low-intensity conflict of the sort the nation had engaged in during the Vietnam era (and was currently reliving in Central America), went against the grain of what had by then become the conventional wisdom of the American military establishment, and of the Army in particular. It prepared him well for the intellectual campaign he was later to wage against the conventional Army on behalf of the theory of counterinsurgency warfare.[9]

Petraeus' intellect, driving ambition, and appetite for work in any case marked him as a rising star. In 1988, as a major, he was selected to be the personal aide to General Carl Vuono, chief of staff of the Army. As a lieutenant colonel, Petraeus commanded a battalion of the 101st Airborne Division at Fort Campbell, Kentucky, and later served on the division staff. His mentor during this period was the division assistant commander, Jack Keane, the future vice-chief of the Army. (Of Petraeus and himself, the general once revealingly remarked: "We're both change agents.") As a colonel, Petraeus took brigade command with the 82nd Airborne Division at Fort Bragg, North Carolina. Following that, he was assigned a prestigious staff job in Washington as executive assistant to the Chairman of the Joint Chiefs (then General Hugh Shelton), before returning to Bragg as a brigadier general and assistant commander of the 82nd Airborne in 1999. By the time of the invasion of Iraq, he was given another star and command of the 101st Airborne.

The sector assigned the 101st centered on Mosul, Iraq's second largest city. Mosul, in north-central Iraq, was the largest Sunni-majority city in the country, but also a volatile ethnic and religious mix. In the early days of the occupation, individual military commanders had significant leeway to manage local affairs as they saw fit, and Petraeus took full advantage of this to launch an aggressive nation-building program, with priority attention to issues of governance and economics. It took him a month to hold elections and establish a

---

[9] For an early manifesto along these lines see John Rogers Galvin and David Petraeus, "Uncomfortable Wars: Toward a New Paradigm," *Parameters* (Winter 1986): 2–8. (General Jack Galvin, then the SOUTHCOM commander, was an important mentor of Petraeus'.) For all this see especially Robinson, 50–60. The phrase quoted in the text is Robinson's.

governor and governing council for Ninewa Province. After the arrival of L. Paul ("Jerry") Bremer as head of the Coalition Provisional Authority, Petraeus succeeded in persuading Bremer to release funds for local economic and infrastructure projects, in the process courting important elements of the provincial elites and putting as benign a face as possible on the American presence. In view of this, Bremer's two initial orders came as an unpleasant surprise. The "de-Baathification" decree, among other adverse effects, put every professor at Mosul University out of work and prevented students from graduating in the spring. Bremer approved Petraeus' request to delay implementation of the order and attempt reconciliation at the local level, but once the national-level Iraqi de-Baathification committee was formed in Baghdad under Chalabi, it blocked the exceptions recommended by the local committee. The second order, abolishing the armed forces, was also resisted by Petraeus, who suggested that former officers in the area be honored at a public ceremony and invited to rejoin a reconstituted Iraqi army. The request was denied by the CPA. The result was a violent demonstration in Mosul, during which several soldiers of the 101st were killed.[10]

The division, with its commander, left Mosul in February 2004. By the end of the year, following the two American assaults on Fallujah in April and November, Mosul and the surrounding area had become a refuge for insurgents fleeing Anbar, and much of Petraeus' work came undone. The governor of Ninewa was assassinated in July; Mosul's police force fell apart in November after many of them were seized and brutally executed. The smaller U.S. force that had succeeded the 101st was unable to cope with this new level of violence.

After a short respite, Petraeus returned to Iraq in June 2004 to head a new command that was to take charge of the training and equipping of the new Iraqi army and police forces, a mission increasingly seen as critical for the stabilization of the country and the eventual withdrawal of American troops. Then, in September 2005, he was brought back from the Middle East to be commander of the Combined Arms Center at Fort Leavenworth, Kansas. Although seen by some in the Army at the time as an indication that the general was out of favor, the appointment was in fact of great significance for the role Petraeus would later play as commander of all U.S. forces in Iraq. The CAC oversaw the Command and General Staff College and other Army education and training programs, including doctrine development. Petraeus used this opportunity to revive classic counterinsurgency theory within the Army officer corps; in particular, he supervised the writing of a new manual on counterinsurgency warfare – something the Army had not done in twenty years.[11]

---

[10] On Petraeus' performance as commander of the 101st see the account of Atkinson, a *Washington Post* reporter the general had invited to "embed" with the division.

[11] For the thinking behind this manual, see particularly John A. Nagl, *Learning to Eat Soup with a Knife: Counterinsurgency Lessons from Malaya and Vietnam* (Chicago: University of Chicago Press, 2002); David H. Petraeus, "Learning Counterinsurgency: Observations from Soldiering in Iraq," *Military Review* (January–February 2006): 2–12; Eliot Cohen, Conrad Crane, Jan

The "surge" is an extraordinary story of political-military decision-making in the United States today, one that amply demonstrates the importance of personality and leadership in this arena as opposed to formal bureaucratic structures and processes. It is not necessary for present purposes to describe this story in detail, which in any case has been done in several well-informed recent accounts. The focus instead will be principally on the personal contribution of General Petraeus.

As indicated earlier, in a narrow sense the surge was about a temporary increase in the number of American combat brigades in Iraq, but in a broader sense it was about the way the United States should actually be fighting the war. The key – though not the only – feature of the latter was the emphasis on counterinsurgency, as distinct from limited counterterrorism operations together with the training and expansion of native Iraqi forces. Politically and strategically, the most important aspect was the outreach and working alliances established with Sunni tribes in the countryside as well as insurgent elements in Baghdad. At the level of military operations, the most significant innovations were probably the establishment of a *cordon sanitaire* in the Baghdad suburbs designed to curb the flow of militants and munitions into the city, and the development of high-value interagency target teams led by special operations personnel.[12] By the time Petraeus had been confirmed as new commander in Iraq in February 2007, these various shifts were to some degree already in motion. Classic counterinsurgency campaigns had been conducted over the previous several years by several Army and (especially) Marine Corps commanders in isolated sectors of the country.[13] In the latter part of 2006, these efforts began to bear greater fruit with the spontaneous turn of Sunni tribesmen against AQI, which enabled various forms of local cooperation with American units and their commanders. With the arrival in Iraq of Lieutenant General Raymond Odierno in December as deputy to General George Casey, the thinking of the senior American commanders began to change regarding the size of the American force in the country and the best way to employ it. In Washington, finally, support for a significant increase in American combat forces was gaining ground both within the National Security Council staff and in the private think tank world. At the American Enterprise Institute, Frederick Kagan, a military historian and former professor at West Point, had developed

Horvath, and John Nagl, "Principles, Imperatives, Paradoxes of Counterinsurgency," *Military Review* (March–April 2006). The manual itself was first published by the Army in December 2006; see also *The U.S. Army–Marine Corps Counterinsurgency Field Manual* (Chicago: University of Chicago Press, 2007). See further Robinson, 76–81, and Ricks, 16–31.

12 The latter has been very inadequately appreciated. See particularly Christopher J. Lamb and Evan Munsing, "Secret Weapon: High-value Target Teams as an Organizational Innovation," *Strategic Perspectives* 4 (Washington, DC: Institute for National Strategic Studies, National Defense University Press, March 2011).

13 For the Marines see Timothy S. McWilliams and Kurtis P. Wheeler, eds., *Al-Anbar Awakening, Volume I: American Perspectives: U.S. Marines and Counterinsurgency in Iraq, 2004–2009* (Quantico, VA: Marine Corps University, 2009).

a detailed plan for a surge of U.S. forces into Baghdad and began briefing it to potential sympathizers. Former Army Vice-Chief Jack Keane was one of these.

The recruitment of this highly respected retired general to the surge cause lent it great credibility and access to senior levels of the government. Keane himself was seized at once with the imperative of action at what he saw as a critical moment in the nation's history, and he was also convinced that no action was likely if matters were left to the senior military leadership as then configured. As a result, he took it upon himself to short-circuit Pentagon bureaucracy and bring the surge concept directly to the White House. On December 11, he was invited to meet with the president, Vice President Dick Cheney, two other retired four-star generals, and two academic experts. One of the latter, Eliot Cohen, author of a well-regarded book about wartime civilian leadership that Bush had read,[14] opened the session with a strong plea for holding the current commanders accountable for the failing effort in Iraq and making a change. Keane then made his case for an increase in troops and a shift to a population-centric counterinsurgency approach. Although the other four stars opposed adding additional troops, Bush apparently was persuaded. He then asked the group who he should pick to succeed Casey. Cohen responded: "David Petraeus." The others immediately supported him. Not long afterward, Keane received a call from a White House official who told him that the meeting had had a decisive effect on Bush's thinking.[15] On January 10, 2007, Bush delivered a somber televised address in which he called the current situation in Iraq "unacceptable" and announced that the United States was changing its strategy and would be sending 20,000 more combat troops there.

But Keane's intervention was not limited to that. He was in constant contact with Petraeus, and spoke frequently with Odierno in Baghdad. Keane himself traveled to Iraq in January and spent some hours being briefed by Odierno's staff on his innovative operational plan. Needless to say, his role in all this was not appreciated by Casey, Abizaid, or the Joint Chiefs. It should be added that Odierno himself deserves more credit than he has received for taking the considerable risk of opposing the views of his immediate superiors and, indeed, working quietly against them in the months prior to Casey's relief by Petraeus. As one observer has said:

If Jack Keane was the spiritual godfather of the surge, Odierno was its biological parent. Petraeus, arriving in Baghdad two months later, would become its adoptive father. In order to position the U.S. for a new strategy – that is, get additional brigades and use them differently – Odierno had to take on his direct superior, General Casey, who in turn was backed by the entire chain of command. It is extraordinary to consider that the new strategy that would be implemented by the U.S. military in Iraq in 2007 was opposed by the U.S. military in both Baghdad and Washington. With the exception of Odierno, it came from outside the military establishment.[16]

---

[14] Eliot Cohen, *Supreme Command* (New York: Free Press, 2002).
[15] Ricks, 94–101.
[16] Ibid., 107, 303–04, citing Odierno's own complaint about Woodward's White House–centric account.

Bureaucratic fortune further smiled on Petraeus when Ryan Crocker replaced Zalmay Khalilzad as ambassador to Iraq in March. Crocker was a seasoned and respected foreign service officer who had spent many years in senior positions throughout the Arab Middle East. Crocker and Petraeus were determined to avoid the problems that had plagued the State–Defense relationship in Baghdad at the outset of the occupation, and worked hard to ensure "unity of effort" in the U.S. Iraq project. But Petraeus' relationship with the military establishment would remain problematic. George Casey enjoyed a soft landing as Army chief of staff, like Westmoreland after his disastrous tour in Vietnam. Casey well knew he had lost the confidence of the president and was no doubt resentful of the part played in this drama by Keane, Petraeus, and Odierno, and from his new position continued to press for a rapid drawdown of U.S. forces. The pliant and ineffective Pace would remain chairman until fall. The new secretary of defense, Robert Gates, had acquiesced in the surge, but seems to have been less than fully committed to it. But perhaps the most unfortunate personnel development was the replacement of Abizaid as CENTCOM commander by Admiral William ("Fox") Fallon. Fallon, the former commander of PACOM, knew little about Iraq or the Middle East, and was abrasive and domineering. He soon bought into the prevailing Pentagon skepticism about the surge and began to throw obstacles in Petraeus' way.[17] In a private meeting with the vice president in August, Jack Keane complained of the lack of support Petraeus had been getting from Fallon in particular, but also from the State and Defense Departments in Washington. As for the Pentagon, Keane apparently told Cheney: "The Joint Chiefs are more concerned about breaking the Army and Marine Corps than winning the war. They don't say it that way.... The fact that the Army is stressed and strained is sort of expected during war," he added. "That's why it exists."[18] After Admiral Michael Mullen replaced Pace, in an effort to reestablish what he felt to be the diminished authority of the chairman and the Chiefs, he tried to cut off Petraeus' access to Keane, telling the general he would no longer be allowed to travel to Baghdad. Cheney intervened personally to have this decision reversed. The president himself felt obliged to send Petraeus a private message through Keane expressing full support for his commander in doing whatever might be necessary to win the war.[19]

On taking command of Multinational Force Iraq (MNF-I) in February, Petraeus had already made it clear to his commanders that he was fully committed to victory.[20] To achieve it, he was prepared to discard established orthodoxies and experiment with new and radical approaches. One of his first steps was to create his own "brain trust," officially known as the Joint

---

[17] Ibid., 230–36.
[18] Woodward, 376–77.
[19] Ibid., 386–90, 399–401; Ricks, 252–53.
[20] One of Petraeus' three-star commanders spoke later of a "blood pact" with his top generals: "It was, we're gonna do this, or we're gonna go down trying. But we're not going to operate so that the next generation of Americans are going to have to go to war to finish this thing. And we're going to have our integrity when we're done." Ibid., 133. Parallels with the Vietnam War were very probably in the general's mind.

Strategic Assessment Team (JSAT). Headed by then–Colonel H. R. McMaster, this extraordinary group of several dozen accomplished individuals included a number of senior Army officers with PhD degrees, civilian academics, several State Department officials, and even the occasional foreigner (notably, the Australian anthropologist and counterinsurgency expert David Kilcullen). This was not an ordinary planning cell; rather, it was tasked to do a fundamental reassessment of the situation on the ground in Iraq and American strategy there. Also directly supporting Petraeus was another unusual organization, the Commander's Initiatives Group, tasked with challenging conventional thinking across the board on a day-to-day basis and acting as the general's eyes and ears and sounding-board; its commander, Colonel Bill Rapp, was one of the general's most important advisers.[21]

One major course correction Petraeus instituted at the very beginning was to press his commanders to be more active and open with the media. "We are in an information war," he reportedly told them; "sixty percent of this thing is information."[22] The general was fully aware of the aversion many military officers felt toward the American press – one of the unfortunate legacies of the Vietnam era. He was also sensitive to the tendency of officials and politicians of all kinds to put a positive face on the state of ongoing military conflicts, with the attendant decline in their credibility that goes with this over time. Petraeus recognized that his immediate predecessors had damaged themselves and the war effort on both counts, and made it a strategic priority of his own to undo this damage. More than that, he understood that the administration itself – and the president above all – had lost a great deal of credibility by its persistent optimism about conditions in Iraq as the situation there steadily deteriorated. Petraeus' own public demeanor was calm, reasonable, and reassuring, but he was also very cautious in predicting progress or success. In the first six months of his tenure, he became virtually *the* public face of the administration on Iraq. The combination of the real progress actually made over these six months and the adroitness with which it was communicated took much pressure off the White House, and greatly strengthened Petraeus' own standing both in Washington and in Baghdad. An important turning point was reached in early September, when Petraeus and Crocker appeared together on Capitol Hill to give a long-awaited progress report on the state of the war. Their lengthy testimony effectively validated the surge in the eyes of enough members of Congress to forestall any serious challenge to the American presence in Iraq and provide the administration added political breathing room to see the new strategy through.[23]

The turnaround in the war began to be noticeable as early as July. By this time, the five surge brigades had been fully deployed in Iraq. At the same time, the JSAT, Petraeus' personal think tank, had produced a sharp-edged report

---

[21] See especially Robinson, ch. 4.
[22] Ricks, 133.
[23] See especially ibid., 241–51.

distilling a new understanding of the violence in Iraq and how the United States should approach it. For the first time in an official document, this study recognized the reality that the nature of the conflict itself had mutated from a counterinsurgency struggle to a low-grade civil war – and one to which the Iraqi government itself was a party. Unlike some voices that were beginning to be heard in Washington, however, it rejected the view that the United States had to pull back from the cities and prepare for an early departure, or for that matter actively encourage the partition of Iraq among the three communal rivals. Its main recommendations were to adopt a political strategy of seeking cease-fire agreements and accommodation with various local actors; to implement a military strategy of protecting the population while stepping up pressure on irreconcilable militant elements of whatever affiliation; to engage in regional diplomacy, especially with a view to neutralizing the Iranians; to continue building Iraqi governing capacity, including a massive increase in the size of the Iraqi army; and to work actively to remove sectarian officials from the government, if necessary by unilateral action. After some internal debate, Petraeus largely accepted this approach, though toning down the last recommendation in particular in response to concerns that it would infringe Iraqi sovereignty. Finally, it is interesting to note that the JSAT team also put forward a radical proposal for organizing the overall U.S. effort. It argued that nothing short of genuine "unity of command," under which military and civilian personnel from the embassy and the MNF-I would be fully integrated in a single staff, would support a strategy in which the political component was so central. In this regard, it appealed explicitly to the Vietnam-era CORDS counterinsurgency organization. Petraeus decided against such a move, probably as a bridge too far, but also no doubt in some measure because of his confidence in working with his State Department counterpart; but he did take significant (indeed, largely unparalleled) steps to improve interagency coordination in the theater – notably, by collocating Crocker's office in the Green Zone with his own and appearing together with him at important meetings with senior Iraqis.[24]

Much of Petraeus' effectiveness in his proconsular role derived in fact from his feeling for the political dimension of warfare. In Iraq, he understood that victory would be won not simply by killing "bad guys" but rather by promoting a process of political reconciliation that would create the preconditions for creating a stable security environment. Unfortunately, little progress had been made or seemed possible at the national level in Iraq, given the historical rivalries in play as well as the deadly animosity arising out of the recent blood-letting between Shia and Sunni. Fortunately, an alternative presented itself – fostering reconciliation from the bottom up through direct negotiations between the American military and hitherto neutral or even hostile local groups. As noted earlier, this had already begun to occur to some extent as the Sunni tribes in Anbar turned increasingly against the AQI elements in the area. But Petraeus

---

[24] Robinson, 114–17.

set out to encourage it systematically. Even more importantly, however, he and his subordinate commanders initiated such efforts in Baghdad itself.[25]

The problem was that this strategy increasingly alarmed the Shia-dominated government. It was one thing for the Americans to enlist the Sunni tribes in fighting Al Qaeda in Anbar, a part of Iraq that was largely desert, lacked oil, and was seen by the Shia as strategically irrelevant. It was quite another to seek alliances among Sunni insurgents or militias in the capital itself, where Iraqi forces and friendly Shia militias were actively engaged in sporadic violence against Sunnis as part of a campaign of "ethnic cleansing" of mixed and Sunni neighborhoods. The critical strategic challenge, then, was not simply cutting political deals with local Sunni entities, but controlling the potential political blowback from these deals. Petraeus was in fact masterful in meeting this challenge – probably his single greatest personal achievement on the ground in Iraq. To do so required developing and maintaining relations of respect and trust with senior Iraqi politicians, beginning with Prime Minister Nouri al-Maliki himself. Initially, Maliki resented Petraeus, and in fact tried to get Bush to remove him.[26] Toward the end of August, this task became measurably easier when relations between Maliki's government and the JAM soured, eventually forcing Moqtada al-Sadr to call on his followers to observe a unilateral cease fire. Petraeus also succeeded in persuading Maliki to make at least some gestures in the direction of reconciliation at the national level – most dramatically, by taking him on a helicopter trip to Anbar (the prime minister had never been there before).[27]

It is often said or assumed that President Bush essentially contracted out America's Iraq policy to David Petraeus. Bush clearly did find it politically convenient to give this impression, but in fact he was personally highly engaged in Iraqi affairs during this period. Strikingly, he conducted weekly video teleconferences with Petraeus and a few of his staff (Crocker also frequently attended). This channel bypassed not only the entire National Security Council but also CENTCOM and Petraeus' immediate military superior, Admiral Fallon.[28] In this regard, Petraeus "probably had a more direct relationship with his president than any field commander in an American war had enjoyed since the Civil War, when Lincoln could summon a general to Washington or board the *River Queen* to steam down the Potomac and up the James and meet with Grant and Sherman. . . ."[29] What transpired in these sessions is not known. Did the president grasp the full implications of Petraeus' new strategy and campaign

---

[25] See, for example, West, ch. 22, and Ricks, ch. 7.

[26] West, 278–79.

[27] Sudarsan Raghavan, "Maliki, Petraeus Visit Insurgent Hotbed in Iraq," *Washington Post*, March 14, 2007.

[28] Before these meetings, however, Petraeus emailed a written version of the verbal report he would deliver to the president to the secretary of defense, the chairman of the Joint Chiefs, and the CENTCOM commander. Ricks, 225–27, remarking tellingly that Petraeus was "skilled at managing upward." Consider the contrast with Jerry Bremer.

[29] Ibid., 231.

plan? There is reason to think that Petraeus never actually sought approval from Bush for the plan to attempt political reconciliation unilaterally at the local level.[30] Even less would it seem that the president realized the extent to which Petraeus was prepared to interfere in the workings of the Iraqi government or to pressure and cajole the Iraqi leadership, particularly Maliki himself. In fact, Bush himself acted to some degree at cross purposes with this strategy, for he also carried on biweekly teleconferences with Maliki personally. The effect of this arrangement was actually to undercut the influence of Petraeus and Crocker on the Iraqi leadership and encourage Maliki to think he could easily play the American side.[31]

By the end of 2007, it was clear that things were looking up in Iraq. But even the scent of victory did not completely quiet the skeptics, either in the Pentagon or Congress. In March 2008, an important corner was turned when Maliki personally led Iraqi army and special forces units in an assault on the JAM stronghold of Basra, which had by that point clearly drifted out of the control of the coalition and the central government. The action was poorly planned and not coordinated ahead of time with U.S. forces, which were then called on to step in to prevent a disaster; but Maliki eventually prevailed, thus greatly enhancing his own and the government's prestige and political standing throughout Iraq, particularly with the Sunnis. Also in March, there was an unexpected development on the U.S. side, as Fox Fallon abruptly resigned as CENTCOM commander as a result of remarks attributed to him that seemed critical of Bush administration policy toward Iran.[32] Petraeus, who had planned on leaving his post in Iraq to become Supreme Allied Commander in Europe, instead found himself assigned to replace Admiral Fallon in Tampa.

As CENTCOM commander, Petraeus assumed overall responsibility for both of America's ongoing wars. The situation facing him in Afghanistan at the end of 2008 was in many ways reminiscent of what he had found in Iraq at the beginning of 2007. The weak central government of Hamid Karzai suffered severe problems of legitimacy and governing capacity, and was increasingly under challenge by a resurgent Taliban movement operating from sanctuaries in Pakistan's Northwest Frontier Province. American military forces in the

---

[30] Ibid., 202–03.

[31] "The Iraqis played hardball because they always did. They were banking on President Bush's steadfast unwillingness to walk away from Iraq, and perhaps on the unwillingness of any U.S. president to abandon Iraq to Iran and the possible resurgence of Al-Qaeda forces. The Iraqis needed and wanted the United States to continue to provide a security blanket, but they knew the administration was just as eager to stay. Bush's frequent conversations with Maliki worked to the detriment of the U.S. bargaining position. He appeared to be at least as eager as the supposed petitioner to reach the necessary agreements." Robinson, 334; cf. also 173–74. For some cautionary remarks on personal presidential diplomacy, see Carnes Lord, *The Modern Prince: What Leaders Need to Know Now* (New Haven, CT: Yale University Press, 2006), 156–58.

[32] For an assessment of this episode from the point of view of American civil–military relations, see Mackubin Thomas Owens, *US Civil-Military Relations After 9/11: Renegotiating the Civil-Military Bargain* (New York: Continuum, 2011), 76–77.

country were spread thin. Supporting forces provided by various NATO and other allies played a larger role than in Iraq, yet often operated under exasperating constraints and had proven largely ineffective in their most important role, training of the Afghan armed forces and police. A case could be made under these circumstances for a "surge" of American troops similar to that in Iraq, and perhaps as well for a shift in the direction of a more robust counterinsurgency approach to the country's security problems.

What would soon be very different, however, was the political environment in which Petraeus found himself. When Barack Obama replaced George W. Bush in the November elections, Petraeus no longer had easy access to the president. More than that, though, Obama had always disliked the war in Iraq, and had specifically opposed the surge. In his first meeting with Petraeus in Baghdad while still a candidate, he had made it very clear that while as commander in chief he would certainly welcome professional military advice, he would make his own decisions on issues such as strategy and force levels. The clear implication was that he believed Bush had been too deferential to his generals, and in particular to the chief military proponent and defender of the surge. Indeed, the Obama White House, together with many Democrats in Congress, continued to view Petraeus with suspicion as a general who had become too politically identified with the Bush administration. More than that, though, there was also an underlying current of distrust relating to Petraeus' own potential political ambitions. During the fall of 2008, there had been much speculation in the media in the wake of the success of the surge and the general's impressive public performances on behalf of Bush's Iraq policy that he might well become a serious contender – perhaps as early as 2012 – for the Republican presidential nomination. Although Petraeus strenuously denied any such ambitions, this was an issue that would refuse to go away. As with earlier American cases, especially MacArthur and Lodge, the importance of this factor in shaping the behavior of the White House toward its proconsul should not be underestimated.

The United States' now decade-long war in Afghanistan has not received anything like the same attention as the war in Iraq, particularly at the level of national and theater-level decision-making. This is true both within the U.S. government and in journalistic and academic analyses.[33] Accordingly, it is difficult to track the American leadership picture in Afghanistan and the Greater Middle East (i.e., CENTCOM's "area of responsibility") with the same fidelity as that in Iraq, not to speak of older historical cases. There can be little question that the spectacular victory achieved by U.S. and friendly Afghan forces over the Taliban regime in November 2002 inspired an unwarranted sense of confidence in American civilian and military officials. After the decision was made to

---

[33] See notably Ahmed Rashid, *Descent into Chaos: The United States and the Failure of Nation Building in Pakistan, Afghanistan, and Central Asia* (New York: Viking, 2008); Seth Jones, *In the Graveyard of Empires: America's War in Afghanistan* (New York: W. W. Norton, 2009); and Bob Woodward, *Obama's Wars* (New York: Simon & Schuster, 2010).

invade Iraq in the spring of 2003, moreover, American attention and resources were soon diverted from the tasks of Afghan security and reconstruction to the new theater of operations. Iraq would remain the United States' key priority in the region for the next five to seven years, while Afghanistan was by and large neglected. As former Chairman of the Joint Chiefs Admiral Michael Mullen once put it: "In Iraq we do what we must. In Afghanistan, we do what we can."

The consequence for Afghanistan was not unlike the trajectory of the second Iraq war, although on a lesser scale. With very limited troops on the ground and little effective assistance from either Coalition forces or the Afghans themselves, the United States was not able to secure the country's porous borders to the south and east or to prevent a revival of the Taliban in its sanctuary in the tribal areas of Pakistan and the gradual growth of an insurgency, abetted by Al Qaeda and supported in some measure by elements of the Pakistani intelligence service. Once again, the United States was slow to acknowledge that its position in Afghanistan had begun to unravel. Counterterrorist operations targeting Al Qaeda leadership rather than a counterinsurgency effort aimed at protecting the Afghan population were the focus of the limited American military effort, along with the recruitment and training of Afghan security forces. As in Iraq, too, the new government under President Hamid Karzai was weak and difficult to work with. Much real power remained with unsavory local warlords, while crime and corruption, much of it driven by an explosion of opium production in these years, were rampant. Although President Bush had once pledged to launch a new "Marshall Plan" for Afghanistan, the funds to support this were never forthcoming and the country remained an economic shambles.[34]

This situation began to change for the better in 2003, when Zalmay Khalilzad was named ambassador to Kabul and Lieutenant General David Barno took over as commander of U.S. forces in Afghanistan. In his previous incarnation as staff member of the National Security Council, Khalilzad had been instrumental in developing a new strategy for American involvement in the country, focusing on building Afghan government institutions, broadening the political base of the government, disarming and otherwise weakening the warlords, and improving the economy, particularly in the rural areas. This would become the template for the robust nation-building effort that Khalilzad would pursue as ambassador, in tandem with the new counterinsurgency or population-centric approach developed by General Barno.[35] To symbolize the new "unity of effort" on the American side, Barno moved his own headquarters from the main Coalition hub at Bagram Air Force Base into a trailer in the

---

[34] Jones, 115–17, as well as Dov S. Zakheim, *A Vulcan's Tale: How the Bush Administration Mismanaged the Reconstruction of Afghanistan* (Washington, DC: Brookings Institution, 2011).

[35] Jones, 134–45. On the latter also see Donald P. Wright et al., *A Different Kind of War: The United States Army in Operation ENDURING FREEDOM, October 2001–September 2005* (Fort Leavenworth, KS: Combat Studies Institute Press, U.S. Army Combined Arms Center, 2010), ch. 9.

embassy compound in Kabul. Khalilzad and Barno seem to deserve considerable personal credit for devising this new strategy as well as for implementing it through a close working partnership on the ground. Unfortunately, Washington, preoccupied with the Iraq situation, was reluctant to make any substantial financial commitment in support of these initiatives.

As discussed earlier, Zalmay Khalilzad was in many ways ideally suited to a proconsular role. A native-born Afghan and a Muslim with an instinctive feel for Middle Eastern ways of doing business yet very much at home in American academic and policy circles, highly intelligent and of great personal charm, Khalilzad was able to establish a close personal relationship with Hamid Karzai and other influential members of the Afghan political elite. He personally involved himself in internal Afghan politics to an extent that would have been impossible for virtually any other American. He was also instrumental in arranging the highly successful elections that took place in the country in October 2004.

"Yet fate took a strange twist. In 2005, Zalmay Khalilzad replaced John Negroponte as U.S. ambassador in Iraq. It was a move symptomatic of the U.S. government's tunnel vision on Iraq. The State Department had taken one of its most seasoned and effective ambassadors, who spoke Afghanistan's two main languages and had a special rapport with its political leaders, and moved him to Baghdad during an extraordinarily fragile period in Afghanistan's history."[36]

This is a particularly glaring, but as has been seen, hardly unique example of the failure of Washington officialdom to give serious attention to the strategic management of America's overseas "empire."[37]

When running for president, Barack Obama had criticized the Bush administration for neglecting America's "necessary" war in Afghanistan in favor of its adventure in Iraq. After assuming office, the new president initiated a major review of U.S. policy toward Afghanistan, and in relatively short order signaled his commitment to enhancing the American effort there by sending additional forces (some 21,000 troops) as well as by several key personnel changes. The replacement of Lieutenant General David McKiernan by Lieutenant General Stanley McChrystal in May 2009 brought to the top of the American command structure in Afghanistan a seasoned special operations officer as well as a creative and dynamic leader. Also noteworthy was the appointment of a special State Department envoy to Afghanistan and Pakistan, the accomplished and ambitious Richard Holbrooke. The U.S. ambassador to Afghanistan remained retired Army Lieutenant General Karl Eikenberry, a former commander of U.S. forces in the country; Petraeus, to repeat, had assumed the leadership

---

[36] Jones, 150.

[37] An interesting coda to the Khalilzad story is the ambassador's apparent flirtation with a run for the presidency of Afghanistan in 2009 should Karzai have stepped aside, and then with the possibility of appointment as a kind of prime minister or national security adviser under Karzai. See, for example, Helene Cooper, "Ex-US Envoy May Take Key Role in Afghan Government," *New York Times*, May 18, 2009.

at CENTCOM. This was an impressive array of political-military talent and experience.

Unfortunately, it failed to mesh as an effective team; nor did Washington encourage it to operate as such. McChrystal, with Petraeus' support and following his example from Iraq (both had in fact served there together), undertook a comprehensive review of the U.S. position in Afghanistan with a view to reemphasizing a counterinsurgency approach to the conflict. Eikenberry, though, disagreed, and at one point sent a lengthy cable to the White House criticizing this approach, without clearing or discussing it with McChrystal or Petraeus – not surprisingly, something that badly damaged their relationship. Throughout the summer of 2009, the White House insisted on conducting its own laborious review of Afghanistan strategy, including a running debate on the merits of a "counterinsurgency" as distinct from a "counterterrorism" strategy, and the linked question of possible requirements for additional U.S. forces. Two distinct factions eventually coalesced in support of one or the other of these options, the latter led (oddly and unprecedently) by Vice President Joseph Biden, the former by Petraeus with the support of Mullen and Gates.[38]

It is altogether understandable that President Obama sought to avoid the mistakes made by the Bush White House (and the Rumsfeld Pentagon) in remaining too distant from the Middle East war theaters. But the outcome in practice was problematic. In the first place, the process (as commonly happens in a new administration) was less than disciplined, reflecting in particular the relatively weak leadership of the National Security Council staff under its new head, retired Marine General Jim Jones; the result was an agonizingly slow and frequently repetitive and inconclusive bureaucratic "churn" (to use another term of art). More important, though, was the distrust so clearly felt by Obama and certain White House aides toward the military leadership. To be sure, the president has the right – indeed, the responsibility – to shape strategic decisions with the help of the political perspective that is uniquely his. It is also entirely proper for him to probe the assumptions underlying the judgments and recommendations of his military leadership. But Obama seemed obsessed with the thought that the military was trying to foist its own preferred force numbers on the White House at all costs. The result was a protracted and unseemly haggling over a relatively insignificant increment of troops – and not inconsiderable political damage as the administration looked to be vacillating and divided over a matter that had appeared all but resolved many months before.

This having been said, there is some substance to complaints voiced at the time and later by the president and others in the White House about the forward-leaning tendencies of the military leadership, particularly McChrystal. In a speech he unwisely agreed to give in London in October, not long after he had delivered his classified assessment to Obama, McChrystal strongly defended the counterinsurgency approach and spoke of the need for resolve and

[38] All of this is chronicled in detail by Woodward, *Obama's Wars*.

the demoralizing impact of uncertainty, while alluding to the ongoing debate in Washington and joking about the risks he might be taking in speaking so forthrightly. Some in the White House, not unreasonably, saw this as an open attempt to tie the president's hands and were outraged.[39] On several other occasions, both Petraeus and Mullen also found themselves targets of White House ire for making public statements that seemed to prejudge the outcome of the policy review or, in Petraeus' case, that smacked of self-promotion.[40] Beyond this, however, it is also fair enough to say that the "options" for increased force levels crafted by McChrystal and endorsed by Petraeus, Mullen, and Gates were structured in such a way that they left the president little real choice other than the preferred middle option of 40,000 troops. Moreover, when the president indicated his displeasure with this figure and interest in alternate scenarios, they were resistant. General Douglas Lute, a senior National Security Council (NSC) aide for Afghanistan inherited from the Bush administration, later said he felt "the military establishment was really rolling the President, though he didn't want to assign motives. It wasn't deliberate on McChrystal's part.... McChrystal didn't have a conspiratorial bone in his body. If there was someone trying to roll Obama, it was Petraeus. But he had done so subtly and with a light touch."[41] In the current state of our knowledge, at any rate, this claim cannot simply be dismissed.

Obama succeeded in forcing a compromise on force levels (30,000 would be the final troop number), but in other respects McChrystal and Petraeus got what they wanted. When the president rolled out the new policy in an Oval Office speech on December 1, 2009, he may have believed he had done enough to deflate the commanders' ambition to pursue an Iraq-style counterinsurgency strategy.

Petraeus saw it differently. Counterinsurgency was alive and well. The core of the decision was 30,000 troops to protect the population. All the issues about what the strategy wasn't – not fully resourced COIN, not nation building – were just words. The reduction from 40,000 to 30,000 allowed the president to save face. It wasn't ideal,

---

[39] Ibid., 193–97.

[40] On November 11, Veterans' Day, for example, Petraeus gave an interview to CNN in the White House briefing room shortly before a meeting with the NSC principals. The interview focused mainly on Petraeus' account of a visit to a badly wounded Army officer at Walter Reed Hospital, but he was also asked about his possible interest in running for the presidency. In doing so, Petraeus ignored a blanket ban on TV appearances that had been imposed by the Pentagon and was unapologetic when confronted by the department's press secretary. Ibid., 266–68.

[41] In Woodward's paraphrase (322), Lute continues as follows: "On the other hand, Mullen had failed to maintain the integrity of the process, which required the serious presentation of something other than the one recommended option. He adamantly wouldn't budge and give a hard look at alternatives. To Lute, Gates also had failed to expand the horizon of alternatives for the president, which in his view was the job of the secretary of defense. The secretary was supposed to give his own advice and bottom-line recommendation, but he was also supposed to be the final window in the larger world of choice for a president.... Lute thought Gates overly deferential to the uniformed military."

but McChrystal could get 10,000 from NATO and other countries. If the president had told him at the beginning that it would come out with this strategy and 30,000 troops, Petraeus would have taken it in a second.[42]

---

[42] Ibid., 324–33. Though he does not say so, Woodward seems to be paraphrasing Petraeus' own words from a later interview, in accordance with his usual practice. He also cites the vice president as saying he believed "the president had put a stake in the heart of expansive counterinsurgency. His orders, in Biden's view, formed a new strategy to stabilize Afghan population centers, such as Kabul and Kandahar, to prevent the Taliban from being able to topple the Karzai government. The military felt they had outsmarted the president and had won, but he believed that the president had prevailed" (332). If this indeed reflected the president's own view, his strategic vision was fundamentally flawed. A major difference between Iraq and Afghanistan is that in the case of the latter, control of the countryside, not the major cities, is the key to successful counterinsurgency.

American Lessons

What conclusions can be drawn from this (necessarily partial) account of pro-consular leadership? In particular, are there any practical lessons that can be learned from it for the conduct of American security policy in today's world? If the United States has indeed become an empire of sorts, is it not of some importance to try to clarify or rationalize the role of its proconsuls abroad, especially in the light of what will generally be agreed to be the mismanagement of recent American experiments in regime change and nation-building in Iraq and Afghanistan? I will try to address these questions briefly.

It is difficult to make large generalizations about the American proconsular experience. This is so in part because of the disparate circumstances in which proconsular leadership has arisen in the United States and in part because of changing organizational and cultural factors in American government and politics. The overarching thesis of this study is that delegated political-military leadership has been a significant independent variable in American national security decision-making from the end of the nineteenth century to the present – or, more simply stated, that it has made a strategic difference. This is not to say that it has made a difference always and everywhere or with the same degree of impact or long-term significance. Indeed, this has clearly not been the case. This study has necessarily concentrated on individuals and particular episodes in American history in which proconsular autonomy and hence leadership have been most marked; it has not attempted anything approaching an overall assessment of the relative contributions of leadership on the periphery and leadership at the center of the empire (to use again our vocabulary of convenience). Nevertheless, it seems safe enough to conclude that the cumulative weight of the cases studied here shows that the proconsular factor in the American story is one that has been widely neglected or underappreciated in standard historical accounts.

Is proconsular leadership then a good thing?

That proconsuls can be dangerous to the health of empires is a lesson all too easily learned, as has been seen from the experience of the later Roman

Republic. At first sight, it is tempting to imagine that this ancient history is of little relevance to the present. Rome's social and political system was in many ways vastly different from that of America today, in spite of the family resemblance of the two polities. So too was the character of its government and elite decision-making. The Romans had no real bureaucracy, but they did have a cohesive (if often internally divided) governing class with a shared and deeply felt set of beliefs and practices, hardened and reinforced by almost constant warfare. This allowed them in the course of several centuries to conquer most of the Mediterranean world with virtually no centralized institutions for the conduct of military planning or operations, diplomacy, or intelligence. They were able to do so by delegating significant authority – and on an increasing scale – to their senior political officials, who functioned at the same time as military field commanders. Though theoretically answerable to the authority of the Senate (and even more theoretically that of the People), Rome's consuls and proconsuls enjoyed wide discretion, and even when their actions were disliked, they were rarely reversed in Rome. In general, command and control of these officials was affected as much by cultural norms and expectations as by the formal commands of the Senate. At the same time, senators were often jealous of the political achievements of their peers and moved to rein them in from time to time. For the most part, however, the power of Rome's commanders was checked primarily by strict limitations on their tenure in office. When these limitations began to break down toward the end of the second century BC, Rome's great consular figures began to emerge as a source of existential threat to the Republic.

The American experience is of course vastly different. Partly because the American Founders were fearful of precisely this Roman precedent, they were careful to subordinate command of the military to a powerful civilian executive, the president, and then to limit the ability of the president himself to conduct warfare without the approval of a representative civilian legislature. In the course of recent American history, the power and scope of operation of its military commanders have been increasingly constrained by the growth of a large civilian defense establishment as well as competing civilian organizations dealing with diplomacy, intelligence, and other matters potentially affecting the conduct of military operations. Another important factor, of course, is the rapid development of electronic telecommunications technologies in the decades prior to the United States' emergence as a global power at the end of the nineteenth century. Today, an era of virtually instantaneous global communications might be thought to impose very severe limits on the ability of any senior American official abroad to play any sort of autonomous decision-making role.

And yet as we have also seen, the dynamics of delegated political-military leadership in the United States today are not after all completely without parallel in the Roman experience. To begin with, and perhaps most strikingly, there is a persisting if little-noticed pattern in the American case of the intrusion of political ambition into proconsular leadership. From the very beginning, Americans attracted to proconsular roles frequently harbored or developed higher ambitions, which in turn affected how they played out those roles and interacted with their superiors in Washington. The first American proconsul, General Leonard Wood, became a vocal critic of his commander in chief Woodrow Wilson while still in uniform and (barely) lost a race for the presidential nomination in 1920. Of the governors-general of the Philippines, William Howard Taft later became secretary of war as well as president and chief justice of the Supreme Court; and no fewer than three others seem to have harbored presidential ambitions. The same was patently true of General Douglas MacArthur, whose assignment to the Philippines by Roosevelt in 1936 was a sort of political exile. And the nadir of the American proconsular story, Ambassador Henry Cabot Lodge, who was dispatched to Vietnam by both Kennedy and Johnson in large part for malevolent political reasons, used his potential presidential candidacy to leverage his proconsular prerogatives, as MacArthur had done in 1944 and 1948. Both men successfully defied the wishes of the president and were able to protect themselves from dismissal, while the latter, in Korea in 1950–51, posed the greatest challenge to civilian control of the U.S. military in American history. Finally, let us not forget that General Wesley Clark also ran for the presidency after his minor triumph in the Balkan wars of the 1990s.

But it would be a mistake to overemphasize this dimension of the American proconsular experience. At least as problematic is a subtler form of distance between proconsuls and the center – one stemming partly from limitations of personality, intelligence, or ideology and partly from a distortion of strategic perspective caused by the proconsul's own limited vantage point or a personal investment in viewing his situation or tasks in a certain way. As an example of the latter, one can cite MacArthur's increasingly deviant strategic perspective in the last period of the Pacific War, particularly as it related to his personal imperative of reconquest of the Philippines. Arrogance or self-righteousness played a large role in MacArthur's case, but it is also in evidence in Lodge's egregious insubordination in Saigon in 1963 and, if in a much more defensible way, in the sharp-elbowed and envelope-pushing behavior toward peers and superiors evident in the personal styles of Wood and Clark. Bremer's errors seem to have resulted from a combination of personal vanity and misapprehension of the strategic situation he faced (that is, viewing Iraq in the optic of the American occupations of Germany and Japan following the Second World War). Harrison's tenure in the Philippines is a prime example of proconsular freelancing fueled by a combination of ideology and ambition.

On the other hand, we have also seen cases of exemplary proconsular leadership where there can be little question that proconsular officials were in significant measure personally responsible for ensuring a better outcome to American decision-making relating to their area of responsibility than would have occurred, other things being equal, in their absence. In this category arguably belong Wood, Taft, Clay, Lansdale, Abrams, Clark, and Petraeus. For all his flaws, the same should probably be said for MacArthur, at any rate during his tenure as proconsul in occupied Japan.

This is a respectable balance sheet. It reflects, above all, the high caliber of these men and others like them who have served the American Republic in high office since the nation's emergence as a great power. They were more than mere imperial functionaries. Though not lacking in personal ambition, they were both American patriots and "change agents" who seized opportunities available to them to shape or steer national policy in the best interests of the United States and what it stands for. In this regard, they exercised "leadership" in the proper sense of that term.

The American proconsular story is not only about individuals, however. It is also about basic aspects of American political culture and the organization and operation of the United States government. The egalitarianism and entrepreneurial spirit so deeply rooted in American life mitigate the hierarchical structure of governmental institutions and nurture initiative in subordinate officials. Space for bureaucratic initiative and maneuvering is in any event provided by the structure of the American institutions themselves – at the political level, by the separation of powers between the executive branch and Congress, and at the administrative level, by the high degree of autonomy generally enjoyed by the departments responsible for national security affairs. A second key point, and one too easily overlooked, is that the American national security establishment has never been structured around a consciously imperial mission. Even in the short heyday of real American imperialism following the Spanish-American War, the management of America's newly acquired overseas territories was an afterthought from Washington's point of view. The United States has never had the equivalent of imperial Britain's colonial office. This has meant that American proconsuls have often had very inadequate guidance or oversight from the center, and almost always have been forced to improvise their own organizational arrangements and relationships. This was true, understandably enough, during the American occupation of the Philippines, when the nation was still in its bureaucratic infancy. Yet our recent experience with the Coalition Provisional Authority in Baghdad should suffice to show that the problem is still very much with us.

The core dynamic of proconsular leadership may be said to be the balancing and integration of political and military decision-making. The fundamental problem facing American proconsuls is that political and military decision-making are institutionally split. This remains the case in spite of the significant reforms put in place after World War II, especially the creation of the National Security Council. Today, after ten years of war and continuing pressures to improve the integration of the political and military dimensions of American counterinsurgency operations in the Greater Middle East, there remain significant disconnects and tensions between a civilian leadership that is increasingly without military experience and a military establishment (embracing civilian professionals as well as the uniformed military) that is increasingly competent to deal with security-related matters beyond the narrowly military sphere.

There is no easy solution to this problem. Proconsular leadership in the proper sense of the term seems to call for unity of command in the field. Roman proconsuls, as we have seen, performed both political and military functions. In the American experience, this has been the exception rather than the rule. Wood governed Cuba briefly essentially by himself. Clay and MacArthur exercised undisputed authority within occupied Germany and Japan respectively, though each also employed a "political adviser" seconded by the State Department and was at least theoretically subject to the writ of Foggy Bottom. In all these cases, it is not accidental that the proconsul was a military officer. Endowing a military officer with civilian or political authority has always been an acceptable institutional solution, while placing military commanders in a non-military chain of command has been considered unacceptable by the military, for reasons difficult to dispute. For the most part, the national civilian leadership has not challenged this position. The most common solution has been a bifurcated proconsulate, with a commanding general and an ambassador (or in the Philippine case, governor-general or high commissioner) sharing authority in a formally undefined but more or less balanced fashion. Finally, though, several other models of proconsular leadership are possible, and in fact have been experimented with in some fashion in the period we are considering. One is the Lansdale model, where the proconsul enjoys no formal authority but exercises great de facto influence through his personal relationship with an indigenous leader or elite, as Ed Lansdale did in both the Philippines and Vietnam. (A comparable example in the British imperial experience is Cromer's role in Egypt in the late nineteenth century.) Finally, there is the solution of an ambassador or governor endowed with authority over all field operations of the imperial power. This solution is most feasible if the ambassador or governor is himself a serving or retired military officer. In the American experience, apart from Wood, we have encountered this only once, when retired general Maxwell Taylor was made ambassador to the Republic of Vietnam, though it might very well also have happened with Ed Lansdale in 1963. Unfortunately, Taylor failed to rise to the challenge and never attempted to establish real authority over the American military commander or American military policy in the country. With Lansdale, it might have been a different story. (In the British experience, consider the highly successful prosecution of the Malayan Emergency by the British High Commissioner Sir Hugh Templeton in 1948–51.[1])

Obviously, the answer very much depends on the strategic environment the proconsul faces. In the case of military occupations following the defeat of an enemy by conventional military means, the American experience as a whole can be said to validate the model of a single military proconsul, as best exemplified by Lucius Clay in postwar Germany. Wood, Clay, and MacArthur all performed effectively, in spite of some frictions with the State Department in particular. Bremer, on the other hand, failed signally to create and manage an essentially civilian occupation authority. Perhaps the clearest lesson from our

---

[1] See the account of John A. Nagl, *Learning to Eat Soup with a Knife: Counterinsurgency Lessons from Malaya and Vietnam* (Chicago: University of Chicago Press, 2002), chs. 4–5.

recent Iraq experience is that an occupation authority should not be improvised from scratch, but should be built around an existing standing military headquarters at the corps level, and then firmly embedded within the military chain of command in the field (not as in the CPA case, through a tenuous link directly to the Pentagon).[2] In the case of counterinsurgency operations in an allied country, on the other hand, what seems needed ideally is a civilian proconsul with plenipotentiary authority, on the model of Taylor (theoretically) or Templeton (in practice). This is because of the need in counterinsurgency warfare for close and constant coordination on the ground between political, diplomatic, military, intelligence, economic, and other operations. Second best, though with the potential for substantial effectiveness, is the political-military tandem option, as seen notably in the cases of Abrams and Bunker in Vietnam and Petraeus and Crocker in Iraq.

An interesting aspect of proconsular leadership, though one only touched on over the course of this study, is the geopolitical reach of proconsular authority. As we saw at the outset in discussing the structure of the British Empire in the nineteenth century, proconsuls in the truest sense may be said to be those presiding over a strategic "paramountcy," an extended area that crosses political boundaries (both internal and external to the empire) and generally entails some degree of diplomatic engagement with other powers as well as some degree of direction or oversight of imperial military forces in the region. During the Vietnam War, it is arguable that the United States would have fared better had it conceptualized Southeast Asia as a single theater of conflict and provided for more centralized direction of American policy on the ground. This could perhaps have been done by granting the U.S. ambassador to South Vietnam the status of a special presidential envoy with some degree of authority over American ambassadors and other operations elsewhere in the region. Very recently, it has been thought useful to create a special representative of the secretary of state – initially, seasoned ambassador and trouble-shooter Richard Holbrooke – for Afghanistan and Pakistan ("Afpak"), in recognition of the vital importance of Pakistan in the ongoing efforts of the United States and its NATO allies to pacify Afghanistan. (Holbrooke apparently pressed for the inclusion of India in this portfolio, but for understandable reasons the Indians declined the honor.) Holbrooke was unable to be effective in this role, at least in part because the precise nature of his remit was ill-defined. But it would be worthwhile to do some systematic thinking about the possible utility of special envoys or super-ambassadors in regions of crisis and conflict in the future.

This brings us back to the question of the regional role of the U.S. military – above all, the proper scope of activity of the regional unified or combatant

---

[2] It has been suggested, for example, that ORHA/CPA could have been based on the headquarters staff of III Corps Artillery at the Army base at Fort Sill, Oklahoma. This would have solved many practical problems later encountered in communications, office equipment and support, and other areas. See Gordon W. Rudd, *Reconstructing Iraq: Regime Change, Jay Garner, and the ORHA Story* (Lawrence: University Press of Kansas, 2011), 396–400.

commanders. Should the regional CINCs properly have the large role in American diplomacy attributed to them by some contemporary observers? As was apparent in the reaction to the creation of AFRICOM, in spite of the ubiquity of the American military presence throughout the world, it is not necessarily viewed in a benign light even by many who are unlikely to be in its crosshairs. After all, no other nation has anything approaching the network of overseas bases, forward deployed forces, and client relationships of the United States. No other country divides the entire world into AORs presided over by generals and admirals. There can be no question that the optic in all this is disturbing – not least because it seems to send an implicit message to foreign leaders and peoples regarding the reality of military power and civil–military relations in the United States and American foreign policy today. Even if one believes that the diplomatic or engagement role of the CINCs is invaluable and that their diplomatic role has been greatly exaggerated, it is not clear by any means that only the current institutional arrangements can ensure that it is carried out effectively.

The case for rethinking the unified commands is in fact a strong one. There are two other powerful reasons for reform of the current system. The first is that it only perpetuates the fundamental problem of poor or unreliable interagency coordination that has plagued the U.S. national security establishment for many decades. The second is that the regional unified commands really are, from a military perspective, in a fundamental sense the product of the Cold War. To put it bluntly, they are in an advanced state of obsolescence.

Let us take the latter issue first. It is obvious that the most pressing security concern facing the United States today is a transnational terrorist threat that takes unexpected forms and does not respect national or regional boundaries. This strategic environment is far different from that of the Cold War, a time when we faced an adversary with a clear return address posing well-defined threats in various yet predictable parts of the world. It is rarely observed, however, that the unified command system was problematic in some ways even during the Cold War. The regional combatant commands are very much what might be called an Army-centric construct. Their primary raison d'être was the support of large overseas deployments of American troops and supporting elements in theaters of potential conflict – most notably, in Germany and Korea, and later in the Persian Gulf. But they were much less relevant to the needs and characteristics of American air or naval forces. The U.S. Navy in particular is essentially a global force. The U.S. Air Force also has substantial global capability in the form of long-range or strategic bombers and ballistic missiles and space assets of various kinds. The needs of these services were accommodated in the Unified Command Plan (UCP) to some extent by the formation of so-called specified commands in addition to the unified commands, most notably the former Strategic Air Command (SAC), now the U.S. Strategic Command (STRATCOM). (Today's other specified commands are the U.S. Transportation Command and the U.S. Special Operations Command.) But this bifurcation of the military command structure was always flawed in significant ways. Today, it continues to cause troublesome problems of coordination and control of military activities spanning the artificial boundaries of the unified commands. And in key respects the problems are worse.

This is so primarily because of several fundamental changes in the strategic environment and in military technology and weaponry over the last several decades. Contemporary war is no longer waged just in the familiar three dimensions of land, sea, and air. Space and cyberspace are increasingly integral dimensions of military competition and conflict. Both are inherently global in nature. In contrast to the Cold War, when military space satellites served primarily as tools of strategic intelligence and communications, today they are deeply embedded in the conduct of military activities at every level, and the primary enabler of America's formidable remote targeting and precision strike capabilities. As such, they have made it increasingly likely that space will in the future become an actual arena of war between the United States and even second-tier military powers. Quite apart from the prospect of direct attacks on satellites, in a major power conflict, ballistic missiles and missile defense interceptors could conduct duels in near space. Cyberspace, too, has rapidly become a critical enabler of contemporary military operations as well as an arena of war in its own right. Finally, it should be noted that in the current strategic environment, the Cold War equation of long-range or global strikes with nuclear weapons no longer holds. Long-range conventionally armed cruise missiles launched from submarines or surface ships are a key weapon in the American arsenal, and they are likely to be joined in the near future by conventionally armed "strategic" ballistic missiles for certain time-sensitive, specialized missions. These missiles are much more likely to be used than their nuclear counterparts – and used as an integral part of American combined arms operations. All of this poses tremendous new complications for a regionally focused system of command and control of American military forces.[3]

Furthermore, a case can be made that the Goldwater–Nichols defense reform legislation of 1986 may well have erred by injecting the unified commands into the process of budgetary and programmatic decision-making in Washington. Everyone knows that the services are prone to take parochial views in such matters. Yet there can be no guarantee that the CINCs will not show themselves at least equally parochial in their short-term and essentially regional perspectives on the world. More radically still, one might question even the venerable practice of leaving war planning mainly to the unified commands.[4] It is unclear what advantage accrues to having such planning carried out not in Washington but in places remote from it and isolated from one another.

[3] In 2002, the former Strategic Air Command, now the United States Strategic Command (STRATCOM), was merged with the United States Space Command, with headquarters at Colorado Springs. This specified command is currently assigned the "global" mission areas of space, cyberspace, and strategic or global strike. USTRANSCOM and USSOCOM also both have essentially global missions that cut across the unified command boundaries.

[4] Note Priest's vignette on COCOM domination of war planning, 98.

It would be one thing if there were a deep pool of resident expertise in the unified commands. Yet this is far from the case. The well-known vagaries of the military personnel system make it very difficult to nurture and retain in place for any length of time officers with special knowledge of a region.

The second argument for reform has to do with the continuing challenge of coordinating U.S. government interagency operations in the field. As Admiral Blair has put it: "We are just not set up right for engagement in the world. It's a tangled mess of people trying to do the right thing, but we'd never resolved the lines of authority" between the Pentagon, State, and the other agencies working abroad. "There was no unified team when it counted."[5] As has been seen repeatedly in the course of this study, this is nothing new. AFRICOM provides a new model of sorts of State–Department of Defense collaboration by giving the CINC a second deputy for non-military affairs of ambassadorial rank and seeding the staff with more civilian officials; other unified commands have experimented with a new construct called a Joint Interagency Coordination Group (JIACG), though this is an advisory rather than an operational body.

All such approaches fall short of addressing the real problem, however, which is the lack of directive authority over agency operations in the field by representatives of other agencies. The historical record shows that this problem has sometimes been finessed by the development of a close working relationship between the senior military and civilian officials in a theater, as remarked earlier. Is there a workable alternative? In the American historical experience, one stands out: CORDS. As we have seen, the Vietnam-era Civil Operations and Revolutionary Development Support organization, originally created by Robert Komer in 1967 and later led by future CIA director William Colby, was a unique experiment in truly integrated interagency operations. It intermixed military officers and civilians from various agencies at every echelon and ensured real integration by giving civilians authority to write performance evaluations of their military subordinates and the other way around. It was headed by a civilian of ambassadorial rank but was embedded in a military structure (the Military Assistance Command–Vietnam) to ensure tight coordination between the pacification effort and regular military operations. There is no reason why this model could not be adapted for use today. And in fact this is being urged with increasing frequency by those frustrated with the persisting shortcomings of the existing system.[6]

What might that mean in terms of the unified commands and the management of military activities overseas? The most radical option would be simply to abolish these commands as such and replace them with new hybrid, regionally focused interagency organizations.[7] These organizations would no

---

6 See, for example, Mitchell J. Thompson, "Breaking the Proconsulate: A New Design for National Power," *Parameters* (Winter 2005–06): 62–75.
7 Jeffrey Buchanan, Maxie V. Davis, and Lee T. Wight, "Death of the Combatant Command? Toward a Joint Interagency Approach," *Joint Force Quarterly* 52 (1st Quarter 2009): 92–96.

longer command military forces but would plan and carry out many of the functions currently discharged by the unified commands relating to theater security engagement or cooperation. They would be substantially smaller and leaner than the current unified commands. They would have a significant but not dominant military component, and they would be headed by a civilian of ambassadorial rank. Command and control of actual military operations, however, would devolve to ad hoc (or in some cases perhaps standing or semi-permanent) Joint Task Forces, which in turn would report directly to the Joint Chiefs of Staff in Washington.

Pursuing the logic of all this is beyond the scope of the present discussion. But it would clearly mean a dramatic recentralization of the U.S. military command structure under a new, globally oriented Joint Staff or component thereof.[8] War planning would once again become a responsibility of the joint and service staffs in Washington. No doubt, the complaint will be heard that this arrangement is a return to an abhorred model – the German "general staff" of old, which supposedly contributed to the militarization of German foreign policy, dysfunctional civil–military relations, and Germany's loss of two world wars. In my opinion, this is a tired canard. The real problem with the German defense establishment in the late nineteenth century and after was that, because it reported directly to the Kaiser (and later to Hitler), it had no effective civilian oversight. In the case of the contemporary United States, it can be argued that civilian control would actually be enhanced by such a step, which would reduce the scope of (proconsular) authority in the unified commands by recentralizing strategic military planning and operational decision-making in Washington under the vigilant eye of the secretary of defense and his large civilian bureaucracy.

None of this is meant to suggest, however, that proconsular leadership in some form will not be necessary in the future. The key point is that it will need to be conceptualized and structured in more imaginative and flexible ways than in the past. The proposed abolition of permanent regional military commands need not mean that regional commands could not be reestablished under certain circumstances on a temporary basis. Such commands could then be adjusted flexibly to take account of changing geopolitical boundaries and circumstances. Within both the Armed Forces and the State Department's Foreign Service as well as at the White House, there is a need to rethink political-military decision

---

Less radical solutions might be to reduce the unified commands to three or two, or replace them with a single global "Strike Command" of the sort that existed for a period in the 1960s. Thus, for example, James Jay Carafano, "Herding Cats: Understanding Why Government Agencies Don't Cooperate and How to Fix the Problem," *Heritage Lectures* (Washington, DC: The Heritage Foundation, July 2006).

[8] G. John David and Paul S. Reinhart, "A Joint Staff to Believe In," Joint Force Quarterly 56 (1st Quarter 2010): 128–33; Stephen L. Melton, "Conceptualizing Victory Anew: Revisiting U.S. Law, Doctrine, and Policy for War and Its Aftermath," *Joint Force Quarterly* 60 (1st Quarter 2011), 8–10.

and command relationships at a fundamental level.[9] Also needed is a reexamination of military and diplomatic personnel and professional education policies with a view to improving the preparation of senior officials for proconsular-type roles. Certain ground truths need to be frankly acknowledged. Perhaps the most important is that the primary home of proconsular leadership must be the uniformed military. The State Department simply lacks the resources, the strategic mindset, and the operational skills to take the lead in postconflict stability and reconstruction operations. The Department of Defense needs to come to terms with this reality and embrace the mission.[10] For its part, however, the Pentagon needs to fully internalize the hard lessons of our recent experiences in Iraq and Afghanistan and institutionalize them in education, training, doctrine, force structure, personnel policies, and command and control arrangements. This includes above all the nurturing of broad political-military expertise at senior levels of the officer corps. It should also involve a rethinking of Army and Marine Corps "civil affairs" doctrines and capabilities as well as the potential utilization of civilian talents in the Reserve Components of our military for postconflict operations.[11]

Finally, however, serious thought should also be given to national-level political-military decision structures and protocols in the light of the proconsular imperative. Integration or fusion of political-military decision-making in the field will never be more than partially successful in the absence of integration or fusion of such decision-making in Washington, and particularly in the White House (though the supporting role of Congress is also worth some attention). To say it once more, in spite of the fundamental changes wrought in the American national security system by the National Security Act of 1947 and the various formal and informal interagency mechanisms to which it has since given rise, most knowledgeable observers believe that problems of interagency coordination in the U.S. government remain a serious obstacle to the effective planning and implementation of U.S. national security policy. In particular, the link between Washington policy-making and the operations of the U.S. government in the field remains deeply problematic, in spite (and perhaps to some extent because) of the marvels of contemporary electronic communications.[12] As we have had ample opportunity to see in the course of this study, the

---

[9] An outstanding example of such rethinking is Christopher J. Lamb and Edward Marks, "Chief of Mission Authority as a Model for National Security Integration," *Strategic Perspectives*, No. 2 (Washington, DC: Institute for National Strategic Studies, National Defense University, December 2010).

[10] See notably Russell R. Hulam, "Stability Operations: An Inherently Military Function," in Harry R. Yarger, ed., *Short of General War: Perspectives on the Use of Military Power in the 21st Century* (Carlisle Barracks, PA: U.S. Army Strategic Studies Institute, April 2010), as well as Melton, 12.

[11] See especially Kurt E. Müller, "Toward a Concept of Strategic Civil Affairs," *Parameters* (Winter 1998): 80–98.

[12] Carnes Lord, "Rethinking the NSC System," *Orbis* (Summer 2000): 433–50, remains a pertinent discussion.

problem is hardly a new one in the American experience. The debacle of the Coalition Provisional Authority in Iraq provides a graphic recent example. It is beyond our present scope to explore the issue further here. Suffice it to say that proconsular leadership, which so plainly offers danger as well as opportunity, is an instrument in need of adult supervision at the imperial center.

Index

Abizaid, John, 194–195, 210–211, 216–217

Abrams, Creighton, 19, 136, 160–166, 230, 233

Acheson, Dean, 100–101, 107, 117–119, 131

Aguinaldo, Emilio, 73, 85

Albright, Madeleine, 175, 179, 181

Alger, Nelson, 53–54

Allawi, Ali, 195–196

Allawi, Iyad, 200, 204, 210

Armitage, Richard, 206

Atcheson, George, Jr., 100

Augustus, 24, 31, 45

Baker, Newton, 83

Ball, George, 150–151

Bao Dai, 137–138, 141

Barno, David, 223–224

Benyon, John, 15

Berger, Sandy, 179, 181–182

Bevin, Ernest, 126, 129

Bidault, Georges, 118, 121, 126

Biden, Joseph, 225, 227

bin Laden, Osama, 209

Blackwill, Robert, 203

Blair, Dennis, 173–174, 236

Blair, Tony, 183

Bloomfield, Lincoln, 174

Bradley, Omar, 124–125, 128, 130

Bremer, L. Paul, 20–21, 191–205, 210, 214, 220, 230, 232

Brooke, James, 57–59, 61, 64

Bundy, McGeorge, 149, 151, 154–155, 157–159

Bunker, Ellsworth, 20, 136, 159, 160, 163, 165–166, 233

Burke, Arleigh, 144

Bush, George W., 186–187, 190–192, 197, 205, 212, 216, 220–226

Byrnes, James F., 111–112, 117–120, 122

Caesar, Gaius Julius, 3, 24, 28, 31–32, 43–46

Card, Andrew, 201

Casey, George, 21, 211–212, 215–217

Castro, Fidel, 145

Catulus, C. Lutatius, 36

Caudex, Appius Claudius, 35

Chalabi, Ahmad, 192–194, 198, 203, 214

Cheney, Richard, 216, 217

Chiang Kai-shek, 106, 107

Chiarelli, Peter, 196

Churchill, Winston, 10, 110, 202

Clark, Wesley, 20, 165, 167, 174–185, 230

Clay, Lucius, 18–20, 71, 102, 109–132, 162, 168, 185, 203, 205, 230, 232

Cleveland, Grover, 52

Clinton, William J., 167, 172, 174, 181, 183, 186, 191

Clive, Robert, 18

Cohen, Eliot, 183, 216
Cohen, Theodore, 93
Cohen, William, 174, 175, 178, 179,
    181, 183
Colby, William, 20, 142, 144, 150, 152,
    154–155, 163, 165, 236
Conein, Lucien, 137, 143, 153–155
Cornwallis, Lord Charles, 17
Crocker, Ryan, 21, 136, 207, 217–221,
    233
Cromer, 1st Earl of, 14, 19, 79, 232
Curzon, Lord George, 14, 19

Diem, Ngo Dinh, 135, 138–148,
    150–156, 197
Dodge, Joseph, 106
Don, Tran Van, 154
Douglas, Lewis, 4, 121, 165, 188,
    226
Dulles, Allen, 89, 137, 138
Dulles, John Foster, 119–120, 137,
    140–141
Durbrow, Elbridge, 21, 143, 144, 197

Eikenberry, Karl, 21, 224–225
Eisenhower, Dwight D., 110, 112, 119,
    121–122, 137, 140–141, 143, 147,
    149, 168–169
Estrada Palma, Tomás, 55, 63, 64

Fallon, William, 173, 217, 220–221
Feith, Douglas J., 191–194, 198, 200
Ferguson, Niall, 7–8
Flamininus, Titus Quinctius, 32, 34,
    38–40
Forbes, W. Cameron, 78–80, 83
Forrestal, James, 129
Forrestal, Michael, 150
Franks, Thomas, 190–191, 205–206

Galbraith, John Kenneth, 118
García, Calixto, 55–56
Garner, Jay, 189, 191, 194–195, 198
Gates, Robert M., 5, 21, 173, 206, 217,
    225–226
Gaulle, Charles de, 4, 116, 202
Gelbard, Robert, 174
Gilpatric, Ros, 144
Gingrich, Newt, 200

Gómez, Maximo, 55–56
Gouin, Félix, 117
Grew, Joseph P., 100
Grossman, Marc, 174

Habib, Philip, 159
Haig, Alexander M., 176
Halberstam, David, 145–147, 150–151,
    153
Hannibal, 30, 33, 37–38
Harding, Warren G., 66, 83
Harkins, Paul, 151, 154–157
Harriman, Averill, 134, 146, 149–151,
    153–154, 156
Harrison, Francis Burton, 21, 80–85,
    230
Hashemi, Aqila al-, 199
Hastings, Warren, 17–19
Heath, Donald, 138, 140
Herbits, Steven, 200
Hilsman, Roger, 146, 150–151, 156
Hinh, Nguyen Van, 140
Hirohito, 102
Ho Chi Minh, 137
Hodge, John R., 108
Holbrooke, Richard, 176, 180, 224,
    233
Hoover, Herbert, 85, 94
Hopkins, Harry, 41, 111
Howley, Frank, 124, 127
Humphrey, Hubert H., 159
Hussein, Saddam, 55, 139, 187–188,
    193, 196, 208–209
Hyam, Ronald, 13

Ickes, Harold, 100

Jackson, Michael, 183
James, D. Clayton, 93
Jefferson, Thomas, 9, 48
Johnson, Louis, 106–107
Johnson, Lyndon B., 9, 136, 150,
    156–163, 165, 169, 230
Jones, Elizabeth, 174
Jones, James, 225

Kagan, Frederick, 215
Karzai, Hamid, 142, 197, 221, 223–224
Keane, Jack, 212–213, 216–217

Kennan, George, 105–106, 115, 119, 122, 126–127, 131
Kennedy, John F., 136, 143–157, 159, 169, 175, 188, 230
Kennedy, Paul, 10
Kennedy, Robert F., 154
Khalilzad, Zalmay, 142, 197–198, 217, 223–224
Khanh, Nguyen, 158
Kilcullen, David, 218
Kissinger, Henry A., 191
Komer, Robert, 160–161, 163–164, 236
Ky, Nguyen Cao, 159

Laird, Melvin, 164
Lansdale, Edward, 19, 88–90, 135, 137–145, 152–153, 159, 165, 197, 230, 232
Lawton, Henry, 53, 56, 124, 140
LeMay, Curtis, 124, 128, 130
Lincoln, Abraham, 206, 220
Lodge, Henry Cabot, 19, 21, 134, 145, 147–157, 159–160, 165, 222, 230
Lodge, Henry Cabot, the elder, 51, 77, 147
Long, Huey, 95
Lovett, Robert, 122, 129
Lugard, Sir Frederick, 14–15
Lute, Douglas, 226

MacArthur, Arthur, 73–74, 77, 100
MacArthur, Douglas, 4, 5, 6, 19–21, 55–56, 86–88, 91–108, 110–112, 115–116, 148, 157, 162, 168, 200, 203, 222, 230, 232
Machiavelli, Niccolò, 63, 71, 142
Magoon, Charles, 64
Magsaysay, Ramon, 89, 137, 142, 197
Mahan, Alfred Thayer, 49, 51
Maliki, Nouri al-, 220–221
Mao Tse-tung, 106
Marius, Gaius, 42, 45
Marshall, George C., 96, 105–106, 112, 119–122, 126, 129, 131
McChrystal, Stanley, 5, 224–227
McCloy, John, 110
McCone, John, 150, 152–153, 155, 161

McKiernan, David, 190–191, 224
McKinley, William, 20, 47, 49, 51–54, 57–59, 61, 67–68, 70–71, 73–75, 83
McMaster, H. R., 161, 218
McNamara, Robert S., 149–155, 157–158, 160–161, 169, 205
McNutt, Paul, 85–87
Mello, Sergio Vieira de, 199
Miles, Nelson, 52, 68
Milosevic, Slobodan, 175, 177–181, 183
Minh, Duong Van, 153, 156
Molotov, Vyacheslav, 118, 121, 126
Morgenthau, Henry, 114, 118
Mullen, Michael, 217, 223, 225–226
Murphy, Frank, 85–86
Murphy, Robert, 86, 112, 123, 131
Murville, Maurice Couve de, 126

Napier, Sir Charles, 14, 23
Naumann, Klaus, 177, 180–181
Negroponte, John, 206, 224
Nes, David, 156, 157
Nhu, Ngo Dinh, 133, 138–140, 142, 147, 151–153, 155
Nimitz, Chester, 96, 98
Nixon, Richard, 136, 147, 163–164
Nolting, Frederick, 144, 149, 151, 155, 159

O'Daniel, John, 137–138, 140, 143
Obama, Barack, 222, 224–226
Odierno, Raymond, 215–217
Osmena, Sergio, 78–82, 85, 99–100

Pace, Peter, 212, 217
Pardo de Taveres, Trinidad, 77–78
Paullus, Lucius Aemilius, 40, 91
Pershing, John, 66, 94
Petraeus, David, 1, 4, 20–21, 136, 172, 207–209, 212–222, 224–227, 230, 233
Phillips, Rufus, 137, 143, 153, 159
Philo, Quintus Publilius, 23, 30
Polybius, 24–25, 34
Pompey, 40, 43–44
Porter, William, 159–160
Powell, Colin, 191, 195, 198, 200

Priest, Dana, 167, 170–171, 173
Prueher, Joseph, 173

Quang, Tri, 147
Quezon, Manuel, 67, 70, 78–81, 84–87, 92, 95, 99
Quirino, Elpidio, 89

Radford, Arthur, 137
Rapp, William, 218
Rayburn, Samuel, 111
Reed, Walter, 60, 226
Regulus, M. Atilius, 36
Reimer, Dennis, 184
Reinhardt, George Frederick, 143
Reuter, Ernst, 128, 130
Rhee, Syngman, 108
Rice, Condoleeza, 190–191, 195, 198, 201, 203
Richardson, John, 151–153
Robertson, Brian, 121, 127–129
Roosevelt, Franklin Delano, 20, 85–87, 95–98, 100, 110–113, 168, 190, 202, 230
Roosevelt, James, 86
Roosevelt, Theodore, 9, 49, 51, 53, 65, 69, 77
Roosevelt, Theodore, Jr., 85
Root, Elihu, 47, 51, 58–59, 61–62, 65, 71, 74
Rostow, Walter, 144
Roxas, Manuel, 99, 100
Royall, Kenneth, 105, 121, 125
Rumsfeld, Donald, 168, 186, 190–192, 194–195, 200–203, 205–206, 212, 225
Rusk, Dean, 144, 148–152, 154, 160

Sadr, Moqtada al., 189, 210, 220
Sanchez, Ricardo, 21, 196–197, 205, 210
Schurman, Jacob Gould, 83
Scipio, Publius Cornelius Africanus, 28, 30, 34, 37–39
Shafter, William, 53–56
Sharp, Ulysses S. Grant, 158
Sheehan, Neil, 145, 151

Shelton, Hugh, 174, 178–179, 181–185, 213
Sidell, Charles, 194
Slocombe, Walter, 180, 195
Smith, Walter Bedell, 112, 122, 126, 129
Solana, Javier, 176–180, 182–184
Stalin, Josef, 110, 129
Stavridis, James, 169
Stephenson, James, 196
Stimson, Henry L., 78, 85, 93, 114
Sulla, L. Cornelius, 28, 43, 44

Taft, Charles P., 100
Taft, William Howard, 19, 64, 67–78, 80–81, 85, 100, 230
Taylor, Maxwell, 19, 150–154, 157–159, 232–233
Templeton, Sir Hugh, 232
Thieu, Nguyen Van, 159, 165
Tho, Nguyen Ngoc, 153
Thuan, Nguyen Dinh, 153
Truman, Harry S, 87, 96–97, 100–101, 104–108, 110–111, 117, 119, 121, 123, 129, 130–131, 168–169

Vuono, Carl, 213
Vy, Nguyen Van, 142

Weber, Max, 3
Westmoreland, William C., 157–160, 162–164, 217
Wilhelm, Charles, 172
Williams, Samuel, 143
Willoughby, Charles, 101
Wilson, James, 58–59
Wilson, Woodrow, 2, 51, 65, 69, 80–82, 96, 147, 161, 230
Wolfowitz, Paul, 192, 200, 202
Wood, Leonard, 5, 18–19, 47, 51–66, 71, 78–81, 83–85, 92, 94, 230, 232
Woodward, Bob, 205–206, 216, 227
Wright, Luke, 78

Yoshida, Shigeru, 92

Zinni, Anthony, 172–173